Sith co nem
Nem co doman
Bennaigid don
Morrigan
Mórda

The Book of the Great Queen

The Many Faces of the Morrigan, From Ancient Legends To Modern Devotions

Morpheus Ravenna

Concrescent Press

For information contact:
Concrescent Press, Richmond CA, USA
info@Concrescent.net

ISBN: 978-0-9903927-1-2

Library of Congress Control Number: 2015940766

In dedication to
the Morrigan, mighty Great Queen,
this book is offered
in fulfillment of the vow

Table of Contents

Acknowledgements

A great many people helped bring this book to life, and I am mightily grateful for their manifold and generous support.

To Brennos Agrocunos, my beloved mate and fellow Coru priest: my gratitude for your endless and passionate support of this project, for caring for the working writer in every way imaginable.

To P. Sufenas Virius Lupus, C. Lee Vermeers, and Segomaros Widugeni: my gratitude for your insightful and learned critiques; and for giving your valuable time to provide informal peer review, making this a much better book than it would have been. To Isolde Carmody, for generously giving your time and worthy scholarship to poem translations and language help for my work with the poems. I cannot offer gratitude enough.

To Rynn Fox, dear friend and Coru Priesthood sister: my gratitude for editing help, constant support and morale boosting, and above-and-beyond aid on the fundraising video and campaign. To all my Coru Priesthood kin: my gratitude for your brilliant collaboration in living devotion, deep magic, and authentic polytheist practice, without which this book and my own practice would be so much the poorer. My thanks also for your vibrant support throughout the project and the fundraising campaign, especially to Amelia Hogan for gorgeous bookbinding.

To Valerie Herron: my inspired gratitude for your honed skill and magnificent ability to capture my vision in exquisite illustrations, and for really stellar professional collaboration. May great success come to you! To Sam Webster, my longtime friend and priestly colleague: thank you for placing your faith and confidence in me to publish this book.

To the many, many other friends and colleagues who constantly reached out to me, sharing wisdom, insights, resources, good cheer, prayers, madhattery, and shenanigans, and in so many other ways helped me to feel like I had an army at my back and a wind in my sails: thank you. To Theanos Thrax, for prayers, divinations, kinship, and wise teachings. To Barbara Cormack, for library magic and corvid cheer. To John F. Beckett, for taking up the call and offering staunch and active support. To the EMBS crew: rockstars Winter, Sharon Knight, and Paul Nordin, for helping me bring poetry to life.

To all those who chose to invest in me by backing the campaign to fund this book project, I have not the words to convey my gratitude for your trust, faith, and generous support, deepest thanks to:
James Andrade, Kris Anton, Morgan Ash, John Bacevicius, John Beckett, Christine L. Berger, James Boyd, Kiarna I. Boyd, Jan Bosman, Jerry Brown, Steven C. Brown, Amber Bruce, Margaret Bruce, Ashley Bryner, Leland Cargle, Virginia Carper, Ben Cislowski, Charles Collins, Owen Cook, Barbara Cormack, Thorn Coyle, Brenda Bradshaw Csonka, Temperance De'lonkcra, Shawna De Puente, Anna DiPietro, Shelly Ferland, Daniel and Sarah FitzGerald, Ellen Francik, Nick Friend, Renee Garner, Patrick Garretson, Rose Gwiniolen, Pamela Haynie, Paula L. Herron, Chrissie Hogen-Esch, Cynthia Iverson, Jo Jenson, Lady Jake Jocelyne, Kelly Kearns, Kimberly Kirner, Anna Korn, Nerys Lewis, Jon Lynn, John Machate, Mairin, Bari Mandelbaum, Samantha Mant, P. McBride-Martin, Dian McDonald, John Medellin, Amber Kay Mildenhall, Jessica Minah, Dale Moss, Jack W. Naranjo, Athelia Nihtscada, James O'Brien, Patrick O'Malley, Gerrie Ordaz, Thomas Parshall, Lisa Paul, Misha Penton, Grey Perkins, Joe Perri, Kurt Piersol, Sandra Pomeroy, H. Wesley Poteet, Katie Quenneville, Anne Randall, Wendy Rapagna, Sara Ahern Sawyer, Joel Schonbrunn, Samantha Shay, Niall Sheehan, J. Fox Sircy, Benjamin Stockton, Ward Trythall, Ilan Weiler, Helen Willey, Rebecca Wright, Evan Young, S. Youngs,

and the many other backers who made this project possible.

There are many, many more dear friends, kin, and community members who have supported my work over the years, and I am grateful to you all. May the blessings of the Great Queen strengthen you.

Map of Ireland

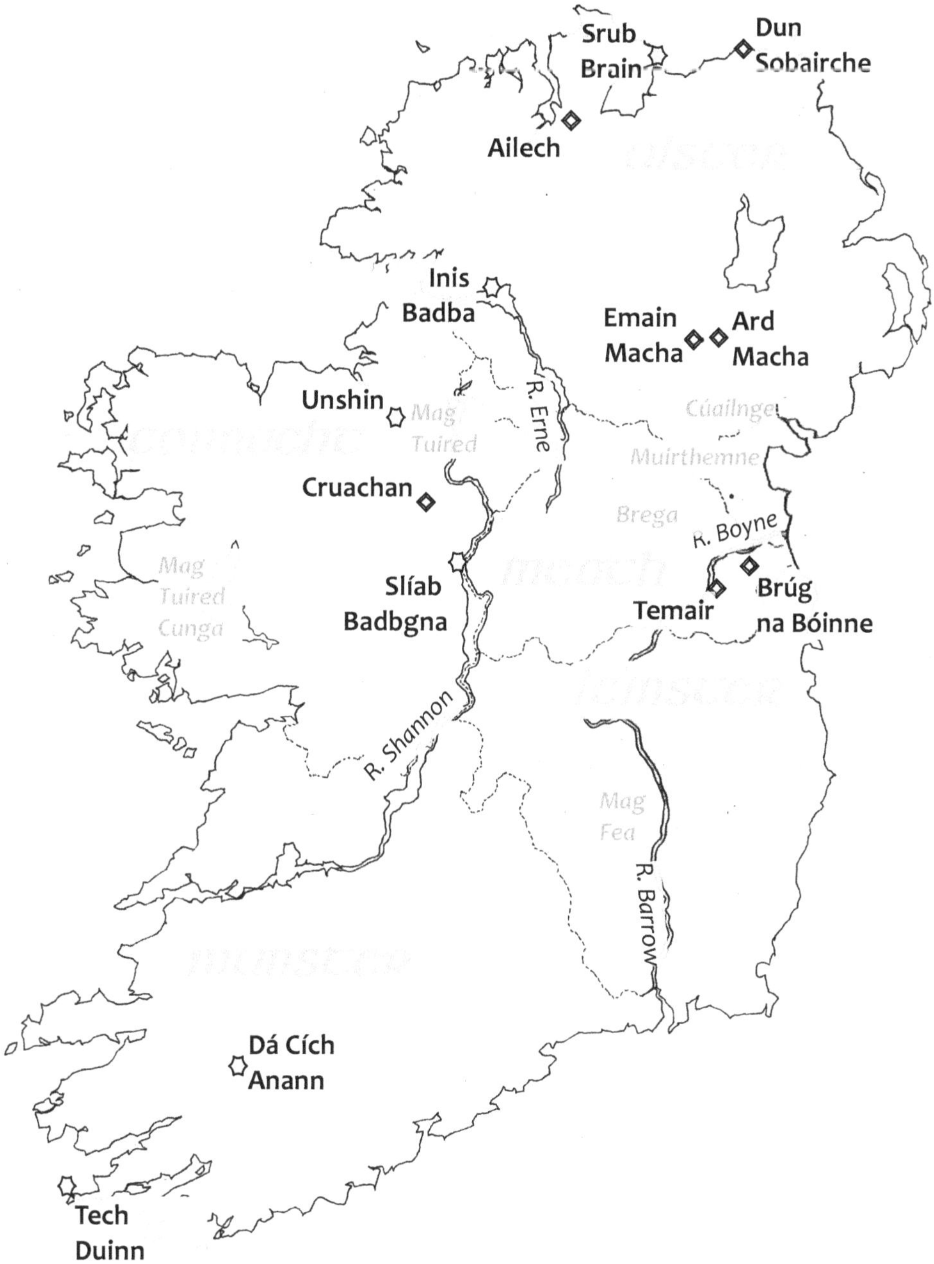

Introduction

I was compelled to write this book. It has been a work of devotion, but one I came to reluctantly at first. My primary work is as an artist and ritualist rather than a writer. Or so I thought, until I found myself writing a book. It is often said that when you look for a book and find it hasn't been written yet, it's up to you to write it. As a devotee of the Morrígan, and a polytheist who deeply values scholarship, I have been voracious in my hunger for learning about her origins and her worship. Since she first spoke to me nearly twenty years ago, I began devouring all the sources I could find about her, across disciplines, from early Irish literature to heady academic dissertations to popular Pagan books.

The Morrígan is a mystery. Complexities and ambiguities always seem to obscure her identity, like the druidic mists and illusions she conjures in her tales. It took me more than a decade of study to begin to feel I understood her voice. As I became more visibly active as a priest in her service, people began asking me what they should read to learn about her, and I wanted a book to recommend that synthesized the knowledge of the many kinds of sources I had been reading. I wanted a book that built in strong scholarship and historical perspective, but also conveyed the experiential understanding that I was constantly being asked for by people looking for guidance in their lived devotional practice. There were books covering each of these areas, but none that brought them together in the way I was seeking. I didn't know where to find that book, until people began asking me when I was going to write it.

I came to this work by inches, saying no for a long time until I realized I had already said yes. I admitted to myself that my research was for a book in about the spring of 2013, and began writing in earnest that summer. The project remained on slow-burn for some months after that, however: constantly pushed to the side in my over-scheduled life as a self-employed artist. In the spring of 2014, the Morrígan intervened. One morning as I entered my ritual space for daily practice, she broke over me like a blinding light and set a *nóinden* on me, a devotional binding with a term of nine months, to complete the book before the end of the year. Everything in my life shifted to make room, and I have spent the rest of the year writing. It is New Year's Day 2015 and I have just completed the first draft of the manuscript.

In truth, I don't think any one book about the Morrígan can be comprehensive. Her roots reach deep into the ancient Indo-European past and connect her, and her cults of worship, to a great constellation of divinities and cultures. Her nature is so complex and so changeable that even could someone capture her history in a volume, the lived experiences of practitioners engaging with her bring constantly new revelations about her relationships with the forces of history, of culture, and with her devotees themselves. So, I do not expect this book to be received as comprehensive, but I have endeavored to be thorough.

My approach to engaging with Gods is neither eclectic nor reconstructionist. In my own religious practice, I believe in delving as deeply into the historical record and the ancient literatures as possible. However for me, the paramount value in religious practice is lived religious experience and authentic relationship with the Gods. The study of the source cultures and histories of the Gods makes that relationship possible—it is how we learn the cultural, symbolic, and theological language of a deity, so that we can enter into that lived relationship with them. In metaphorical terms, it's like dating someone from a different country: you need to have a shared language to be in relationship, but you can't conduct a relationship following a script or a textbook. You need to become fluent in their language and then let the relationship itself guide you as it unfolds. Just so, for me scholarship is how I have sought to become fluent in the language of the Morrígan, sought to understand her the way one would want to know as much as possible about a lover's culture, background, and life history: so that I can love her well.

For that reason, this book weaves together both focused historical study and modern, experiential devotional practice. It is my hope that everyone who is interested in the Morrígan and her cult of worship, whether coming from a reconstructionist or modern polytheist perspective or simply wanting to learn about her history, will find something of value in this work. The book is divided into two parts. Part I seeks to address the questions of who the Morrígan is, what are her functions and her relationships to other divinities, and to place them in a cultural and historical context. Part II seeks to explore her cult of worship, addressing the questions of how people have engaged with her historically, and how they can do so now. It breaks down cult practice into a group of related subject areas, and, for each ,looks first at historical cult practices, followed by an exploration of how we can bring this aspect of cult practice into modern polytheist devotion.

The historical sections draw heavily on the early Irish literatures, along with other early literary and mythological sources, combined with archaeology, contemporary historical and literary scholarship, folk belief, and a variety of other kinds of evidence. The sections on lived practice combine insights drawn from my own personal practice of nearly two decades of devotional polytheism, priesthood service, and modern witchcraft, as well as the insights of colleagues and fellow priests in these traditions, including the Coru Cathubodua Priesthood. Readers may also recognize the influence in these areas of my training and background in the Anderson Feri Tradition of witchcraft. In this book, most of the sections on practice assume a basic level of experience, as I could not make this book as in-depth as I wanted it to be while also teaching how to start with the very basics of polytheist religious and magical practices. My primary goal in these sections is to help people deepen their practices.

As there has been much ambiguity, especially in popular Pagan literature, about the Morrígan and about the notion of Celtic cultural identity, it will be helpful here to briefly lay out the cultural geography of the Celtic peoples within which the cults of the Morrígan developed, and to define some of the ways I use language.

When we come to speak of the Celts, we are referring to a collection of tribal groups who emerged in Europe in the late Bronze Age around the beginning of the last millennium BCE, developing an identifiable culture and speaking an early form of Celtic language. These tribes are characterized by distinctive decorative art and metalwork, a warrior aristocracy, a polytheistic and ritually active religion, and other notable cultural patterns. We have varying theories as to where Celtic language first became differentiated from earlier Indo-European language, but what is known is that by the middle of the last millennium BC, a recognizable ethno-linguistic family of Celtic tribal cultures had emerged and spread themselves through a great swath of old Europe. During the Iron Age and before the expansion of the Roman Empire, these Celtic tribes held and controlled a large part of the European continent, although they were not organized into an empire or nation.

The Celtic lands in the early Iron Age, generally speaking, included Gaul, covering much of modern France and parts of Germany and Eastern Europe; Celtiberia, extending into much of modern Spain; and the Insular Celtic lands of Britain and Ireland. Galatia, a region of modern Turkey, was also colonized by Celtic tribes in the late Iron Age. When we speak of "Insular" elements, we mean Celtic culture as it was expressed in the islands—Britain and Ireland. When we speak of "Continental" elements, we mean Celtic culture as it was expressed on the European mainland. In each of these areas, unique evolutions and syntheses of Celtic culture with other local cultures occurred. Communication and trade was maintained both within the Celtic world and between Celts and neighboring cultures and empires, but geographic and cultural separations also brought much regional variation. The early, common Celtic language differentiated into the Celtic language groups: Gallo-Brittonic (ancestor of modern Welsh and Breton), and Goidelic (ancestor of Irish, Scots Gaelic, and other dialects). Early styles of Celtic material culture are sometimes referred to as Hallstatt culture; somewhat later (though overlapping), another style developed which is often called La Tène culture—and it is the latter which most characterizes what we typically think of as "Celtic" art, with its complex, mesmerizing spiral patterns and interlocking forms.

This is the world from which the Morrígan begins to emerge into the light in early Ireland. During the period of Celtic emergence, most of the Celtic peoples did not employ writing, or employed it on a limited basis only. Thus from the Celtic Iron Age itself, most of our evidence regarding the Gods and cult activity is archaeological, or comes indirectly by way of neighboring cultures such as the Greeks and Romans who wrote down observations of their experiences with and opinions about the Celts. In terms of mythological literature, the stories of the Gods, little is preserved until near the end of the first millennium CE, when Christian clerics, primarily in Ireland, began collecting and recording what remained of the pre-Christian oral literature. Thus the Irish medieval literature represents our closest approach to the mythologies of the ancient Celtic peoples, but it is filtered through nearly half a millenium of Christianization. In Gaul and the rest of the Continent, where Roman conquest began to substantially alter the religious and cultural practices before the advent of Christianity, most of the mythologies are lost and we can only piece together glimpses from archaeology and comparative studies with Insular mythology.

In this book, the language I use to speak about the Morrígan is flexible and sometimes ambiguous. This is because ambiguity is inherent to her. The Irish literary sources speak of her as a Goddess who is sometimes individual and sometimes triple or multiple. They speak of a group of divinities who may be manifestations of a single Goddess, or may be distinct, related Goddesses: Morrígan, Badb, Macha, Anu, Némain, Féa, Bé Néit. They speak of a collective, the Morrígna, which is to say "the Morrígans". I explore the questions raised by this confusing multiplicity in Chapter 2. But just as no single source text is definitive, neither are my ideas and conclusions definitive. In respect for that inherent ambiguity and the reader's place in drawing their own conclusions, I have sought to preserve some of that flexibility of perception in my language when speaking about the Morrígan. I often refer to the Morrígna as a group of divinities, but those divinities can be thought of either as distinct faces or identities of one Goddess or as separate, individual Goddesses, depending on the reader's perspective. It belongs to the reader, to the individual practitioner, to explore this material for themselves and discover what their relationship is to the Morrígan, to her identity and multiplicity.

Part 1
Herself

In this first part of the book, we look at the Morrígan in mythology, seeking to illuminate her identity, roles, and functions within the mythological and cultural context, her relationships with other divinities, and her history.

To begin this inquiry, we first need to become familiar with the source materials which record her lore—primarily, the early Irish literature. Chapter 1, therefore, is dedicated to an exploration of the major story cycles: the *Dindshenchas* tales, the Mythological Cycle tales, the Ulster Cycle tales, the Finn Cycle tales, and a few other groups of texts. We will look at each of these groups of stories, placing them in their historical context, and identifying the roles and actions of the Morrígna in each of the tales.

Armed with this knowledge of the source literature, we can begin to tease out patterns within the lore cycles. Chapter 2 engages questions about the multiple nature of the Morrígan: whether she is a singular Goddess within a sisterhood of related Goddesses, a triple Goddess, or one face of a collective. We will look at how the nature and relationships among the Morrígna have been portrayed distinctly within different regions and story cycle and attempt to resolve some of the ambiguities surrounding their identities and relationships.

Chapters 3 through 7 then take each of the Morrígna in turn, examining each of them individually with respect to their identities, roles in mythology, relationships, and cultural histories. We will meet and come to know the Morrígan, Badb, Macha, Anu, Némain, and Féa individually through this series of chapters.

Expanding beyond the Irish mythic landscape, in Chapter 8 we trace the threads of cultural connection to illuminate the relationships of the Morrígna with related divinities in ancient Celtic Britain and the Continent.

Finally, in Chapter 9, we give voice to the Morrígan herself, devoting this chapter to a deep study and analysis of her poems as recorded in several of the Irish texts. Through this study, the poems serve as a lens which illuminates the character, voice, and perceptions of the Morrígan, as well as the cultural and spiritual landscape within which she moves.

1

The Irish Lore

The Morrígna are known to us from the medieval Irish literature: the group of Irish mythological and heroic tales which were collected from the oral tradition by medieval Christian scholars and recorded into manuscripts. As we will be frequently referring to various tales throughout this book in our discussions of the Morrígna, this chapter will provide a review of the texts in which they appear, to provide for a common understanding of these tales and their essential contents and contexts. Readers may find this chapter slower reading than the rest of the book, but I hope you will bear with me as we lay the groundwork for the deep explorations of myth, culture, and religious practice that we will undertake in chapters to come.

Context and Source in Medieval Irish Literature

When reading the medieval Irish literature, it is critical to keep context and source in mind. We need to remember that the Irish medieval texts were originally an oral literature, recorded and often extensively reworked by Christian monastic scholars. Even in the earliest texts, this process was taking place several centuries after the conversion of Ireland to Christianity as the dominant religion. The ethos of the monastic scholars was conservative, treating these texts as the foundational lore of their heritage and preserving a great wealth of detail. However, with regard to the pagan magical and religious content of the lore, in many cases the practiced religious understanding of that pagan content had already been lost by the time the material was being committed to text. In some cases, it may have still been understood but was deliberately obscured in order to legitimize the act of recording the lore within a Christian institution and society.

As an example of these changes, many characters who in earlier times may have been understood as Gods were recorded as pseudo-historical or legendary human characters, and given deaths. These characters' lives and deaths are then highlighted within a lineage of ancestry. In part, this reading of Gods as mortal beings with human lives and deaths may be reflective of a cyclical quality inherent to Celtic religion—a non-linear relationship with time in which the Gods are born, live, and die many times, endlessly playing out variations on the themes of their stories, and whose death tales themselves serve to enhance their mythic status. At the same time, framing the Gods as mortal characters may also have served to make the literature more acceptable to medieval Christian patrons, by divorcing it from contamination with paganism and placing it firmly in the past. This re-framing of Gods as ancestors also may have made the literature more useful to the kings and lords who were in many cases the patrons behind the production of the literature, giving them semi-divine ancestors to claim descent from, in order to legitimize authority. It is important to remember that in the early medieval period, most of the scholars who worked this material worked for someone—that is to say, the Church in medieval Ireland was not independent of the political landscape.

The Pagan Past

For all these reasons, and more, we must read the medieval Irish texts as imperfect sources on pre-Christian Celtic Irish culture, especially its polytheistic and ritual dimensions. Whenever we are working with medieval literary sources, we must remember that what they show us most directly is what medieval Irish Christians had received, believed, and wished to record for posterity about their perceived Iron Age pagan heritage.

That pagan past itself was likely not a consistent, easily communicated system of practice or belief. Celtic peoples, in Ireland as elsewhere, were tribally organized societies, and this tribal configuration lasted well into the medieval period in Ireland. As such, there would never have been a uniform system of religious ideology or practice. The myths of the Gods, their cults of worship, and the reflection of religious ideas in social customs will have varied widely between tribal groups. The oral traditions which were recorded and worked into literary form by the scholars, while internally highly conservative, would likely not have been consistent across different regions and tribal groupings. We therefore see an enormous amount of variety in the stories, relationships, iconography, and practice of the pagan Irish and other Celtic peoples, in addition to the changes brought about in this material in the process of becoming literature.

The literary evidence should therefore be looked at much in the same way that an archaeologist views physical evidence of the ancient past; carefully, contextually, and with the assumption that it can only ever illuminate a part of what was.

Story Cycles

What follows here is an index, as complete as I have been able to make it, of the medieval Irish literary texts within which the Morrígna appear, grouped into major narrative cycles or families of related texts. The story cycles into which these tales are grouped are:

- the *Dindshenchas*, lore about important places in the Irish landscape
- the Mythological Cycle, which contains the mythic foundation stories about the origins of the land, Gods, and peoples of Ireland
- the Ulster Cycle, a series of sagas centering on Cú Chulainn and other heroes and kings of the province of Ulster
- the Finn Cycle, stories about the hero Finn mac Cumhaill and the Fianna warrior bands
- the Cycle of Kings, stories relating to the lives and reigns of various mythic and historical kings of Ireland

Along with these, we include a few other texts which do not fit neatly into any of the story cycles. In some cases, stories or parts of stories appear in more than one narrative context.

There is, of course, no substitute for reading the tales themselves, and I encourage every reader to also access the full text of the tales as companion material to this book. Many of the tales are available in translation online for free; sources for reading are given in the appendices. As well, each of these groups of tales represent a rich wealth of lore about ancient and medieval Celtic societies. In this book, there is not space to delve into all the meaningful dimensions of these stories; we will instead focus on what they can tell us about the Morrígna. Recommendations for further analytical readings on the tales can also be found in the appendices.

Dindshenchas: the Lore of Places

The *Dindshenchas* are a large body of short tales and poems texts recording ancient folklore about the stories attached to culturally and spiritually important places in the Irish landscape—the meaning of the word is "stories of high places". They are usually constructed so as to explain the origin of the name of the place. *Dindshenchas* stories and poems represented an important genre of story for the early Irish, and there are hundreds of them. Collections of these tales were included in several of the medieval manuscripts, and there are also *dindshenchas*-type stories embedded within many of the narrative sagas. The manuscripts in which the *Dindshenchas* are found generally date from about the 11th century and later, but analysis of the texts reveals that the material contained in them is far older, much of it likely prehistoric in origin and preserved orally into the medieval period. The *Dindshenchas* materials are grouped by scholars into the prose texts and metrical (poem) texts. I have grouped the relevant stories here by place rather than by manuscript source for clarity.

Ailech Néit | Grianán of Ailech

Ailech Néit is an ancient site with a stone ring-fort at the far northern tip of Ireland, in Ulster province. It has features dating back as far as the Neolithic, and is variously called Ailech, Ailech Néit, Ailech Imchell, or its modern name, Grianán Ailech.

A series of three *Dindshenchas* poems convey the mythical histories of Ailech. In these poems, the Goddess Némain is described dwelling there as wife to Néit, a war God, and stories about the building of the ring-fortress are told.[1]

1 Gwynn 1924 pp. 96, 103, 115

Ard Macha | Armagh

Ard Macha (the modern city of Armagh) formed part of the ancient royal center of the Ulster province, along with nearby Emain Macha (now known as Navan Fort). Many of the tales consistently link the two sites within related stories.

Several different *Dindshenchas* stories of Macha exist, both in collections and embedded in narrative tales. These Macha tales may represent distinctly different individuals simply sharing the same name,[2] or may represent "incarnations" of the same Goddess.

A long *Dindshenchas* poem links three different tales of Macha, connecting each to the establishment of Ard Macha as a sacred center. This poem briefly mentions Macha, the wife of Nemed, a mythical founder of Ireland who is said to have cleared the plains within which this Macha was buried. The poem then goes on to describe how the warrior woman Macha, daughter of Áed (elsewhere Macha Mongruad), shaped the fortress of Emain Macha with her brooch. We learn of her death and burial at Ard Macha, and that the Assembly of Macha was held each year in her honor. The rest of the poem is devoted to the story of Macha, the wife of Cruinn, also called here by the name Grian, who is forced to race the king's horses at Emain Macha while pregnant to prove her husband's boast about her ability. Dying in the trauma of childbirth at the finish line, she gives birth to twins and curses the men of Ulster with the pain and weakness of childbirth. She too is said to be buried at Ard Macha.[3]

A prose tale about Ard Macha from another manuscript parallels the poem above with some additional details. It first gives Macha, wife of Nemed, adding to her story a vision in which she prophesies the *Táin* and all the destruction that would come with it. Her heart breaks with the horror of the vision, and she is buried at Ard Macha. The story of Macha, daughter of Áed (elsewhere Macha Mongruad) is then told, followed by Macha, wife of Cruinn, closely following the poem version.[4]

---

2 As many as four distinct Machas can be found in the various tales: Macha, wife of Nemed; Macha, daughter of Áed, also called Macha Mongruad; Macha, wife of Cruinn; and Macha, daughter of Ernmas. We explore the relationships of the different Machas in Chapter 5, devoted to her. Here, we simply note this multiplicity in the context of laying out the story cycles.

3 Gwynn 1924 124-131. We cover these stories in more detail in the narrative texts of the Ulster Cycle.

4 Stokes 1893 481

Emain Macha | Navan Fort

Emain Macha was the ancient royal center of the province of Ulster. It is the location around which a great number of the Ulster Cycle tales revolve, and corresponds to the site now known as Navan Fort, where a mound, rath (earthen bank fortification with boundary ditch), and many other archaeological sites are found.

A *Dindshenchas* poem associates much of the same mythic material with Emain Macha that we have just seen connected to Ard Macha, above. The poem reiterates parts of the story of Macha Mongruad, but relates a different story for her founding the fortress of Emain Macha. In this poem, she tricks and enslaves the sons of her rival for the kingship, Dithorba, forcing them to build the rath of the fortress following the the path laid out by her brooch. This poem also continues with the story of Macha, wife of Cruinn, in a shortened form, describing her race against the king's horses and dying curse against the men of Ulster.[5]

Brúg na Bóinne | Newgrange

An important sacred landscape, the valley of the Boyne River contains many important ancient monuments, including the Neolithic chambered tomb now called Newgrange. Built long before the arrival of the Celtic-speaking peoples, it was nonetheless adopted as an important sacred site associated with the Gods of the Celtic Irish, and called Brúg na Bóinne, the Palace of the Boyne.

A series of *Dindshenchas* poems about the Brúg na Bóinne sites speaks of the Morrígan as the wife and "great lady" of the Dadga and associates her with landforms in the area.[6] Another verse mentions a mound where she was "smitten" in violence, which may be a reference to a death-tale whose full narrative is now lost.[7] An extensive section of prose *Dindshenchas* also covers the Boyne region. It primarily constitutes a list of named sites without substantial narratives, from which shreds of information on folk tradition may be gleaned. The list is extensive and touches on a variety of mythologies; several relate to the Morrígan in her partnership with the Dagda.[8]

5 Gwynn 1924 308-311
6 Gwynn 2008 11
7 Gwynn 2008 19
8 Stokes 1894 292

Odras - Slíab Bodbgna | Slieve Bawn

A story about the River Odras is referenced in two *Dindshenchas* stories, a poem and a prose text. This river name does not seem to have a counterpart in modern maps, but a mountain also referenced in the story, Slíab Bodbgna, is the one now known as Slieve Bawn, in eastern Connacht.

The poem tells that this river Odras is named for a woman who was cursed by the Morrígan. Odras, the wife of Buchat, "lord of cattle", falls asleep while tending the cattle. The Morrígan takes away a bull from the herd and brings it to the Síd (fairy mound) of Cruachan to mate to a cow in another herd. Odras comes after her to seize the cattle back, but when she again falls asleep along the way, the Morrígan curses her, transforming her into a pool of water that becomes the river Odras.[9] The somewhat simpler prose version of this tale of Odras and the Morrígan parallels the poem, varying in a few details.[10]

Mag mBreg | Plain of Brega

Mag mBreg means "plain of Brega" and refers to the kingdom of Brega, a central Irish kingdom containing the sacred royal site of Temar (Tara), within the ancient central province of Meath.

A prose tale relates the naming of this plain. A druid named Tulchine prays to the Morrígan to give him a cow whose name is Brega, because this cow is spiritually linked by simultaneous birth to Dil, a *síd* woman he wants to marry. The tale suggests that his prayer is answered; "the Morrígan was good unto him," and the woman marries him and brings her cattle with her.[11]

Berba | River Barrow

The ancient name of the River Barrow was Berba. This river flows southward through the ancient province of Munster to the sea in the southeast of Ireland.

A prose *Dindshenchas* tale gives the story of the naming of the river after the death of the Morrígan's son, Méche. Méche has three hearts with three adders growing in them, and these adders are a threat to the land. The warrior Mac Cécht slays Méche, burns the hearts, and casts the

9 Gwynn 1924 196-201
10 Stokes 1894 113
11 Stokes 1892 471

ashes into the stream, where they boil the river and kill all the animals in it.[12] Another version of this tale from a different manuscript adds that the river's name, Berba, means "slow water", a reference to the water of the river becoming sluggish and murky with the ashes of Méche.[13]

Mag Féa | Plain of Féa

This name appears alongside Mag Femen and Mag Fera, referring to the plains of southern Leinster.

Two prose *Dindshenchas* stories explain the name of the plains. In the first version, Féa, Femen, and Fera are three brothers who clear the three plains and give their names to each of the plains respectively. In the second version, Féa, the wife of Néit who is elsewhere related to the Morrígna, is given as the source of the name. This version also associates the oxen belonging to Dil (the fairy woman mentioned in the *Dindshenchas* of Brega, above) with the naming of these plains.[14]

The Mythological Cycle

The texts in this group contain the remnants of the foundation myths of the Irish: stories of the mythic origins of the Irish landscape and civilization, described in several waves of "invasions". These tales are called the Mythological Cycle by many scholars, as they focus on the arrival, conflicts, and adventures of the Gods and mythic beings who make up the Irish pantheon. Central among the characters of the Mythological Cycle are the Túatha Dé Danann, or "People of the Goddess Danu",[15] a family of Irish Gods, including the Morrígna. The stories were heavily altered by medieval monastic authors, in an attempt to present a pseudo-historic narrative that fit native Irish mythology into their understanding of Biblical history. There are some dozen or so tales in this

---

12 Stokes 1894 483

13 Stokes 1894 304. This is a folk etymology which does not align with modern linguistics on the origin of the name, but which nonetheless still teaches us something about how ancient people understood the meaning of the name.

14 Stokes 1894 436

15 Throughout this book I also use the shortened form Túatha Dé to refer to this group of divinities. It should also be noted that the meaning of the name Túatha Dé Danann is contested; some scholars regard it as referring not to a Goddess Danu (whose name is never documented in that form) but rather to the word *dán*, "skill", referring to Gods of art and skill—values certainly enshrined in the mythology of the Túatha Dé. See Chapter 6 for further exploration of this issue.

group; here we deal only with the three central texts within which the Morrígna appear.

Cath Muige Tuired Cunga | The Battle of Mag Tuired of Cong; also known as the First Battle of Mag Tuired

The name Mag Tuired (commonly anglicized as "Moytura") means "Plain of Pillars" and refers to the location of the battle. Several versions of the story are found in manuscripts from around the 15th century, though the mythic material likely represents a much older oral tradition. The story focuses on the coming of the Túatha Dé Danann to Ireland and their battle for sovereignty of Ireland against another tribe of primal beings who preceded them, called the Fir Bolg.

In the story, the trio of Badb, Macha, and Morrígan are named as sorceresses among the Túatha Dé, and they attack the Fir Bolg with sorcery on the nights before the battle, pouring down magic showers of fire and blood.[16] At the time of the battle, the same trio muster along with other sorceresses and the chieftains of the Túatha Dé in the vanguard of their battalions.[17] Badb is also referred to individually in this story as "the Red Badb", who is eager for battle and the carnage that will ensue. She is mentioned as part of a group of battle spirits who raise a dreadful outcry with their voices over the scene of the battle.[18] Through a very bloody battle, the Túatha Dé take possession of Ireland, offering the Fir Bolg one of the four provinces, Connacht, to remain settled in.

Cath Maige Tuired | The Second Battle of Mag Tuired

This text is derived from a 16th century manuscript containing material dated, based on its language, from the 12th to as early as the 9th century. It relates the continuing story of the Túatha Dé following their taking of Ireland, and their struggle with the Fomoiri, a shadowy Otherworld race of adversaries who are said to have been in Ireland from very ancient times or possibly to have originated from the sea.

The driving conflict of the story is a contest over kingship. The Túatha Dé king Nuada has been disqualified for the kingship due to the loss of his hand in the battle with the Fir Bolg (in the *First Battle of*

---

16 Fraser 1915 27
17 Fraser 1915 45
18 Fraser 1915 33

Mag Tuired, above). A blemished king could not rule, according to Irish custom, so the kingship is granted to Bres, a relative who is half Túatha Dé and half Fomoire by birth. But Bres reigns poorly and without generosity, allowing his Fomoiri relatives to oppress the Túatha Dé with heavy taxation and deprivation. The Túatha Dé then overthrow Bres, returning the kingship to Nuada. With the backing of his Fomoiri kin, Bres attempts to take back the kingship, resulting in a great battle between the two tribes. It is within this tale that the warrior Lugh comes to the Túatha Dé and is raised up to lead them in battle. The Túatha Dé are again victorious in the end, and the closing of the tale focuses on the re-establishment of natural order, peace, and agrarian fertility.

The Morrígna in The Second Battle of Mag Tuired

The Morrígna, and especially the Morrígan herself, loom large in this tale. Here, the Morrígan's famous sexual tryst with the Dagda is described. The encounter takes place near Samhain and just before the battle, where she is washing in the river Unshin, with one foot on each of its banks and her hair in "nine loosened tresses". The Dagda meets her there and they mate, leaving a mark in the landscape named "the Bed of the Couple" from their union. Afterwards, the Morrígan gives the Dagda crucial information about where their Fomoiri enemies will land, saying that she will meet their forces there, destroy the Fomoire king, take his blood, and give it to the hosts.[19]

Another episode follows which partly echoes the Dagda's tryst with the Morrígan. The Dagda encounters a Fomoire woman named only as "the daughter of Indech" (the same Fomoire king the Morrígan has promised to kill in the above episode). The Dagda and this woman engage in a series of highly ritualized verbal exchanges leading to a fight and then a sexual tryst. The episode has a bawdy character to it, with scatological humor and frank language about the couple's sexual anatomy. The character of Indech's daughter is paradoxical: she begins by threatening the many ways she will hinder the Dagda from going to the battle, but ends with a promise to hinder and attack her own Fomoiri kin on behalf of the Dagda, in language that echoes the Morrígan's promises.[20] It has been suggested that this episode may represent a folk variant of the same tale, perhaps composed for a different and

19 Stokes 1891 85
20 Gray 1982 47

more informal audience; but this is far from clear.

In the preparation for the great battle, the Morrígan incites Lugh to lead the Túatha Dé, advising him in the attack.[21] When Lugh is asking each of the Túatha Dé what power they will bring to assist in the battle, she promises to pursue, kill, and destroy adversaries.[22] During the height of the battle, she chants a poem of incitement which turns the battle in their favor.[23] At the end of the battle, the Morrígan, with Badb,[24] comes again to proclaim the victory and the tale of the battle, and she gives two poems, one a benediction of peace, strength, and prosperity, and the other a dark prophecy of a time of sorrow, anarchy, and violence.[25]

Macha, as a sister of the Morrígan, is also mentioned in this text; she is said to have been killed, along with Nuada, by the monstrous Fomoire warrior Balor.[26]

Lebor Gabála Érenn | The Book of the Taking of Ireland (also known as "Book of Invasions")

This text is recorded in several manuscripts dating from the 12th century to as late as the 17th century. It compiles tales about the earliest mythic founders, the peoples of Cessair, Partholon, and Nemed, who shaped the landscape of Ireland. It also contains versions of the Mag Tuired tales regarding the battles of the Túatha Dé Danann with the Fir Bolg and the the Fomoiri, and finally, the the arrival of the Sons of Mil. The text exists in several different versions called recensions (re-workings of earlier versions by medieval monastic compilers). The earliest version, Recension 1, is itself a compilation of a number of different textual sources, woven together with medieval and Biblical pseudo-history. Later Recensions 2 and 3, and derivative versions continue this pattern of rearranging and reworking the texts. The *Lebor Gabála Érenn* seems to have been produced to meet medieval Irish society's need for a legendary historical narrative that would parallel and

---

21 Gray 1982 45
22 Gray 1982 53
23 Stokes 1891 101
24 Where the Morrígan is credited with these poems, it is implied that either she is identical with Badb, or that they are united in the function of retelling the heroic deeds of great battles.
25 Gray 1982 71, Stokes 1891 109
26 Stokes 1891 101

stand beside books such as the Bible (with its story of wandering tribes returning to retake the promised land), while also presenting a mythic ancestral narrative for the origins of Irish civilization. As such, it is very much a patchwork of many pieces of Irish mythography, much altered and rationalized to fit the narrative. The manuscripts also include some of the material in verse form. An additional text called the *Roll of Kings* follows in some of the manuscripts, detailing a list of mythic and historic kings of Ireland with stories of their reigns.

Here, the Morrígan and her sisters, the daughters of Ernmas, appear several times in the form of name lists and genealogies. Brief descriptions are given in some of the texts, but most lack the narrative depth of the Mag Tuired tales.

Macha is mentioned among the founding tribes. In several versions, she is described among the Túatha Dé as one of the daughters of Ernmas, and her death along with Nuada is recorded.[27] In Recension 2 and the verse texts, she is listed as one of ten daughters of Partholon, as well as one of the four wives of Nemed, and as the tutelary figure for which the royal center at Ard Macha was named.[28] Recension 3 identifies her with Macha, wife of Cruinn who gave birth to twins at the horse race at Emain Macha.[29] The story of Macha Mongruad is also given in another of the verse texts, as well as in the Roll of Kings.[30]

Badb is mentioned independently in a verse text about the Battle of Allen. Here she is described in the form of a "red-mouthed sharp-beaked scald-crow", singing warnings about the head of the hero Fergal.[31]

Féa and Némain (or in some variants Badb and Némain) are mentioned in the texts as the two wives of Net, a war god, and identified with Ailech Néit (Grianán Ailech) in far northern Ireland.[32] Féa also appears here as one of the first of the people of Partholon to die in Ireland, and for whom the plain of Mag Féa is named.[33]

---

27 Macalister 1956 119, 229

28 Macalister 1940 27, 131

29 Macalister 1941 189

30 Macalister 1956 263, 461, 513

31 Macalister 1956 539. This story is expanded in more detail in the text *Cath Almaine*, "The Battle of Allen".

32 Macalister 1941 123, 155, 161, 183, 217, 237

33 In this case, Féa is given as a man. It is not at all clear whether we can recognize this as a gender-altered version of the Féa who is associated with the Morrígna, or whether this is a completely different person. Macalister 1939 269, Macalister 1940 13.

Ulster Cycle

The Ulster Cycle tales[34] center around the reign of King Conchobor mac Nessa, the life story and exploits of the great hero Cú Chulainn, and related characters within the ancient northern Irish tribal grouping known as the Ulaid. Tradition places the Ulaid in the territories in the northern and eastern parts of Ireland during the late Iron Age. The stories correspond roughly to a period closing the last few centuries BCE to the first few centuries CE (though they are, of course, mythic rather than historical). This cycle contains some of the earliest texts within the Irish literature. They appear in manuscripts primarily from the 10th-12th centuries, but some contain material dated based on language to as early as the 7th century CE, shortly after the conversion period. As with the rest of the Irish literature, the pre-Christian material is interwoven with medieval Christian literary ideas and material, as well as some influence from Classical Latin and Greek epics.

The central epic of the Ulster cycle is the *Táin Bó Cúailnge*, or Cattle Raid of Cúailnge, a long, detailed, and dramatic narrative of the great war between the provinces of Ulster and Connacht. The *Táin*[35] exemplifies a genre of Irish tales centering on tribal wars fought over cattle and borders. It centers on the theft of an important bull, the *Donn Cúailnge*, ("Brown Bull of Cúailnge"), and highlights the heroic exploits of Cú Chulainn. Associated with it are collections of additional stories that prefigure and lay the background for the conflicts played out in the *Táin*. These back-stories are known as the "Foretales". The Morrígna loom large throughout the *Táin* cycle. The Morrígan herself is significantly involved in most of the major narrative threads of the cycle, taking a special interest in both Cú Chulainn and the *Donn Cúailnge*.

Foretales: *Tochmarc Emire* | The Wooing of Emer

This story is found in 11th-15th-century manuscript versions, and includes material dating to as early as the 7th century, making it among the earliest of Irish texts. It recounts the story of Cú Chulainn's courting of Emer, a young woman of Ulster. Before Emer's father will allow the marriage, he sends Cú Chulainn on a long and arduous journey to

---

34 Sometimes also called the Red Branch stories in earlier usage.

35 As the exemplar of its genre, the abbreviated title "the *Táin*", always refers to the *Táin Bó Cúalnge*.

the stronghold of Scáthach, a legendary warrior woman who gives him martial training and a prophecy of his future. Scáthach herself is a mysterious figure linked with the mythology of the Morrígan. In this tale, however, the Morrígan and her sisters are mentioned within kennings spoken by Cú Chulainn and Emer in their courting speech. These kennings function as coded phrases containing compressed *Dindshenchas*-style references to the lore of places in the landscape.

Among these *Dindshenchas* kennings, Badb is named in association with the land of Ross ("Forest"); she is then equated with the Morrígan and the title Wife of Néit.[36] The Morrígan is also mentioned in association with another place, "The Garden of the Morrígan", a field given to her by the Dagda.[37] In kennings referring to Emain Macha, two stories of Macha are told: an abbreviated version of the story of Macha, wife of Cruinn, followed by the tale of Macha Mongruad. These stories parallel closely with versions found in the *Dindshenchas* and may have been copied from them.[38]

Foretales: *Tochmarc Feirbe* | The Courtship of Ferb

Found in the 12th-century *Book of Leinster*, this tale illuminates part of the history of conflict between Ulster and Connacht. In it, Badb incites the two kingdoms against each other by appearing to each sovereign respectively.

Badb appears to King Conchobor of Ulster, in the form of a fair, queenly woman with golden hair and rich clothing. She incites him to attack Connacht now and thus prevent the devastation of the coming *Táin*.[39] She then visits Queen Medb of Connacht and warns her that the Ulster forces are attacking and her son Mani, who is shortly to marry a woman named Ferb, will be killed, and that Medb should go to avenge him.[40] A battle is fought between the two kingdoms, the young prince Mani is killed, and Connacht is defeated by the Ulster forces.

Badb is also mentioned in several poems within the text, in the context of warnings about destruction and carnage.[41]

36 Meyer 1888 231
37 Meyer 1888 153
38 Meyer 1888 151
39 Leahy 1902 11
40 Leahy 1902 25
41 Leahy 1902 11, 41, 89

Foretales: *Echtra Nerai* | The Adventures of Nera

This legend describes the Otherworldly exploits of Nera, a warrior of Connacht, and includes a brief encounter between the Morrígan and Cú Chulainn. It dates to 14th century manuscript sources.

Nera goes out on Samhain night to put a willow binding on the foot of a dead hanged man, acting on a challenge from King Ailill. This contact with the dead initiates a series of adventures which lead Nera into the Síd of Cruachan (the fairy mound, an entrance to the Otherworld), wherein he meets and marries a fairy woman. While he is in the Otherworld, the fairy woman gives birth to their son, and a cow born on the same day is given to the child. Later, while Nera is tending the cattle, he falls asleep, and the Morrígan appears and takes his son's cow to Ulster to mate it with the Donn Cúailnge, the mighty Brown Bull over whom the *Táin* will be fought. Coming back toward Connacht, Cú Chulainn challenges her to prevent her taking the cow out of Ulster.[42] The encounter with Cú Chulainn is not described in detail, but the text mentions that this is the same encounter described in the *Táin Bó Regamna*, another foretale (below). The story also previews the fight of the two bulls which will come at the end of the *Táin Bó Cúalnge*.

Foretales: *Táin Bó Regamna* | The Cattle Raid of Regamna

This 14th-century text details an encounter between the Morrígan and Cú Chulainn, touched on in *Echtra Nerai* (above) and revisited in a third version within the *Táin Bó Cúailnge* itself. In the *Regamna* version, it begins when Cú Chulainn is awakened by a terrifying cry that echoes across the country.[43] He runs out and encounters the Morrígan at a ford, all in red, with red horse and chariot, and a man also in red driving a cow. As in the *Echtra Nerai* version, Cú Chulainn challenges her, saying that the cows of Ulster are under his care. They exchange a ritualized series of verbal threats and poetics:[44] in frustration with her cryptic speech, Cú Chulainn threatens her, springing into her chariot and placing his spear-point on her head, demanding her name. She tells him she is a poet, and has come with the cow as her fee for a poem.[45]

---

42 Meyer 1889 223

43 Leahy 1906 130

44 I refer to this as "ritualized" as it parallels similar cryptic exchanges in other texts: see the exchanges of the Dagda and Indech's daughter in *Cath Maige Tuired* (Gray 1982 47), and of Cailb and Conaire in *Togail Bruiden Dá Derga* (Stokes 1910 70).

45 Leahy 1906 132

He demands to hear the poem, and she performs it—a prophecy of Cú Chulainn's own doom and death after the *Táin*. Again he springs at her chariot, but she changes form into a black bird on a branch. In this form, she issues a series of threats, saying she will attack him in three forms—as an eel, a wolf, and a heifer—when he is in combat with a warrior whose strength equals his. He counters with the feats he will do against her to win the battle. They then separate, and the Morrígan continues with the cow to the Síd of Cruachan.[46]

Táin Bó Cúalnge | The Cattle Raid of Cúailnge

The central epic of the Ulster cycle, the *Táin Bó Cúalnge* is found in several versions. The earliest, Recension 1, was compiled in the 11th-12th centuries and includes material as old as the 8th century. The slightly later Recension 2, also known as the Book of Leinster *Táin* (from the *Book of Leinster*, its major manuscript source), was compiled in the 12th century using materials from Recension 1 and other sources. Two somewhat later recensions exist, Recensions 3 and 4. For this work, I will draw primarily on the earlier material in Recension 1 and the Book of Leinster.

The Morrígan and her sisters appear as central characters driving the action of the *Táin* narrative. Medb, queen of Connacht, raises all the other provinces of Ireland against Ulster in a war over possession of a mighty, highly valued bull, the Brown Bull or Donn Cúailnge. The Donn Cúailnge is himself one of a pair of magical characters who are reborn again and again through several human and animal forms until taking the form of two mighty bulls. Cú Chulainn is the central warrior-hero of the tale, holding the borders of Ulster alone through most of the tale by virtue of his mighty prowess and capacity for heroic battle fury.[47] The forces of Connacht are at the last defeated, but they take with them the Brown Bull; he is then brought against his adversary, the White-Horned Bull, and the two mighty creatures fight to the death, marking the landscape with their destructive combat. Scholars recognize based on structural elements in the *Táin* that in composing the narrative, medieval scholars may have been influenced by the Clas-

46 Leahy 1906 136

47 He fights alone because all the other Ulster warriors are suffering from the debilitating curse of Macha and cannot rise to their province's aid until the final, full-scale battle in the story.

sical epics in the construction of the long-form narrative saga; however, it is clear that the components of the saga reflect a wealth of quite ancient Irish lore.

While the invasion is gathering force, the Morrígan visits the Brown Bull in the form of a bird and perches on a pillar-stone to speak to him. She delivers a prophetic poem warning him of the danger of capture should he remain in that place; her poem also prefigures the carnage of the battles to come.[48]

The next we see the Morrígan in the tale, she visits Cú Chulainn in the form of a beautiful young woman calling herself the daughter of Búan the king; bringing her wealth and her cattle, she offers herself to him, apparently for marriage. He refuses the offer, saying that he is in the midst of strife and not seeking a tryst. In response, she threatens that she will come against him when he is in the midst of fighting his enemies, and she will attack him in the form of an eel, a she-wolf, and a heifer. He responds with counter-threats to break her ribs, eye, and leg.[49] This episode represents a third iteration of the same encounter also described in the *Echtra Nerai* and *Regamna* foretales (above).

A few skirmishes later, she makes good on the threat, while Cú Chulainn is fighting a formidable hero called Lóch. She attacks him three times in sequence as an eel, a she-wolf, and a heifer. Each time he counterattacks and breaks her bones as he had said he would; but at the same time he is grievously wounded through fighting both enemies at once.[50]

Following the brutal fight with Lóch and several other warriors after him, Cú Chulainn lies wounded and exhausted. The Morrígan comes to him again, in the guise of an old woman milking a cow with three teats. He asks her for a drink to restore him, and with each drink of the milk that she gives him, he blesses her, so that the three wounds are healed.[51]

Several instances within the *Táin* show us the Morrígna acting as war Goddesses, inciting and attacking the hosts. Némain appears in the night on two occasions and attacks the camps of the warriors prior to battle.[52] In one instance, she attacks as part of a triad of war-goddesses: "Badb and Bé Néit and Némain shrieked above them that night in Gáirech and Irgáirech so that a hundred of their warriors died

48 O'Rahilly 2011 152
49 O'Rahilly 2011 176
50 O'Rahilly 2011 180
51 O'Rahilly 2011 181
52 O'Rahilly 2011 130, 220

of terror."[53] Also on the eve of the final great battle between the two armies, the Morrígan appears speaking a poem warning of bloodshed and battle, and which appears to incite the two armies against each other.[54] The story also shows us Cú Chulainn's heroic battle fury associated with appearances of the Morrígna. In one episode, he gives a "hero's shout", which is answered by a host of battle spirits and the appearance of Némain who cause terror and confusion in the enemy encampment in the night.[55] In another episode, his battle fury and accompanying physical distortion is described in language that associates it with Badb in particular.[56]

Also nested within the *Táin* is a series of tales called the *Boyhood Deeds*, flashback-style retellings of the exploits of Cú Chulainn in his early youth and the markers of heroism that he showed. In one tale, his foster-father, the king Conchobor, is lying wounded on the field after a battle. Cú Chulainn ventures out to carry him home, but is attacked by a revenant dead man on the battlefield and thrown to the ground. The Badb is heard "crying from among the corpses", mocking him. This provokes Cú Chulainn to his feet, and he slaughters the revenant and succeeds in retrieving the wounded king.[57]

Other Ulster Tales

Nóinden Ulad | The Debility of the Ulstermen

This story features Macha and gives the mythic background for the curse of the Ulstermen. The present text dates from 14th-century manuscript sources and is perhaps the most detailed, but its story is told in several other places as well, including parts we have noted in the *Dindshenchas* (above).

A man of the farming class, Crunniuc (a variant of the name; elsewhere called Cruinn) lives alone after the death of his wife. A beautiful Otherworldly woman appears mysteriously one day and without explanation, enters his house and begins to do the housework. She sleeps with him that night and becomes his wife; his household and farm gain

53 O'Rahilly 2011 231
54 O'Rahilly 2011 229
55 O'Rahilly 2011 182
56 O'Rahilly 2011 187. The association between Badb and the battle distortion will be explored in full in later chapters.
57 O'Rahilly 2011 138

in wealth and fertility under her care, and she becomes pregnant by him. When the time comes for the annual fair at the royal center of Ulster, the woman warns him not to speak of her. Crunniuc, however, goes to the royal fair and to the horse-race, and there boasts that his wife could outrun the king's horses. The king demands that the woman be brought to him to prove the boast by racing against his horses, and Crunniuc is held on pain of death should she fail. She begs for compassion and a stay of the demand to race until after she has given birth; but her appeal is twice refused. She comes to the race and identifies herself: "My name, and the name of my progeny will for ever be associated with this place. Macha, daughter of Sainreth, son of Imbath, is my name." She races and outruns the king's horses, proving the boast, but her labor comes at the finish-line. She gives birth to twins and, dying from the trauma, with her final screams she lays a curse on the men of Ulster that whenever they were most needed they would suffer a debility with the pain and weakness of a woman in childbirth, continuing to the ninth generation.[58]

At the time of the *Táin*, as we have seen, Macha's curse comes into effect and all the men of Ulster fall under the debility. Cú Chulainn, for mysterious reasons which various sources attribute either to his youth or to his semi-divine status, is not affected by the curse, and this is the reason he undertakes the defense of Ulster alone.

Aided Con Culainn | The Death of Cú Chulainn

The story of Cú Chulainn's death exists in two primary forms. This, the earlier version, is found in 11th-12th-century manuscript sources and contains material dated to the 8th century. This is the ancestor to later versions of the story.

The kin of two adversaries, Cú Roí and Calatín, slain by Cú Chulainn in earlier parts of his saga, now bring about his death in vengeance for the killings of their fathers. The Morrígan attempts to prevent Cú Chulainn's going to the battle with his enemies by breaking his chariot.[59]

On his way to the battle, Cú Chulainn encounters three hags, blind in their left eyes, who have cooked a dog on rowan stakes, to entrap him into breaking his *geis* (ritual prohibition) against eating dog flesh.

58 Henderson 1898 304
59 Tymoczko 1981 42

Since it is also *geis* to him to refuse to eat at a hearth where he is invited, he cannot escape their curse entirely. He accepts the dog meat, but does not eat it; however, simply by touching it, he begins to lose his strength.[60] While these crones are interpreted by some as an appearance of the Morrígan or of Badb, this is a matter of scholarly debate, a question we will explore in more depth in later chapters.

Finally, after his enemies have mortally wounded him, Cú Chulainn ties himself to a pillar-stone so that he may die standing. It is not until a bird lands on his shoulder, indicating that he is dead, that his enemies dare approach him and cut off his head. In this earliest version, this bird is not identified specifically as anything other than a bird.[61]

Brislech Mór Maige Muirtheimne | The Great Defeat on Muirtheimne Plain

Based on the above *Death of Cu Chulainn* text, this later version elaborates and expands the tale. It occurs in manuscripts from the 15th-century onward.

In this later form of the story, the daughters of Cú Chulainn's enemy Calatín are described in terms that recall the classic war-fury: shrieking, frightful voices that strike terror, birdlike flight, magical capacities for shapeshifting, illusion, and battle sorcery. One of Calatín's daughters is named Badb.[62] They work to bring about his death and in this tale, it is these three who appear in hag form and trap him into breaking his *geis* by eating the dog-meat. As with the above version, some read these hags as a manifestation of Badb the Goddess; however, others read them as separate and clearly malevolent characters who simply share the name Badb.

Here we also have Badb appearing before the battle as an omen of Cú Chulainn's doom, in the form of a woman washing bloody armor in the ford.[63] At Cú Chulainn's death, the bird that descends on him is identified as Badb, in crow form.[64]

---

60 Tymoczko 1981 49-50

61 Tymoczko 1981 61. Tymoczko translates this bird as "raven" , though the Irish word is indennach, "bird". Stokes gives "birds" (Stokes 1876 181).

62 O'Grady 1898 241, 243

63 O'Grady 1898 247

64 O'Grady 1898 260

***Togail Bruidne Dá Derga* | The Destruction of Dá Derga's Hostel**

This story derives from 11th-15th-century manuscript sources, including material dating to as early as the 7th century. It relates the kingship of Conaire Mór, a high king of Ireland, set around the same period as the Cú Chulainn saga. The story includes his birth and accession to kingship, and then tells how failures of his judgment as king lead him to breaking all his *gesasa*, and thus to his downfall and death in a battle at a location called Dá Derga's Hostel.

One of the major supernatural figures in the story, the hag who visits Conaire at his arrival at the hostel, is interpreted by many scholars as a guise of Badb herself. She identifies herself first as Cailb, but also gives a long string of 32 names, including Badb, Némain, and Macha.[65] There is a ritual exchange between Cailb and Conaire involving curse threats, prophecies, and strings of cryptic names, and she entraps Conaire into breaking his *geis* by means of a dilemma: to break his *geis* against refusing hospitality to anyone, or break his *geis* against receiving a solitary woman after sundown.

Later in the story, a watcher of the approaching enemy forces looks into the Hostel and identifies each room and all its occupants, including three who are named Badb, described as naked, with ropes of slaughter on their necks and streams of blood running through them, suggesting a coded reference to human sacrifices.[66] Eventually, the king's enemies surround the Hostel, and a battle ensues in which he and almost all his retinue are killed.

***Bruidean Dá Chocae* | Dá Choca's Hostel**

A similar tale to *Dá Derga's Hostel* above, and likely based on it, this 12th-century text tells of the downfall of Cormac Connlongas, a prince who was selected for kingship following Conchobor, just after the time of Cú Chulainn.

While on the journey to Ulster for his coronation, Cormac encounters the Badb in the form of a "red woman", washing gore and blood from his chariot in the river, with prophecies of doom.[67] When they come to the Hostel for the night, a hag visits just as in *Dá Derga's Hostel*, and her physical description is lifted nearly verbatim from the ear-

65 Stokes 1910 70
66 Stokes 1910 87
67 Stokes 1900a 157

lier text. Here, however, she is identified clearly as Badb. She gives a prophecy of death and destruction, and then mysteriously disappears.[68] As in the earlier narrative, Cormac has broken all his *gessi* along the journey and is eventually slain in a final battle.

Tóruigheacht Gruaidhe Griansholus | The Pursuit of Gruaidh Griansholus

A late, somewhat fantastical story of Cú Chulainn, this 17th-century tale follows a model more characteristic of the medieval adventures of Finn. There are several mentions in this text of classes of beings called *badba*; this term is inconsistently translated by O'Rahilly as "war-goddess", "vulture", or "scald-crow" within the same text. In several instances, the *badba* are mentioned as part of a litany of battle-spirits, raising dreadful cries, prophesying bloodshed and carnage.[69]

The episode of Cú Chulainn's combats with Lóch and the attack of the Morrígan at the ford is also mentioned, but here she is not named. She is mentioned only as "the fairy".[70] The Washer at the Ford is also seen washing bloody accoutrements and lamenting, but in this instance she is also not named.[71]

Other Ulster Texts: Incidental Mentions

In the following Ulster texts, the Morrígan or her sisters are not active in the story, but are mentioned. We can still learn something from the context and language used in these mentions.

Fled Bricrend | Bricriu's Feast

An Ulster story found in 11th-century manuscript sources, with material dating to the 8th century. It relates a contest between warriors for the Hero's Portion. Medb gives a poem about the hero Loegaire in which she calls him a *barc bodbae,* translated as "fury of war" or "fury of Bodb"; contextually, the phrase can also be read as "champion of the war Goddess".[72]

68 Stokes 1900a 315
69 O'Rahilly 1924 27, 29, 47, 125
70 O'Rahilly 1924 75
71 O'Rahilly 1924 105
72 Henderson 1899 56

Serglige Con Culainn | The Wasting-Sickness of Cú Chulainn

This 10th-11th-century text about one of Cú Chulainn's adventures contains a poem written in the margin of the manuscript as commentary on the story. This poem refers to Badb as *mna tethrach .i. badb*; "Tethra's wife, that is, Badb"; Stokes here translates *badb* as "she-scald-crow". Tethra was a king of the Fomoiri, with whom the Morrígan is also elsewhere identified.[73]

Scéla Muicce Meicc Da Thó | The Tale of Mac Da Thó's Pig

A satirical tale from 12th-century and later manuscript sources, using material dated to the 9th century. It relates another incident in the rivalry between Ulster and Connacht in the reigns of Medb and Conchobor. Badb is mentioned in a poem, "the brooding *bodb* was met" referring to a war-fury appearing in the battle between heroes.[74]

Finn Cycle

The stories in the Finn Cycle center around the poet-hero Finn mac Cumhaill, the Fianna warrior bands, and the kings and heroes of his age. The time period they appear to describe falls after the stories of the Ulster Cycle, in the early medieval period, though as with the other story cycles, much of the material is mythical and reflective of ancient customs.

Reicne Fothaid Canainne | The Dirge of Fothad Canainne

Recorded in the 8th-9th century, this poem is spoken by a dead hero to his bereaved lover after a battle. A verse describes the apparition of the Morrígan in the form of the Washer at the Ford as an omen of his death:

> "There are around us here and there many spoils whose luck is famous; horrible are the huge entrails which the Morrígan washes.
> She has come to us from the edge of a pillar, 'tis she who has egged us on; many are the spoils she washes, horrible the hateful laugh she laughs.
> She has flung her mane over her back, a stout heart ... that hates her; though it is near us here where she is, let not fear attack thy shape."[75]

---

73 Strachan 1900 17
74 Leahy 1905 48
75 Meyer 1910 16

***Seilg Síth na mBan Finn* | The chase of Síd na mBan Finn**

A 13th-century poem detailing some exploits of Finn and his death. During a battle, Finn is described in heroic fury with the "bird of valour" arising over him, along with *badba belderga*, "red-mouthed battle demons", and the host of battle spirits shrieking over his head and waging strife in the battle.[76]

***Cath Finntrágha* | The Battle of Ventry**

This 15th-century text tells of a battle led by Finn and the Fianna warriors against an invasion of Ireland led by Dáire Donn. As the battle commences, *badba* appear with the host of demons and battle spirits, shrieking and foretelling the devastation that will be done that day.[77]

Cycle of Kings

This story cycle (also called the Historical Cycle) contains tales relating to the lives and reigns of various mythic and historical kings of Ireland. The stories blend mythology into history, written by medieval poets to celebrate the lives, reigns, and lineages of their royal patrons.

***Cath Muighe Rath* | The Battle of Mag Rath**

A text of about the 12th century, from a 15th-century manuscript, it tells of a massive battle fought in the 7th century between High King Domnall mac Áedo and King Congal of Ulster. In the dispute that causes the battle, Congal's rage is ascribed to the influence of three furies, "Electo, Megaera, and Tesiphone". In Irish texts where Classical figures are referenced, Alecto or Tisiphone are often identified with the Morrígan or Badb, and the descriptions in this text align strongly with the character of these appearances.[78] During the battle, a fury shrieking over Domnall's head is identified by name as the Morrígan.[79] Diviners attempt to predict the outcome, seeking to learn "which of them the battle-terrific Beneit would more inspire with her vigors."[80]

---

76 Meyer 1910 94-95
77 Meyer 1885 40
78 O'Donovan 1842 33, 167. Further analysis in Bernhardt-House 2007.
79 O'Donovan 1842 199
80 O'Donovan 1842 243

***Cogadh Gáedhel re Gallaibh* | The War of the Irish with the Foreigners**

This 12th-century epic relates King Brian Boru's conflicts with the Vikings and allied Irish kings, and the famous battle of Clontarf. A *badb* appears in the height of the final battle, screaming and fluttering over the heads of the warriors, along with a host of demons and battle spirits.[81]

***Cath Almaine* | The Battle of Allen**

This text from about the 14th century describes an 8th-century battle between High King Fergal mac Máele Dúin and the Leinster forces of Murchad mac Brain. The Badb is described appearing over the battle, "red-mouthed, javelin-armed", uttering a poem around the head of Fergal and rejoicing in the slaughter.[82]

***Cath Mhuighe Leana* | The Battle of Mag Lena**

This 17th-century Irish text tells of a series of battles between High King Conn Cétchathach ("of the Hundred Battles") and rival kings. A *badb* named Siomha attacks King Eoghan and is killed in this combat. Here *badb* appears in the generic sense, common in later texts as a term for a malevolent magical female, translated "witch" by O'Curry.[83]

In another episode, Eoghan meets a triad of *badba*, venomous, hideous hags, and in a prophetic poem, they tell of the destruction and slaughter to come in the battle, as well as his death. Following this, they then appear to Fráech, another combatant, and give a similar prophecy of his death and destruction. Finally, the three go to Conn, and they incite him to the battle and tell of the victory that he will achieve.[84]

In the battle sequence, terrific descriptions of carnage and blood ensue, and "blue-mouthed, loud-croaking badbs" are said to rejoice over the feast of corpses. The context of *badba* here suggests carrion birds, however, "red-mouthed, deep-black raven-birds" (*brain-eóin*) are mentioned separately and their bird form is emphasized, so it the *badba* may be intended as supernatural creatures.[85]

---

81 Todd 1867 175
82 Stokes 1903 52, 54
83 O'Curry 1855 33
84 O'Curry 1855 119
85 O'Curry 1855 131

Chronicles & Other Collections

***Annála na gCeithre Máistrí* | Annals of the Four Masters**

This 17th-century compilation contains chronicles of kings and events spanning from pseudo-historical Biblical flood events to the year 1616. It contains a brief mention of Macha, the wife of Nemed who died on arrival in Ireland, also said to be one of the wives of the four sons of Nemed.[86]

A version of Macha Mongruad's story appears; she is said to have defeated Dithorba and Cimbaeth in battle and captured Dithorba's sons "by virtue of her strength", then forcing them in servitude to build the fort of Emain. The religious and symbolic elements of her story are minimal in this version.[87]

Annals of Ireland: Fragments

A 17th-century compilation of chronicles for two Irish kingdoms, this text contains a description of Badb appearing at a battle between the Laigin and Osraighe forces, accompanied by battle din, tumult, and bloody massacre on both sides.[88]

***Banshenchas* | The Lore of Women**

Composed in the 12th century, this text gives a list of legendary and historical women of Ireland, in prose framing a series of verse texts. Set forth as a pseudo-historical text, much of the material closely follows that in the *Lebor Gabála Érenn* and the *Dindshenchas*. "Gentle" Macha is mentioned as one of the four wives of Nemed.[89] A brief version of Macha Mongruad's story also appears.[90]

The seven sorceresses of the Túatha Dé are listed, including "Némain, Danand, Bodb and Macha, Morrígu who brings victory", along with Étain and Be Chuilli.[91]

A "venomous" Némain is also mentioned on her own, mother of a son called Colman.[92]

---

86 O'Donovan 2002 M2850
87 O'Donovan 2002 M4532
88 Mac Firbisigh 1860 191
89 Dobbs 1930 317
90 Dobbs 1930 320
91 Dobbs 1930 318
92 Dobbs 1930 330

***Trecheng Breth Féne* | The Triads of Ireland**

This text is a compilation of traditional sayings in the form of "triads", dated to the 9th century. The Morrígan appears in Triad 120: "Three things that constitute a blacksmith: Nethin's spit, the cooking-hearth of the Morrígan, the Dagda's anvil." The language used for cooking-hearth is *fulacht na Morrígna*.[93]

***Cóir Anmann* | Fitness of Names**

The *Cóir Anmann* is a 16th-century text on the meanings and derivations of names. Here the story of the Morrígan attacking Cú Chulainn during his combat with Lóch and the subsequent healing exchange are reiterated nearly verbatim from the *Táin*.[94]

Glossaries

Glosses were often written into the margins of medieval texts, giving additional interpretation of material in the body of the text. Collections of these in the form of glossaries were also made. Many of their entries contain folk etymologies which no longer align with linguistic science with regard to word origins, but these folk etymologies are still valuable as they reflect the beliefs of people at the time.

***De Origine Scoticae Linguae* | O'Mulconry's Glossary**

This glossary contains passages from as early as the 7th to as late as the 14th century. Bé Néit is mentioned as wife of Néit, and "venomous were the pair." An entry for Macha gives "Machae, that is Badb; or she is the third Morrígan; whence Macha's fruit crop (*mesrad Machae*), that is, the heads of men that have been slaughtered."[95] Another gloss mentions Némain as part of a phrase, *nemain dega*, apparently an idiom meaning "sparks of fire".[96]

***Sanas Chormaic* | Cormac's Glossary**

An early glossary dated to the 10th century, *Sanas Chormaic* contains many relevant entries.

---

93 Meyer 1906 17

94 Stokes 1897 149

95 Stokes 1900 271. The spelling used here, Machae, is an archaic one, possibly indicating that this entry derives from the older stratum of the text.

96 Stokes 1900 273

An entry for Ana identifies her as "mother of the Gods of Ireland", and who nursed the Gods. Her name is linked to *ana*, "plenty", and associated with the hills called Dá Chich Anainne, "Two Paps of Ana", west of Luachair.[97] Anu occurs again under an entry for Buanann, where Cormac equates the two, "from their similarity to each other, for as the Anu was mother of gods, so Buanann was mother of the heroes"; along with a folk etymology reading Buanann as "good mother".[98] It should be noted that Búanann is also one of the names of Scáthach.[99]

An entry for *gúdemain*, "false demons", glosses the word as *úatha 7 morrígnae*, "terrors and Morrígna".[100] This gloss is likely based on an earlier one from the *Bretha Nemed Dédenach*, an 8th-century law text, in which gúdemain are called *fennóga 7 bansigaidhe*, "scald crows or women of the síd", and *na morrígna*, "the Morrígna". The gloss goes on to explain that these demons are "false" because "it is a falsehood so that the women of the *síd* are not demons; it is a falsehood so that the scald-crows are not demons of hell, but demons of the air."[101]

In an entry for Bé Néit (Be Net), the title is given to Badb, and she and Néit are called "evil". A saying is quoted, *"be net fort"*, indicating use as a curse " Bé Néit on thee!" or "evil upon thee!". Entries for the alternate spelling Beneid, and for Néit, repeat the gloss from O'Mulconry, here naming the wife Nemon.[102]

Macha appears in an entry for Emain, deriving Emain from *eo-muin*, her neck-brooch with which she measured the outline of the rath at Emain Macha. In a variant manuscript, a note in Latin derives Emain from *ema-unus*, "emanation" and "one", and adds "the emanation is blood… of one man was shed at the time of its creation". This is again a folk etymology, but suggests a contemporary belief about sacrifice in association with important structures. A second entry under "Emuin" alludes to the twins born to Macha there.[103]

---

97 O'Donovan 1868 4

98 O'Donovan 1868 17

99 Macalister 1919 323

100 Meyer's translation, quoted in Borsje 2007 82. O'Donovan's edition gives *úatha* as "spectres" and *morrígnae* as "fairy queens" (O'Donovan 1868 87).

101 *Bretha Nemed Dédenach*, Binchy's translation, quoted in Borsje 2007 88.

102 O'Donovan 1868 25, 26

103 O'Donovan 1868 63

O'Davoren's Glossary

A 16th-century glossary, it contains an entry giving Anann as an alternate name for the land of Ireland, and calls her *bandea .i. sofis fri fileda*, "a goddess, i.e. knowledge to poets".[104] Another entry mentions *bodba*, a synonym for *crufechta*, "scald-crows".[105]

Classical Adaptations

Several important Classical works of epic literature were translated into Irish by medieval scholars, including reworking some of the material using native literary forms and imagery. The Morrígan, or sometimes Badb, are often inserted in place of Classical figures such as furies, demonesses, or war Goddesses.[106]

In Cath Catharda | The Civil War of the Romans

In this 15th-century Irish adaptation of the sections of Lucan's *Pharsalia* on the Roman civil war, the Badb makes several appearances equated to Roman and Greek deities and spirits of war.

In a series of omens prefiguring war, "the Badb of battle Erinys" appears at night over the city of Rome, with serpents for hair and carrying a burning torch.[107] In Lucan's original, the description is of a giant Fury; the serpents and torch are Classical images rather than Celtic.[108] The term "Erinys" is Greek, meaning "avenger of perjury", and signifying an infernal spirit or Goddess involved with the punishment of oath-breakers. The *badba* appear in a group of demonic battle-spirits causing terror in the two camps. The term in the Irish text is *na m-badb m-bélderg*, "the red-mouthed Badb".[109]

In another passage, the Badb is associated with Caesar. In a poetic description that could fit perfectly into an instance of Cú Chulainn's distortion, a battle frenzy comes upon Caesar with "heat and burning and madness and fury", and he is compared in this frenzy to the Badb.[110]

---

104 Stokes 1901 204
105 Stokes 1901 256
106 Bernhardt-House 2007
107 Stokes 2010 71
108 Duff 1928 44
109 Stokes 2010 327
110 Stokes 2010 435

Togail Na Tebe | The Destruction of Thebes

This 15th-century Irish text is based on the *Thebaid*, an epic Latin poem by Statius, based on an early Greek original describing the battle between Argos and Thebes.

In the Irish work, the Badb appears as a *baidbi bruthmaire bellдeirgi,* "fiery red-lipped scald of war", again with serpent hair and fiendish traits. She is called Tisiphone, one of the Furies, and she causes horror and fear when she emerges from a "door of hell" adjacent to a stream.[111] Her image is a Greek one, but the emergence from an underground Otherworld strongly resembles descriptions of the Morrígan emerging from the Síd of Cruachan.

Elsewhere, the Badb appears as a "contentious war-goddess", red-mouthed, brandishing torches and shrieking over the war-camps.[112] In the Latin original, this war goddess is Bellona; she incites warriors to valour but does not engender horror—an element of the Irish model which has been inserted here.[113]

A final intriguing instance equates Badb, as the wife of Néit, with Enyo, a Greek war goddess. The Irish text mentions "the warlike disturbing wife of Néit, that is, Enyo, sister of Mars, the god of war."[114] Interestingly, the Latin original does not mention the war god husband, describing Enyo instead as wielding a torch and bearing serpents. The Irish adapters have equated this Enyo to Badb, as the wife of Néit, and then added the mention of Enyo's relationship to Mars—himself a Roman war god who has in turn been conflated with the Greek Ares.[115]

---

111 Calder 1922 13
112 Calder 1922 87
113 Mozley 1928 507
114 Calder 1922 209
115 Mozley 1928a 243

2

One, Three, and Many

Who is the Morrígan? Many names are associated with the Morrígan: Badb, Macha, Anu, Danu, Némain, Fea, and Bé Néit. Are they all aspects of one divinity, or separate, independent sister Goddesses? Is the Morrígan a single, triple, or multiple Goddess? Who are the Morrígna and what does this collective term mean? Confusion has dominated the popular perception of this constellation of Irish divinities. In part this arises from the tendency in popular treatments to not distinguish between the various streams of lore, nor to recognize the evolution of the material over its history. By examining the evidence for patterns based on historicity and source, I hope to offer some clarity as to the identity of the Morrígan and her relationships to other divinities.

Three-in-One: The Early Morrígna

The earliest strata of textual material about these Goddesses is, generally speaking, where they seem to present themselves as multiple names or faces of a triple divinity. This is most visible in the Ulster texts, since a great deal of the earliest material pertaining to the Morrígna comes from this cycle. A trio of Badbs is mentioned in *Dá Derga's Hostel*, implying triplicity under one identity.[1] In the same text we see the Otherworldly hag Cailb name herself Badb, Némain, Macha, and a host of other names besides, suggesting that many of these names may have been understood as bynames for the same Goddess—or alternate forms in which she might choose to appear. In another early Ulster text, *The Wooing of Emer*, Cú Chulainn equates Badb and the Morrígan as a singular entity: "In the Wood of Badb, i.e. of the Morrigu, for that is her wood, viz. the land of Ross, and she is the Battle-Crow..."[2] Again in the early version of the *Death of Cú Chulainn*, Cú Chulainn's chariot is smashed by the Morrígan to prevent him going to battle; in the verse text immediately following, the same action is ascribed to Badb as though they are one person.[3] In the *Táin* itself, the Morrígan and Badb are used interchangeably with reference to encounters with Cú Chulainn—first the Morrígan is described in the narrative text, then Badb is attributed her actions in the verse text.[4] This equation of Badb and Morrígu in Ulster materials is not seen beyond the time period of the *Book of Leinster Táin* (around the 11th century). Máire Herbert theorizes that Badb was originally understood as an aspect of the Morrígan when appearing in bird form but that this distinction was later lost and the two came to be treated as fully interchangeable.[5]

Outside the Ulster texts, this ambiguity also shows in the early Mythological Cycle text, the *Second Battle of Mag Tuired*. The text tells of the Morrígan arising after the battle to proclaim the victory in poetry, and then tells us "that is the reason Badb still relates great deeds."[6] Additionally, an early gloss gives us the collective term *morrígna* for a trio of divinities, "three Morrígans", while at the same time equating Macha and Badb as names for a member of this trio.[7]

Taken together, these early sources paint a picture of a powerful,

---

1 Stokes 1910 87
2 Meyer 1888 231
3 Stokes 1876 175-176 and Tymoczko 1981 42
4 O'Rahilly 2010 194-195
5 Herbert 1996 145
6 Gray 1982 71. Note that Stokes translates this as "the Badb also relates great deeds" (Stokes 1891 109).
7 Stokes 1900 271

Otherworldly Goddess who might triple herself, appearing as both three-and-one: three who are all Badb, three who are all Morrígan; and whose names might be fluidly interchangeable. This fluidity is expressed most consistently in the identification of Badb and the Morrígan as one in earlier Ulster texts, but hints at the inclusion of Macha and Némain as well. As the literary tradition develops, this fluidity or ambiguity seems to resolve itself into a more differentiated picture, and after the 11th century or so, we no longer see the identification of Badb and the Morrígan as one.

In the early materials, Macha's identification as one of the Morrígna is at best loose, consisting only of the mention of her name, whereas elsewhere, she already has a story of her own that seems to run parallel and perhaps separately from her identification with the primal triad. This material is seen in its early form in detailed *Dindshenchas* stories embedded within the *Wooing of Emer*, giving her as the source for the foundation stories of Emain Macha.[8] It is also notable that apart from her name being one of the list of Cailb's names in *Dá Derga's Hostel*, everywhere else within the Ulster Cycle preserves her distinct identity.[9] This is also the case in the earliest Mythological cycle text, the *Second Battle of Mag Tuired*; here Macha has a separate identity as the wife of Nuada, not identified with Morrígan/Badb.[10] Thus, apart from one early gloss, it is only in the later Mythological Cycle and related materials where we see Macha begin to be firmly gathered into the triad.

The triad of war Goddesses begins to develop with the first recension of the *Táin*, in material from the 8th-9th century. The triad here is Badb, the Morrígan (also identified as the wife of Néit) and Némain. Each of these appears both together in the triad and individually, and seems to display specialization of functions. These three are consistent with the later Book of Leinster *Táin*, but in the first recension we see them acting only individually, not together a triad. Notably, in Ulster texts this triad is never specified as a group of sisters. In the *Death of Cú Chulainn*, a triad including a Badb also appears (collectively called the daughters of Calatín), but the two other sisters are not named, and it is not made clear that these sisters are the war Goddesses.

---

8 Meyer 1888 151-152
9 Stokes 1910 70
10 Stokes 1891 101

Three Sisters: The Mythological Triad

It is in the middle and late Mythological Cycle texts that the triad of sisters crystallizes most fully and consistently. Here the consistent triad configuration becomes Badb, Morrígan, and Macha. In the *First Battle of Mag Tuired*, they are simply a triad of sorceresses.[11] In the *Lebor Gabála* and related texts, they are usually spoken of as a group of sisters who are all daughters of Ernmas. In a handful of cases, one of the sisters is given the name Anann; this is listed as the personal name of the Morrígan in particular.[12] In later recensions Anann is appended to the triad as an additional sister; in at least one case this is clearly an error as four names are listed as "three daughters".[13] In a few cases the triad is included within a larger group such as seven daughters of Ernmas, or nine women of the Túatha Dé.[14] However, within these larger groups the essential triad remains intact.

Thus while there may appear to be an incredibly confusing array of different configurations represented in the lore, the essential triad within the Mythological Cycle texts is clear: Badb, Macha, and the Morrígan, whose name in this stream of the tradition is also Anann. This triad would appear to be the result of literary attempts to rationalize and systematize regionally and tribally variant mythological groupings. This triad holds within the Mythological Cycle texts, beginning with 12th-century materials and continuing right through to late texts of the 17th century. Frequently associated with this Mythological triad are paired Goddesses, also members of the Morrígna group, often identified as wives of the war God Néit. In the Mythological texts, these two appear as either Féa and Némain or Badb and Némain. When the pair is grouped within a specific collective that includes the triad, the pair appears as Féa and Némain, sensibly avoiding the contradiction of listing Badb twice in one group. We will explore the nature of Néit and the Morrígna Goddesses identified as his wives in more detail below in Chapter 7.

Outside the Mythological tradition, and in all Ulster materials dating from the 12th century onward, we tend to see primarily single appearances of one of the Morrígna, presented independently of each

11 Fraser 1915 27

12 Macalister 1941 123, 131, 161 etc. There is one exception where Macha is the name given for the Morrígan, but this is likely due to scribal error.

13 Macalister 1941 123

14 Macalister 1941 155, 217.

other. These texts typically include either Badb or the Morrígan acting as war Goddesses, but never both together; Macha appears separately as a heroic legendary figure with her own story.[15] Annals and texts in the Cycle of Kings, typically describing battles for kingship, give appearances of either the Morrígan, Badb, or in some cases an impersonal, undefined collective of *badba,* interpreted as a generic class of war-furies or battle spirits. Most Finn cycle texts including any of the Morrígna are late medieval, featuring only Badb or generic war-furies; with the exception of one early poem in which the Morrígan is named.

Patterns in the Lore

Thus to summarize this wealth of material we can identify a few core patterns, around which variations occur, as would be expected in a body of lore that is the distillation of localized, tribal, and changing religious ideologies.

1. Very early materials tend to show triads under the same name: three Badbs, three Morrígans, with additional bynames.
2. The Ulster tradition tends to equate Badb and the Morrígan as one Goddess, or to present a triad of Badb, Morrígan, and Némain. Macha is treated separately as a tutelary figure.
3. The Mythological tradition tends to present a triad of Badb, Morrígan, and Macha. An overlapping, related pair are presented as wives of Néit (usually Némain with Féa).
4. Late materials across traditions tend to present a single Badb or Morrígan only, or a depersonalized generic collective of *badba* war-furies.

We of course recognize that this summary glosses over the inherent variation of the source materials, in the interest of highlighting patterns and trends.

Should we recognize the Morrígan as a single multiform Goddess with many aspects? Should we recognize each of these Goddesses as individual in their own right? Angelique Gulermovich Epstein argues for the view that, for the medieval scholars at least, they were all un-

15 This reading of their relationships is supported by Herbert 1996 142.

derstood as aspects of one Goddess, the Morrígan.[16] If the lore tells us anything, I think what it makes clear is that this question has been approached differently by people throughout history. We can see regional patterns in the approach to these divinities as well as patterns that have changed with time and the encroaching influence of Christianity. Which among these early peoples represents the "authentic" way to approach the Morrígna? My own experience in studying this material has been that the deeper I delved, the more detailed my study, the more ambiguity I found. Like the druidic mists and smoke she conjures, like her love of constantly changing shape, the Morrígan has continually eluded attempts to define her and her relationship to other divinities in concrete terms.

In my own relationship to the Morrígna, I tend to encounter them as theophanies rather than separate Goddesses (a theophany meaning a visible manifestation of a divinity). They are to me distinct identities and appearances adopted by the great and ancient war Goddess we know best as the Morrígan. This is primarily because she has presented herself to me in that way. As a practicing polytheist, I think experience is the best guide. We need to study the lore and history of her worship, to train our perceptions, to learn the iconographic and mythical language in which she speaks. But old texts are not religion—religion is lived, and authentic polytheism means recognizing the agency of the Gods and responding to their lived communications and revelations in the here and now. Thus, I encourage readers to pursue what yields fruit in devotional practice. If the divinities respond best to separate worship, let us give them separate worship. If they present themselves to us as integral, let us worship them in that way. Some may find this leads them to a rich, diverse practice engaging all the daughters of Ernmas as distinct, separate Goddesses. Some may find they seem to be looking at a familiar, beloved face wearing many masks. As with so much of Celtic spiritual practice, to thrive in this we must be at home with paradox. Just as our own identities are complex, just as we may have our own singular personhood and yet also possess identities that are collective, so the Morrígna can be understood to be at once both individual and collective.

16 Epstein 1998 65

The Modern Triple Goddess

Popular books, websites, and other modern treatments of the Morrígan have often referred to her as "a triple Goddess", and this has been the source of much confusion and misinformation. While it is true that there is a clear pattern in the sources where she is presented in the context of a triad, the modern conception of "the triple Goddess" as composed of Maiden, Mother, and Crone archetypes does not apply to the Morrígna group and should be abandoned by any serious student of the Morrígan.

The triple Goddess archetype is quite modern and rather Victorian in its ethos. It defines the roles, functions, and symbolisms of its three Goddesses based on socially constructed female roles in relation to sexual and reproductive life: Maiden, a pre-sexual or at least pre-motherhood female; Mother, a fully sexual and reproductive woman; and Crone, a post-menopausal and grandmotherly "wise woman". It is crucial to note that all of these archetypes are defined by the woman's relationship relative to reproductive functions and motherhood, a social role. This archetypal model assumes that women will progress through each of the three stages and it defines the status, meaning and function of womanhood in a heteronormative procreative context. It centers sexual reproduction in the identity of these Goddesses.

In contrast, the triads of Goddesses that we see in ancient Celtic religions are very different from this archetype. Rather than being defined based on temporal social roles for women, these triads tend to personify related specializations of a shared larger function, such as war, fecundity, sovereignty, wealth, or a combination of such functions. For example, the Morrígna triads typically present a pattern of three related specializations of war, such as victory, heroic battle ardor, and carnage; or three related archetypes such as Queen, battle crow, and war-fury. In other cases, the triad is simply an amplification of one personality, such as the "three Badbs" of *Dá Derga's Hostel* or the three one-eyed crones of *The Death of Cú Chulainn*.[17] Similarly, we also see triads such as the three tutelary Goddesses of Ireland, Ériu, Fotla, and Banba, whose identities emerge as variations of their land and sovereignty functions.[18] Elsewhere in the ancient Celtic and Germanic worlds we often find triads of this

17 Stokes 1910 87, Tymoczko 1981 49-50

18 Macalister 1956 53

sort, such as the Matres or Matrones, typically three mothers who typically carry various symbols of fertility, wealth and protection (though in some cases, they appear as more than three).[19]

In none of these cases can we actually map a Maiden, Mother, and Crone group onto these triads. While it is true that we can find the Morrígna appearing in the shapes of youthful women, as mothers, and as crones or hags, the three roles never appear together as such. Most of the Morrígna appear in more than one of these forms as it suits them, so that no individual theophany can be clearly linked to any of the three archetypes. The triple Goddess archetype is too tidy to contain our fighting queens and wild war furies, our pregnant sorceresses and lascivious hags. Most importantly, the identities and roles of the Morrígna Goddesses are never primarily defined by reproductive status. Motherhood tends to be incidental to their function; we are told the names of sons borne by the Morrígan and Macha, but these acts of motherhood are peripheral to their narratives. Even where sexuality takes center stage in their narratives, it is in the context of granting sovereignty, victory, or another form of Otherworld favor, rather than a socially defined reproductive role.

19 Irby-Massie 1999 148

3
The Morrigan

Queen Goddess

We meet the Morrígan in a great range of sources throughout the Irish literature, from the earliest material continuing into the late medieval period. Her name appears in several other forms: Mórrígan, Morrígu, Morrígna, and many variant spellings. In many cases it is given with the definite article, *an Morrígan* "the Morrígan" and appears to be a title rather than a name; in other cases, it is presented as a name. In a few instances, it is pluralized as a name for a class of beings: Morrígna, "Morrígans".

The meaning of the name (or title) *Morrígan* is given by some scholars as "Phantom Queen"; other scholars also give "Great Queen". The element *rígan* is unambiguous: "queen". This element appears in many related Celtic Goddess names: Gaulish Rigani, Welsh Rhiannon, etc. The element *mor* is contested, in part because of differences in how it is written. Accented *mór* is "great", in the sense of large, powerful or mighty.[1] Unaccented *mor* may refer to the concept of "phantom, shadow", as appearing in names such as that of the Fomoiri. According

1 A related form, *már*, is older.

to some scholars, this term traces to a common root found in other Indo-European languages such as Germanic *mara* (Old High German/ Anglo Saxon), indicating a baneful or frightful spirit (inherited in English "nightmare").[2] These scholars make the argument that the original form of the name was unaccented, Morrígan, and that the length mark has been added by medieval transcribers, and a popular etymology then created to link it to *mór*, "great". Charles Donahue notes that, other than as a part of names such as Morrígan, Fomoire, and similar, the unaccented element *mor* is not found in Irish, and suggests that it may therefore be of very great antiquity, tracing back to continental Indo-European roots: "... the naming of the goddess must have taken place very early and probably on the continent."[3] Indeed, looking at her alignment with similar Continental divinities, Epstein suggests we should look on the Morrígan as descended from a very ancient "Germano-Celtic war goddess" combining aspects of the medieval Irish war Goddesses and the Norse-Germanic valkyries.[4]

When it comes to the medieval literature in which her stories are contained, both forms (Mórrígan and Morrígan) are attested, and her identity both as a great Queen, and in association with phantoms, are not in doubt. Throughout this book, when I am not quoting a source directly, I employ the spelling Morrígan for the sake of consistency.

A Síd: From the Fairy Mounds

In many instances when the Morrígan appears, she is said to either emerge from or travel into the *síd*, or fairy mounds. The *síd* are, generally speaking, ancient mounds, caves, or other subterranean structures existing in the Irish landscape, which in most cases predated Celtic civilization. Many of them are funerary mounds—megalithic chambered tombs covered with great cairns of stone and earth, over which vegetation has regrown, creating a human-made hill. These sacred subterranean places were understood to be entrances to the Otherworld territories, inhabited by the fairy tribes. Her association with these sites points to her identity as an Otherworldly being; in general, the Túatha Dé are associated with the *síd* mounds where the tales say they

2 Donahue 1941 11-12, Stokes 1891 128

3 Donahue 1941 12

4 Epstein 1998 viii

retreated when the Milesians overtook the land of Ireland.[5]

The Morrígan is repeatedly described as "from the fairy mounds". In the *Táin* episodes of her prophecy to the Brown Bull, her combat with Cú Chulainn at the ford, and the healing of Cú Chulainn, it is mentioned that she comes out of the "fairy mound" on these forays.[6] In the *Second Battle of Mag Tuired*, the character identified as Indech's daughter (who is not named here but whose tale in some ways parallels that of the Morrígan in her meeting with the Dagda) says that she will "summon the sons of Tethra from the síd-mounds"; sons of Tethra referring to Fomoiri entities.[7] This again suggests a close relationship with Otherworldly people.

The *síd* she is most closely associated with is Cruachan; stories tell of her emerging from this site on her errands to orchestrate the movement of cattle and the instigation of the *Táin*. In the *Cattle Raid of Regamna* and Odras *Dindshenchas* tales, it is to the Síd of Cruachan that she takes the cattle.[8] A cave still exists at Cruachan, now called Oweynagat (an anglicization from the Irish Uaimh na gCat, "Cave of Cats"), which enduring folk traditions still attribute as the home of the Morrígan and Otherworldly chthonic powers, and from which she is said to emerge every Samhain.[9]

In addition to residing in the Síd of Cruachan, the Morrígan also associates herself with certain other mounds. In the *First Battle of Mag Tuired*, it is from the Mound of the Hostages at Tara that she, along with Badb and Macha, conjure druidic mist and violent showers against the Fir Bolg.[10] Though we don't see her enter into or emerge from the Mound of the Hostages; as a funerary mound and also a high place in the landscape, it seems to provide both a sanctified place from which to conjure, and a vantage point for access to the war camp of the Fir Bolg in Tara. As it was known as a grave mound, the choice of this site also may suggest that the spirits of the dead within the mound may have been understood to play a role in the type of battle magic the sorceresses were there to conjure. In the Brúg na Bóinne *Dindshenchas*, the Morrígan is also associated with the mound of Áed Lurgnech. It is implied that she was struck down or killed at this site.[11]

5 Hennessy 1889 3
6 O'Rahilly 2010 174, 194, 196
7 Gray 1982 49
8 Leahy 1906 136, Gwynn 1924 196-201, Stokes 1894 113
9 Waddell 2014 67
10 Fraser 1915 27
11 Gwynn 2008 19

Banchaínti: Poetess

In almost every story in which she makes a significant appearance (as opposed to simply being mentioned), the Morrígan can be found reciting poetry. In many cases, the poems are oracular prophecies; in some, they are also warnings, incitements, or enchantments. In the *Second Battle of Mag Tuired*, she recites three poems: a battle incitement, and two prophecies. In the *Táin*, she appears to the Brown Bull and gives him a warning poem, and she speaks a poem of incitement and warning between the Ulster and Connacht encampments. In the *Cattle Raid of Regamna*, she delivers a prophetic poem to Cú Chulainn, prophesying his death. Here she identifies her title as a poet: *"Am banchainti-sea em"*, "I am a female satirist in truth."[12]

The term "satire" in the Irish context means something very different than it would in modern Western culture. Here she speaks not of humorous mockery in the way that we might now think of as satire. She refers to the poetic tradition of satire, a specialized form of magically aggressive poetry—a type of cursing, in short. Fragments of ritual lore surrounding the practice of satire are found in the Irish texts, and place it within a spectrum of ritual poetic forms which also includes prophecy. Satire poetry, that designed specifically to bring harm and destruction on the recipient, bears close parallels with prophetic poetry—it is often not possible to tell whether a poem telling someone's doom is a passive foretelling or an active casting of a spell of doom. It is this tradition and range of practices with which the Morrígan identifies herself when she names herself "a female satirist".

In practice, her work as a poet seems to be primarily prophetic. As measured by Epstein, whenever the Morrígan speaks in the literature, almost without exception her speech either foretells the future, or is intended to bring about future consequences—and in very many cases these speakings take the form of poetry.[13] Her speech is never passive and rarely conversational. We can observe her practicing both aspects of magical poetry: prophetic delivery (e.g. to Cú Chulainn, to the Brown Bull, and at the end of the *Second Battle of Mag Tuired*) and active cursing (e.g. to Odras). A third form of poetry which she also performs is incitement (e.g. in the *Second Battle of Mag Tuired* and the *Táin*). The poetry of the Morrígan will be examined in detail in Chapter 9.

12 Leahy 1906 132
13 Epstein 1992 187

Dia Sóach: Shapeshifting Goddess

Another primary attribute of the Morrígan is shapeshifting. She changes form at will, and is named "the shape-shifting Goddess" in a *Dindshenchas* poem.[14] As we will see, several of these forms overlap with forms taken by other Morrígna, such as Badb typically appearing in crow form. What is distinctive to the Morrígan is the sheer variety and range of the forms she takes, and the specific linkage with the act of changing shape. When one of the Morrígna appears in a story and actively changes shape within that same story, it is always the Morrígan. This shapeshifting behavior is one of the hallmarks of an Otherworldly personage, and is often linked to characters who are said to reside in, or emerge from, the *síd* or "fairy mounds". As well, the color of many of these appearances signals Otherworldly identity: the all-red clothing, and the white, red-eared description are typical of many Otherworldly characters. Here we summarize the shapes in which she appears; the significance of each particular shape is explored in more depth elsewhere.

Red woman: A woman dressed all in red, with red eyebrows and hair. Beings wearing red or animals colored red are classic signals of Otherworldly status in the Irish literature. In the *Cattle Raid of Regamna* episode, she is also accompanied by a man all in red, and a chariot with a red horse.[15] Similar Otherworldly beings all in red appear as omens in *Dá Derga's Hostel* and *Dá Choca's Hostel*.[16]

Young woman: A young woman "of surpassing beauty", dressed in many colors, she appears bringing her wealth and cattle, to offer a liaison with Cú Chulainn.[17] It is likely that here, the array of many colors is a signifier of wealth and especially status; medieval Ireland had customs prescribing the colors that people of varying social status were allowed to wear.

Hag or crone: An old woman, often lame and/or one-eyed. This form appears to Cú Chulainn during the *Táin* as well as his death-tale.[18] She is also seen as a skinny, gray-haired hag shrieking over the weapons in

---

14 Gwynn 1924 196
15 Leahy 1906 132
16 Stokes 1910 41, Stokes 1900a 157
17 O'Rahilly 2011 176
18 O'Rahilly 2011 181, Tymoczko 1981 49

battle.[19] One-eyed or lame beings are another signal of Otherworldly status. In essence, it is an expression of the malevolent aspect of Otherworldly power, and is often also a form adopted by Badb.

Black bird: A raven, crow, or simply a black bird. The Morrígan is primarily seen taking this shape within the *Táin* and foretales, in which literature she is also identified as Badb.[20] Thus this form is more properly connected with the Badb. These birds are deeply linked with battle and slaughter as carrion birds, and also take part in prophetic and magical functions, as well as being associated with the phenomenon of the warrior's fury. These functions and the bird forms are discussed in full detail in the section on Badb.

Eel or serpent: A black eel in a river.[21] The eel appears in the symbolism and language of sorcery, in particular, cursing and binding practice. This aspect is explored in more depth below, in the section on sorcery. Possibly related, serpents are loosely associated to the Morrígan through her son Méche, who has three hearts with three serpents in them.[22] It seems medieval scholars may have regarded eels and serpents as iconographically equivalent, and perhaps this is part of the reason the Morrígan (and Badb) are sometimes identified with demonic serpent-haired divinities in Classical translations into Irish.[23]

She-wolf: A wolf, shaggy and russet in color (or sometimes gray).[24] The wolf, and by extension the dog, are animals closely associated with warriors and especially warrior bands such as the Fianna, with their seasonal patterns of hunting and raiding. The identity of Cú Chulainn, of course, is tied to dog iconography and the rituals of warriorship. An interesting medieval gloss also links the Morrígna with wolves and foxes under the rubric of "howlers", linking their vocalizations with those of scald-crows as demonic creatures.[25] The wolf identity and its expressions in warriorship will be explored in full in the section on the warrior cults.

Cow: A heifer, either red and hornless, or white with red ears. This is the form she takes in her attack at the ford, and she is accompanied

---

19 O'Donovan 1842 199
20 Leahy 1906 136, O'Rahilly 2011 152
21 O'Rahilly 2010 194, O'Rahilly 2011 180
22 Stokes 1892 483
23 Stokes 2010 71
24 O'Rahilly 2010 194, O'Rahilly 2011 180
25 *Bretha Nemed Déidenach*, quoted in Borsje 2007 88.

by fifty heifers linked in pairs by chains.[26] As mentioned above, the red animal shape is an indicator of Otherworldly status, as are the paired chain-linked animals. The Morrígan's relationship to cattle and cattle iconography is explored in more detail below.

Ban-Túaithech: Sorceress

Sorcery, including battle magic, enchantments, weather effects, cursing, and confusion are consistently attributed to the Morrígan throughout her lore. She is named as one of the *ban-túaithecha*, "sorceresses" of the Túatha Dé, and she and her sisters are called "springs of craftiness".[27] These sorceries are not, per se, a unique capacity of the Morrígan, but a manifestation of her function as one of the druids of the Túatha Dé, and in most cases examples of similar spells can be seen from other characters.

We have a few fascinating glimpses into the forms her sorcery may take. In the *Dindshenchas*, she transforms the woman Odras into a pool of water by chanting spells of power over her "with fierceness unabating".[28] This scene evokes a passionately chanted magical charm, a practice which is consistent with the *rosc* poetic form she often uses. Versified charms and spells recorded in curse texts and tablets have been found that link this practice to the *rosc* form, a topic we will explore in more depth in the chapter on the Morrígan's poetry.[29]

Another form of sorcery employed by the Morrígan seems to be binding magic, and this would appear to be particularly associated with her appearance as an eel. Her action against Cú Chulainn in eel form is to "draw a noose" about his feet, evoking the notion of magical binding.[30] Similarly, the druid Mug Ruith conjures an eel in a stream which binds and constricts his enemy. Bernard Mees notes that the word for eel, *escong*, may in fact be related to the word *escaine*, meaning "to curse", and to *nascad*, "binding".[31]

The Morrígan's most notorious type of sorcery may be her battle magic. In the *First Battle of Mag Tuired*, with her sisters she conjures magical mist and showers of blood and fire down onto the warriors of

26 O'Rahilly 2010 194, O'Rahilly 2011 180
27 Dobbs 1930 318, Macalister 1941 217
28 Gwynn 1924 196
29 Mees 2009 77
30 Leahy 1906 136
31 Mees 2009 140

the Fir Bolg.[32] Such showers of blood and druidic fire are attributed to Mug Ruith as well. Druidic battle magic is linked in quite a few places in the lore with pillar stones. Druids and poets are said to station themselves atop pillar stones to ply sorcery during a battle—a position that would grant a vantage point, while also likely drawing on supernatural forces inherent in the stone itself.[33] This positioning atop a pillar is a characteristic behavior of the Morrígan, and from here she incites warriors to battle (as in the *Fothaid Canainne* poem),[34] and delivers prophetic poetry (as in the *Táin* poem to the Black Bull.)[35] Pillar stones are also employed by the Túatha Dé sorcerers, including the Morrígan and her sisters, as some form of battlefield binding in the *First Battle of Mag Tuired*, where "they fixed their pillars in the ground to prevent any one fleeing till the stones should flee."[36]

Ba Slóg-Dírmach Sámda: Whose Pleasure Was in Mustered Hosts

All the Morrígna are associated with warfare, but their individual functions within the sphere of war vary. The Morrígan in particular is called a Goddess of battle in sources from the earliest to the latest; she "whose pleasure was in mustered hosts",[37] bringer of victory,[38] and of "bitter fighting".[39] In the Mythological Cycle, she takes part in battles with sorcery and magical attack as well as incitement to warriors for ferocity. Here she is placed clearly on one side of the battle, strengthening and fighting on the side of her people, the Túatha Dé. She musters with the war-chiefs of the Túatha Dé in both *Mag Tuired* stories. She also suggests specific war powers she will bring to bear directly, pursuing, killing, and destroying adversaries in the battle, including the king of the Fomoiri (in the *Second Battle of Mag Tuired*).[40] Here as well, she takes a significant role as observer of the battle and its outcome, and it is she who announces the

32 Fraser 1915 27
33 Fraser 1915 43
34 Meyer 1910 16
35 O'Rahilly 2010 174
36 Fraser 1915 45
37 Gwynn 1924 196
38 Dobbs 1930 318
39 Macalister 1941 217
40 Gray 1982 53

battle and the victory to the whole of Ireland at its end.

In the Ulster Cycle, her role is more ambivalent and complex. She orchestrates the coming of the *Táin*, instigating the battle by arranging the mating of the cow from the Síd of Cruachan with the Donn Cúailnge in Ulster, to bring about the conception of the calf that will challenge the two bulls to fight.[41] She still seems to take a side—and she is listed among the chieftains who will be asked to muster on behalf of the Ulster forces in the final *Táin* battle.[42] But when full scale warfare between the armies is imminent, she stirs dissension and fear between the camps—appearing to both bless and warn each side.[43]

The apparent ambiguity of her role and motives in the instigation of warfare is a key mystery. On the most direct and surface level, she seems to instigate and escalate warfare. On a deeper level, she is also taking part in a larger cycle and fulfilling a predetermined role within it. The two Bulls of the *Táin* were destined to fight, and represent two great Otherworld houses of Ulster and Connacht. The fight of the Bulls is a cosmological one, linked to themes of the destruction and re-creation of the cosmos through conflict and sacrifice. Similarly, the great battles of the Mythological Cycle have a cyclical and seasonal quality, reflective of deep cosmological underpinnings of Celtic culture in which great Otherworld battles are fought at seasonal points, and in which conflict and bloodshed are seen as periodic necessities to restore order and to feed the forces that uphold the cosmological cycle. The Morrígan's role seems primarily to be in orchestrating that inevitable and perhaps necessary conflict; as war Goddess, to bring it to a head; as tutelary Goddess of heroes, to make it heroic; and as poetess, to prophesy, speak destiny, and incite to victory.

Yet her relationship to warfare appears to be personal, too. There is a persistent sense in the literature that the Morrígan is not only active in war as part of her ordained divine function, but in fact actually enjoys it. This is reflected in sources both early and late. In the early *rosc* poem she chants during the *Second Battle of Mag Tuired*, she compares her experience of battle to that of a hound shaking its kill to and fro.[44] In the *Fothaid Canainne* poem, we meet her laughing spitefully at the carnage

41 Meyer 1889 223
42 O'Rahilly 2010 248
43 O'Rahilly 2010 229
44 Carmody 2013

as she incites warriors on toward death.[45] In the *Battle of Mag Rath*, we see her nimbly dancing over the spear-points in battle.[46] Again and again is expressed the sense that she takes pleasure in war—an ethos that we see even more intensely in the person of Badb, with whom she is closely identified. For Badb, as battle crow, the pleasure seems more specifically oriented toward the carnage, on which as carrion bird she would feed. The Morrígan seems to take a different pleasure, the "pleasure in mustered hosts". To make sense of this, we will need to take a deeper look at how she was venerated in war and by warriors, a topic we take up in Chapters 16 and 17.

Oitin do Bá'is-siu: Guarding Your Death

Beyond her association generally with the sphere of war, the Morrígan involves herself in an intimate and complex relationship with individual warrior heroes. This occurs not just in the context of battle, but in an ongoing tutelary relationship between war Goddess and warrior. Cú Chulainn represents the best example of this relationship, and in the Ulster Cycle we see his connection with the Morrígan (as well as Badb and Némain) developed into full depth and complexity.

We see Badb, inciting him to courage even as a youth, and elements of the war Goddess's identity and symbolism are suggested in his training with Scáthach. In the *Táin* and related tales, the Morrígan engages in a complex sequence of relations with Cú Chulainn including offering sexual love and aid in battle, prophesying his fate and death, challenging and attacking him in physical combat, exchanging healing with him, and finally involvement with his death. Her relationship with heroes is tutelary and erotic, and at the same time challenging and potentially destructive. It is strongly suggestive of an initiatory relationship linked to the Celtic traditions of warriorship and the training, rites of initiation, and customs of warrior societies. The Morrígan's complex relationship with the hero, at once tutelary and threatening, may be encapsulated with the expression she speaks to Cú Chulainn: "It is at the guarding of thy death that I am; and I shall be."[47] This phrase, "guarding your death", has been variously interpreted to mean "work-

45 Meyer 1910 16
46 O'Donovan 1842 199
47 Leahy 1906 136

ing to bring about your death", "guarding the manner of your death", or even "guarding you from death". Whether this is read as protective or malevolent—or both—it is clear from its delivery and context that the Morrígan is personally interested in the life story and manner of death of this warrior.

The subject of the relationship between the Morrígna and Cú Chulainn and its reflection on warrior customs of the ancient Celts is an expansive one we will explore in more depth in Chapter 17.

Nobered Búaid: Bringer of Victory

The *Banshenchas* poem calls her "Morrigu who brings victory"—a key element of her relationship to warfare.[48] In addition to specific descriptions of this kind which tell us directly that she is responsible for bringing victory in battle, we also see several instances in narrative lore where this action is played out. In the *Second Battle of Mag Tuired,* she appears to act as an awakener or initiator; in Isolde Carmody's words, "the opening call for Lug to 'awake' and 'undertake a battle of overthrowing' points to her role as the awakener of the young warrior to his heroic destiny."[49] She appears at another critical moment and turns the battle to a rout favoring the Túatha Dé by inciting them "to fight the battle fiercely and fervently", with her poem beginning "Kings arise to the battle."[50] In this story, it is implied that she has given a promise of victory to the Dagda for his people, at their tryst on the river Unshin on the eve of the battle; she offers personally to destroy the king of the Fomoiri and gives the Dagda strategic information to assist in the victory.[51] The *Táin* and related Ulster stories make her victory aspect somewhat more understated, but a similar dynamic is implied. She comes to Cú Chulainn as King Buan's daughter offering him a marital tryst and martial aid in the battle.[52] This offer is rejected by him, but the underlying dynamic is parallel.

In each of these stories, aid and victory in battle are coupled to a sexual tryst (or offered in conjunction with one). Thus what we are seeing here is a mythic process parallel to sacred kingship, but with respect

48 Dobbs 1930 318
49 Carmody 2004 105
50 Stokes 1891 101
51 Stokes 1891 85
52 O'Rahilly 2011 176

to war in particular. In the lore of sovereignty and sacred kingship, the king ritually marries the sovereignty Goddess who is an embodiment of the land itself and its power; through this sexual union, his right relationship to the land is established, his rule sanctified, and the benefit of the land and people ensured. Here, a warrior or war-leader ritually marries the war Goddess, who carries the fate of the battle and its warriors; through this sexual union, he secures her aid in the battle, both supernatural and physical, and she grants victory to her chosen. Both patterns are exemplary of the fundamental Celtic belief that prosperity and a positive fate are secured by means of a contract with the Otherworld powers, and in many cases, that contract is sealed through erotic union with an Otherworldly being who is a vessel and embodiment of those powers.

Her appearance between the two camps on the eve of battle in the *Táin* expresses the victory aspect in an interesting way. Here she seems to both tell of victory and warn of defeat to both camps simultaneously—suggesting that this is not prophecy. Instead, her verses imply that the victory may go to either side.[53] Is this simple incitement to battle? It seems not: for the warriors listening to the spectral voice, hearing their forces both hailed as victors and warned of slaughter and defeat, there would naturally be an element of fear and dread to the message. It conveys a powerful sense that the victory has not been decided, that it perhaps lays in her hands.

In Mórrígan Mórda: The Mighty Great Queen

Among the most ancient and enduring of our lore for the Morrígan are stories of identification with the land. The *Wooing of Emer* identifies her with landscapes including Gort na Morrigna and the forest land of Ross.[54] *Dindshenchas* tradition situates her in the landscape of the Brúg na Bóinne and its complex of monuments and sacred hills and rivers, as well as the mighty cave at Cruachan.[55] Of course, *Dindshenchas* tradition overflows with stories placing hundreds of characters into the landscape, so this in itself does not make her a land Goddess. It is the nature of her identification with the landscape that points to an ancient

53 O'Rahilly 2011 229
54 Meyer 1888 153, 231
55 Gwynn 1924 19, 196

identity as Goddess of the land and sovereignty. The land itself takes her shape at Brúg na Bóinne, with its two hills identified as the "Two Paps of the Morrígan".[56] Landscape sites are named and linked to her partnership with the Dagda: the Bed of the Couple near the Mag Tuired battle site[57] and sites named for their bed and dwelling-place at Brúg na Bóinne.[58]

The coupling of the Morrígan and the Dagda is at once an example of her victory-bringing function and also illustrative of her as sovereignty Goddess. For the Dagda is not just a warrior and war-leader, but one of the kings among the Túatha Dé, and what is contested in the battle is the sovereignty of Ireland itself. It is this that she grants to his people through her aid, engendered by their coupling at the river. The lore that links her to sovereignty bespeaks some ambiguity about her origins, too. If she is acting here as a sovereignty Goddess granting victory and rulership of Ireland to the Túatha Dé, then her identification with the land of Ireland would tend to place her as a member of a pre-existing group. And in fact a few references throughout the lore do suggest a connection of the Morrígna with the Fomoiri: Badb, closely identified with the Morrígan, is sometimes called the wife of Tethra, a king of the Fomoiri.[59] And as we have seen, the element *mor* in her name may be cognate with the name of the Fomoiri, indicating "phantom", shadowy Otherworld people. Yet in so many other places she is identified as one of the Túatha Dé. This ambiguity may be reflective of differing local traditions about her identity and it may reflect a shift over time as well.

Goddesses with names reflecting queenship and regality are found among many of the ancient Celtic cultures, and are pervasively linked to sovereignty. The Gaulish Rigani, whose name also means "divine queen", is thought to be related to the Welsh Rhiannon, whose lore bespeaks sovereignty and a close parallel with horse-related sovereignty and battle Goddesses including Macha and Epona.[60] These British and Continental Goddesses and their relationship to the Morrígan are explored further in Chapter 8. The tutelary Goddess of the land and its sovereignty, of course, naturally may take on a warlike aspect when

56 Stokes 1894 292
57 Stokes 1891 85
58 Gwynn 1924 11
59 Borsje 2007 49
60 Waddell 2014 89-90

threatened, and tribal warfare was a means by which early Celtic warrior societies maintained their identity and social structure.

Bóaire: Lady of Cattle

As the wealth of the land, the Morrígan displays an active and dynamic engagement with cattle both as symbol and object of value. We have seen her shape-shifting into the form of a hornless red heifer to attack Cú Chulainn during his combat with Lóch at the ford. Interestingly, this action seems to have a significance beyond simply making Cú Chulainn's fight harder: it displays significant parallels to a druidic curse practice. Here a druid Dill, in an attempt to repel an invading tribal enemy, transforms himself into an identical hornless red cow and runs over a ford from east to west, with incantations and the burning of magical ingredients.[61]

The Morrígan's involvement with cattle goes beyond taking their shape. She actively involves herself in the movement of cattle, orchestrating the mating, movement, and protection of significant cows and bulls, initiating cattle raids, and even receiving and answering prayers related to cattle herding. In a *Dindshenchas* tale, a druid named Tulchine prays to the Morrígan to let him marry a woman, Dil, by giving him her cow; because by virtue of being born at the same time, the woman is magically tied to the cow.[62] In a tale found in varying forms in the *Adventure of Nera* and the *Cattle Raid of Regamna*, the Morrígan takes a cow from Nera to mate with the Donn Cúailnge, the Brown Bull; while she is traveling with the cow, she is challenged by Cú Chulainn in a pivotal encounter in the setting up of the story that will become the *Táin*. Here, the calf that will be born from this mating is prophesied by her to have the same lifespan as Cú Chulainn.[63] In the *Táin*, she takes a special interest in the Donn Cúailnge himself, perching in bird form on a pillar-stone and delivering a prophetic poem to warn the Bull of his danger should he remain there.[64]

In these stories, the movement and reproduction of cattle function as levers for the manipulation of large-scale events on both a magical and

61 O'Curry 1873 207
62 Stokes 1892 471
63 Leahy 1906 136
64 O'Rahilly 2011 152

social level. Cattle, of course, were central to both the economy and sacred iconography of the Celts in Ireland as elsewhere. Their economic function as wealth and currency are reflected in another *Táin* episode where the Morrígan offers herself to Cú Chulainn for marriage, in the shape of a young woman bringing her cattle herds and wealth.[65] Cattle are also deeply connected to cosmological themes within the Celtic worldview. Examples of this can be seen in the connections between Goddesses in cow form and mythic themes of creation and landscape formation (e.g. the Goddess Bóann), and the cosmological themes embedded in the epic battle between the two great bulls, whose birth and eventual combat the Morrígan is carefully arranging in the events leading up to the *Táin*. The combat of the bulls, culminating in their death and dismemberment and the shaping of the Irish landscape from the parts of their bodies, expresses a deep mythic theme found throughout Indo-European cultures. It also hearkens back to the practice of ritual bull sacrifice, also thought to be Indo-European in origin.[66] The bull sacrifice in Ireland takes the form of the *tarb feis*, "bull feast", a druidic oracular ritual in which bull sacrifice is used for divination specially related to kingship.[67]

Fulacht na Morrígna: the Morrígan's Hearth

A minor and often-overlooked aspect of the Morrígan is her connection to the hearth, cooking, and hospitality. The primary expression of this is found in the *fulacht fiadh*, or "wild hearth". Often called "burnt mounds" by archaeologists, these sites (dating from late Neolithic to early Iron Age) are found throughout Ireland and typically include a trough where water was boiled using fire-heated stones, and the used fire-blacked stones tossed into a midden, forming the "burnt mound". Theories as to what these outdoor hearths were used for include cooking game and curing hides from hunting expeditions, brewing beer, and heating sweat-houses or primitive saunas—and there may well have been multiple uses. Folklore has long associated the *fulachta* with both *fianna* warrior bands and the Morrígan. An alternate name for these sites, especially the larger ones, is *fulacht na Morrígna*, or "hearth of the

65 O'Rahilly 2011 176

66 Lincoln 1991 34

67 Waddell 2014 137. See chapters 12 and 14 for further exploration of this ritual.

Morrígan". The identification of these sites with the Morrígan by that name is an enduring one, reflected in folk usage right up to the present day, and also found in texts dating as far back as the 9th century.[68]

A *fulacht* figures significantly in the death-tale of Cú Chulainn: it is there that a trio of Otherworldly crones (closely resembling a guise in which the Morrígan visits him in the *Táin*, and in the later version, specifically named Badb) entrap him into breaking one of his *gessi*, and so bring him closer to his death. The hags have cooked dog-meat on a spit and offer it to Cú Chulainn, apparently knowing that he will have to accept it and thus break his *geis* against eating the flesh of his sacred name-animal. The *geis* that this conflicts with appears to be one compelling him to eat at any *fulacht* where he is invited.[69] In light of Cú Chulainn's close relationship with the Morrígan as her chosen hero, and if we are reading the *fulacht* hag as a guise of herself, this *geis* becomes very interesting. It may suggest something more specific than a *geis* against refusing hospitality at any *fulacht*, but rather a ritual requirement not to refuse hospitality at a hearth of his tutelary Goddess.

The *Triads of Ireland* associates both the Morrígan and the Dagda with the hearth and hospitality functions as well as the role and tools of a blacksmith, a highly mythologized occupation, and one belonging to Cú Chulainn's namesake Culann: "Three things that constitute a blacksmith: Nethin's spit, the cooking-hearth of the Morrígan, the Dagda's anvil."[70] The spit may be significant: we have seen this in the form of the spit on which the crones have cooked the dog-meat to curse Cú Chulainn. Beyond its use to prepare the cursed meat, in the later version of the death-tale, Badb attacks him directly with the spit, throwing it at his head; he catches it and throws it back, but a drop of blood from the spit touches him and delivers the curse.[71] Here, a cooking-spit is associated with her as both a magical and physical weapon. It may be meaningful that an iron flesh-hook decorated with ravens and swans was found in northern Ireland, dating to the late Bronze Age. While the Dunaverney flesh-hook cannot be directly associated with a cult of

68 Coyne 2006 34

69 Stokes 1876 176. Stokes' translation reads this as Cú Chulainn being bound not to consume the food at a *fulacht*; but this makes no sense as there would be no conflict between *gessi* and no compulsion for him to visit the crones and take the meat. Tymoczko corrects this in her translation (Tymoczko 1981 49).

70 Meyer 1906 17

71 Epstein 1998 130

the Morrígan, Waddell and others suggest the possibility; at the least, its paired bird symbolism may relate to themes of death and life or plenty, and its design seems intended for the serving of meat.[72]

Medieval Irish law texts provide some intriguing detail relating to hospitality and the *fulacht na Morrigna*. Such a hearth must have "three kinds of victuals on it, i.e. dressed victuals, and raw victuals, and butter"; the text is careful to specify that the cooked food must not be burned, and the butter not melted but "proper".[73] One might be tempted to note that this fairly well resembles the modern idea of a full and balanced meal—cooked meat, uncooked foods (perhaps vegetables?) and dairy. In another Brehon text, it is said that nine persons might be fed at the Morrígan's hearth, and that they went to her because they were outlaws.[74] Her *fulachta*, then, provide hospitality especially to warrior bands (*fianna*) operating in the wild outside society—tying neatly to the other name of the *fulachta* as hearths of the Fianna. This helps to explain why we would see hearth and hospitality associated with an otherwise rather un-domestic Goddess: it is primarily within her relationship with warriors and warrior culture that the hearth and hospitality role is expressed.

In Ben Mór, in Dagda Donn: The Great Lady and the Dark Dagda

As we have seen, the Morrígan's primary consort is the Dagda (though there are others, as we shall see). In almost all cases where the Morrígan by name is given a husband, it is the Dagda. This is seen in the earliest Ulster texts, including the *Wooing of Emer*, where the landscape called the Garden of the Morrígan is said to have been given to her by the Dagda.[75] The pairing is reiterated in the *Mag Tuired* texts, the *Dindshenchas* material, and in many other sources including the *Banshenchas*, where the Morrígan is one of three wives (along with Badb and someone named Asachu who is otherwise unknown.)[76]

The Dagda merits a book unto himself, and we can do little more than outline his features here. His name is, like hers, as much a title as

72 Waddell 2014 47
73 Petrie 1839 212
74 Petrie 1839 213
75 Meyer 1888 153
76 Dobbs 1930 168

a name, appearing with the definite article *in*, "the". Dagda is typically translated "Good God", though alternate translations are possible.[77] Another of his names, also something of a title, is Eochu Ollathair: *eochu* is a variant of *ech*, "horse"; Ollathair is from *ol*, "great"; athair is "father". This name is thus something like "Horseman Great-Father".[78] A primary attribute of the Dagda is his huge club (or sometimes forked staff, hammer, or axe) which has the power to kill with one end, and to bring life with the other. The Dagda, and this club, are involved in land formation acts, as reflected in the *Mag Tuired* episodes in which he is put to work building raths, and in the Indech's daughter exchange.[79]

He functions as a war-leader in both *Mag Tuired* battles, and he is also among the kings of the Túatha Dé to rule Ireland both before and after the mythic battles.[80] It is to him that the Morrígan gives the promise of aid in battle and victory at their tryst at the river. Here the language suggests a standing appointment: "the Dagda had to meet a woman". It seems clear that he has not chanced upon her, but gone to an appointed meeting. That there is a place at the river called "the Bed of the Couple", along with the seasonal symbolisms inherent in the *Magh Tuired* battles, suggests that their coupling was part of a seasonal mythic cycle of sovereignty and battle celebrated there.

He is also called *in Dagda deirg* "the red Dagda"[81] and *Ruad Ro-fhessa*, "Red one of Great Knowledge".[82] The red color identification here may signal Otherworldly status. When the Morrígan appears to Cú Chulainn as the "red woman", she is accompanied by a great man in red, with a "forked staff of hazel", driving her cow. A similar, but distorted and ugly, man with a forked pole and swine accompanies the Otherworldly hag who we know to be Badb in her malevolent form in *Dá Derga's Hostel*.[83] And indeed, the hostel is named for a mysterious person called Dá Derga, "red God", who may well be the Dagda himself.[84]

---

77 *Dag*, "good"; *da* may also be "good", which would render an intensive by repetition, something like "the most good". Alternately, *da* may be from *día*, "a God".

78 Macalister 1941 102

79 Gray 1982 47

80 O'Donovan 2002 23

81 Stokes 1894 292

82 Stokes 1897 150

83 Stokes 1910 41

84 This idea is explored in more detail in Chapter 10.

Ancestry and Relations

The Morrígan's maternal lineage in particular is very consistent. In every case where maternal lineage is mentioned, she is said to be the daughter of Ernmas. These references occur throughout the *Second Battle of Mag Tuired,*[85] all recensions of the *Lebor Gabála,*[86] as well as ancillary sources such as the *Banshenchas*, where they are applied to the whole Mythological triad—Badb, Macha, and Morrígan are the daughters of Ernmas.[87] This lineage is also consistently given in both versions of the *Táin*, where the Morrígan appears solitary (and frequently identified with Badb) as the daughter of Ernmas.[88] Ernmas is a female divinity essentially known only from these mentions as the mother of various Túatha Dé Goddesses. Where she is described any further as to character and function, Ernmas is a "she-husbandman". The name, however, counters this agrarian image; it is from the word *ernbas,* meaning "slaughter, violent death", or literally, "death by iron": *iarn* "iron", *bas* "death". The *First Battle of Mag Tuired* also gives two foster-mothers of the Morrígna triad: Bechuille and Danann, also "she-husbandmen".[89]

Paternal lineage for the Morrígna is less emphasized, but when it is mentioned, it is usually given that they are the daughters of Delbáeth (who is sometimes also called a son of Néit, the war God).[90] The name Delbáeth is likely from *delbaid,* "to shape, form, or fashion"—perhaps a kind of creator God. It is also possible that the name is a compound of *delb* "shape, form" and *áed* "fire"; it would then be something like "form of fire" or "fire-shaped".

The primary progentors of the Morrígna triad, then, are Violent Death and the Shaper, or Shape of Fire. This in itself suggests that their primal identity is that of war-Goddesses.

Clann na Morrígna: the Children of the Morrígan

Dindshenchas literature gives the Morrígan a son, Méche. Méche is a monstrous and terrible son, possessed of three hearts and serpentine quali-

85 Stokes 1891 101, 109

86 Macalister 1941

87 Dobbs 1930 168

88 O'Rahilly 2011 176 etc

89 Fraser 1915 45

90 Dobbs 1930 168, Macalister 1941 189

ties: "The shapes of three adders' heads were on the three hearts that were in Méche, and, unless his death had occurred, the adders would have grown in his belly till they would not have left an animal alive in Ireland."[91] The hero Mac Cecht kills him in a highly ritualized manner suggestive of sacrificial rites: he is slain, his three hearts burned, and the ashes cast into the river Berba (Barrow), boiling it and killing all the creatures within. No clear translation or etymology seems to be evident for the name Méche, but as we have noted above, the link between eels or serpents and sorcery and binding magic may be relevant here.

A comparison has also been suggested between Méche and the great monstrous serpent Matha, of whom several stories exist in the *Dindshenchas* and later material.[92] Slain by a great hero, its bones and body parts make up the shapes of the land, and its bones pollute the sea, similar to the remains of Méche polluting the river. The grave of Matha is associated with Brúg na Bóinne sites named for the Morrígan and the Dagda.[93] Matha too is repeatedly called "sluggish"; similarly, the river into which Méche's remains are cast is said to become sluggish or slow.[94] Both creatures share serpentine attributes, monstrous hugeness or multiplicity, and sacrificial deaths that simultaneously shape the land and poison the water. It may be not be appropriate to view them as identical, but it seems likely that there may be a relationship—both may derive from similar mythic origins.

The Morrígan has other children, about whom we also have little information. A brood of warriors are ascribed to her in the Finn cycle text *Acallam na Senórach*: "the children of the Morrígan daughter of Ernmais, with her twenty-six female warriors and her twenty-six male warriors."[95] These children are not named as individual characters but simply as her *clann*, "children", and apparently her troops. Finally, in one late *Lebor Gabála* text, the Morrígan is attributed three other sons by Delbaeth, her own father: Brian, Iucharba, and Iuchair. This is, however, the same text in which she is conflated with Danann, so this is likely an error.[96] Most other sources list another Goddess as the mother of these sons (in some cases, Brigid). Additional confusion has some-

91 Stokes 1892 483, Stokes 1894 304
92 Carmody & Thompson 2014
93 Gwynn 2008 13
94 Gwynn 2008 25
95 Cited in Epstein 1998 184.
96 Macalister 1941 189

times arisen regarding supposed children of the Morrígan as a result of the Dagda having another wife, the Goddess Bóann. Thus references to the Dagda's wife and children including Cermait, Brigid, Óengus Mac ind Óc and others have occasionally been mistakenly assumed to be children of the Morrigan, when in fact they are his children with Bóann. Epstein points out that in every case where children are clearly attributed to the Morrigan, they are children who bring forth war and destruction—the warrior bands, the son whose serpent hearts threaten the world. For this reason, though mother she is in the strict sense, she does not fit the archetype of the "mother Goddess".

4

Badb

She of the Battle

The name Badb is from the Irish word *badb*, generally translated as "crow", though its meaning and usage in ancient times with reference to birds was generally less specific and could indicate any carrion bird (crow, raven, or vulture), or occasionally even a bird of prey. The older stratum of Irish literature often uses the earlier spelling *bodb*. When used in context of the Irish Goddess, it appears as both Badb or "the Badb", indicating that it may in some cases have been seen as a title for a war Goddess, rather than a proper name.

In Gaulish and early Brittonic Celtic, the cognate word is *bodua*, appearing in many personal, religious, and tribal names (e.g. Boduos, Bodua, Boduognatus, Maroboduus, Cathubodua).[1] Related names occur in early Germanic (Baduhenna, also a war Goddess; Baudihillia, *beadu*, "battle") as well as Norse languages (Old Icelandic *boð*, "battle").[2] The root **bodu-* can thus be seen as a very ancient Indo-European root standing for concepts related to carrion birds and battle. This very an-

1 Delamarre 2003 81
2 Donahue 1941 7

cient identification of the root throughout Celto-Germanic civilizations suggests that her identity as a war Goddess reaches back to the common Indo-European roots of these cultures on the continent. As we will see, across a very broad swath of ancient Europe, war deities in the shape of crows or ravens appear to have been worshiped.

Scholars believe that the original meaning of this root **bodu-* was in fact war, and its application to carrion birds came about by virtue of their association with battlefields.[3] This goes some way to explaining the non-specificity of the Irish word *badb*, being translated by scholars of the Irish literature as "carrion crow", "scald crow", "hooded crow", "raven", "vulture", or "bird of prey". In later usage within the Irish literature, the word *badb* takes on further dimensions of meaning and is used to mean "witch", or one of a class of malevolent non-personalized entities *badba*, translated as "war-fury" or "demon" and appearing in company with a host of battle spirits and frightful Otherworld beings. In addition, *badba, bodba,* or variants are also commonly used in Irish texts as adjectives which, depending on context, may mean "warlike", "violent", "pertaining to war", or may signify identification with Badb herself, "of the war-goddesss".[4]

Thus the picture that emerges from the etymological history of the word is the transformation of an ancient war Goddess associated with the battlefield and appearing in carrion bird form, to a broader usage that included impersonal classes of beings viewed in a more demonic light.

Badb Catha: Battle Crow

Early textual mention of Badb in crow form is found in the encoded *Dindshenchas* lore in the *Wooing of Emer*, where she is called *an bodb catha*, "the battle crow" and identified as a Goddess of war (simultaneously identified with the Morrígan).[5] Similar references continue throughout the lore from early to late.

One of the most prominent features of Badb as battle crow is her voice. In many cases where Badb appears, and particularly when associated with the battlefield, it is her voice that is first characterized, and sometimes it is her only described feature. It is not always clear

3 Delamarre 2003 81, Donahue 1941 8
4 Borsje 1999 234
5 Meyer 1888 231

whether or not a given instance of Badb's voice is meant to be read as the intelligible voice of a Goddess or simply the screaming of carrion crows; this ambiguity suggests that in the mind of the ancient Irish the two were equivalent, and indeed, as we will see, the voices of corvids were treated in some instances as oracular.[6]

Among the earliest texts in which the Badb of battle speaks are the Ulster Cycle tales. In one of Cú Chulainn's boyhood tales, he is walking a battlefield at night to rescue the wounded Conchobor, and he hears "the Badb crying from among the corpses".[7] She proceeds to incite him with taunts, making clear that this Badb is not just a carrion crow, but a war Goddess. Elsewhere, the phrase "ford above which the Badb will shriek" is invoked, the ford here referencing that many of the important combats take place at fords, which are boundary-crossing places.[8] Badb also shrieks over the camps of the Connacht armies (in the triad with Bé Néit and Némain, in this case).[9] In a great many instances, the epithet used is *Baidbi béldergi*, "red-mouthed war Goddess". This colorful phrase suggests a mouth red with blood from feasting on the carnage, and ties the Badb further to carrion bird imagery.[10] Sometimes the bird imagery is made even more explicit, as in *badb belderg birach* "red-mouthed sharp-beaked scaldcrow".[11] In almost every case, the action associated with this form is shrieking, screaming, or occasionally singing, in the air over battlefields.

Badb as battle crow is pervasively linked in the literature to the carnage of war—a natural reflection of the action of carrion birds. She is said to hunger for slaughtered bodies, to feast and revel among them, and to be thankful for the carnage. The carnage itself is named for her in idioms like "the sorrow-heaps of Bodb".[12] These descriptions of Badb enjoying carnage are present across nearly all groups of texts (e.g. Ulster, Mythological, Kings, etc.) with the exception, perhaps, of the *Dindshenchas* tradition. However, these descriptions tend to be most prominent in the later sources, starting around the 11th century. Early references link Badb to the battlefield more in terms of the combat it-

6 See Chapter 14, below, for citations on this.
7 O'Rahilly 2011 138
8 O'Rahilly 2011 202
9 O'Rahilly 2011 231
10 O'Rahilly 2010 231
11 Macalister 1956 539
12 Macalister 1941 279

self, or the action of the warriors within it, than simply to a hunger for carnage; the earliest references to death and bloodshed in association with the Badb suggest sacrifice rather than war.[13]

Coinnli Bodba: Fire of the War Goddess

Badb, like the Morrígan, has a special association with heroes—but Badb's role is a specific and unique one. Her association with heroes is particularly linked to the heroic fury or battle frenzy, and the phenomena which accompany it. This is most vividly described in Cú Chulainn's heroic *ríastrad* or "distortion": his body contorts, one eye bulges frenziedly, his jaws draw back grotesquely, and fiery emanations radiate from him. "The torches of the Badb, virulent rain-clouds and sparks of blazing fire, were seen in the air over his head with the seething of fierce rage that rose in him." Associated with the fiery "torches of the Badb" is the phenomenon called the "hero's light" (*lúan láith*): a mighty pillar of light "as long and as thick as a hero's fist", rising from his forehead.[14]

The hero's light is shown by a handful of heroes and warriors in the literature, and it is very often associated with a bird form. This bird apparition is seen fluttering over the head (or on the breath) of a warrior in possession of heroic fury, as in the poem in the *Death of Cú Culainn*, "a glossy bird/ flutters over the chief/ of that chariot".[15] The phrase typically used in the case of the bird form is *én gaile*, "bird of war-fury" or *lon gaile* "black bird of battle". The word *gaile*, from *gal*, "valor" is significant—it is a term that appears widely in idioms describing aspects of warriorship, and refers to seething heat that rises to become warrior's rage, and is expressed in acts of valor and warriorship. Thus *én gaile* may be translated "warrior's bird", "bird of battle", etc; I tend to use "bird of valor". Language used to describe the bird form here is sometimes ambiguous, but the suggestion is of a glossy, shining black bird emerging round the head of a warrior in connection with the radiant, fiery hero's light and possession of battle frenzy. Related phenomena are recorded in other Indo-European (Roman, Greek, and Iranian)

13 Stokes 1910 87
14 O'Rahilly 2011 187
15 Tymoczko 1981 52

as well as Etruscan cultures.[16] We have here a fundamental and quite ancient concept of a heightened heroic state of war-fury, expressed as fiery light emanation and the presence of a divine war-bird spirit hovering over the warrior.

That war bird may be read as the Badb, as evidenced by her mention in Cú Chulainn's case. In almost every instance in which the heroic fury is described in terms of its bird form, the Badb (or *badba* as a collective) are also invoked into the scene. The rising of the heroic fury, with its heat, fiery emanations, and hero's light, brings the bird of valour; and she seems either to emerge from him with the hero's light, or perhaps is drawn down from above, to hover over him in his battle ardour.

Badba Bélderga: Red-Mouthed Battle Spirits

A recurring feature of stories in which the Badb appears is a group of spectral creatures or spirits associated with battle, violence, and terror. I refer to this group as "the battle spirits". Wherever they are mentioned, these battle spirits are evoked in rhythmic runs of descriptive text in which a variety of types of spirits are listed. A typical run in terse early Irish style is something like this, "the goblins and sprites and spectres of the glen and demons of the air gave answer..."[17] Later texts elaborate these runs into long, evocatively dramatic sequences in high medieval style:

> "And there arose a wild, impetuous, precipitate, furious, dark, frightful, voracious, merciless, combative, contentious, vulture, screaming and fluttering over their heads. And there arose also the satyrs, and the idiots, and the maniacs of the valleys, and the witches, and the goblins, and the ancient birds, and the destroying demons of the air and of the firmament, and the feeble demoniac phantom host; and they were screaming..."[18]

Creatures variously included in these groups of battle spirits include *badba*, already familiar to us as carrion birds, war furies, or manifestations of the war Goddess; along with *ammaiti* "hags", *arrachta* "specters", *bánánaig* "pale creatures", *boccánaig* "horned creatures", *demna aieóir* "demons of

16 Campanile 1988 92
17 O'Rahilly 2011 182
18 Todd 1867 175

the air", *gelliti glinne* "mad creatures of the glens" or *geniti glinne* "witches or spectral women of the glens", *siabra* "sprites", *urtrochta* "phantoms", *uatha* "horrors". Some of these terms may hint of Christian ideologies toward Otherworldly spirits, but it is clear that these entities belong to a native Celtic stratum of mythology associated with battle. In one episode of the *Táin*, they are specifically identified with the Túatha Dé.[19]

The typical context in which the battle spirits arise is in association with a hero's expression of battle fury, when he is rousing himself to fight or in the fray itself. They are, again and again, said to "raise a cry about him" or to "scream from the rims of their shields and from the hilts of their swords".[20] Incitement to violence, howling for blood, terrifying warriors, comparing the valor and strength of armies, and prophesying victory and death are all functions ascribed to the shrieking and screaming of the battle spirits. This screaming onslaught of the battle spirits rarely occurs absent an appearance of one of the war-Goddesses, and it is Badb with whom they are most closely associated. In some instances, we may see Némain or another of the Morrígna appearing just before or after the battle spirits arise, but it is only the Badb who ever rises among them and whose voice they seem to echo. In later texts, where the Badb becomes depersonalized and relegated to the status of a generic collective term, it is only in such contexts that she appears.

Fáistine na Fola: Prophetess of Blood

The shrieking of Badb as carrion bird and her appearance with the battle demons in connection with heroic fury evoke with them another of Badb's functions: that of prophecy. As with heroes, prophecy is also a domain of the Morrígan, but her prophecies are typically chanted poems with meter and structure and are usually performed by her in formal contexts contexts where she is acting in an official poetic capacity. The forms of prophecy associated specifically with the Badb are somewhat distinct from this, in that they tend to occur in the madness and bloodshed of war itself, or in a hostile visitation to prophetically incite battle.

The prophetic manifestation is characteristically seen in association

19 O'Rahilly 2010 217
20 O'Rahilly 2010 217, 228

with the battle spirits as mentioned above. The Badb arises, often surrounded by the host of frightful spirits, shrieking or chanting warnings over the heads of kings and heroes entering battle. The crying of these spirits tells of the carnage to come, and in many instances is said to foretell who will live and be victorious, whose blood will be shed, and who will die on the battlefield. We also see them "screaming and comparing the valour and combat of both parties."[21] As mentioned above, there is a particular association between Badb and the battle spirits and the onset of heroic fury—in at least one case following the performance of a "hero's shout" vocalization by the warrior, implying that the battle host may be arising in response to an invocation. They are also said to shriek and scream from the special weapons and armor of warriors, suggesting empowered or ensouled battle-gear were also seen to be connected to the emergence of these prophetic war-furies.[22]

There are cases where Badb herself is associated with prophecy in a more formal poetic context. One occurs in the *Second Battle of Mag Tuired,* where she takes part with (or as) the Morrígan in performing the two poetic prophecies after the battle. But here, because of the identification with the Morrígan, it is not clear whether it is as *Badb* per se that the prophecies are given.[23] A second type of prophetic manifestation occurs in the *Courtship of Ferb* as well as the *Battle of Mag Lena,* in which Badb appears separately to both hostile parties prior to a battle, to warn and incite them to war. In the case of the *Courtship of Ferb,* the prophecy is intermixed with incitement.[24] In the *Mag Lena* case, the prophetic visitation to one side appears to be as much a curse as a prophecy, and her visit to the opponent is more an incitement than a prophecy.[25]

Amait Arrachta: Spectral Hag

A consistent feature of Badb's appearances is her use of sorcery for battle magic as well as personal cursing. We see acts of sorcery in the *First Battle of Mag Tuired,* where she appears in the mythological triad with Macha and Morrígan, and conjures "magic showers of sorcery and compact clouds of mist and a furious rain of fire, with a downpour of

21 Todd 1867 175
22 O'Rahilly 2011 182, 201
23 Gray 1982 71
24 Leahy 1902 11
25 O'Curry 1855 119

red blood from the air on the warriors' heads".[26] This description typifies her acts of battle sorcery. However, she does not engage in this type of sorcery alone, tending to appear either in the above triad, or in the Ulster sources with Némain and Bé Néit (likely here the Morrígan).[27]

Outside battle magic, Badb's characteristic expression of sorcery is in the form of malevolent prophetic visitations which carry a distinct suggestion (in some cases made explicit) that the prophecy is not simply a vision of the future but in fact a curse. In these instances her appearance is usually as a grotesque hag, a visage which signifies the Otherworldly malevolence that underlies her function. We see this most clearly in *Dá Derga's Hostel* and the later, related text *Dá Choca's Hostel*. *Dá Derga's Hostel* names the visiting crone Cailb, but Badb is also among the names she gives, and later in the text the presence of a triple Badb inside the hostel makes her identity clearer.[28] She approaches the Hostel with a distinctly malevolent demeanor, "casting the evil eye on the king and the youths who surrounded him", and in reply to a request for prophecy from the King Conaire, she gives a prophecy of doom: "Truly I see for thee that neither fell nor flesh of thine shall escape from the place into which thou hast come, save what birds will bear away in their claws." A prophecy, but this is not simply a seer passively declaring a vision she has seen, for she has taken up a ritualized posture, "on one foot, and holding up one hand, and breathing one breath", and proceeds to chant a ritualized list of her names. The act is immediately recognized as a hostile one by the king and his attendants, because the posture, and her one-eyed visage, are associated specifically with cursing and Otherworldly malevolence throughout Celtic tradition.[29] Similarly, in *Dá Choca's Hostel*, her first appearance is prophetic, in the form of a red woman washing gore from a chariot at a ford who gives Cormac a prophecy of doom.[30] She then appears at the hostel as a hag, lame in one leg and blind in one eye, leaning her shoulder against the door-post and uttering ill words. In both the *Hostel* tales, the Badb's visitations include another curse in the form of inducing the king to break a *geis*.

26 Fraser 1915 27

27 O'Rahilly 2011 231

28 Stokes 1910 70, 87

29 Borsje 2003. Another example of this cursing posture is seen in Lug, who goes on one foot with one eye open chanting curses against the Fomoiri in the second *Mag Tuired* battle (Stokes 1891 99). Cú Chulainn also employs it in the *Táin* when deploying *ogam* battle magic (O'Rahilly 2010 150).

30 Stokes 1900a 157

Similar visitations of *badba* as malevolent cursing hags occur in other texts: usually blind in one eye and lame or standing on one leg, sometimes appearing in a triad, and always a harbinger of doom. These may or may not be *the* Badb, but they certainly constitute a recognizable type of character. In the *Battle of Mag Lena*, Eoghan and Fráech each are approached by a trio of hideous *badba* who prophesy their undoing and death; in the case of Fráech they threaten him directly: "The hideous woman who looks/ Upon your host at this time,/ Horrible shall be the force with which she will scream/ In a terrible shriek at you."[31] (Here interestingly suggesting that the three are in fact one, just as in *Dá Derga's Hostel* and other appearances of the Badb.) In the death-tale of Cú Chulainn, this characteristic trio also appears; in the earlier version, the crones are not named, but their description matches—three crones, blind of the left eye. Their verbal cursing is subtle, but threatening; they deliver a curse to Cú Chulainn by way of forcing him to break one of his *gessi* (either to eat dog meat, or to refuse hospitality from a hearth).[32] In the later version, they are identified as the three daughters of Calatín, each a one-eyed, one-legged hag, one of them named Badb. She curses Cú Chulainn by throwing a cooking-stake at him on which dog meat has been cooked, again transgressing his *geis* by contact.[33] Again, it is not made clear that these are a visitation of *the* Badb, but they replicate many aspects of her pattern: the tripled being who acts as one, the cursing hag shape and behavior, and the name Badb.

This cursing crone form of Badb is in almost every case linked to the enforcement and breaking of *gessi*. The *gessi* are in essence magical contracts with the Otherworld; it is through their observance, and the attendant Otherworldly assistance that heroes and kings maintain their powers, and it is when these *gessi* are broken that the influence of the Otherworld turns malevolent. Badb stands at the heart of this dynamic: she is at once the catalyst of *geis*-breaking, and the agent of the doom that inevitably pursues the hero who has failed his *gessi*. Why, if her concern is to enforce the observance of the Otherworldly contract, would she entrap these heroes into breaking their *gessi*? In most of these cases, the onset of the Otherworld's malevolence has already been triggered by previous transgressions; in *Dá Derga's Hostel* and *Dá Choca's Hostel*, both

31 O'Curry 1855 119-127
32 Tymoczko 1981 49
33 O'Grady 1898

targets have already broken several of their *gessi* before Badb appears. In the case of Cú Chulainn, he seems to have been marked for death because of warrior transgressions against enemies he has killed (Calatín and Cú Roi). From this, we can see that Badb seems to arise as an agent of the cascading process of magical downfall—once the hero begins to break his contracts with the Otherworld, its powers turn upon him, entrapping him into continuing the breaking of his *gessi* until they bring about his undoing and finally his death.

Thus it can be seen that the Badb's special association with cursing as the agent of the Otherworld's malevolence toward a transgressing hero is simply the other side of her special association with the heroic and sovereign powers granted to the favored hero by the Badb as battle fury and by the Morrígan as bringer of victory.

Depersonalization: Witch, Crow, War Fury

As we look at the Irish material from early to late, the Badb of battle is gradually depersonalized, separated from the identity of the war Goddess to become simply a generic witch, battle demon, or ordinary carrion bird. The transformation from war Goddess and battle crow toward witch may be evident in the later version of Cú Chulainn's death tale. Here a character called Badb, one of a trio of witches who are daughters of Calatín, an enemy killed earlier by Cú Chulainn, shifts to and from bird form and is seen flying and shrieking over the land, causing terror.[34] Her identity with the war Goddess is ambiguous and her motives framed as more personal and vengeful, less related to transpersonal forces. In the 17th century *Battle of Mag Lena*, we have a human witch with a name of her own, Siomha, who is called a *badb* simply in reference to her use of sorcery to attack one of the central characters.[35] Other late sources give us only carrion birds, absent the spiritual functions of war Goddess, and depersonalized war-furies or battle demons.[36] Where Badb as a fully divine Goddess of war does still appear in these late sources, her individual functions and modes of action have often been blurred, or her attributes have been assigned to a classical entity (such as Bellona, Enyo, or Tisiphone).[37]

---

34 O'Grady 1898 240

35 O'Curry 1855 33

36 O'Curry 1855 131, O'Rahilly 1924 27

37 Stokes 2010 71, Calder 1922 209

Ancestry and Relations

In much of her literature, Badb's ancestry is not described. Nowhere in the Ulster cycle texts is she attributed parents. Mentions of her ancestry appear primarily in texts where she appears in the Mythological triad of Badb, Macha, and Morrígan, the three daughters of Ernmas. This includes all recensions of the *Lebor Gabála*.[38] The same maternal ancestry is also implied in the *Second Battle of Mag Tuired* where she is identified with the Morrígan as daughter of Ernmas.[39]

Her paternal lineage is ambiguous. The father of the daughters of Ernmas triad is generally said to be Delbáeth (as described above in the section on the Morrígan) and in most instances in the Mythological tradition this is the paternity she is given. When she is listed as one of the two wives of Néit, her father is Elcmar of the Brúg. However, this is an exception to a pattern in which the pair is usually Féa and Némain, daughters of Elcmar and wives of Néit, so this may represent a separate mythology into which she has been inserted.[40] Occasionally, Badb is linked with a character called Bodb Derg ("Red Crow"), a *síd* king and a member of the Túatha Dé identified with the mound known as Síd Bodb, in Munster. In a couple of instances, references to *ingen Badb* are found, which may be read as "Badb's daughter"; sometimes this seems to be intended as "the daughter Badb", as in the case of Badb as one of Calatín's children, in Cú Chulainn's death-tale.[41] In the case of one such reference in the *Táin*, however, Windisch suggests it be read as referring to Bodb Derg as the father of Badb.[42] Bodb Derg himself has a distinct identity and a set of narratives of his own, so while he may or may not be a relation of Badb, the two should not be confused with one another.

Badb also seems to lack a firm connection with any consort. A few instances do link her with a husband, but never in any consistent way, and never with accompanying narratives as we find with most other divine couples in the literature. In a few places we find Badb listed as a wife of the Dagda; this occurs in the *Banshenchas*: "Badb wife of the

38 Macalister 1941 123, 131, 161, 183, 217 etc.
39 Gray 1982 71
40 Macalister 1941 155
41 O'Grady 1898 247
42 Windisch 1905

Great Dagda", along with the Morrígan and a third wife, Asachu.[43] In another version of the same text, she is also called the wife of Indai, the father of the war God Néit. As mentioned above, there are also couple of instances where Badb is also given as the wife of Néit himself, seemingly by way of being conflated with Féa or Némain.[44] And the marginal poem from the *Wasting Sickness of Cú Chulainn* calls Badb the wife of Tethra, a king of the Fomoiri.[45] In each of these cases, her role as wife seems to have been attached to a pre-existing mythological tradition.

Notwithstanding the obscure references to "Badb's daughter" mentioned above, I have found no names mentioned in Irish texts of any children of Badb. She seems at best only loosely connected to any suggestion of divine family and lineage, and in this is she quite distinct from most of the other Morrígna Goddesses. We might wonder whether this solitariness is a reflection of her ancient, primal identity as a divine personification of war and warrior fury. Whereas several of the other Morrígna, most especially the Morrígan and Macha, have substantial sovereignty, land, wealth, and related functions, Badb seems to live on the battlefield alone, and perhaps this is the reason that her family ties are at best fragmentary.

---

43 Dobbs 1931 168

44 O'Donovan 1868 25, Macalister 1941 155. More on this in Chapter 7, below.

45 Strachan 1900 17

5

Macha

She of the Plain

The name Macha is from *macha*, an Irish word meaning an enclosed field used for livestock, such as a milking-yard or horse paddock. The word *mag*, "plain", frequently appearing in place-names such as Mag Tuired, is related. Both trace to an ancient root that is connected to measures of land. The older form of the name, rarely seen in the Irish literature, is Machae.[1]

Macha's many entangled legends have been the source of much confusion for students of the Irish deities. Depending how you identify her, there are as many as four different Machas in the lore: Macha, the oracular seer and wife of the ancestral founder deity Nemed; Macha, the daughter of Ernmas, member of the Mythological triad of Morrígna war Goddesses, and wife of Nuada; Macha, Otherworldly wife of Cruinn and author of the *nóinden*, or curse of the Ulstermen; and Macha Mongruad, mythic Queen of Ulster by right of arms and founder of the fortress of Emain Macha. Appearing throughout the range of literary sources as well as significant place-names and legendary associations,

1 Toner 2010

Macha's identity nevertheless presents some consistent features: links with sovereignty, its symbols, powers, and pitfalls; with land and the foundation of royal sites; and with the tense dynamic between war and fertility in the warrior society. Though these various characters have their own stories, as we shall see they are not entirely distinct from one another, and may represent varying oral traditions surrounding a central Goddess Macha.

In the earliest textual sources, Macha's legends are already well developed as origin stories for the sacred royal site of Ulster, Emain Macha. Separately from these stories, her name does appear in early sources as identified with the Morrígna, but that identification remains vestigial—the mention of a name, such as in *Dá Derga's Hostel* where her name appears as one of the names of the cursing hag Cailb,[2] or the early glossary in which she is called "one of the three Morrígna".[3] Her presence in the Mythological Cycle remains somewhat separate from the other Morrígna until we come to the *Lebor Gabála Érenn*, where she begins to be firmly patterned into the Mythological triad of Badb, Macha, and Morrígan. Thus from these many interweaving threads of story, what emerges clearly is an ancient identification of Macha as tutelary Goddess of the land of Ulster and the royal center at Emain Macha, an identity which seems to have been gradually fused into the war Goddess trinity.

Óenach Macha: Gathering-place of Macha

Macha's legends as eponymous founder and tutelary Goddess of Emain Macha retain their vividness and detail remarkably consistently throughout the source literature from early to late. The essential narratives of these stories include Macha of Cruinn racing the horses at Emain Macha, Macha Mongruad fighting for kingship of Emain Macha, and Macha carving the rath of Emain Macha with her brooch (usually, but not always, attached to the tale of Macha Mongruad). This *Dindshenchas* material is found among the oldest text collections as well as embedded within other texts, such as the *Wooing of Emer* and early glossaries. Its persistence and wide distribution suggest that it is mythic material of very ancient origin.

Macha's identification with the royal site of Emain Macha runs so deep that some scholars have suggested that in fact Macha herself may

2 Stokes 1910 70
3 Stokes 1900 271

be named for the sacred enclosure, rather than the other way round, in a parallel fashion to the way that the name of the Gaulish Nemetona may have arisen from the consecrated sanctuaries dedicated to her.[4] For Macha, as we have seen, also means "land enclosure", and she exemplifies a pattern in Irish myth of Goddesses who share their names with sacred sites for which they also give origin legends (such as Tea, Tailtiu, Carman, etc).[5] The great mound at Emain Macha, now called Navan Fort, shows evidence of a huge shrine structure with concentric rings of large vertical posts or timbers, which may have been either a great roofed temple or a wooden ceremonial "grove" like the constructed *nemetona* seen elsewhere in Celtic antiquity and often, as is the case with Emain, also connected with sacred horses.[6] More details of this structure will be discussed below in Chapter 10. Here, what is important to note is that at the royal center named for Macha, pervasive archaeological evidence displays a deep history of ritual use, including evidence of kingship rituals, processions, feasting, sacrifice including horses, and funerary ancestor veneration.

These ceremonial gatherings alluded to in Macha's legends—like those of the other tutelary Goddesses attached to royal sites—tell that after her death, funeral games were established in her honor: the *Óenach Macha*, Assembly of Macha. From that gathering and from her tomb there, the place took its name.[7] A very ancient link also can be traced between the horse-racing element of Macha's story, funerary practices, and royal sites. The term *óenach* itself means "funerary games", and refers to an ancient tradition of holding large ceremonial gatherings at ritual centers where horse-racing in particular and other games were enacted in a belief that they honored the ancestors attached to the site. And while Macha, as a mythological figure, cannot be tied to a specific tomb, archaeological excavations at Navan fort have established the presence of burial sites, and these burial sites would likely have been objects of reverence in the ritual practices of the ancients at the Assembly of Macha.[8]

Macha, wife of Nemed, the latest to appear in the texts but the first in mythological terms, also presents herself as an ancestral figure involved in the formation and claiming of the land. Nemed is a primal

---

4 Waddell 2014 96
5 Sjoestedt 1994 39
6 Waddell 2014 96
7 Gwynn 1924 124-131, Stokes 1893 481
8 Waddell 1983 21

ancestor figure, the progenitor of the People of Nemed who become the Fir Bolg, mythical inhabitants of Ireland before the coming of the Túatha Dé; his name means "sacred" or "privileged". The poems and texts that mention Macha together with him speak of the many plains cleared by Nemed, plains "where our horsemen ride".[9] Nemed who clears plains for the raising of horses is married to Macha whose name means "field"; hers was the first death of the people of Nemed in Ireland, and the establishment of her tomb is given as the basis for the name of Ard Macha, another ancient sacred center near Emain Macha.[10] The establishment of a burial site physically embeds ancestry into the land, serving as marker of identity, sacral orientation, and territorial claim for the descendants.

Banflaith: Lady of Sovereignty

A crucial feature of these origin tales that we should note is that they each feature encounters with sovereignty and the institution of sacral kingship. Both Macha Mongruad's and Macha of Cruinn's stories explore complex social themes relating to the Celtic warrior aristocracy. Macha Mongruad in some ways exemplifies the "bride of sovereignty" motif; representing the land as its tutelary figure, it is through marriage to her that kingship is granted. She protects the sovereignty by force of arms, refusing to grant it to Dithorbae and his five sons, whose names mean "profitless, foolish, boastful, wanton, arrogant, and ignorant"—which is to say, those unworthy of the sovereignty.[11] As Gregory Toner points out, by forcing these men into servitude to build the rath of Emain, she effectively moves them from royal status into the status of commoner, damaging their claim to kingship. By this means, she establishes the dynasty of Ulster and its claim to the sacred royal center, and creates a class of commoners who will support the wealth and status of the kingship through their labor. It is through marrying Macha that Cimbaeth becomes "first prince of Emain" and "head of battle of the Red Branch", according to the poem in the *Roll of Kings*, founding a dynasty that traces itself to divine ancestral origins and holds the kingship

9 Gwynn 1924 124
10 Macalister 1940 131
11 Toner 2010 100

through its connection to the tutelary Goddess of the land.[12]

Macha of Cruinn in her story illustrates other aspects of sovereignty. She herself is not exemplary as a bride of sovereignty per se—she marries a member of the free farming class, a commoner. But her encounter with the king, in which she races the king's horses to prove her husband's boast, displays the latent conflict between social classes in the warrior aristocracy and illustrates the institution of kingship itself. The racing of horses at the Ulster gathering is, in Toner's words, "a form of proxy combat—a means by which warrior-nobles can display their prowess and status", and the potential for a common farmer to overturn that status represents a threat to the warrior aristocracy itself, a threat of being overpowered by a commoner as well as a woman.[13] We can see how crucial martial dominance is in the severity of the punishment threatened against Cruinn; if she cannot prove his boast, he will be put to death. In a sense, through Macha, Cruinn is laying a claim to kingship, or at least king-like elite status, she brings him wealth, fertility, and the possibility of establishing dominance in the elite warrior class by out-competing them in the martial display of the horse-race.

Even Macha of Ernmas reflects a subtle link to sacral kingship. Though her action is primarily as a member in the war Goddess triad, she is also seen independently as the wife of Nuada, the original king of the Túatha Dé, and a figure whose story presents the essential features of the sovereignty theme. Nuada exemplifies the Celtic ethos of sovereignty—that the well-being of land and people are invested in the person and physical body of the king, so that when he sustains a blemish by losing his hand in the first *Mag Tuired* battle, he voluntarily relinquishes leadership to Lugh. Nuada is, in this sense, the archetype of sacral kingship, and Macha is his wife.

Gabor: White Mare

Macha's equine identity is expressed most clearly in the person of Macha of Cruinn: she can run faster than the best of the king's horses, even while pregnant; her identity is revealed in connection with the ceremonial horse-race; and she gives birth to twins who, in some versions, are twin foals. In other parts of the Ulster Cycle, these twin hors-

12 Macalister 1956 461
13 Toner 2010 93

es are identified as the special horses belonging to Cú Chulainn which were born on the same night as him and therefore tied to his fate. One of the pair carries her name, Liath Macha, "the Gray of Macha", and this Liath Macha has heroic and supernatural qualities of its own. We also see a more subtle link with horses expressed for Macha of Nemed, who is associated with the clearing of plains for horse-riding.

Macha's links to sacral kingship and to horses are of course not incidental to each other. Horses are iconic of sovereignty throughout Celtic, and Indo-European cultures generally. Irish rituals of sacred kingship feature horses prominently. The rites of inauguration for a high king, according to medieval texts, included unbroken horses being yoked to a chariot, and the requirement of the king to demonstrate mastery of the horses and chariot.[14] Another account of kingship rites by the medieval historian Giraldus Cambrensis describes the consecration of the king by a ritual copulation with a horse, followed by a sacrifice and consumption of horse meat. This account which has been considered outlandish by some, and its agenda clearly was to portray the Irish as barbaric and thus justify Norman conquest. However, the ritual itself is closely paralleled in other Irish accounts, as well as related kingship rituals elsewhere in the ancient Indo-European world, and which may be corroborated by the discovery of evidence of horse sacrifice at Navan mound in Emain Macha.[15]

This association of horses with kingship is reflective of ancient structural elements of Celtic and Indo-European societies generally: the ruling kingship maintained through the military power of an elite warrior class, supported by an agrarian and craftsman class, and legitimized and sanctified through the action of a priestly class. Kingship held obligations to all three functional parts of society, but kings were drawn from the warrior elite and reliant on its military prowess to maintain position. The horse was both symbol and vehicle of this elite military power, its mode of action expressed in the patterns of mounted and chariot warfare as well as the rituals attendant to warriors and kings. Horses too were both symbol and vessel of the wealth and influence necessary to maintain kingship; the horse is the highest-value animal

14 Petrie 1839

15 Waddell 2014 102. We will explore the details of the Irish horse ritual in greater detail in Chapter 12; here we mention it as simply one more example of the relation of horses to kingship.

that can be produced on grazing land, and as such represents the concentrated values of land, wealth, and military power in living form. To possess horses was to demonstrate control of land, wealth, and the means of warfare so important to the Celtic warrior aristocracy. We can see the centrality of horse-lordship in the title Eochaid, which was given to many kings both historical and mythical (including the Dagda himself): it means "horseman".[16]

Thus Macha is an embodiment both of the horse itself as living symbol of sacral kingship, and the land from which its power is derived. White horses in particular seem to have been especially sacred; there is even a special word *gabor*, meaning a white horse or mare, which is found attached to sacred landscape elements associated with Irish royal sites.[17] Waddell suggests the white horse carved in the chalk at the British site of Uffington may be reflective of similar ritual patterns seen in Ireland.

Badb na mBerg: Raven of the Raids

Macha, for all her identification with land, wealth, and sacral kingship, also remains a battle Goddess, and her complex symbolism speaks to the relationship between fertility and war in Celtic thought. She has a clear and well-developed tutelary mythology relating to territorial Ulster, but from the earliest sources she is also seen at least loosely identified with the group of war Goddesses.

An early gloss gives her name in its archaic form, Machae, and interprets it thus: "Macha, that is Badb, or she is the third Morrígan, from whence Macha's fruit crop, that is the heads of men that have been slaughtered."[18] We cannot treat this as anomalous, for she is identified with the Morrígna again and again throughout the sources. In *Dá Derga's Hostel*, hers is among the names given by the cursing hag Cailb, who also names herself Badb.[19] A *Dindshenchas* poem about Macha Mongruad calls her *badb na mberg*, "the raven of the raids", apparently as a descriptive rather than a name. In the Mythological Cycle materials, her identity with the Morrígna becomes firm: daughter of Ernmas, she joins Badb and Morrígan on the battlefield of the first *Mag Tuired* battle and pours

16 Macalister 1941 102

17 Waddell 2014 124. Gabhra river, Sgiath Gabhra, and Loch nGabor are all associated with royal sites.

18 Stokes 1900 271

19 Stokes 2009 70

down showers of sorcerous fire, blood, and druidic mist on the Fir Bolg.[20] We might wonder whether these are entirely separate Machas; however, at least in the minds of medieval scholars who encoded this material, it seems they were not. Macha, daughter of Ernmas is directly stated to be the same Macha who gave birth to the Liath Macha.[21] Among her epithets in the *Lebor Gabála* material is *met n-indbais*, "greatness of wealth", evoking the associations with land and wealth we have seen above.[22]

The phrase *mesrad Machae*, "Macha's mast" or "Macha's fruit crop", as a kenning for the severed heads of the slain perhaps best encapsulates the complexity of Macha's identity as both fertility and war Goddess. We have here an image of carnage, presented in the language of harvest. What this points to is that even where Macha is a land Goddess, her relationship to land is one of territoriality rather than simple fertility. She is identified with the land, as the embodiment of its sovereignty, and therefore as part of her tutelary protective function, she enacts that protective function through battle. Macha exemplifies both external warlike protective functions, in the person of Macha of Ernmas who attacks the Fir Bolg on behalf of her people, and internal protective functions, in the person of Macha Mongruad, who fought to defend the sovereignty from unworthy contenders within the dynasty.

Mná Trogain Tres: Woman in Birthing Strife

Macha's stories are also stories about gender, transgression, and the Otherworldly power of women. We are, of course, unsurprised to meet a female divinity concerning herself with battle. But the particulars of Macha's engagements with kingship, motherhood, and battle reveal something unique and interesting about gender in the Celtic paradigm. Macha Mongruad's tale, while clearly hearkening to a mythic foundation story, also presents her as the only queen to rule by her own right among a long line of kings in the annals. Her story has been given a gendered light; her male relatives try to refuse the kingship she should inherit from her father, because "they would not give sovereignty to a woman".[23] She will not stand down but fights for it, and gains the

20 Fraser 1915 27
21 Macalister 1941 189
22 Macalister 1941 217
23 O'Curry 1861 527

battle. Her story is remarkable in that she rules in her own right and by her own sword, but also acts in the role of bride of sovereignty—transgressing the normal gender divide in which a woman representing the land bestowed the sovereignty to a male ruler, just as she also transgresses social class in forcing the sons of kings to labor for her as slaves.

Gender and transgression are themes in the story of Macha of Cruinn, too. She represents a conflict, in Toner's language, between "the warrior code, which shields the existing hierarchy, and natural justice, which protects all members of society."[24] The compassion and fairness she asks for, to delay forcing her to race until she has delivered, is denied her by the king; he is thinking only of the threat to his position. In denying her justice, however, he breaks contract with the Otherworld, the spiritual powers by whose consent any Irish king held the sovereignty. Her curse is the Otherworld's retribution for this breaking of the spiritual contract—in short, for his violation of *fír flathemon*, kingly justice. And this is the second transgression against an Otherworld contract leading to her curse—the first was committed by Cruinn himself, when he boasted of her at the horse-race against the terms of their marital arrangement. Like Cailb/Badb, appearing as the malevolent Otherworldly crone to curse the king who has violated his sovereign's *gessi*, Macha exacts the vengeance of the offended Otherworld on the Ulster warrior society which has failed to uphold the terms of its relationship.

A margin poem in a 16th century manuscript draws together these threads vividly:

"Rough the dwellings in which we are,
where men strip Macha's mast,
where warriors drive floods [of blood] into the courtyard,
where women in childbirth stir up strife."[25]

Strife as battle is here linked with strife as the struggle of childbirth, and associated with both Macha's harvest of carnage and with a menacing ability of birthing women. It was believed that women in childbirth gained a special status of powerful speech; the triads record that "the oath of a woman in birth-pangs" required no substantiation.[26] She was understood to be in a liminal place, in direct contact with the Otherworld, and thus her word carried additional power. This may be the reason that

24 Toner 2010 96
25 TCD Ms. H 3.18, quoted in Toner 2010 103.
26 Meyer 1906 23

some of the tales present the sound of Macha's birthing scream alone as carrying the force of the curse against all who heard it, even before she was to speak it.[27] She was in a sense conveying the force of the Otherworld through her body and in her voice—the same power, perhaps, that screamed through the voices of the other Morrígna, too, and could cause hundreds of warriors to die of terror simply from the sound.

The sound of her scream may not have been the only menacing aspect of Macha's travail at the end of the race. In a variety of contexts, female nudity and female sexuality are presented as threatening, or as conveying a force which limits the martial capacities of warriors.[28] For example, an alternate story explains the Ulster curse as coming from another woman, the seeress Fedelm, who bares herself to the Ulstermen in vengeance for a different slight, and her nakedness brings the debilitating curse on them. Elsewhere, the women of Ulster bare their breasts to counteract the battle-rage of Cú Chulainn.[29] Here women's bodies are presented as vessels of fertility, which seems to have been seen as the counter-force to the deadly warrior power. Additionally, the curse may also be connected with the transgression of normal sexual boundaries and propriety concerning the bodies of women.

Ingen Áeda Rúaid: Daughter of Red Fire

The paternal line of Macha Mongruad is from a king Áed Rúad, which means "red fire". *Áed* appears to be a divinity in his own right, likely to be identified with the *Áed* of the Túatha Dé. *Áed Ruad Ró-fhessa*, "Red Fire of Great Knowledge" is also an epithet of the Dagda, and on this basis a few scholars have linked the two and suggested that we might see Macha as a daughter of the Dagda.[30] Her own epithet Mongruad means "red-haired", evoking the color of fire at least. Macha of Cruinn, in the *Dindshenchas* version of her tale, also called Grian, "sun", and called "sun of womankind". Here, she is said to be the daughter of Midir, a faery king of the Síd of Bri Leith.[31] Some have, from these threads, concluded that Macha is a sun Goddess. "Sun of womanhood", daughter of Red Fire—it can seem a compelling image. However, the

27 Henderson 1898 304
28 Toner 2010 94
29 O'Rahilly 2011 147, Tymoczko 1981 37
30 Ó hÓgáin 1999 109
31 Gwynn 1924 124-131

evidence for Macha as a sun Goddess is very slim. In fact, it is limited to those two epithets, which do not appear together with reference to the same incarnation of Macha. The *Dindshenchas* poem seems to associate Macha-as-Grian with the west of Ireland, and may represent a local legend related to a sun Goddess Grian associated with the Síd of Bri Leith, which has been absorbed into Macha's legend.[32] In the *Banshenchas* version, Macha and Grian are two different wives of Cruinn, which may support the notion that we are dealing with two different Goddesses who have been fused in some of the literature.[33]

Multiplicity and Duality

Some scholars have argued that the several incarnations of Macha represent her identity being refracted through the three functional divisions of Celtic society, following Dumézil: Macha of Nemed, a seer representing the priestly function, Macha Mongruad, a warrior representing the military function, and Macha of Cruinn, a farmer's wife and mother representing the agrarian function.[34] In my view, this is too simple and too neat; apart from leaving out Macha of Ernmas, the war Goddess and one of our most active manifestations of Macha, it also leaves out the ways that each of these stories crosses functional divisions. Macha of Nemed is a seer, but she is also tied to agrarian land foundation. Macha Mongruad is a warrior, but also acts as sovereignty bride. Macha of Cruinn is a mother and wife but also performs a transgressive curse reminiscent of Badb, and reflective of the tensions of a warrior society. John Carey suggest that the multiplicity of Macha resolves itself to two primal functions: that of war, and the oracular and aggressive magics associated to it, and of land, with wealth and fertility as its modes of embodiment.[35] These two domains can be further seen as two aspects of the sovereignty Goddess: fecundating, protective, and blessing, and malevolent when wronged.

32 "Her two names, not seldom heard in the west, were bright Grian and pure Macha... in her roofless dwelling in the west she was Grian, the sun of womankind." Gwynn 1924 124-131.

33 Dobbs 1931 174

34 Quoted in Carey 1982 263.

35 Carey 1982 275

G

Anu

The Wealthy One

This Goddess appears as Ana and Anu, with the genitive form Anann or Anand; according to Carey, the earliest form of the name is Anu.[1] Several etymologies have been proposed for the name. The most well-established etymology links it to *ana* (*anae* in the plural), "wealth, riches, prosperity, treasure". The 10th-century *Cormac's Glossary* interprets the root *ana* as "plenty".[2] Alternate proposed etymologies connect the name to *án*, "bright, splendid" or to its alternate meaning, "cup, vessel" or "womb", although this is uncertain. It is possible that these terms in far antiquity derive from a common Indo-European root relating to wealth, plenty, and fertility.

In textual sources referring to the Goddess, the name does not appear until documents dating to the 10th century, and then it is restricted to versions of the highly systematized *Lebor Gabála Érenn*, along with a few glossaries and name-lists. Anu as such has no narrative literature attached to her at all—there are no actual stories given to that name

1 Carey 1982 270
2 O'Donovan 1868 4

in extant texts.[3] The nearest we come to any action ascribed to her is Cormac's description that "she nursed the gods".[4] In the *Lebor Gabála* materials, she appears among lists of Goddesses of the Túatha Dé, as one of the daughters of Ernmas. Here she never appears independently of the Mythological triad (typically Badb, Macha, and Morrígan), and in several places is Anu is explicitly identified with the Morrígan, as the personal name of the divinity carrying that title.

Bandía an tSónusa: Goddess of Prosperity

The single item of lore that is always attached to Anu, in nearly every instance in which she appears in the Irish texts, is her identification with the twin hills in Kerry, in the old province of Munster, called the Dá Chích Anann or Two Paps of Anu ("paps" being a Victorian word for breasts, an artifact of archaic English usage). Those twin hills are to this day still identified with her in folk belief, although none of these stories appear in the *Dindshenchas* texts, nor any about Anu herself. As her strongest and most consistent identification is with land-forms and the land itself, Anu appears most clearly as a tutelary land Goddess associated with plenty and prosperity. An entry in *O'Davoren's Glossary* gives her name as meaning "abundance", and identifies her with the land of Ireland as a whole;[5] all the other references to land-form identification are to the Dá Chích Anann and the province of Munster.[6] The entries for Mumu (Munster) in the *Fitness of Names* identify an Ána as a Goddess of prosperity, centering her worship in Munster, and explain that it was because of this worship that Munster's wealth (*ána*) was greater than any other province.[7] Thus it can be seen that her primary identity is as tutelary land Goddess of Munster, providing nourishment (symbolized by the breast-shaped hills) and wealth coming from the land.

Two sources in the Finn cycle provide some interesting material about the two hills. A poem in the *Acallamh na Senórach* mentions a warrior of the

3 Anu has sometimes been confused with Áine, due to the similarity of names and the fact that both are local Goddesses associated with the land of Munster, but the names are etymologically unrelated (Beck 2009 248).

4 O'Donovan 1868 4

5 Stokes 1901 204

6 Macalister 1941 123, 155, 161, 183, 189

7 Stokes 1897 288

Fianna undergoing testing at the Dá Chích Anann.[8] In another poem, Finn himself undertakes a journey, on Samhain, to various mountains about Ireland; the journey has traces of ritual about it (he is said to be "racing with the deer"). A feast is occurring at the Dá Chích Anann, and there Finn kills an adversary, Ua Fidga, in revenge for the slaying of a poet. From the mound of the Pap above him, a voice is heard speaking poetry which tells of the death and the spear used in the deed, "Venom is the spear".[9] In addition to suggesting seasonal ritual behavior linked to the site, we may wonder whether the Otherworldly voice that is heard announcing the death may be that of Anu—an action reminiscent of the Morrígan's role in the announcing the deaths and the victory after the second *Mag Tuired* battle. Poetry is indeed mentioned in connection with Anu in one of the glosses, where she is called by a kenning "knowledge to poets".[10]

Another land-form exists that closely parallels the Dá Chích Anann: two hills in the Boyne valley associated with the Brúg na Bóinne complex, called the Dá Chích na Morrígna, Two Paps of the Morrígan (possibly also to be identified with the hills called the Comb and Casket of the Dagda's Wife, from the same site).[11] The parallel between the two names is striking, especially given that in the Mythological Cycle materials, Anu is explicitly identified as the personal name of the Morrígan. In a *Banshenchas* text, this identification is repeated, and Anu is directly listed as a wife of the Dagda, reinforcing this connection.[12]

Daghmatair: Good Mother

The embodiment of Anu in the form of breasts and concepts of plenty and fertility can suggest a mother-Goddess identity, and indeed she has sometimes been associated with *Danu, the mother Goddess for whom the Túatha Dé Danann are thought to be named.[13] In textual sources, the identification of Anu as the mother of the Gods shows ear-

8 MacLeod 372

9 Meyer 1910 47

10 Stokes 1901 204

11 Stokes 1894 292

12 Dobbs 1931 168

13 The only known form of this name is in the genitive as Danann (and variant spellings). It has been presumed that the nominative form would have been Danu, but no known textual sources actually attest this name; thus we mark it as a reconstructed, provisional name with the asterisk, *Danu (Kondratiev 1998 2).

liest in *Cormac's Glossary*, where he calls her *mater deorum hibernensium*, "mother of the Gods of Ireland".[14] He then goes on to also identify her with Buanann, "mother of the heroes", by similarity and folk etymology.[15] We next see the phrase "mother of the Gods" applied to her in a late recension of the *Lebor Gabála*, where Anu and *Danu have become equated—one which is not seen in earlier material in the Mythological Cycle. This identity of Anu and *Danu as one and the same and the mother of the Gods is repeated twice in 3rd recension texts.[16]

*Danu, apart from these brief instances, appears to have a compelling presence of her own, particularly in the Mythological Cycle materials. She is associated as foster-mother to the triad of Badb, Macha, and Morrígan and musters with them in the *First Battle of Mag Tuired*.[17] She also appears in separate, often triad groupings, with entities such as Bé Chuille and Bé Theite, sometimes described as "she-husbandmen," or sorceresses. Her identity as the tutelary mother Goddess of the tribe of the Túatha Dé is repeated in several places.

However, it is a matter of scholarly debate as to whether or not she should be recognized as separate from Anu, or whether her existence may be purely literary. The name Danann does not appear in any textual source earlier than the *Lebor Gabála* materials beginning in the 11th century, and here it is thought possible that it was introduced as a linguistic accident. In early Irish, similarities between the sounds of words such as nAnann "of Anu" and nDanann "of *Danu" could have introduced the confusion at the time the tales were being compiled.[18] Additionally the phrase Túatha Dé Danann can be read as not speaking of a Goddess at all, but rather as the "people of the Gods of skill", based on the word *dána*, "skill, art, or gift". Due to this and to her absence from earlier texts, some scholars dismiss the existence of *Danu as a literary invention.

Traces suggestive of *Danu can be found, however, in imagery, etymology, and place-names. A triad of Gods appear among the Túatha Dé, called the *tri dée dána*, "three Gods of skill", likely identified with the three craftsmen Gods Goibniu, Crédne, and Luchta (blacksmith, brazier, and carpeter). These three are in some sources read as three

14 O'Donovan 1868 4
15 O'Donovan 1868 17
16 Macalister 1941 183, 189
17 Fraser 1915 45
18 Kondratiev 1998, MacLeod 367-368

sons of *Danu by her stated father, Delbaeth, "shaper".[19] In their turn, the three Gods of skill have descendants Écna, "wisdom, knowledge", and Érgna, "understanding, discernment". While this does not establish *Danu as a real presence, there is a compelling mythic logic to the image of a primal pair called Skill and Shaper (*Danu and Delbaeth) from whom come all the Gods of skill, embodying craftsmanship, knowledge, and understanding. At the very least, these figures do present an image that seems accurate to the high values placed on craftsmanship, skill, and knowledge within the mythical world of the Túatha Dé.[20] Further, we also find notable parallels in the Welsh Dôn, whose name is cognate to *Danu, and who is herself the mother of a tribe of Gods, several of whom share these skill-oriented identities, including Gofannon, directly cognate to the Irish Goibniu.[21]

Another trace finds hints of *Danu in etymological links with river names throughout ancient Europe: the Danube from *Danuouios, the Rhône from *Rodanos (with the intensive particle *ro-*), the Dniester from *Danu-Nazdya, the Dnieper from *Danu-Apara, the several rivers Don in Britain and Russia, and more. A few Goddesses in the Indo-European family preserve hints of the name as well, the Vedic Danu, the Welsh Dôn as mentioned, and others.[22] The root of her name can be tied to rivers, waters, and concepts of flow throughout Indo-European sourced languages—cultures in which acts of creation are often linked to rivers which can be seen to literally shape the land, a mythic pattern also reflected in the Irish literature.

How can we reconcile these different images of *Danu—as literary fiction, as the source of knowledge and the mother of the Gods of skill, and as primal river Goddess? If we look to the Irish lore of rivers, the mythology often focuses on sacred Otherworldly wells which are seen as the source of the rivers, and from which wisdom and knowledge were conceived of as flowing in streams. Several prominent origin narratives tell of a Goddess who, seeking the source of knowledge, delves into such a well which floods out to form the river; in the process, she dies and is merged with the river as its tutelary Goddess, and the

19 MacLeod 340. Note: Some texts name a different trio as the *trí dée dána*; for reasons compellingly argued by MacLeod, notably that the other trio of Brian, Iuchair, and Iucharba are not Gods of skill. I follow the above attribution.

20 MacLeod 342

21 Kondratiev 1998 7, MacLeod 345

22 Ó hÓgáin 1999 65, MacLeod 350

rivers also shape the landscape. This essential narrative is conveyed in the stories of Sinann (the Shannon River) and Bóand (the Boyne River).[23] In it is also encapsulated the association of sacred waters with knowledge and skill. This mythic pattern fits both images of *Danu as the source of knowledge and as a primal river Goddess. Interestingly, Sharon Paice Macleod notes that the region where the Proto-Indo-European language (ancestor to the Celtic languages as well as the other languages in the Indo-European culture family) is thought to have developed centers on the same region where the concentration of river names linked to *Danu are found. This suggests a deep cultural reflex recalling a wellspring in the landscape of memory from which knowledge originally flowed.[24]

I think, then, if we look beyond Cormac's imaginative glosses and the confused patchwork of the *Lebor Gabála Érenn* 3rd recension, the Irish *Danu emerges as a memory of a very ancient primal ancestress, river Goddess, source of wisdom and knowledge, and mother of the tribe of Gods. It seems to me that the literary artifact is not the invention of either *Danu or Anu, but their equation with one another in the context of an artificially rationalized, systematized, pseudo-historical narrative. The reader should note, of course, that some scholars differ from me on this point.

To return to Anu, once we have disentagled her from the shadow of *Danu, we can more easily recognize her own maternal identification as a territorial land-goddesss and provider of wealth and plenty through the land itself—that is, the land of Ireland, and especially Munster. This is distinct from *Danu's maternal identity as primal ancestress, creatrix, and river of knowledge. Anu is a mother not in the sense of primal creatrix, but in the sense of one who nurses, nourishes and sustains: the richness and wealth swelling from the land itself as a mother's breast. In the phrase of *Cormac's Glossary*, "it was well she nursed the gods.[25]" Her tightly localized identity points to a history not as mother in some vague cosmic sense, but rather the manifest life and plenty of the land of Munster itself.

23 MacLeod 353
24 MacLeod 355
25 O'Donovan 1868 4

Crobh Dearg: Red Claw

Taken together, the evidence suggests Anu may originally have been a localized Goddess identified with the fertility and territorial landscape of Munster, whose identity was absorbed into the collective identity of the Morrígan (and of *Danu as well) in the middle Irish period. Anu and the Morrígan share some similar features, including their tutelary and territorial functions; the Morrígan's identification with cattle and thus wealth provides another indirect parallel. It is also possible that in the folk traditions behind Anu's legend lay stories containing more detail that have not been preserved in our textual sources, which may have more clearly articulated the link between them.

Localized folklore and *Dindshenchas*-type material are often the most enduring. Landforms remain, and place-names create stable identities around which stories are built and continue to be told. As the folklore identifying the two hills in Munster as the breasts of Anu is the most enduring and consistent of Anu's lore, we may imagine that this reflects a very ancient tradition. If the same may be true of the two hills at the Brúg na Bóinne, their identification as the breasts of the Morrígan may also be quite ancient—as indeed, place-names figure among the earliest of the Morrígan's lore, as we have seen above in the examination of *Dindshenchas* material in the *Wooing of Emer*. We may speculate that the existence of landscapes in different parts of Ireland, each identified with the breasts of a territorial land Goddess and serving as a focal point for ritual activity, points to very ancient cults of worship which may have been typical throughout pre-Christian Celtic religion, but expressed locally using different names. This would fit well into our understanding of the social organization of the early Celts as tribal, rather than nationally organized cultures.

In the case of the Dá Chích Anann, prehistoric cairns built on both hills give the appearance of nipples on the breasts; these cairns have been the focal point of ritual activity, including placing of offerings by women at or near Beltaine, fertility symbolism and processional rites.[26] Vestigial links to folklore of the Morrígna remain attached to several sites near the Paps, including two *fulachta* and the megalithic complex of Caher Crobhdearg, to whose stones and holy well cattle were brought

26 Coyne 2006 13, 21

for blessing, also at Beltaine.[27] Local folklore links this Crobh Dearg, "Red Claw", one of a triad of sister "saints", to the Morrígna, traditions which suggest the persistence of a folk belief in the connection between Anu and the Morrígan, as well as possibly Badb, if the evocative image of the "Red Claw" may be followed by association.[28]

27 Coyne 2006 21

28 Coyne 2006 47. The "saints" appear to be pagan Goddesses thinly veiled; they do not appear in the Christian calendar, and are linked to pre-Christian ritual sites.

7

Némain, Féa and Bé Néit

Némain: The Sacred One

Némain is among the most mysterious of the war Goddesses appearing with the Morrígna. The etymological meaning and source of her name remain contested and ambiguous, and the quantity of material concerning her is scant in comparison with some of the other Morrígna divinities. Yet the traces we do find seemingly lead us deep into the Celtic worldview and the heart of its conception of sacredness.

The term *nem* in Irish refers to "sky, heaven", or that which is above; when accented as *ném*, it means "luster, radiance". These two meanings are likely connected to each other, as the sky is the source of natural light and the place where the radiance of heavenly bodies is seen. Word-roots related to *nem* are found in many of the Celtic languages and appear to trace to a very ancient, likely Indo-European concept of sacredness.[1] In adjectival form *nemed* is "sacred, consecrated, privileged", a meaning likely derived from its ancient usage to refer to a consecrated place (as in the Gaulish *nemeton*, or sanctuary). From this developed the medieval Irish usage of *nemed* for elite, protected social status.[2] The DIL also defines *nemain* as a noun meaning "battle-fury, warlike frenzy, strife", based on usage in some early and middle Irish texts; however, these usages appear not to be based on the etymological meaning of the name, and are likely derivative from the identity of Némain as a war Goddess.

Another possible link is *neim*, an Irish word meaning "poison, venom", and in a broader sense, "baneful or malefic power", with related concepts of "virulence, fierceness, intensity", all of which are associated with Némain in her lore.[3] This semantic group might seem to be distinct from *nem* as "heaven". It is possible that both groups derive from a common, ancient concept of numinous, powerful sacredness that was recognized as both separate from ordinary reality, and also possessed of a power so potent that it was dangerous and deadly to encounter. Ancient, Continental worship structures and patterns suggest something along these lines, where the sacred groves of Gaul were called *nemeton*, "sacred place", and were described by contemporary authors as places of dread. Constructed sanctuaries across Ireland, Britain and Gaul were consistently accompanied by apotropaic systems of protection built specifically so as to contain and to protect the outside world from the power within.[4] The *nemed* status in Irish thought, exemplified in the person of the king, was accompanied by binding taboos, or *gessi*, again reflective of the belief that sacred power carried with it a potentially destructive force.[5]

Where does this lead us with regard to Némain, the Irish Goddess? We cannot say with certainty, but the evidence suggests that she is a very ancient deity whose roots trace back to common ancestry with Gaulish figures, and possibly Indo-European origin. Many scholars point out the etymological linkage of her name to the Gaulish Nemetona, and we may note also that Némain, like Nemetona, is in almost every instance where

1 Also seen in the Latin *nemus*, "sacred grove"; as in the grove of the Goddess Diana Nemorensis (Alfoldi 1960 141).
2 Waddell 2014 134
3 Royal Irish Academy 2013: entry neim.
4 Waddell 2014 72, Brunaux 1988, 25-33, 24
5 O'Connor 2013 76

she appears, stated to be the wife of a war God.[6] In the Irish literature, Némain only appears in fully active form with distinct characteristics in the early Ulster sources and to a lesser extent, the *Dindshenchas* material, with her place attributions clustered distinctly into the north of Ireland. Outside of these sources, she appears only in lists of Goddesses, as in the Mythological Cycle and related materials, where she is mentioned almost incidentally as one of the sorceresses of the Túatha Dé, or as a wife of the war God Néit. Thus the picture that emerges may suggest that the Irish Némain is a descendant of a very ancient Celtic Goddess linked to concepts of sacred space and numinous, otherworldly power, whose Irish cult was centered in the northern part of the country.

Úathbas: Terror-Death

The sources which give us the most detailed and active picture of Némain are the various recensions of the *Táin*. Here she actively takes part in war, and is called "the war-goddess". Her particular actions are attacking the forces of Connacht which are arrayed against Ulster, in association especially with phenomena of terrific noise and confusion.[7] With her entrances come the noises of clashing of arms and shouting of hosts, and most especially her shrieking in a voice so fearsome that "a hundred warriors among them fell dead of fright and terror" from hearing it. Her voice causes confusion, awe and panic and strikes warriors with *úathbas*, which means "terror-death"—a terror so profound that they fall dead on the spot. The noise and clamor in particular suggest the descriptions of battle practice from contemporary Classical authors describing Gaulish use of noise and clamor to add to the terror of war: "For there were among them countless horns and trumpets which were being blown simultaneously from every part of the army. The sound was so loud and piercing that the clamor didn't seem to come from trumpets and human voices, but from the whole countryside at once."[8]

In the earliest recension of the *Táin*, Némain usually appears alone engaged in this action of terrifying the hosts of Ulster's enemies. Of four incidents in the first recension, she only appears in company with other Morrígna once, on the night before the final full-scale battle of

6 Stokes 1862 34, Waddell 2014 96, Olmsted 1994 408
7 O'Rahilly 2011 130, 182
8 Polybius, quoted in Koch & Carey 2003 9.

both armies. Here she is in company with Badb and Bé Néit, ("wife of Néit" or "woman of battle") who in context of the story is likely the Morrígan.[9] In the *Book of Leinster* recension, she acts alone. Perhaps significantly, every one of these visitations to terrify the armies occurs at night. Each time, we are reminded that the sleep of the armies is disturbed; the characteristically wry Irish prose says "that was not the most peaceful night for them".

An interesting, possibly related mention occurs in the *Dindshenchas*, where a poem about a place called Fich Buana mentions a woman called Buan. The story resembles in some ways the King Buan's Daughter episode in the *Táin*, in which the Morrígan comes in this guise. Némain here is mentioned as part of a place called Fich Némain "of the anguish-cry".[10] The tale lacks enough detail to draw any clear conclusions, but once again the name Némain is here linked with the sound of baneful voice.

Búadris: Trance-Speech

If we examine the attacks of Némain in the *Táin* cycle more closely, another feature emerges. She appears in conjunction with, and apparently in response to, acts of speech on the part of warriors. In all but one of these instances, her attack is preceded by a warrior's "trance-speech" (*búadris*). These trance-speeches share certain characteristics: they are performed by warriors at war camps, during the night; they are often performed after rising from sleep or from a sleep-like trance; they are chanted in verse form and involve prophetic visions about the impending battle, exhortations to readiness, or in a few cases laments.[11] In each case, the next thing that is described is the onslaught of Némain, either alone or in a triad with other Morrígna, bringing confusion and striking warriors dead of terror from the dreadful shrieking of her voice. The language is often suggestive of the trance-speech causing Némain's attack. For example, after Dubthach's trance-speech, the text goes on, "thereupon the Némain, that is, the war-goddess, attacked them", or in the *Book of Leinster* version, "then Dubthach awoke from his sleep and

9 O'Rahilly 2011 231, Epstein 1998 52
10 Gwynn 1924 181
11 O'Rahilly 2011 130, 220, 231. A similar instance of trance-speech occurs in Da Derga's Hostel (Stokes 1910 82).

the Némain brought confusion on the host…"[12]

The single instance of Némain's attack which is not preceded by a trance-speech is the one associated with a vocal act of Cú Chulainn. He is encamped overlooking the hosts of Connacht at a place called Breslech Maige Muirthemne, and the sight of his enemies massed before him enrages him:

> "He shook his shield and brandished his spears and waved his sword, and he uttered a hero's shout deep in his throat. And the goblins and sprites and spectres of the glen and demons of the air gave answer for terror of the shout that he had uttered. And Némain, the war goddess, attacked the host…"[13]

Here, instead of following a trance-speech, Némain's attack follows the hero's shout of Cú Chulainn, along with the collective of battle spirits that typically attend him. Thus in its difference this episode still seems to confirm a pattern: trance-speeches or vocalizations from warriors in their camps at night are followed by an attack of the war Goddess on the opposing camp.

What seems to be suggested here is an invocation, habitually performed at night, which can take the form of a chanted poem given in trance, or in Cú Chulainn's case, an invocatory shout accompanied by battle fury. This association of Némain with incantatory invocations may be the reason why, in the *Lebor Gabála Érenn* poem, she is called "Néman of prophetic stanzas," highlighting her connection with prophetic poetry.[14] Might it also be part of the reason we see so little narrative about her outside of these invocations? In the name Némain are contained meanings of numinous, Otherworldly power held sacred and protected apart from the ordinary world, a power which could be deadly and perhaps was seen only when invoked against the camps of one's enemies.

Bé Néit: Wife of the War God

Outside the *Táin* episodes concerned with Némain's attacks, she is consistently associated with a war God Néit, as his wife. *Dindshenchas* materi-

12 O'Rahilly 2010 250
13 O'Rahilly 2011 182
14 Macalister 1941 217, Epstein 1998 62

al speaks of the couple at some length, in poems giving the lore of Ailech Néit, the stronghold of the war God, a place now known as Grianan Ailech on the far northern point of the Irish isle. Némain in these poems is a "winsome woman", a "law-giver", called *Némain na ened cathach,* "Némain of the wounds of war". Ailech Néit is a "sharp-crested stronghold", envied among the Túatha Dé, and "guarded by weapons".[15]

This association with Néit, and with Ailech Néit the place, is repeated in the Mythological Cycle materials. Here descriptions are for the most part lacking, but she is in several places mentioned (along with Féa, or in one case, Badb) as one of the two wives of Néit.[16] This pairing appears to extend beyond Ireland, as we see British and Continental Gods and Goddesses with related names showing as divine couples as well. Nemetona, whose name is thought to be etymologically related to Némain as discussed above, is usually found in British and Gallo-Roman inscriptions paired with a Celtic God of war, syncretized as Mars-Neto or a similar epithet.[17] We explore the identity of this war God in more detail below, in the section on Bé Néit.

Nemain ocus Neim: Murder and Poison

A persistent association between Némain and venom or poison occurs in the glosses and folklore materials. The *Banshenchas* and *Cormac's Glossary* entries call her "venomous".[18] She is associated with the idea of poison in a *Dindshenchas* poem telling of a woman who poisoned her enemies, where the name is used in a phrase *nemain ocus neim*, "murder and poison."[19] It is interesting to note that *nemain*, here used as a noun, is translated "murder". As this is not one of the usual meanings of words derived from *nem-*, it would seem to be a folk etymology arising from the deadliness of Némain herself, reflecting a perception linking her with death and poison. It may be worth noting that *neimnech*, "poisonous", is a term also used to describe other characters with the power of striking enemies dead or paralyzing them with fear—notably, Balor, the Fomoire king who possessed a single evil eye.[20] His eye is

15 Gwynn 1924 96, 115
16 Macalister 1941123, 131, 155, 161, 183, 189
17 Sjoestedt 1994 31, Olmsted 1994 408, 415
18 O'Donovan 1868 25, Dobbs 1930 330
19 Gwynn 1924 14
20 Borsje 2003

called poisonous, and its destructive ability resembles the capacity of Némain's voice to strike down warriors in paralysis or death. Thus it may be that the "poisonous" nature ascribed to Némain is not so much a reference to physical poisons, but metaphorical of destructive Otherworldly power which could render people helpless.

Féa

Féa is an identity associated with the group of war Goddesses, but lacking any clear narrative literature giving her action or voice. Even the name itself is mysterious in its etymology and origin. An old Irish word *fé* exists, which is essentially a vocalization of grief, and is used by Lugh in his battle magic in the *Second Battle of Mag Tuired*.[21] According to *Cormac's Glossary*, it had funerary and magical associations—a *fé* is described as a wooden stave used to measure graves, which caused ill if someone was struck by it, and which was evoked in verbal curses of the form "*fé* to it!"[22] We do see this word used in the sense of woe or calamity—in the *Siege of Howth* the battle is said to be "*fé* on this side and *fé* on that", suggesting woe befalling both sides of the conflict.[23] There is, however, no direct association between Féa as a divinity and any of these usages.

In the literature, Féa appears primarily in the *Lebor Gabála*, with a couple of additional instances in *Dindshenchas* and annals.

Mag Fea: the Plain of Féa

The earliest material is likely that recorded in prose *Dindshenchas* tales, where she is associated as a tutelary Goddess with a plain called Mag Fea, in south Leinster (County Carlow).[24] This text also includes a confused tale of three apparently male founder-ancestor characters Femen, Fera, and Fea, clearing plains of Ireland; this Fea is also mentioned in the *Lebor Gabála Érenn* among the people of the founder Partholon, as either the first to be born or the first to die in Ireland.[25] Scholars tend to treat this Fea as unrelated to Féa, the Goddess, due to their gender, although this could be the result of a scribal error. A further land refer-

21 Royal Irish Academy 2013 entry: *fé*; Ó Tuathail 1993.
22 O'Donovan 1868 75
23 Stokes 1887 57
24 Stokes 1894 436
25 Macalister 1939 269

ence to *sídaib Féa,* “the mounds of Fea”, is mentioned in the *Lebor Gabála* as well; this may be a hill elsewhere given as Oilre in Mag Fea (possibly Ullard in Kilkenny, according to Macalister), but the identification is by no means clear.[26]

Féa emerges, absent any further information about her, as a Goddess associated with the region of south Leinster. She would appear to be a tutelary Goddess identified with the land and possibly eponymous ancient ancestral figures who cleared primordial forests and established the plains of Ireland, and may be identified with burial mounds.

Dam Dil: Faithful Ox

A folk-etymology in the Mag Fea *Dindshenchas* appears to link Féa to cattle. These oxen are named Fe and Mæn and associated with the place-name Mag Femen, along with Mag Fea.[27] Again in the *Lebor Gabála Érenn,* a Fea is identified as one of two royal oxen also associated with Mag Fea.[28] It is not clear whether this is the same as the Goddess Féa also appearing in the same paragraph—as the *Lebor Gabála* is a compilation of a variety of materials, we may be seeing differing local traditions reflected here.

The particular word used is *dam,* and with regard to cattle, *dam* refers specifically to oxen, that is, cattle used as draught animals for ploughing fields, again linking us back to the agrarian land association. However, *dam* is also used of stags; the phrase *dam díli,* “stag of flood” or “ox of flood” occurs in a number of texts and shows links to male virility and kingship. In particular, these two are identified with the two oxen of Dil, referring back to the *Dindshenchas* story of the druid Tulchine who prayed to the Morrígan to help him win Fairy woman’s hand in marriage.[29]

Da Mnai Néit: Two Wives of Néit

In almost every instance where Féa is mentioned, she is said to be the wife of the war God, Néit. This is consistent through every source text, including the *Dindshenchas, Banshenchas,* and *Lebor Gabála Érenn* texts. In most of these cases, she is associated with Némain as one of the “two

26 Macalister 1940 215
27 Stokes 1894 436
028 Macalister 1941 123
29 Stokes 1892 471

wives of Néit". Together, Féa and Némain are included among the sorceresses of the Túatha Dé, and said to be daughters of Elcmar of the Brugh.[30] This seems to represent a consistent tradition at least within the extant literature—and Féa's association with Néit and Némain is, in fact, her only link to the Morrígna group.

Bé Néit

As we have now seen Bé Néit among the group of Morrígna Goddesses in a variety of contexts, as well as syncretized to Classical entities, it bears looking at this name to see what we can determine about who she is. Bé Néit is not a name, per se, so much as a title: its primary meaning is simply "wife of Néit". As such it tells us very little directly about the Goddesses who are known by this title, other than that they were mated to a war God by the name of Néit. In some sources, the names of these Goddesses are also given: variously, they include Badb, Morrígan, Némain, and Féa—though never more than two are identified as the wives in any one text. In a few places, the title is treated as if it is a name in itself (e.g. Beneit) and no other name given. As a title Bé Néit can also be read "woman of battle",[31] a title which could be appropriate to any of the Morrígna (except perhaps Féa).

Néit in Airm Lebair: Néit of the Long Weapon

Who is this Néit? His name is an Old Irish word, *néit*, meaning "combat, battle". It derives from the same root that gives words such as *nia*, "warrior, hero" and *níth* "spirit, conflict", and compounds such as *níthcharpat*, "war-chariot". Néit seems to be a classic God of war. He is only given any detail in the *Dindshenchas* material; here we find the story of his association with the stronghold of Ailech Néit (Grianán Ailech). From these tales we learn that he is "surly of temper", that he is identified with a "long weapon", and that his stronghold was guarded by weapons.[32] The son of one Indúi, he is also called "the stranger" (*in allaid*, a term that indicates wildness and is more usually applied to animals), possibly suggesting the idea that he had a cult originating

30 Dobbs 1931 168
31 Epstein 1998 52
32 Gwynn 1924 115

outside Ireland. In the *First Battle of Mag Tuired*, he is called "the Fomorian," related to both Bres and Balor.[33]

Némain is Néit Dremuin Dúairc: Némain and Néit Wild and Grim

The Goddess most consistently mated to Néit, and for whom the most detailed lore about the pairing exists, is Némain. Poetic *Dindshenchas* texts that provide this more detailed lore also are notable for their lack of attestation of a pair of wives—it is simply Némain and Néit, war Gods identified with the stronghold at Ailech Néit, whereas in many of the other sources, Néit has two wives.[34] This single-pairing is also reflected in glosses, where the pair are called "a venomous couple," with no mention of a second wife (although in these sources, the identification of Némain is less clear, and she is sometimes conflated with Badb in the role).[35] In instances where two wives are named, Némain is always one of the pair—without exception. Thus the strongest mated pair identity is Némain and Néit.

Numerous dedications to a war God Neto synctretized to the Roman Mars have been found in Britain, Gaul, and Celtic Iberia; in many cases Mars-Neto is paired with Nemetona.[36] Etymological and iconographic links suggest a connection between this Continental divinity pairing and the well-attested Irish couple of Néit and Nemain.[37] In light of the "stranger" status of Néit, it begins to look very much like these Gods may have been brought together as a divine pairing from the Continent, and the identification with other Goddesses as additional wives of Néit developed as their cult was integrated with local ones.

If this is the case, it may also explain why the title Bé Néit is occasionally applied to another divinity, such as Badb or Morrígan, or used as a name in itself. Resonances or similarities between Némain and other war Goddess theophanies—such as shrieking and battle terror—may have led ancient and medieval people to interpret them as aspects of the same war Goddess. This seems to have been the process especially in the Ulster cycle, where early material in the *Wooing of Emer*

33 Fraser 1915 45
34 Gwynn 1924 96, 103, 115
35 Stokes 1900 240, O'Donovan 1868 25, 26
36 Olmsted 1994 327, 344, 408, 415
37 Stokes 1862 34, Sjoestedt 1994 74

identifies Badb and the Morrígan as one Goddess and calls her the wife of Néit.[38] The early *Táin* expands the identification to a triad, including Némain alongside Badb and an unnamed Bé Néit, but who context suggests is the Morrígan, since elsewhere in the saga she is the third war Goddess who appears. Similarly, an identification with Badb occurs in the *Cormac's Glossary* (which also notably, in the same text, gives the title to Némain).

Da Mnai Néit: The Two Wives of Néit

Elsewhere and especially in the *Lebor Gabála Érenn* materials, we find the consistent appearance of Néit with the two wives. Most commonly, the pairing is Némain and Féa. Two instances of the Badb-Némain pair occur, but the overarching pattern remains Némain and Fea when two wives are indicated.[39] Both of the pair, but Féa especially, seem to have distinctly localized, and quite ancient, traditions tying them to place. This might suggest that Féa was originally a local tutelary land and ancestral Goddess in Leinster, who was drawn into association with the other divinities. Whether this reflects an actual devotional tradition or an artifact of medieval scholarship we do not have the information now to determine. Carey suggests that it may be reflective of an ancient pattern whereby the triads seen in the literature ultimately derive from paired Goddesses where one is a tutelary and fertility figure and one a war Goddess.[40] This primal duality embodies sovereignty as both war Goddess and as tutelary land Goddess and can also be seen existing as a parallel, overlapping pattern to the triplicities also expressed by the Morrígna Goddesses.[41]

---

38 Meyer 1888 231
39 Macalister 1941 155, 237
40 Carey 1982 272-3
41 O'Donovan 1868 25, 26

8

Deep Roots: British and Continental Sisters

As we have seen above, the Irish Morrígna show significant linkages to related divinities seen elsewhere in the ancient Celtic and Indo-European worlds. It is worth taking a look at these related divinities for what they can suggest or reveal about the relationships between local, regional, and pan-Celtic patterns of worship and religious ideology. While important local, regional, and tribal differences in myth and religious practice clearly existed, it is equally clear that well-defined and consistent patterns in cosmology, identities of Gods, and in ritual practice can be traced across not only the Celtic world, but threading through the whole of the Indo-European culture family, touching Germanic, Scandinavian, Hellenic, Italic, and Vedic cultures as well as the Insular and Continental Celtic cultures.

Particularly strong parallels can be seen in the regions of the Celto-Germanic border cultures, and this should not surprise us, given the profound contact and sharing of culture that would have taken place there. Scholars suggest that this region would have seen many bilingual people in ancient times, allowing for significant cultural exchange.[1]

Within the Celtic world, significant parallels in religious structure, priesthood function, and ritual patterns can also be seen. The language used of the Irish priestly classes show fairly precise cognates in Gaulish; for example Irish *bard* parallels Gaulish *bardos* (poet); Irish *druí*, Gaulish *druis* (druid); Irish *fáith*, Gaulish *vatis* (seer, priest); Irish *fili*, Gaulish *velets* (seer, poet).[2] The functions of these various priestly classes were not identical across Celtic societies, but their cognate relationships demonstrate at least a pattern of similar divisions in religious roles and functions. Likewise, Gods with etymologically related names and often similar iconography can be found between Insular and Continental Celtic societies, such as Gaulish Lugus, Irish Lugh; British Brigantia, Irish Brigid; British Nodons and Irish Nuada.[3] Again, we would not assume these divinities are identical, but clearly relationships existed at some time in the past. Given that members of the priestly classes had rights to travel freely between different tribal areas and studied with one another in a collegiate fashion, and that specialized religious knowledge was shared between druids and poets of Ireland and nearby Britain and Gaul, it is reasonable to imagine that at least some shared development of cult practice, iconography, and belief about these divinities may have occurred.[4]

The Great Queen

Several inscriptions have been found in Gaul and Britain dedicated to Goddesses by names meaning "Great Queen" or variants on this theme. These appear to be divinities whose identities are centered around sov-

1 Donahue 1941 7
2 Delamarre 2003 67, 149, 308, 311, Ó hÓgáin 1999 72
3 Beck 2009 223, Macalister 1941 97, 101. Though, it should be noted, the relationship between Brigantia and Brigid is the subject of debate.
4 Kelly 2003 46, Aldhouse-Green 2010 17, Ó hÓgáin 1999 94

ereignty and its personification in a mighty, queenly figure, who as a protector of sovereignty often also shows martial attributes.

A votive bowl from the early first century CE was dedicated to two Goddesses, Rigana and Rosmerta.[5] Inscriptions on altars from Gaul and Britain include the names Regina (a Latinized form) and Riigina. The latter includes an image in relief which shows a Goddess with a knee-length robe, radial, halo-like hair, and with a column and pointed staff or spear, attributes which convey regality, sovereignty, and martial power.[6] This depiction is parallel to and often compared with depictions of Brigantia, tutelary Goddess of the Brigantes tribe in northern Britain, and a cognate to the Irish Brigid.[7] Sculptural portraits like this one post-date Roman conquest and clearly do show Classical influence. However, the imagery used in these dedications aligns closely with the combined tribal/tutelary, land and sovereignty, and martial functions we are familiar with from the Irish literary portrait of the Morrígan and clearly also reflect a native Celtic tradition about the identity and attributes of these protective tutelary Goddesses.

Several related names or bynames of Goddesses incorporate the Queen element. Dedications from Gaul to Camuloriga, "Queen of Champions", and Albiorica, "Queen of the World" may be related to Rigana as bynames or epithets for the same Goddess in varying aspects, or local cult forms of related Goddesses.[8]

Scholars studying the Morrígan's name have more recently tended to favor the idea that the unaccented form Morrígan, meaning Phantom Queen, is the older and therefore "original" one. However, the existence of these Great Queen Goddesses in Britain and the Continent, and whose names are cognate to Morrígan, would seem to point toward a very ancient origin for the Great Queen as a title and divine identity in Celtic cultures as well. Several scholars have pointed out that many of the oldest Irish land Goddesses have the epithet *Mór* as part of their names or titles (e.g. Mór Muman, Mag Mór) and argued here based on this and the epigraphic evidence from Gaul and Britain that the title "Great Queen" may be of equal antiquity to "Phantom Queen".[9] The inferred ancient name which is thought to lay behind known deity

5 Olmsted 1994 362
6 Beck 2009 262
7 Beck 2009 331
8 Beck 2009 536
9 Beck 2009 262, Olmsted 1994 185, 203

names including Rhiannon, Rigana, and Mórrígan is reconstructed as *Rigantona, "Divine Queen" or "Queen Goddess."[10]

The Horse Goddess

The etymological connections between the Queen Goddesses such as Rigana and Morrígan and the Welsh Rhiannon in particular suggest that at the period in antiquity when these mythological identities were developed, the sovereignty Goddess in horse form must have been part of the picture. There are striking parallels between the myths of Rhiannon and Macha as we know them. Each tale includes a horse race which is a contest between a Goddess and a king, followed by a double birth (twins for Macha, or simultaneous human and horse birth in Rhiannon's case); the Goddess in both is brought to a humiliated condition "that blurs the distinction between horse and woman" by the boasting or foolishness of a mate.[11] Macha herself is, as we have seen, deeply tied to kingship and sovereignty not just in her mythological stories, but in the ritual life of Ulster as recorded in the lore and reflected in the archaeological record.

Waddell argues that the sovereignty Goddess in horse form can be seen in Rhiannon, Macha, and the Gaulish Epona as well as Róich, the mother of the Irish mythological king Fergus mac Róich, and whose name means "Great Horse" (*ro-ech*).[12] Epona too means "Divine Horse" (*epo* being the Gallo-Brittonic form of the Indo-European root **ekuo*, "horse"), and she was sometimes given the double title Epona Regina, connecting her to the Great Queen Goddesses.[13] She was very often depicted with paired horses or foals, a feature which may suggest mythology paralleling the twin foals of Macha and the double birth associated with Rhiannon. As well, among Epona's bynames we find Imona, "Swift One", a name that is etymologically cognate to the Irish Emain (of Emain Macha, the royal center of Macha's tutelary domain). Thus a name like Emain, or its possible root *Imonis, may have been part of the ancient horse Goddess's title. Olmsted's suggested reconstruction of the title as we know it in Irish, Emain Macha, is "Swift One of the Plain".[14]

---

10 Beck 2009 265, Waddell 2014 89

11 Waddell 2014 90

12 Waddell 2014 91

13 Olmsted 1994 158, 172

14 Olmsted 1994 158. On this name, however, see also Ó hÓgáin, who derives

Epona, like Macha and the Great Queen Goddesses, also has recognizable martial attributes. Many of her dedications are found in the stables of Roman military sites where Gaulish cavalry units had been stationed, demonstrating an association not just with horses, but with military power.[15] Epona's native Celtic identity has been questioned by some, as she is best known from these Roman military dedications. Her alignment with clearly Celtic figures such as Rhiannon and Macha is beginning to emerge, however. Armed, warlike horsewomen are shown on a large number of pre-conquest late Iron Age coins from Gaulish tribes, and scholars suggest that prior to conquest, a more strongly martial Goddess associated with armed horse-warriorship and sovereignty may have been venerated, who gradually shifted to become the more beneficent Epona of fecundity and prosperity known from Roman times.[16]

Crow of Battle

As we discussed above in the chapter on Badb, her roots reach beyond Ireland to a shared Celtic religious pattern of war divinities in female form. Cognate to Badb are a group of Goddesses from Gaul and the Germanic border region whose names are all derived from a common Celtic root *bodu-*, meaning "combat, war, violence", which in turn may derive from Indo-European **bhu-dh-wa*, "to warn" or "to awaken".[17] The prophetic functions of the war Goddesses as harbingers of death and battle thus may be among their earliest attributes. According to this theory, the connotation of the words *badb* in Irish and *bodua* in Gaulish to mean "raven" or "crow" are later and derived from the association of the war Goddesses with these carrion birds in their presence on the battlefield. Warriors will have seen the crows and ravens hovering over the fields of war, their presence indicating an anticipation of carnage, and recognized them as avatars or visitations of the Goddess of battle.[18]

Inscriptions showing the existence and veneration of the war God-

---

Emain from the early Celtic *isomnis*, "sturdy posts", based on the name Isamnion appearing on the map of Ptolemaeus, and possibly referring to the great wooden post temple structure of Emain Macha (Ó hÓgáin 1999 172).

15 Olmsted 1994 158

16 Aldhouse-Green 2010 243, Beck 2009 282

17 Beck 2009 251

18 Beck 2009 251

dess in this form have been found in Gaul. An altar dedication from Mieussy, France, is dedicated to "the August Cathubodua", an exact Gaulish cognate to the name Badb Catha known in Ireland.[19] The altar, incidentally, was dedicated by a woman and a Roman citizen. Likely related, a Victoria Cassibodua is honored on a dedication from a nearby Germanic location. The first element of the name *cassi-* is debated as to its meaning, but the second element *bodua* clearly links her to this group of war Goddesses.[20] *Cassi-* may be a tribal identifier, or may mean "sacred", "exceptional", or has even been suggested to mean "bronze". Of these, "Sacred Crow" seems to me the most likely name.[21] The epithet Victoria is a Latin addition showing she had been syncretized with the Roman Goddess Victoria, and suggesting she was being worshiped in her capacity to grant victory in battle.

Textual evidence from the accounts of Tacitus describes a Goddess by the name of Baduhenna, who had a grove dedicated to her in Frisia in the Germanic border area, where Roman soldiers were killed, possibly in sacrifice.[22] Baduhenna incorporates the element *badu*, the Germanic form of the same root. According to some scholars, the names of deities such as Baduhenna and Cathubodua will have been recognizable by members of both Celtic and Germanic tribal groups well into the late Iron Age, and represent evidence of parallel cult development or cultural diffusion between neighboring tribes.[23]

Several items of war-gear adorned with ravens have been found from Gaul and other Celtic territories, including helmets with bronze decorative crests in the shape of crows or ravens. While the most ornate of these are likely to have been ceremonial gear rather than anything actually worn in battle, they still demonstrate the widespread association of corvid birds with warfare and their use in religious iconography of war.[24] Similarly, Gaulish personal names and titles of war leaders

---

19 Beck 2009 252

20 Beck 2009 253

21 Beck 2009 252, Delamarre 2003 109. Elsewhere, we also have Ancasta, a deity name Olmsted translates as "the Sacred One"; it is possible that the element *cassi-* is identical with *casti-*, which is consistent with spelling changes often seen in the transcription of the Gaulish Ð or tau Gallicum, a sound transcribed as both ts- and st-. See Delamarre 2003 96 and Olmsted 1994 410.

22 Beck 2009 252

23 Donahue 1941 8

24 Beck 2009 254

often contain the element *bodua* in filial constructions meaning "Born of Bodua" or "Son of Bodua"; as in Boduagnatus, Boduogenus.[25] Gaulish warriors seem to have been keen to identify themselves with the battle crow in ways that recall the close association of Cú Chulainn with Badb and the battle spirits who shrieked from his helmet and his war gear.

The Victorious

The identification of Cassibodua as Victory highlights a further theme running among the Celtic war Goddesses—names, epithets and attributes as Goddesses of victory and victory-bringers. This is seen in two inscriptions to a Goddess Boudina or Boudena, and one to a Tutela Boudiga, all from Gaulish locations in France and Germany.[26] The root *boud-* is "victory", and these names are usually read as "Victorious One". *Tutela* is a title meaning "protectress" and used with tutelary Goddesses identified with a place or tribe. Boudiga is also sometimes paired with a nurturing land Goddess, the pair together exemplifying the supportive and protective functions of the tutelary Goddess.[27] Another group of inscriptions give related names such as Segeta and Segomanna, "Victorious One" and "Victory Giver", from another Celtic root *sego-* also meaning victory.[28] Brigantia, best known from Britain, is also identified with Victory in some of her dedications as well.

Readers familiar with Celtic histories will have noticed the resemblance of the deity name Boudiga to Queen Boudicca, a famous war leader of the British Iceni tribe who led a violent uprising against Roman occupation in the first century CE. We can look at this as an example of a pattern seen in many instances in Celtic history of a female spiritual leader who is identified with and often named after a tutelary Goddess of the tribe, and who in many cases would have served as the persona of the Goddess in sovereignty rites, political or religious leadership, or in war. Instances in both mythology and history of powerful women with a succession of husbands acceding to kingship through them instantiate this, such as Medb of Cruachan, as well as Queen Cartimandua of the Brigantes.[29]

25 Olmsted 1994 411
26 Olmsted 1994 411
27 Beck 2009 139
28 Beck 2009 331
29 Waddell 2014 113, Koch and Carey 2003 45

Queen Boudicca only emerges into the historical record after the death of her husband and the beginning of her conflict with the Romans, so we know little of what her role would have been in relation to leadership and sovereignty outside the context of war and rebellion. If, as many scholars suggest, she represents a case of this pattern, her name would tend to indicate that the tribal Goddess she was identified with may have been named Boudiga or some variant of the name. Historical accounts tell of Queen Boudicca praying to and invoking a Goddess Andraste upon the battlefield; this name is translated "Invincible One" or "Unconquerable" from *an-*, a negative prefix and *drastos*, "to vanquish."[30] The name thus carries very similar meanings to Boudiga as "Victorious One", and may simply be the fiercer byname that Boudicca chose to invoke in her war of vengeance. In either case, both Boudiga and Andraste clearly fit into the pattern of Celtic tutelary and war Goddesses identified with Victory.

The Slain-Choosers

The functional resemblance between the Morrígna and the Germanic and Norse valkyries is often remarked on: both kinds of being show a special relationship with heroes, appear in bird form, female form, or as frightful battle demons, and may sometimes be evoked in groups of three.[31] In medieval literature dealing with both groups, Classical war-furies and Goddesses such as the Erinyes: Tisiphone, Alecto, and Bellona are used as glosses. The valkyries in Scandinavian and Germanic literature are also specifically associated with ravens in a number of sources. Both groups also involve themselves in the psychopomp function of conveying the souls of the slain in battle into their Otherworld afterlife, though the evidence linking the valkyries to this function is more direct than in the case of the Morrígna.[32] The resemblance in both image and function points to something quite ancient in the relationships of these cultures to war, death, and concepts of fatality.

The Old Norse *valkyrja* means "slain-choosers" (from *valr*, "slain", specifically used to indicate valorous dead who died in battle, and *kjósa*,

30 Beck 2009 184
31 Donahue 1941 1
32 Epstein 1998 272

"to choose").[33] We see some intriguing parallels with the Greek *keres*, conceived as malevolent death-spirits or death Goddesses who would haunt battlefields and who were tied to the fates of warriors, claiming them at their foretold moment of death.[34] It has been suggested that the element *ker* "death, fate" in the Greek *keres* may be etymologically related to the element *kyr* in the Norse *valkyr*, by way of an interrelationship between the meanings of "choice" and "fate", though this may be modern folk etymology. Certainly these groups of divinities show marked functional parallels, being involved with the choosing of warriors who would die in battle and appearing in the form of malevolent and bird-like female spirits.[35] We do not see Celtic battle divinities appearing to be related to this group by name; I have seen no direct cognate to "slain-chooser" as a byname of any Celtic divinity or spirit. However, several individual *valkyr* divinities have names including the element *badu*, a Germanic cognate of the familiar Celtic *bodua/badb*, and an element in the names of Germanic war Goddesses such as Baduhenna. On this basis, it has been argued that the *valkyrja* and Germanic and Celtic war Goddesses may all trace back to an ancient Germano-Celtic divinity, the root of whose name would have been *Badu; although a singular ancestral deity is not the only possible explanation.[36]

The Battle of Clontarf presents an interesting lens through which to view this connection. Clontarf was a major historical battle which took place in Ireland near Dublin in the year 1014, involving the Gaelic Irish against a Viking-Irish alliance. It is somewhat special in that we have surviving narrative sagas telling its story from both Irish and Scandinavian perspectives: the Irish *War of the Gaedhel with the Gaill*, and the Icelandic *Saga of Burnt Njál*. In both sagas, female battle-spirits involve themselves with the fate of battle and of the heroes, though they take a different role in each. In the Icelandic tale, one of the warriors at the battle sees a vision of twelve women weaving on a loom built of weapons, with entrails for its warp and weft; they chant a baneful song about weaving the fates of men and the carnage of battle.[37] In the Irish tale, Badb appears along with the host of frightful battle-spirits, screaming

33 Donahue 1941 3
34 Homer 1924 II 18 535
35 Donahue 1941 6, Atsma 2011
36 Epstein 1998 289 citing Lottner and others.
37 Dasent 1861 242

over the heads of the warriors and comparing their valour in combat.[38]

In the *badba*, *valkyrja*, and *keres*, we are likely looking at the refraction through different cultures of a very ancient type of female battle spirit whose mode of action is fatality: death in war, foredestination, and the prophetic knowledge of that fate, originating in the Indo-European level of antiquity. These traits and functions are expressed in distinct but related ways among the Irish and other Indo-European peoples.

Triplicities

There is some evidence to suggest that the British and Continental war Goddesses who are cognates of the Morrígna may also have shared the triplicity we so often see in the Irish materials.

At a Romano-Celtic temple at Benwell, along Hadrian's Wall in Britain, an altar was dedicated *Lamiis Tribus*, "to the three Lamiae".[39] *Lamia*, a Latin word denoting "demoness, monster, or fury", is very frequently used in Irish literature in reference to the Morrígna, and seems to have become, in the post-Roman world, a term used in literature for any frightful, female spirit, such as the war Goddesses.[40] The Benwell altar was fire-reddened from cultic use, and was found in the subterranean level of the temple, suggesting an association with chthonic, Otherworldly forces accessed beneath the ground. While the term *lamia* is Latin and refers to a type of being known in Roman literature, there has been no evidence found of any actual Roman cult reverence toward *lamiae* anywhere else; that is to say, the term may be Latin, but the altar and the cult associated with are local and probably Celtic.[41]

At the same site, another dedication was found at surface level to a triad of maternal Goddesses associated with the military space, *Matribus Tribus Campestribus*, "the Three Mother-Goddesses of the Training Ground".[42] Dedications such as this to triads of mother Goddesses styled Matres or Matronae are found virtually throughout the ancient Celtic and Germanic worlds, and are often identified as the Mothers of a given tribe, or are associated with fertility attributes such as iconography of

38 Todd 1867 175
39 Ross 1996 285
40 Bernhardt-House 2007 52, Ross 1996 285
41 Epstein 1998 215
42 Beck 2009 102, Bernhardt-House 2007 52

bread, fruits, and infants.[43] They illustrate a pervasive pattern in Celtic thought in which sacredness is triadic and divine powers are expressed in triple form, each member of the triad embodying a variation on the central function—a pattern also seen with the three Brigits and other triads in Celtic myth.[44] The pairing of the two dedications at Benwell to the chthonic triad of demonesses or furies, and the protective triad of mother-Goddesses linked to the military training-ground, is suggestive of the way that the triplicity of Celtic divinity may have been recognized to manifest in both fertilizing and destructive forms simultaneously.

The Lady in the River

Another Goddess often captures the curiosity of students of the Morrígan's lore due to her association with ravens: Nantosuelta, a Gaulish Goddess, is depicted and named on several altar dedications from the Gallo-Roman period. As her attributes are notable and distinct, we are also able to recognize her in reliefs where no written dedication is included. She typically appears with a crow or raven near her, or in one case has wings herself; she carries a staff with a distinctive small house atop it, and she sometimes also has symbols of plenty such as a cornucopia, patera, or beehive-like object. She appears in several of these reliefs alone, but when paired with a consort God, it is always Sucellus.

The name, Nantosuelta, is interesting in that it bears no direct relationship to the visible symbols of her iconography. The name is from *nantu-* "valley, watercourse, river" and the element *suelta*, which may either be from **suel*, "sun", or **swel-*, "to curve". Thus her name is variously translated "Sun-warmed Valley" or "Winding River".[45] The little house on the pole that she carries has been read as a dovecote or a miniature tomb; in the first case this would indicate domesticity, in the second, a funerary aspect. Honeycombs, cakes, patera, and other symbols of domestic plenty are also common.[46] The raven or crow appearing with her may also be indicative of a funerary connection, as well

43 Beck 2009 63
44 Irby-Massie 1999 148
45 Beck 2009 130. Alternate etymologies have attempted to link the element *nanto* to *neto*, denoting warriors and seen in the names of the war Gods Néit and Neto, but most scholars treat these as unconvincing.
46 Beck 2009 125, Olmsted 1994 301

as appearing as oracular messenger or Otherworld guide for souls.[47] Thus she would seem to embody some combination of land and river Goddess, bringer of life and plenty, Otherworldly knowledge, as well as funerary attributes related to the care of the souls of the dead.

Her coupling with Sucellus tends to align her with an archetype of fertile river Goddesses coupled to tribal warrior Gods. Sucellus, "Good Striker", appears with a large club or hammer and a cup or dish. The hammer conveys warrior functions and is also reminiscent of the Dagda's great club with which he could equally strike dead and revive; the dish calls to mind his cauldron.[48] In Irish myth, we see the Dagda fulfilling this pattern as tribal warrior God mating with Goddesses in association with rivers, in two instances: the Morrígan and Bóann. Bóann is the stronger candidate for a river Goddess; her name is attached to the Boyne. Her story tells of the creation of the Boyne river from a holy well of wisdom whose waters she released, and in so doing, died and became merged with the river.[49] The Morrígan, on the other hand, is never herself identified with a river, but appears again and again at rivers during important parts of her narrative. Interestingly, both Bóann and the Morrígan sustain three wounds resulting from conflicts in their association with rivers, and they are virtually the same three wounds: to the eye, the hand (or in the Morrígan's case, since an eel has no hands, a rib), and the leg.

Thus while neither Bóann nor the Morrígan present themselves fully as cognates of Nantosuelta, they all appear to instantiate a pattern: a tribal war God identified by his mighty weapon and both warrior and fatherly or sustaining qualities, mated to a Goddess associated with rivers, land and fertility, wisdom, and funerary qualities, which may also be expressed in a martial form.

Goddess of the Sanctuary

We have touched on the Gaulish Goddess Nemetona in the previous chapter in the context of her apparent connection to Némain. Nemetona appears to have her origins as a tutelary Goddess in Gaul, in close association to the Nemetes tribe.

---

47 Beck 2009 133

48 Ross 1996 314

49 Stokes 1894 315

The Nemetes occupied a tribal territory in the Rhine region of Gaul. Here, inscriptions have been found to a group of deities associated with the tribe, and it is from this region that the greatest concentration of dedications to Nemetona are found. An instance of the Matres, mother Goddesses so often seen in triple form, appears here in an inscription to the *Matris Nemetialibus*, "Mothers of the Nemetes".[50] Most of the other dedications in the region to Nemetona (or Nemeta) position her as a singular Goddess.[51]

Many of Nemetona's dedications pair her with a war God; he is sometimes named only by the syncretized Roman name of Mars. When this "Celtic Mars" is given a native name along with the Roman, it is most frequently Neto, "warrior", a name of the war God known far beyond the tribal area of the Nemetes, including Ireland, Britain, and among the Celtiberians of Spain.[52] Mars Neto appears to have also been known by a related byname Segomoni "Victor" or "Victory-bringer"; *ogam* inscriptions from Ireland give Neta Segamonas. This links him to the Irish mythological character Nia Segamain, whose name in Irish still means "victorious warrior".[53] At Bath in Britain we also find *Loucetio Marti et Nemetonae*.[54] The close pairing of Nemetona with Neto in Gaul and Britain provides strong parallels to the pairing of Némain with Néit in Irish lore.

The name Nemeta or Nemetona appears to derive from the term *nemeto-*, which has meanings of "sacred" and also denotes the *nemeton*, sacred grove or sanctuary, with the *-ona* suffix typically used to identify names of Goddesses. In addition to the tribal identifier of the Nemetes, it also appears in place-names, such as Nemetobriga.[55] However, it is not directly obvious from these facts whether the meaning of sacredness, or the sanctuary which is the locus of sacredness, or the tribe who honors these things, is the primary meaning from which these names derive. If sacredness is the origin of the term, then her name might be "the Sacred

50 Beck 2009 237, Olmsted 1994 415

51 Beck 2009 237

52 Olmsted 1994 344

53 Olmsted 1994 327, Beck 2009 186. This would seem to be the correct etymology, contrary to speculative folk etymologies given in medieval lore such as "milk-giver" or "little deer".

54 Olmsted 1994 415

55 Olmsted 1994 415. *Briga* is a high place; this would then be something like "sacred height", "high sanctuary", or possibly "high place of Nemetona/the Nemetes".

One", and the *nemeton* is the home of the sacred, and the tribal name can perhaps be read as "the people of Nemetona". The linguistic evidence might tend to support this view, as *nemeð*, a cognate term in Irish, refers to holy or privileged status, and *nem* is the heavens or a sanctified space. This also accords well with patterns seen with other tribes who appear to have derived their names from their tutelary Goddesses, such as the Treveri and the Matres Treverae, the Nervinii and the Nervinae, and possibly the Brigantes and Brigantia.[56] It is, however, possible that the original locus of meaning is the *nemeton* itself, in which case her name would be read as "She of the Sacred Grove" or "Goddess of the Sanctuary", and the Nemetes the "people of the sanctuary". Indeed, the distinction may be a product of modern thought.

Nemetona appears to have a distinctly local character in origin—as mentioned above, most of her dedications come from the Rhine region of the Nemetes tribe. Another group of dedications was found at Bath, in Roman Britain, including one dedicated by a member of the Treveri tribe, another tribe originally from the same region as the Nemetes, near the Rhine in the Celtic-Germanic border regions.[57] The Bath dedications are interesting because they at once reinforce the local and tribal origins of Nemetona and her warrior God consort, and at the same time show evidence of how their worship traveled to the Insular fringes of the Celtic world. Though it cannot be demonstrated, it is possible that in the mythical journey of the Nemedians or "people of Nemed" in the Irish Mythological Cycle, we have a faint folk-memory of the coming of the Nemetes or a related tribe to Ireland, who may at one time have brought the worship of the divine pair who came to be known as the Irish Némain and Néit.

56 Beck 2009 250
57 Beck 2009 238

PEACE
to the sky
sky to the earth
earth under sky strength in each
A cup very full a fullness of honey
mead to fullness
summer in winter
Spears upon shields shields upon fists
Forts fierce for battle
strongholds of earth
Rights of descendants woods full of stags
horns of cattle
encircling palisades
Mast upon trees heavy with growth
wealth for children
children well learned
A mighty yoked bull a bull from a song
plenty in wood wood for fires
fire from a stone stone from earth
Young born from cows cows from an earth womb
mound exalted in song new growth in
spring Autumn with abundant grain
warriors for the land land held secure
tales told in poetry
might to the eternal high places
peace to the sky
be it nine times eternal

9

In Her Words: The Poems

The Irish mythological literature provides us with that thing most treasured by students of a pantheon—the direct speech of the deity. Lore records a wealth of poems and speeches spoken by the Gods, including several long poems, given by the Morrígan herself.

Can we honor these words as the words of the Morrígan herself? It is of course true that the poems were composed and recorded by human beings, not Gods. The poems of the Morrígan are in truth human works of religiously-inspired creativity represented as her own speakings in the stories. In this sense, the poems of the Morrígan are not, per se, her own direct speech in any verifiable way. Yet the poems still offer something very special that reaches beyond the narrative and mythological value of the stories within which they are embedded.

Readers of the Irish mythological and heroic literatures will have noted that the stories alternate between passages of narrative and descriptive text, and passages of verse usually framed as the spoken poems and speeches of the mythic characters themselves. These passages of verse are often marked and introduced in this fashion:

> "Then the Morrigan, daughter of Ernmas, came, and was heartening the Tuatha Dea to fight the battle fiercely and fervently. So then she sang this lay below :
> "Kings arise to the battle", etc.
> Thereafter the battle became a rout, and the Fomorians were beaten to the sea."[1]

Language such as this signals the transition to verse text. Verse text passages are often cryptic and highly archaic in their language, to the extent that many translators, as in the example above, do not even attempt to translate the verse texts. These archaic verse texts are often in a form known as *rosc*, and this is the poetic form of most of the Morrígan's poems.

Ralph O'Connor describes *rosc* poetry so: "a traditional metrical form characteristically used for prophetic utterances and typified by a succession of vivid haiku-like images. *Rosc* does not offer detailed explication, but rather a calculated obscurity."[2] This poetry is characterized by short, terse lines, usually non-rhyming, with poetic alliteration prominent (words that contain similar sounds, such as the line *fri fur fo abad líni Fomoire*). This linking of words by alliteration is called *úaim*, "stitching".[3] The style is rhythmic, but employs an archaic pattern in which stressed words are counted to form the meter, instead of syllables.[4] The typical *rosc* meter employs two stressed syllables to each half-line, a meter that generates a rolling rhythm similar to many nursery rhymes.[5] This rolling, cyclical quality is enhanced as lines interweave with one another through alliteration. Commonly, the final word or syllable of one line alliterates with the first of the next line (such as in the lines *sith co nem/ nem co doman/doman fo ním*). This cyclical alliteration pattern is called *conachlonn*, literally "paired" or "fastened".[6] Many more

1 Stokes 1891 101
2 O'Connor 2013 140
3 Carmody 2004 18
4 Corthals 1996 29
5 Meyer 1909 2
6 Mees 2009 187

complex alliterative patterns than this are also used which interweave the poems in multiple ways.

The language of these poems is archaic to the point of obscurity, showing every sign of being much, much older than the narrative passages which frame them in the tales. Although some forms of *rosc* developed following Latin influence in the Christian era, it is thought that the genre itself derives from a native Celtic poetic tradition whose signature metrical forms can be traced to ancient Indo-European ritual verse patterns.[7] P. L. Henry notes that by the time many of the oral tales were being composed into written sagas, in the 10th-12th centuries, understanding of this genre of visionary poetry was already being lost, as signaled by its treatment in the narrative texts.[8]

The alliterative, rhythmical, and cyclical qualities of the poems, together with the archaic language style, point to the origins of *rosc* as poetry in an oral, ritual context. O'Connor describes *rosc* as an "incantatory rhythmical form".[9] Mees characterizes the origins of *rosc* poetry in the "dreamy mantic utterances" of visionary practices such as *imbas forosnai*, where the poet accesses intensive meditative or visionary states and brings forth inspired verse.[10] This accords well with our understanding of Celtic cultures in general, and in particular the early Irish, as an oral culture placing a very strong emphasis on both memorized oral literature and inspired performative poetry as the modes of transmission for cultural knowledge. The Irish traditions of poetic and religious learning taught a set of practices in which the highest level of divine inspiration was understood to confer direct transmission of poetry from the Gods, as well as practices to inculcate the ability to memorize vast amounts of poetic lore. This poetry, and its performance, represented the primary vessel of cultural transmission and memory for the lore and literature of the culture.

What we see in the *rosc* poems are the traces of an ancient core of Irish ritual lore regarding the Gods and their speakings. We can imagine that in the pre-literate days, poems would have been performed in a ritual context as part of the retelling and transmission of the myths, and other ritual contexts such as prophetic incubation. We can picture

7 Corthals 1996 28, citing Watkins.
8 Henry 1995 35
9 O'Connor 2013 10
10 Mees 2009 188

how the rhythmic, alliterative quality of the poems lends itself perfectly to incantation in the swaying rhythm of ritual trance, as the stories of the Gods and heroes were perhaps re-enacted through poetic recitation in an inspired state. Thus, the *rosc* poems represent for us the shape of early devotional ritual speech, and our best trace of the words and speakings of the Gods as they were understood by practitioners of ancient Irish religion.

Rosc is employed by a great variety of characters in early Irish literature, very often in a poetic or legal context. It is, in Stacey's words, the language "of prophecy, of supernatural insight, and of verbal contestation generally.[11] The poetry attributed to the Morrígan is primarily prophetic in nature. Six major poetic recitations are attributed to the Morrígan in the extant Irish literature: three are given in the *Second Battle of Mag Tuired*, one in the *Cattle Raid of Regamna* foretale, and two in the *Táin Bó Cúailnge* proper. Of these six poems, four fall clearly into the genre of prophecy; the remaining two are battle poems oriented primarily to incitement.

The Battle Poem: "Kings Arise to the Battle"

This poem is given during the great battle between the Túatha Dé Danann and the Fomoiri for the sovereignty of Ireland, in the *Second Battle of Mag Tuired*. At the point when the Morrígan delivers this poem, the battle is already underway and great slaughter has already been occurring. Heroes of the Túatha Dé have already fallen in the battle, including the former king Nuada. Lugh and Balor have just fought one another and Balor has been killed, along with many Fomorians, and the Fomoire king Indech has been struck a blow. At this point the Morrígan rises and chants her battle poem, to hearten the Túatha Dé. Following her incantation, the battle turns from an even slaughter cutting down both sides to a victorious rout in which the Túatha Dé drive the Fomoiri back to the sea.

In other words, she comes at the turning point of the battle, and there is a strong suggestion in the text that her delivery of the poem is itself the pivot that turns the battle. The language used is *boi oc nertad*, "strengthening" them to the fight, by means of her poem.

11 Stacey 2007 11

The poem is given here with Carmody's translation.[12] Notes follow where I have additional thoughts about interpretation of the language.

	Original		Translation (Carmody)*
1	*afraigid rig don cath*	1	kings arise to [meet] the battle
2	*rucatair gruaide*	2	cheeks are seized
3	*aisnethir rossa*	3	faces [honours] are declared
4	*ronnatair feola*	4	flesh is decimated
5	*fennátair enech*	5	faces are flayed
6	*ethátair catha -rruba*	6	[incomplete word] of battle are seized
7	*segatar ratha*	7	ramparts are sought
8	*radatar fleda*	8	feasts are given
9	*fechatar catha*	9	battles are observed
10	*canátair natha*	10	poems are recited
11	*noatair druith*	11	druids are celebrated
12	*dénaitir cuaird*	12	circuits are made
13	*cuimnitir arca*	13	bodies are recorded
14	*alat ide*	14	metals cut
15	*sennat deda*	15	teeth mark
16	*tennat braigit*	16	necks break
17	*blathnuigh[i]t [cét] tufer*	17	[a hundred] cuts blossom
18	*cluinethar eghme*	18	screams are heard
19	*ailitir cuaird*	19	battalions are broken
20	*cathitir lochtai*	20	hosts give battle
21	*lúet ethair*	21	ships are steered
22	*snaat arma*	22	weapons protect
23	*scothaitir sronai*	23	noses are severed
24	*At ci[ú] cach ro genair*	24	I see all who are born
25	*ruad cath derg bandach*	25	[in the] blood-zealous vigorous battle
26	*dremnad fiach lergai fo eburlai*	26	raging [on the] raven-battlefield [with] blade-scabbards
27	*fri uabar rusmebat*	27	they attempt our defeat
28	*re nar már srotaib sinne*	28	over our own great torrents

---

12 Carmody 2013. Line division and bracketing are following Carmody; brackets indicate gaps, implied words, or uncertain translation. I have removed capitalization and punctuation to convey the *rosc* style.

* Carmody, Isolde. 2013. "Poems of the Morrigan: Poem A." Story Archaeology Podcast. http://storyarchaeology.com/poems-of-the-morrigan/ Reprinted with grateful permission.

29 *fri fur fo abad líni Fomoire*	29 against your attack on the full [complement] of Fomoire
30 *i margnaich incanaigh*	30 in the mossy margins
31 *copraich aigid fiach*	31 the helpful raven drives
32 *dorar fri ar solga garuh*	32 strife to our hardy hosts
33 *dálaig for m desigter rodbadh*	33 mustered, we prepare ourselves to destroy
34 *samlaidh derg bandaib dam*	34 to me, the full-blooded exploits are like
35 *aim critaighid conn aechta*	35 shaking to-and-fro of hound-kills
36 *sameth donn curidh*	36 goodly decay of muddy war-bands
37 *dibur fercurib fristongarar*	37 your violations are renounced

Notes:

Line 2: *rucatair gruaide* | "cheeks are seized"

This phrase may simply be a colorful way of describing hand-to-hand violence. However, to "grasp the cheeks" may be a cultural reference to seeking protection. Similar language appears in the *Wooing of Emer*: "When now Emer was brought to Lugaid to sit by his side, she took in both her hands his two cheeks, and laid it on the truth of his honour and his life..."[13] Here Emer, promised in marriage to Lugaid against her will and against her own promise to Cú Chulainn, is seeking protection of her honor from Lugaid. Her action is to take his cheeks in her hands and pledge him on his honor not to force her to forswear Cú Chulainn. The story implies that this gesture may have been recognized as one that a person in need might do to pledge protection from someone of a more powerful status. This admittedly speculative notion might yield an alternate interpretation here such as "protections are pledged".

Line 3: *aisnethir rossa* | "faces [honours] are declared" Alt: "Incitements are declared"

The term *rossa* here may be a reference to satire or incitement. EDIL gives "the face or countenance, esp. the cheeks; a blush, blushing; shame".[14] Insulting speech is routinely used in the tales as a means to incite warriors to peak displays of valor in combat, and is something that friends and allies would do for each other. Cú Chulainn asks his charioteer, Laeg, to insult him in his combats; Badb also uses such shaming speech to incite Cú Chulainn in the *Boyhood Deeds* tales.[15]

13 Meyer 1888 300

14 Royal Irish Academy 2013; entry *rus*.

15 O'Rahilly 2011 139, 207

Line 6: *ethátair catha -rruba* | "[?] of battle are seized"

The indeterminate word here appears to come from the element *ruba* which is related to concepts such as "wounding or killing", or alternately "attack and defence". Thus depending on the form of the word, it might yield something like "wounds of battle are taken" or "battle-kills are taken". However, it also appears as an element in place-names, as an element indicating terrain, so perhaps it is intended here as a reference to the seizing of terrain in battle.

Line 7: *segatar ratha* | "ramparts are sought"

The verbal term *segatar* has multiple meanings including "approaches; seeks out, strives after", as well as "attacks". It is the latter interpretation "attacks" that I think seems most suitable here. In either case we have another line appearing to deal with the seeking, attacking, or claiming of territory in a battle.

Line 8: *radatar fleda* | "feasts are given"

Here we are perhaps speaking of a victory feast which would come after the battle. Additionally, this may also suggest funerary feasts in honor of those slain in the battle. In fact, both functions occur together in the lore.[16] Feasts following battles might entail retelling of heroic exploits, drinking and feasting, the singing of songs for the slain, and other funerary functions. Of course, the battlefield with its carnage is often spoken of as a feast for ravens. In the context of a battle poem, the mention of feasts likely alludes to all these functions together.

Line 9: *fechatar catha* | "battles are observed"

Fechatar is "observed, looked at". One might ask who is she speaking of—who observes the battle? Given that the single other reference in the poem to viewing the battle is spoken in the first person ("I see all who are born…"), this suggests that it is she herself who is observing the battle. The term used here is related to a word *féchadóir* which means "beholder", but also "seer" or "diviner". The concept seems to be seeing through divination, a function of the Morrígan herself, and perhaps a reference to pre-battle prophetic practices undertaken to foretell the outcome.

Line 10: *canátair natha* | "poems are recited"

The verbal term here *canátair*, has a wide range of applications, including the more technical sense of a type of poetic composition, but also has reference to "chanting of spells, prophecies". Another refer-

16 Stokes 1903 59

ence links the term to specifically funerary poetic forms such as elegy or threnody. Here again we have a function which may relate to pre-battle divination and prophecy, and/or to post-battle, funerary ritual custom and memorializing of the dead. Of course, the more immediate association is the poem that is currently being chanted in the midst of battle, within which all this is embedded—a poem of incitement.

Line 12: *dénaitir cuaird* | "circuits are made"

This suggests the practice of Irish kings traveling the circuit of their lands, taking tribute and hostages. This practice was known in medieval Ireland (as described, for example, of Brian Borumha).[17] It suggests the victor receiving submission from the defeated—again something that would occur after the battle. Alternately, sorceries such as *corrguinecht* could be performed in a circuit around the object of the curse, so this could also refer to such action in the context of battle.[18]

Line 13: *cuimnitir arca* | "bodies are recorded"

The translation here is "recorded", but the term also has the connotation of remembering. Thus the poem suggests both recording the numbers of slain as well as memorializing the dead. These functions are also both associated with the Morrígan later in the same text, where her two prophetic poems are given immediately following the recording of deaths and the clearing away of corpses.[19]

Line 14: *alat ide* | "metals cut"

Directly, *ide* is a torch or candle; more broadly, qualities of shining and light. It is found as an alternate term for "metal" as a result of the shining, reflective quality of metals. As we would call a metal which cuts a blade, this line could also be read "blades cut".

Lines 24-25:

at ciú cach ro genair | "I see all who are born"

ruad cath derg bandach | "in the blood-zealous vigorous battle"

These lines initiate a pivot in the thrust of the poem. Here, for the first time, the Morrígan speaks clearly in first-person, actively placing herself within the frame of the battle scene. The vision of the poem suddenly deepens. We are now clearly looking beyond the physical action into the spiritual realities of the event. Carmody describes this shift as a movement from incitement to prophecy, noting also that the meter

17 Todd 1867 135

18 See Chapter 15 for a discussion of *corrguinecht* and related sorceries.

19 Stokes 1891 109

shifts here to longer, more complex lines.[20] The language is evocative of similar prophetic utterances by the seeress Fedelm in the *Táin*; asked to divine the future of Medb's army, Fedelm repeats the line *atchíu forderg, atchíu rúad,* "I see it bloody, I see it red."[21] In the present poem, the Morrígan's lines echo and expand on Fedelm's phrases: *at ciú… ruad… derg…* "I see… red… bloody…", both employing similar patterns of prophetic ritual language.[22]

In these lines, I see the crux of the poem, centering on the phrase "all who are are born". Who are these "born" on a battlefield? Since we are obviously not speaking of birthing infants, I think spiritual birth is indicated. Warriors may be said to be born (or reborn) on the battlefield, as a new identity is forged in the ordeal of war. Her phrase also may suggest the dead: warriors who die in battle. As they die to the world of the living, in the Celtic worldview, they are born into the Otherworld. Though the spirits of the dead are invisible to us, the living, under normal circumstances, here the Morrígan seems to attest that they become visible to her eyes. At the same time, the "seeing" is prophetic seeing, with, as we have noted, the prophetic formula *at ciú*.[23] She may also be conveying her vision of who will fall in battle and be born to the Otherworld, and in a sense, to her.

Line 26: *dremnad fiach lergai fo eburlai* | "raging on the raven-battlefield with blade-scabbards"

As a continuation of the statement beginning "I see all who are born", this clause suggests that it is those born on the battlefield who are raging with blade-scabbards. Does this argue for the first interpretation, that it is the warriors surviving the ordeal of war who are "born on the battlefield" and then unleash their rage? Perhaps. On the other hand, a phantom may express rage, and it is in part because of his unearthly battle-rage that Cú Chulainn is often called a "sprite" or "phantom", according to William Sayers.[24] The interplay of these ideas expresses the entanglement in the Celtic worldview between performance of battle-rage and Otherworldliness, that when undergoing the transformative rage, the warrior is understood to be in contact with the Otherworld.[25]

---

20 Carmody 2004 40
21 O'Rahilly 2011 126-127
22 Carmody 2004 92
23 Carmody 2004 39
24 Sayers 1991 53
25 This concept is explored in more detail in Chapter 17.

Line 27: *fri úabar rusmebat* | "they attempt our defeat"

The term *úabar* is "pride, arrogance"; it has a sense here of outrage. The attempt of the adversary to defeat the Túatha Dé is framed as an arrogation: perhaps, "they dare attempt our defeat". The word used for defeat is a compound; *rus* is related to *rossa* in line 3, suggesting shame or loss of face, and the second term *mebat* derives from a verb for "to break"—taken together, perhaps "breaking in shame".

Line 28: *re nar már srotaib sinne* | "over our own great torrents"

Srotaib here merits exploration. It means "torrents", but beyond a naturalistic sense of flooding waters, the word is used in many contexts implying blood, floods of warriors, or the rising of a warrior's rage. Words for warriorship often include images of either passionate heat or torrential force. Thus the phrase here suggests at once a torrent of warriors crashing against the adversary like a wave; the torrential power of the warriors' fury; and the torrents of blood being shed in the action.

Lines 31-32:

copraich aigid fiach | "the helpful raven drives"

dorar fri ar solga garuh | "strife to our hardy hosts"

Who is the "helpful raven"? While at some times the Morrígna are identified as ravens, crows, or vultures, it is curious that she speaks of this raven in the third person. Ravens are often seen feasting upon the dead or celebrating carnage, but here she suggests the raven is directing the battle, "driving" the combat to the armies. In most cases where a corvid spiritual entity is attributed such powers, they are called *badb*, a term which often refers to members of the Morrígna. We may imagine that this is an ally in raven form, an avatar of herself in bird form, or perhaps a reference to the Badb as her sister, distinct from herself.

Line 34: *samlaidh derg bandaib dam* | "to me, the full-blooded exploits are like"

Here the phrase echoes the *derg bandach* of line 25. There, it was translated as blood-zealous or bloodthirsty. Here, contextually, we have its alternate meaning of bloody deeds or heroic exploits. This phrase, and complex of ideas, is clearly important—each time in the poem where the Morrígan mentions herself directly, this phrase occurs. The recognition of bloody, heroic deeds and the battle rage or blood-zealousness that gives rise to them is central to her perspective in the poem.

Line 35: *aim critaighid conn aechta* | "shaking to-and-fro of hound-kills"

This evocative line conjures the image of a hound viciously shaking captured prey in its jaws to snap its neck. It is revealing for its emotional force; the visceral delight a hound takes in reveling in its kill is inescapable. She suggests that she herself takes a similar pleasure in the heroic exploits. The hound, of course, can also reference the warrior performing the mighty and bloody deeds that she delights in. The name Cú, usually translated "hound" but which can mean dog, wolf, or any canid, is often given to heroic warriors throughout the literature (Cú Chulainn, Cú Roí, etc.) The action of the shaking of the prey seems to be the warrior hound's, but she places herself in the frame with "to me", sharing in the experience of visceral bloody delight.

We may note that in this poem, the Morrígan frames herself as both observer and active participant. She references prophetic sight and knowledge of the fates of warriors, and she connects herself to the action spiritually and emotionally. At several points, she alludes to her own active participation, as the speaker of poems, the observer of battles, the inciter of deeds, and perhaps the raven who "drives strife". She also shifts temporal frame of reference several times between the exploits of the battle itself and events that take place before and after. This time-shifting conveys an Otherworldly perspective from which time is illusory and shifting; events take place in time, and yet all are happening simultaneously. The Morrígan places herself as deeply engaged and central to the action and emotion of the battle—it is her action in speaking this poem that turns the tide of battle by inciting the Túatha Dé to victory. Yet at the same time her poetic voice also seems to stand outside it, creating the frame within which the combat takes place. In the world conjured by this poem, she frames herself both as the battlefield and the soul of battle itself.

The Two Prophecies

The next two poems are given by the Morrígan at the end of the *Second Battle of Mag Tuired*.

> "Now after the battle was won and the corpses cleared away, the Morrigan daughter of Ernmas proceeded to proclaim that battle and the mighty victory which had taken place, to the royal heights of Ireland and to its fairy hosts and its chief waters and its rivermouths. And hence it is that Badb also describes high deeds. 'Hast thou any tale ?' saith every one to her then. And she said..."[26]

26 Stokes 1891 109

Here we see the Morrígan acting as the poet of the Túatha Dé, in the function of recording the great deeds and the outcome of the battle for all to hear. The victory—which is to say the sovereignty of the Túatha Dé over Ireland—is announced to the ruling powers of society ("the royal heights of Ireland") and to the powers of the Otherworld ("to its fairy hosts"). This is significant—both worlds must affirm and uphold the sovereignty for it to stand.

She then chants a poem which begins "Peace to the heavens," followed by a second poem which begins "I do not see a world of the living". These two poems stand in highlighted contrast to one another. The first, a prophecy and benediction of peace, strength, plenty, and longevity. The second, a dystopian prophecy of ominous warnings, decay of social conventions, suffering, loss, and destruction. Why would she give both these two poems together? If they are prophecies—and they are indeed framed as such—how can they both be true prophecies?

She may be seeing both prophecies as possible outcomes. Remember, the event precipitating these prophecies is the taking of the sovereignty of Ireland by her people. The lore of sovereignty teaches again and again that the well-being of the land and the prosperity of the people are directly dependent on the justice and rightness of the sovereign. Thus she may be warning the Túatha Dé that the outcome of their struggle for sovereignty is measured not just in the battle itself, but in how they rule after taking the sovereignty. It is their actions now and into the future which will determine whether the land has peace, plenty, and fertility, or suffering, want, and degradation. Thus both prophecies may be true seeings in the sense that both may come to pass. In this sense the two together serve to convey the gravity and consequence of the sovereignty.

From another perspective, both prophecies are simultaneously true. As a foundation myth, the *Second Battle of Mag Tuired* can be seen as cyclical. That is to say, the battle between the Fomoiri, the primordial tribe of shadowy Otherworld beings, and the Túatha Dé, Gods of civilization, skill, and the high arts, is a conflict whose action is cyclical and never-ending, alternating between open battle and peaceful alliance. It is, in a way, the same dynamic that is constantly being negotiated in the Celtic cosmology between the warrior society of the living, and the mysterious forces of the Otherworld, the people of the *síd*. This archetypal conflict/alliance dynamic stands at the crux of Celtic cosmology, and in fact is reflected in that of many Indo-European societies of the ancient world: the Aesir/Vanir and the Jotun (giants) of the Norse cosmology; the Olympians and the Titans of the Hellenic cosmology; the Devas and Asuras of Hindu cosmology.

In Ireland, myths expressing the conflict between these worlds and forces are often seasonal in nature. The coming of the Tuatha Dé and the battle with the Fir Bolg occurs around Beltaine; the battle with the Fomoiri occurs around Samhain. These magical hinge points in the year, when the gateways are breached between the world of the living and the Otherworld, create a cyclical oscillation. As the separation of human from *síd* is dissolved, the two worlds are brought into conflict which must then be re-fought, resolved, and stabilized again for the continuation of life and the natural order. In this sense, both prophecies are constant and true: Peace and plenty will come, and so will conflict and death. Both are eternal.

The Peace Poem: "Peace to the Heavens"

The first of the two prophecies is given here with variant transcriptions and translations by Carmody[27] and Mees.[28] I have added commentary only where I have additional thoughts on interpretation, or where the two readings are markedly contrasting, in order to explain some of the differences. In some places, the line divisions proposed in the two translations differ; I have followed Mees as I think it better preserves the metrical pattern throughout the poem.

Original

1 *sith co nem*
2 *nem co doman*
3 *doman fo ním*
4 *nert hi cach*
5 *án forlann*
6 *lan do mil*
7 *mid co saith*
8 *sam hi ngam*
9 *gai for sciath*
10 *sciath for durnd*
11 *dunad lonngarg*
12 *longaiter tromfoíd*
13 *fod di uí*
14 *ross forbiur*
15 *benna abu*
16 *airbe imetha*
17 *mess for crannaib*
18 *craob do scis*

27 Carmody 2013

28 Mees 2009 187. Brackets are retained from the translators' text, and indicate gaps, implied words, or uncertain translation; punctuation and capitalization have been removed to preserve the feel of *rosc*.

19 *scis do áss*
20 *saith do mac*
21 *mac for muin*
22 *muinel tairb*
23 *tarb di arccoin*
24 *odbb do crann*
25 *crann do ten*
26 *tene a nn-ail*
27 *ail a n-úir*
28 *úich a mbuaib*
29 *boinn a mbru*
30 *brú lafefaid*
31 *ossglas iaer*
32 *errach foghamar*
33 *forasit etha*
34 *iall do tir*
35 *tir co trachd*
36 *la feabrae*
37 *bidruad rossaib*
38 *śtraib rithmár*
39 *nach scel laut?*
40 *sith co nemh*
41 *bidsirnae s[ith]*

Carmody*

1 peace to [the] heaven[s]
2 heaven to [the] world / earth
3 earth under sky / heavens
4 strength in each
5 cup on a plate
6 full of honey
7 mead to [one's] satisfaction
8 summer in winter
9 spear upon a shield
10 shield upon a fist
11 blade-bristling fort
12 consumption of solid earth
13 rights of [the] grandchildren [descendents]
14 forest on a point
15 horns from a cow
16 encircling fence
17 mast upon trees
18 weary [its] bough
19 weary from growth
20 wealth for a boy

Mees†

1 peace up to heaven
2 heaven to earth
3 earth under heaven
4 strength in everyone
5 a cup overfull
6 full of honey
7 mead aplenty
8 summer in winter
9 spear upon a shield
10 shield on a fort [i.e. a warrior]
11 a fort bold and fierce
12 great grieving is banished
13 fleece from sheep

14 wood [i.e. game] on a spit
15 horned beasts in a yard
16 fenced-in abundance
17 nuts on trees
18 a branch drooping down
19 drooping from growth
20 wealth for a son

* Carmody, Isolde. 2013. "Poems of the Morrigan: Poem B." *Story Archaeology Podcast*. http://storyarchaeology.com/poems-of-the-morrigan/ Reprinted with grateful permission.

† Mees, Bernard. 2009. *Celtic Curses*. Woodbridge: The Boydell Press. Reprinted with grateful permission.

21 boy on a neck
22 neck of a bull
23 bull from a watch-dog
24 knot for [on] a tree
25 tree for fire
26 fire from a stone
27 stone from earth
28 [young] from cows
29 cows from a womb

30 [river-]bank with birdsong
31 grey deer before
32 spring, autumn
33 whence grows corn
34 flock [of birds, warriors, people] for [the] land
35 land [extending] to the shore
36 with sharp edges
37 the great run [time] to the
38 eternal woods / promontory will be fierce
39 have you any story?
40 peace to the heavens
41 it will be eternal peace

21 a son on a shoulder
22 the neck of a bull
23 a bull for slaughtering
24 knot to a wood
25 wood to a fire
26 fire in a stone
27 a stone in the soil [i.e. a memorial]
28 salmon [i.e. wisdom] their winning
29 the Boyne [i.e. Newgrange] their dwelling
30 a dwelling bounded by prosperity fair
31 green growth in the air
32 [in] spring [and in] autumn
33 crops abound
34 held secure the land

35 land as far as the shore
36 surrounded by a foreshore fair
37 [with] ever-sturdy woodlands
38 extensive and ranging far

39 have you any news?
40 peace up to heaven
41 it will be eternal peace

Notes:

Line 1: *sith co nem* | "peace to the heavens"

The word *sith* means "peace" in the general sense, but also can mean a compact of peacemaking. It is related to *síd*, the word for a fairy hill or mound. *Nem* is "sky", but also can mean "heaven" in the metaphysical sense, the abode of blessed or numinous beings, particularly in the post-Christian period. As we have seen, this element also appears in the name Némain, as well as the Gaulish Goddess Nemetona, and the name for sacred groves, *nemeton*. It carries a sense of holy, sanctified place. This line alludes to a compact of peace being established between all the worlds; from the Otherworld beneath the mounds to the heavens.

Line 2: *nem co doman* | "heaven to the earth"

Doman is "world" or "earth" in the sense of the earth we walk on, and its root is found woven into concepts such as "depths", "the bottom", "underworld", as well as primal matter (out of which things are made). Paired with *nem,* it suggests a notion of the full expanse of the cosmos from the highest to the deepest places. It is to this extent of totality that the peace is being established.

Line 4: *nert hi cach* | "strength in each"

We have established that there is peace between the upper and lower realms. Strength rests in each realm. What is being established here is a sense of balance. The cosmological conflict between the worlds has been fought and we have returned to an equilibrium of shared peace and strength.

Line 5: *án for lann* | "cup on a plate" or "a cup overfull"

Án is a cup, drinking-vessel. *Lann* is a term that is used for various kinds of plate—a plate or pan for food, as well as the plates of armor, shields, or blades. It also has a meaning of trophy or award. Alternately, *lan* is fullness. There is also an expression *forlann,* which indicates relative superiority in strength or numbers, "more than a match for [an opponent]". The vessel in fullness can be seen as an image of sovereignty and abundance; at the same time, the line can be read as alluding to great martial strength.

Line 7: *mid co saith* | "mead to satisfaction"

Mid is translated "mead"; however, in poetic usage, it is sometimes used to convey honor or renown. These meanings are likely not separate—honors would be conveyed by means of offering a ritual mead-cup, as in the hero's portion ritual seen in *Bricriu's Feast,*[29] reinforcing *lann* as trophy or award (from line 5). *Saith* is wealth, sufficiency, fill (as in getting one's fill).

Thus the series of three lines *án for lann* | *lan do mil* | *mid co saith* circle around a series of multi-layered allusions to cups and honors, honey and mead, fullness, strength, and satisfaction. All this tends to evoke the doings at the feast that would typically occur following a victory: cups would be offered, mead would be shared, valorous exploits would be acclaimed, honors and rewards would be given, and martial strength would be celebrated. These are central images of sovereignty in the context of kingship and warrior bands.

Line 8: *sam hi ngam* | "summer in winter"

This curious line is sometimes read as simply meaning winter without bite—a mild winter. This may be, but it also conveys the cosmo-

29 Henderson 1899 95

logical theme that time in the Otherworld is opposite or alternate to time in the living world. Thus during summer here, it is winter there, and vice-versa. The *Adventure of Nera* exemplifies this, as Nera brings back summer flowers from the *síd* to his people at Cruachan where it is Samhain, the onset of winter.[30] Folkloric belief in this Otherworldly reversal of time persisted at least into the early Modern era in nearby Scotland, as described by Robert Kirk in 1691.[31] This line in the poem suggests a continued contact between the two worlds.

Line 11: *dunad lonn garg* | "blade-bristling fort"

The fort (*dunad*) in this line is described: *lonn,* "fierce, strong, violent, vehement, eager, bold" and *garg,* "rough, blunt, mettlesome, fierce". We have almost a redundancy of words here, evidently to emphasize the idea of fierceness and readiness for battle.

Line 12: *longait trom foíd* | "consumption of solid earth" or "great grieving is banished"

There are two distinct translations here, one alluding to the fertility of the earth bringing forth food, the other speaking of relief from the heaviness of grief. In part the difference hinges on the verb *longait* which can be "banishes, drives out", or "eats, consumes". *Trom,* as an adjective, would be "heavy, severe, grievous", or as a substantive it can also appear as "weight, heaviness, burden". It appears in figures of speech referring to the concept of "solid earth" or "heavy earth". *Faíd* is "outcry", especially referring to lamentation. In the context of the poem, either reading—or both—could be intended.

Line 13: *fod di uí* | "rights of descendants" or "fleece from sheep"

Úi (accented on the first vowel) is a name term indicating descent. The singular *úa* is "grandson" or "granddaughter". When used in a collective sense, it indicates "the descendents of"—as in Uí Neill, the descendants of Niall. Alternately, *uí* (accented on the second vowel) may be a vairant on *oí,* "sheep". As *úi* "descendants" can refer the young of livestock, this may be a kenning which weaves both meanings together.

Line 14: *ross for biur* | "forest on a point" or "game on a spit"

Carmody's translation is literal: *ross* is a wood or forest, frequently appearing in place-names, and particularly of a wooded promontory or high place. *Biur* is "point", and is used of all manner of pointed things—stake, spear, cooking spit, or even antler. We may be speaking of a high wood-

30 Meyer 1889 221
31 Kirk 1893 6

land place—and we might here recall that a woodland called Ross has been claimed as a sacred site belonging to the Morrígan (and Badb) in the *Wooing of Emer*. Mees's reading takes *ross* as a poetic allusion to game which might be hunted in a woodland and cooked on a spit.

A speculative, possibly occult reading, can arise from *ros*, which also appears as a poetic kenning for knowledge. According to the DIL, this meaning of *ros* is possibly derived from *ro-fhis*.[32] This kenning also appears in one of the names of the Dagda, Ruad Rofhessa, "of great knowledge".[33] We could playfully read this line as something like "knowledge of spears", i.e. mastery of the arts of warriorship. If a kenning for knowledge is intended, it is again possible that the "point" is the point of a tongue: "knowledge at the tip of one's tongue", an apt description of the highly valued poetic art.[34]

Line 21: *mac for muin* | "boy on a neck" or "a son on a shoulder"

Direct translation of this line evokes a boy riding the neck (*muin*) of an animal or carried on a parent's shoulders. We can look further and see alternate meanings: *Mac* also has an alternate meaning of a bond or surety, likely tracing to the Celtic custom of client families sending children to patron families in fosterage. This practice served to guarantee the client family's loyalty, while also providing education and greater opportunities for the youth, and more strongly bonding the families to one another. This alternate meaning of *mac* may be relevant if we read *muin* in one of its alternate usages "patronage, guaranty, protection". Thus the line might also be alluding to "sons for fosterage" or similar. Additionally, as Carmody points out, "*macc for muin* is also a food-portion or ration, deemed appropriate for a free person,"[35] a further allusion to plenty in food.

Line 23: *tarb di arccoin* | "bull from a watch-dog" or "a bull for slaughtering"

What could be meant by a bull that comes from a dog? The key may be *di* which can have a connotation of separation or parting. Thus we might look at it as something like "bull apart from a watch-dog". Remembering that cattle-raiding was common practice in early Ireland, this image of valuable herd animals safely roaming without guard may be a poetic device evoking a land at peace. Further, the watch-dog itself may be a poetic kenning for a dog-warrior who acts as guardian to a bull,

32 Royal Irish Academy 2013, entry 3 *ros*.

33 Stokes 1897 152

34 This reading was suggested to me by P. Sufenas Virius Lupus.

35 Carmody 2013

such as Cú Chulainn does. Mees's reading "a bull for slaughtering" seems to be based on taking *arccoin* as *ar-guin*, "wounding, slaying". The image of bull-slaughter evokes the *tarb feis*, one of the rituals of kingship.

Line 26: *tene a nn-ail* | "fire from a stone"

The natural inference here is flint, a stone from which one strikes fire. We can read this sequence of lines as a recitation of primal needs: wood for fire, fire struck from stone. Also, the expression "fire from a stone" appears in the *Triads of Ireland*: "Three wealths in barren places: a well in a mountain, fire out of a stone, wealth in the possession of a hard man."[36] The triad frames fire as a form of abundance; to strike fire from a barren stone is to conjure wealth from barrenness.

Line 27: *ail a n-utr* | "stone from earth" or "a stone in the soil"

Utr refers primarily to earth as substance—soil, clay, mould—rather than earth as land or territory. *Utr* particularly figures in phrases related to the grave: "the abode of clay", "going into the mould", in later times, the churchyard. There is an allusion here to an ancestral connection, to the funerary pillar-stones used as grave-markers—pillar-stones, of course, being a favored spot where the Morrígan perches on more than one occasion.

The preceding series of lines (a bull for slaughtering/ knot of wood/ wood for fire/ fire from a stone/ stone from earth) also form a series invoking the creation of a feast of plenty. This is most apparent if the series is looked at retrospectively: an ancestral stone, which made the spark, which lit the fire, which burned the wood, to cook the bull for the feast.[37]

Lines 29-30:

boinn a mbru | "cows from a womb" or "the Boyne their dwelling"

brú la fefaid | "(river)bank with birdsong" or "a dwelling bounded by prosperity fair"

Carmody takes *boinn* as a collective for cattle; Mees reads it as a proper name, referring to the Boyne river area of the Brúg na Bóinne, with its ancient mound of Newgrange. As *brú* can refer to belly or womb, or an interior space generally, either reading is possible. I would also note that *boinn a mbru* creates a poetic sound-allusion or back-rhyme to Brúg na Bóinne, where the *Dindshenchas* tell us the Morrígan and the Dagda lived together after the battle in the present text.[38] In the next line, the same word seems to be used differently: *brú* can also mean edge, bank,

36 Meyer 1906 21

37 Credit to Segomaros Widugeni for pointing out the significance of this series of images.

38 Gwynn 2008 11

or border. The sense of "riverbank" emerges especially if we do read *boinn* as an allusion to the Boyne. *Fefaid* is an obscure compound; the element *faid* means a cry, such as lamentation, animal cries, or the cries of birds.

Line 36: *la feabrae* | "with sharp edges"

The "edges" indicated by *feabrae* may be specifically blade-edges, weapons—a reference back to the troops of warriors in line 34. The sequence of three lines seems to parse best when read together, expanding to something like "flock of warriors securing the land, from land to shore, protecting with sharp weapons".

The poem contains several ritual markers denoting its prophetic nature. As we have seen, the alliterative *rosc* poetic form is characteristic of prophetic utterances. This poem also contains a poetic formula that marks prophetic trance utterances: the line *nach scel laut*, "have you any story?" signals a ritual request for prophecy.[39] We might compare it to the prophetic question repeatedly posed to the seeress Fedelm in the *Táin*: "Look once more for us, and tell us the truth."[40]

It is notable that the poem's structure is circular on multiple scales. At the smallest scale, the form of the poem follows the *conachlonn* linking pattern for much of its length.[41] The poem also employs the common poetic device of *dúnad*, closing with the same sounds or words of its opening.[42] This circular device is standard in much Irish poetry, but its use is particularly emphasized here, as it is a triple *dúnad*: a word *dúnad* formed by *sith* being the first and last word, a line *dúnad* in the return to the talismanic opening phrase *sith co nem*, and a third *dúnad* in which the line *nach scel laut* repeats the prophetic question that initiates the poem.[43] This tripled circling closure evokes peace and order on the level of totality, and contrasts with the lack of such closure employed in several of the Morrígan's other poems.

Throughout this poem, we can also note a recurring theme of phrases that allude at the same time to land and wealth, and to warriorship and its rewards. This is of course no coincidence. It reflects the classic Celtic social order which privileges warriorship as the means

39 O'Connor 2013 189
40 O'Rahilly 2011 127
41 Mees 2009 187
42 Carmody 2004 22
43 Carmody 2004 72

through which status, wealth, and well-being are secured, and it conveys a worldview in which peace is equated with martial strength and the ability to defend the land and its wealth. It also reflects the dual identity of the Morrígan herself: land and sovereignty Goddess, and Goddess of warriors and of battle.

It is interesting that nowhere in this poem does the Morrígan herself appear; she does not speak of herself here. In this poem, she speaks as pure oracle—giving voice to the prophetic vision without interpolating her own view. This contrasts with the battle poem, above, as well as the third poem from the story, which comes immediately after.

The Dark Prophecy: "I do not see a world of the living"

The second *Mag Tuired* poem is introduced by the following narrative:

> "Then, moreover, she was prophesying the end of the world, and foretelling every evil that would be therein, and every disease and every vengeance. Wherefore then she sang this lay below…"[44]

The poem is given here with Carmody's translation.[45] I have added notes where I have additional thoughts about interpretation of the language.

Original		Translation (Carmody)*	
1	*ni accus bith no mbeo*	1	I do not see a world of the living:
2	*baið sam cin blatha*	2	summer will be without flowers
3	*beti bai cin blichda*	3	Cows will be without milk
4	*mna can feli*	4	women without modesty [/generosity/pudenda]
5	*fir gan gail*	5	men without valour [semen]
6	*gabala can righ*	6	conquests without a king
7	*rinna ulcha ilmoigi*	7	walls of spear-points [on] every plain
8	*beola bron*	8	sad mouths

44 Stokes 1891 111

45 Carmody 2013. Line division and bracketing are following Carmody; brackets indicate gaps, implied words, or uncertain translation. I have removed capitalization and punctuation to convey the *rosc* style.

* Carmody, Isolde. 2013. "Poems of the Morrigan: Poem C." *Story Archaeology Podcast*. http://storyarchaeology.com/poems-of-the-morrigan/ Reprinted with grateful permission.

feda cin mes	forests without mast
muir can toradh	sea without fruit
tuirbain(b)thine	tower-wall of white metal /// a multitude of storms
immat moel rátha	around bare fortresses
fás a forgnam locha	empty their dark buildings
di ersitir dinn	high places cannot endure
at rifiter linn	a lake has attempted
lines sech ilar flaithie	to flood past a multitude of kingdoms
faoilti fria holc	welcome to its evil
ilach imgnath	howling occupies
gnuse ule	every face
incrada docredb	great unbelievable torments
gluind ili	many crimes
imairecc catha	battles waged everywhere
toebh fri ech delceta	trust in spiked horses
imda dala	many (hostile) meetings
braith mac flaithi	treacherous princelings
forbuid bron	a shroud of sorrows
sen saobretha	on old high judgements
brecfásach mbrithiom	false maxims of judges
braithiomh cech fer	every man a betrayer
foglaid cech mac	every son a brigand
gignitir cen mair	[people] will be born without surviving
olc aimser	evil time
i mmera mac a athair	in which the son will derange his father
i mera ingen …	in which the daughter will derange…

Notes:

Line 1: *ni accus bith no mbeo* | "I do not see a world of the living"

The poem opens with a variation of the prophetic formula "I see…", signaling an oracular visionary utterance (*at ciu*, of which *accus* here is a variant).

The word *beo,* "living", can mean any living being. In this sense, the line evokes a ghostly landscape—a world not of the living. Poetically, it suggests the idea of a world we would not wish to live in, i.e. a world "not for the living". In mythological contexts *beo* often refers to a specific sense of "the living" as the immortals, the Ever-Living Ones, i.e. the Túatha Dé Danann. In light of the poem's context—the taking of the sovereignty by the Túatha Dé, she may be giving a picture of the world without the Túatha Dé, without their beneficent rulership, should they fail to maintain the sovereignty of the land.

Line 2: *baið sam cin blatha* | "summer will be without flowers"

It is significant and likely not accidental that this line presents a natural contrasting opposite image to the line *sam hi ngam* "summer in winter" from the previous poem.[46]

Line 4: *mna can feli* | "women without modesty [generosity/pudenda]"

Féle has several meanings: modesty or propriety; generosity; or "that which causes shame, nakedness, pudenda". It is related to *fíala*, meaning a veil or curtain. Carmody notes that *"féle* is a defining 'virtue' of women".[47] *Féle* evokes idea of the power of female nudity—a concept that arises more than once in the Irish tales. The female body represents a powerful sexual force that was felt to require social control through modesty and veiling. At other times, that sexual power is linked to generosity, as when women in the tales provide sexual hospitality to guests. The essence of female virtue was seen in both the woman's sexual power, and the appropriate containment and deployment of it.

Line 5: *fir gan gail* | "men without valour [semen]"

Gal is "warlike ardour, fury, valour", as well as "steam, vapour, mist". The DIL notes that the earlier, original sense of the word may be "seething heat, passing into that of mental excitement or rage."[48] Throughout Celtic languages, a close link is maintained between words indicating heat and those indicating passion, ardor, fury, and the qualities of a warrior. As Carmody says in her translation notes, this notion of heat identified with male vigor is "a defining 'virtue' of men, hence my reference to semen as male essence."[49] The two lines both contrast and link the defining virtues of men and women as understood in the early Celtic worldview.[50]

Line 6: *gabala can righ* | "conquests without a king"

The word used here, *gabál*, is the same one occurring in the title *Lebor Gabála Éirenn*, popularly known as *The Book of Invasions*. Its direct meaning is "taking"—the seizure of goods or territory. What is notable here is the illumination of the Celtic view of armed conquest, as distinct

46 Carmody 2004 77

47 Carmody 2013

48 Royal Irish Academy 2013, entry *gal*.

49 Carmody 2013

50 Interestingly, while heat is a defining quality of Cú Chulainn's battle distortion, in a great many other respects he does not conform to the dualistic male/female gender essentialism seen in much of Celtic culture—rather, he highlights the limitations of this gender paradigm by transgressing it.

from a modern view. To seize territory is not in itself framed negatively—in fact, such takings are foundational in the Irish origin narratives of the Túatha Dé and the sons of Míl. What we are warned against here is specifically takings without a king—in other words, reaving by bands unsanctioned by kingship. Conquest as the act of a sovereign is contrasted with conquest which is outside the social order and not controlled by the logic of sovereignty.

Line 7: *rinna ulcha ilmoigi* | "walls of spear-points on every plain"

The language here is delightfully vivid: *ulcha* is literally "beard", conjuring a picture of masses of armed men—a plain bristling with pointed spear-tips as thick as a beard, or perhaps bristling with the pointed beards of dead men.

Line 9: *feda cin mes* | "forests without mast"

Again, this line's image of trees barren of mast contrasts directly with the line *mess for crannaib*, "mast upon trees" from the previous poem. It is abundantly clear that these two poems function together as paired, contrasting images of peace, plenty and strength against images of destruction, suffering and barrenness.[51]

Line 11: *tuirb ainbthine* | "a multitude of storms" | Or: *tuir bainb thine* | "tower-wall of white metal"

Depending how the words are parsed, this can be read differently. My inclination is toward the first reading. A tower of white metal is the sort of image one might see in a description of the Celtic Otherworld, where shining great houses and palaces made of fine metals are common; but it says little that contributes to the sense of the poem as a whole. On the other hand "a multitude of storms" carries an ominous thrust that fits well into the poem. In addition, if the words are parsed this way, additional meanings surface. *Tuirb*, from *turba*, a Latin loan-word, is translated "multitudes", but originally carried the sense of hosts or crowds of people. *Ainbthen* likewise translates "storm, tempest", but also "violence, fury, rage", and is closely related to *ainféth* "unrest, turmoil". Thus while we have storms in the sense of weather, the line also connotes angry crowds, anarchy, unrest, and social turmoil—following on the earlier image of violence without the control of kingship.

Line 12: *immat moel rátha* | "around bare fortresses"

Moel is from *mael*, literally "bald". When spoken of places, it means bare, exposed, defenseless, or in a state of disrepair. A related compound, *maolrátha*, is "a dismantled or outworn earthen fort". Thus, paired with

51 Carmody 2004 77

the previous line, we have the sense of crumbling forts, abandoned defenses, unshielded from oncoming storms or violent anarchy.

Line 14: *di ersitir dinn* | "high places cannot endure"

The word *dind* here is "height, hill", as well as more specifically "fortified hill, citadel, stronghold". This recalls the pervasive ancient practice of establishing fortified towns on hilltops. Again the sense here is not just of high places crumbling, but of defenses failing against incursion, strongholds that cannot stand.

Line 17: *faoilti fria holc* | "welcome to its evil"

Many are familiar with the term *fáilte* in Modern Irish used to mean "welcome". In older Irish texts, the word is also used as "joy, happiness, rejoicing". Thus another way to read this line is "rejoicing in evil". The sense of *olc*, "evil", is derived from the idea of wanton violence rather than a dualistic moral evil; it is thought to be etymologically linked to an Indo-European root meaning "wolf".[52] "Wolves" who perpetrate violence are often metaphorical for raiding warrior bands in Irish literature, so this line subtly reinforces the threat of reavers expressed through much of the poem.

Line 21: *gluind ili* | "many crimes"

The word for "crimes" here specifically refers to warlike, treacherous, or violent deeds. *Glond* is elsewhere used to refer to any deed of martial prowess, including in the heroic sense. The word draws our attention to a central paradox of Celtic societies: that the violent martial capacities of the elite warrior class so central to the ethos of the society, when unmoored from social control (evoked this poem by loss of kingship and fair judgement), becomes the violent destructive force which tears that society apart.

Line 23: *toebh fri ech delceta* | "trust in spiked horses"

We might be curious about these "spiked horses". A popular trope about the Iron Age Celts supposes that they attached scythes to the wheel-axles of their chariots. There has been no physical evidence found to support this in Ireland, but it is certainly a part of Irish literary tradition—Cú Chulainn's chariot sports not only sickles on its axles, but spikes, nails, and hooks attached all over it. The line could describe spikes on the horse-gear as well.

Line 24: *imda dala* | "many (hostile) meetings"

Dáil is commonly used of assemblies or meetings (hostile or otherwise); it also may refer to a legal conference or court, or a dispute that would

52 Bernhardt-House 2002 59. The related Irish word is *folc*, "wolf" or "landless brigand".

be brought before a court. The principal house of the Irish parliamentary assembly is still called the Dáil. Here the word seems to point to the breakdown of social cohesion, manifested in an abundance of disputes.

Line 27: *sen saobretha* | "on old high judgements"

The translation of "old high judgements" takes *saobretha* as a compound of *sár* "excellent" and *breth*, "judgement", making sense when this line is read with the previous one, "a shroud of sorrows". A related phrase is *sáibretha*, "false judgement", from *saeb* "crooked, false, unjust". Further, *sen*, when it occurs in a legal contexts means not just old but also "long-standing", thus *senbreth* is a long-standing judgement, i.e. a legal precedent. This line may thus also imply false judgments that are allowed to stand and become precedent—a great wrong according to the values of Irish society.

Line 31: *gignitir cen mair* | "people will be born without surviving"

More literally, this is "birthing without remaining", which may allude to women dying in childbirth, as well as to infant mortality. Both, of course, are indicators of suffering and loss.

Lines 33-34:

i mmera mac a athair | "in which the son will derange his father"

i mera ingen … | "in which the daughter will derange…"

The verb here is obscure but appears to be from *mairnid*, "betrays, deceives". The text ends here, but it it may once have continued. We can speculate that the symmetry implied in the two lines between son and daughter may have continued with father and mother, "the daughter will deceive her mother", but without the missing text it cannot be known.

The structure of this poem is less progressive than some of the others; that is, it does not seem follow an ordered progression of ideas, but instead cycles repeatedly through themes of violent conflict and physical insecurity, moral and social destruction, emotional grief and shock, and loss of natural fertility. Its rapid turning from sorrow to fear to loss evokes a sense of distraught bewilderment. The poem appears to be incomplete, cutting off mid-line with its ending missing. It is just possible that this lack of proper closure is intentional and metatextually "illustrates its dire predictions by being what is unthinkable in a good and proper state of the world", an incomplete poem.[53] If this is the case, it

53 A possibility suggested by P. Sufenas Virius Lupus (pers. comm.) by comparison to the similarly incomplete Anglo-Saxon poem "The Ruin".

would further contrast the fractured, dystopic vision of the poem with the perfect order and multiple circularity of the Peace Poem's closure.

This poem is deeply evocative and carries a great sense of empathy for human suffering: sad mouths, wailing faces, death in childbirth, betrayal tearing families apart. It speaks to the sense of fear people feel in the perception that social contracts, institutions of justice and sovereignty, are failing, that chaotic and violent forces approach, that the wolf is at the door. It is dystopic in a manner that is timeless, as relevant to the fears of people today as it would have been a thousand years ago. In particular it touches on many of the deepest concerns and prevailing themes in ancient Irish culture: the importance of the social order, the making and upholding of true judgements, the function of sovereign as both vessel of justice and armed protector, and the roles of men and women.

In its context within the *Mag Tuired* text, as one of two prophecies given at the point of the taking of sovereignty by the Túatha Dé, the poem voices a central narrative that is threaded throughout the Irish literature: that peace, safety, justice and prosperity utterly depend on the impeccable and just wielding of sovereignty—the *fír flathemon*, truth of the sovereign. In the first prophecy, we are given a vision of the blessings that flow from that justice. In this prophecy, we glimpse the Irish nightmare wherein all things unravel and fall to hunger, sorrow, violence, and suffering in the absence of that justice.

The Prophecy to Cú Chulainn

The poems which follow derive from the Ulster Cycle, centering on the great *Táin Bó Cúailnge* and peripheral tales about the Ulster kings and heroes. The first in this series of poems is the Prophecy to Cú Chulainn, recorded within the *Táin* fore-tale called the *Cattle Raid of Regamna*. In this story, the Morrígan is bringing a cow back out of Ulster after mating it to the Donn Cúailnge; Cú Chulainn challenges her, and she identifies herself as a professional poet. He leaps into her chariot and threatens her with his spear, demanding that she perform a poem for him, and this is the poem she then sings to him.[54] The poem appears to contain a prophecy of his death and elements of the *Táin* conflict. After delivering the poem, she transforms into a "black bird upon a branch",

54 Leahy 1906 132

and continues her warnings, telling him of the time of his death.[55]

The poem is, again a very archaic *rosc* with dense, obscure language. Most translators of the tale have not even attempted to translate the poem. I reproduce here a new translation by Carmody.[56] In many places, the text is quite unclear and allows for multiple translations, some quite divergent, and I include my own interpretation, based on Carmody's, with variation in some of the lines. I have added notes below where I have additional thoughts about interpretation of the language.[57]

	Original	My adaptation
1	*doermais nomgaib*	I grant arms to the one who seizes me
2	*gaib eti eblatar*	seize the herd to be driven
3	*tairichta muirtemniu*	beyond Muirthemne
4	*mo rochrat romlec*	my great shaking released me
5	*dia-n-edim fiach*	so I become a raven
6	*am ainsi nachach toarbair*	skills of the battlefield subdue
7	*adomling airddhe*	a portent springs upon me
8	*oenmairb maige sainb*	a mighty peerless death
9	*croí chengach*	marching gore
10	*cocbith mestin- glinne let*	grievous wounding is promised to you
11	*leiss finn fri*	brightness illuminates
12	*thoiss do beoib*	rest for the lively ones
13	*brectith reth tuasailg*	whose lives spatter and disintegrate
14	*os dum arai*	upon the mound of charioteers
15	*airdd cech lastair cuailngne*	omens, all aflame in Cúailnge
16	*a chuchuluinn... ...arindlindsi*	O Cú Chulainn prepare for it
17	*ar soegaul de an-tuaith*	for the world of the great Túatha Dé
18	*.i. cluas indairmgretha*	hear the clash of arms

55 Leahy 1906 136

56 Carmody 2014. Line division is my own, endeavoring to reconstruct the tripartite meter of the original *rosc*. Bracketing follows Carmody; brackets indicate gaps, implied words, or uncertain translation. I have removed capitalization and punctuation to convey the *rosc* style.

57 Primary translation is from the Egerton 1782 (E) manuscript version of the poem (Flynn 2010). An alternate version of the poem is found in the Yellow Book of Lecan (Y) manuscript, and I refer to some lines of that version for additional interpretation of the poem.

Carmody*

1 may I give arms [to that / the one] which seizes me
2 seize the herd [who] will be driven
3 unnaturally [?] [into] the dark sea / [out of] Muirthemne
4 my great injury released me,
5 so that I become [? lit. "obtain"] a raven
6 skills of the [battle-]field subdue
7 [that which] springs up to [i.e. ambushes] me
8 a mighty single special [death?]
9 corpse, proceeding / marching gore / ravens
10 so that whatever seems good to you may be uncertain to you
11 it seems fair to him as opposed to
12 rest for the lively ones
13 whose lives spatter, disintegrate
14 in front of me
15 noble charioteers will be heard [in] Cúailnge
16 O Cú Chulainn… …for [the sake of] this pool
17 for the [sake of the] life [descending] from a great kingdom / because of the world of the great Túatha Dé.
18 i.e. hearing the clash of arms

Notes:

Line 1: *doermais nomgaib* | "I grant arms to the one who seizes me"

This reads *doermais* as a form of the verb *ernaid*, "bestows, grants". The Y manuscript version supports this, giving the verb *doernais*. The "one who seizes me" would be Cú Chulainn, who has just leapt into the Morrígan's chariot, seized her and pointed his spear against her, demanding a prophetic poem. This seems to highlight a tradition, for Cú Chulainn similarly leaps upon, seizes, and threatens the warrior-teacher Scáthach, for which she agrees to give him training in special warrior-feats, along with a prophetic poem outlining his destiny. As we discuss in Chapter 17, this pattern seems to reflect the remnants of warriors' training and initiation practices, with which the Morrígan is deeply connected. We have no material directly showing the Morrígan "granting arms" to a warrior in such a context. However, Scáthach does grant Cú Chulainn his legendary spear, the *gae bulga*; thus she does "grant arms" to him.

* Carmody, Isolde. 2014. "Rosc from *Táin Bó Regamna*." Unpublished translation. Reprinted with grateful permission.

Line 4: *mo rochrat romlec* | "my great shaking released me" or "my great injury released me"

Rochrat may be from *crád*, "torment, anguish, persecution", following Carmody's translation and pointing to Cú Chulainn's attack against her in the chariot. Alternately, similar constructions in early texts also derive from *crothaid*, "shakes, trembles". As this line leads a segment of the poem in which the Morrígan describes her transformation into raven form and her prophetic vision of Cú Chulainn's death, I think it possible that the line describes entry into a visionary oracular state—in which trembling might be one of the observed signs of trance.

Line 5: *dia-n-edim fiach* | "so I become a raven"

The verb here is literally "take, obtain" (from *ethaid*). The reading "become" might seem a stretch, but the Y manuscript version illuminates this for us. Here the phrase *fiachanma*, "raven-soul" appears in place of the single word *fiach*, "raven", giving the reading "so I take a raven-soul". The sense of this seems to that she takes on a raven's essence or soul in order to change her shape into the visible shape of a raven. This, of course, has profound implications for the human practitioner of shape-shifting.

Line 6: *am ainsi nachach toarbair* | "skills of the battlefield subdue"

This line is very obscure. The reading "skills of the battlefield" seems to be from *áines*, "splendor, skill, sport, play", and *achad*, "field". Alternately, we could be looking at a form of *áinsid*, "lampoon, censure, reproach"; perhaps referring back to the raven, the line could be read something like "scolding on the field of battle".

Line 7: *adomling airddhe* | "a portent springs upon me" or "[that which] springs up to me"

The term *adomling* is a verbal compund from *lingid*, "leaps, jumps, attacks", and may be Cú Chulainn's leaping upon her in the chariot, giving "that which springs up to me" or less literally, "that which ambushes me". As *airddhe* can be "sign, token, portent", and as the poem's context is prophecy, I lean toward a prophetic reading of this line in which it may also be the vision or portent which "springs upon" her.

Line 8: *oenmairb maige sainb* | "a mighty peerless death"

Oenmairb is clearly a compound from *óen*, "only, unique, without equal, peerless", and *mairbe* "deadness" or *marb* "dead, dying". She speaks of a special death—a memorable one perhaps, such as a hero's death, possibly also of dying alone. Carmody reads *maige sainb* as further emphasizing this image, suggesting that the original phrase was *maige sainbás*: from *maige*, "great, mighty", *sain*, "different, special", and *bás*, "death". Alternately, *maige sainb* may well simply be a place-name: "a peerless death in Magh Sainb". Magh Sainb, alternately spelled Magh Samh, is a historical place located by Lough Erne in County Fermanagh, Ulster. Notably, Cú Chulainn is supposed to have died beside a lake. Other local traditions place his death elsewhere, at the site of the Clochafarmore stone outside Rathiddy, County Louth. As with all mythologies, multiple traditions locating a mythic event are simultaneously possible.

Line 9: *croí chengach* | "marching gore"

Carmody gives three related, possible translations here. *Croí* is a variant of *crú*, "gore, blood", or in a metaphorical sense, corpses. The term *chengach* may be from the verb *cingid*, "marches, paces, proceeds". Thus the primary reading of the line is of blood or gore moving; the use of "marching" could evoke the rhythmic pulsing of blood. Also, *cingid* is from a common Celtic root *cing*, meaning "warrior" (e.g. Irish *cing*, Gaulish *cingeto*); a nuance toward "warriors' blood" may also be intended here.

Line 10: *cocbith mestin- glinne let* | "grievous wounding is promised to you" or "whatever seems good to you may be uncertain to you"

Carmody's translation may suggest the confusion wrought by the illusions of Calatín's sorcerous daughters in Cú Chulainn's death tale. Exploring further layers, we find that the compound *cocbith* may derive from *ceó*, "confusion, uncertainty, gloom, grief", and *bíth*, "striking, wounding". *Mestin* appears to be from *mesta*, "to be judged, esteemed" and *glinne* is a "pledge, promise, obligation, surety". In the prophetic context of the poem, she may be stating her judgment that confusion and wounding are a certainty for Cú Chulainn, as we know them to be.

Line 11: *leiss finn fri* | "brightness illuminates" or "it seems fair to him as opposed to"

Leiss may be a prepositional compound "to him" or "with him", and *finn* is "white, bright, fair". Thus a simple translation "it is fair to him". We have no clear referent for "him", as the rest of the poem addresses Cú Chulainn directly. Alternate possibilities for *leiss* are "uncovered, bare", or a form of the verb *lésaigid*, "illumines"; this meaning is particularly interesting as it would emphasize the brightness of *finn*. We might have "brightness illuminates", or "bare and white". The illuminating brightness could be the radiance of the Otherworld, shining on those who dwell there, a meaning that aligns well with the following line.

Line 12: *thoiss do beoib* | "rest for the lively ones"

These "lively ones" who find rest may be the dead, and this sense is emphasized if the line is paired with the following one, "whose lives spatter..." Alternately, as we have seen, "the ever-living" is a kenning for the people of the Otherworld, and especially the Túatha Dé. We seem to be exploring themes around what comes with the death she is here predicting for Cú Chulainn: resting with the dead, or with the Gods in the Otherworld.

Line 13: *brectith reth tuasailg* | "whose lives spatter and disintegrate"

We return to the image of blood running out at the end of life. This reading is metaphorical; *reth* is a verbal noun from "run, course" and so can speak of a life in a symbolic sense. Alternately, *brectith* may relate to *bricht*, "incantation, charm, spell", yielding a reading such as "running incantations are released", perhaps referring to funerary chants.

Line 14: *os dum arai* | "upon the mound of charioteers"

Os dum can be a prepositional phrase "in front of me". Alternately, *dum* is "mound, tumulus, barrow". Carmody's translation attaches *arai*, "charioteers" to the following line, whereas I bring it into this line, based on the alliterative pattern. This construction suggests "the mound of charioteers". As the previous several lines speak to death and funerary processes, the image of a funerary mound does not seem unwarranted here.

Line 15: *airdd cech lastair cuailngne* | "omens, all aflame in Cuailnge"

Again, the reading of this line depends somewhat on where line breaks are placed. *Airdd* may be from *ard*, "high, noble", and may be descriptive of the charioteers in the previous line. Alternately, it may be *airde*, "sign, token, portent"; appropriate in my view for a prophetic poem. Here the Morrígan has moved from describing Cú Chulainn's death to a vision of fire and destruction throughout Cúailnge, and in this is reminiscent of her poem to the Brown Bull.

Line 16: *a chuchuluinn... ...arindlindsi* | "O Cú Chulainn prepare for it" or "O Cú Chulainn for [the sake of] this pool"

Here she addresses Cú Chulainn again directly. Carmody's reading parses *arindlinsi* as *ar ind lind si*, centering around the key word *linn*, "pool"; this can also refer to a larger body of water such as a lake or sea; or may be metaphor for "peace". Alternately, we may have a compound of *indlid*, "prepare, arrange", especially in the sense of "preparing for battle". Given that she begins the poem speaking of giving him arms, and closes it speaking of the clashing of weapons, an instruction to prepare himself for battle would not be out of place here.

At this point in the poem, the Y manuscript version inserts several more lines, directly addressed to Cú Chulainn following the above. I have seen no published translation, but I offer the lines here with my own notes:

acuculaind fri burach mbuaid arcuailgi | O Cú Chulainn for triumphant rage in Cuailnge
acuchulaind cair buidi | O Cú Chulainn favored of face
ben basa clæncuil | a deadly, crooked, violating woman
arm deisi | arm in battle-gear

The first two lines seem to simply be honorifics; she seems to address him as a warrior, and perhaps affectionately. The second two lines clearly become warnings. The "deadly, crooked, violating woman" is most likely the cursing hag, daughter of Calatín, who will be the agent of his destruction. Each epithet here makes reference to the specifics of his death-tale: the hag is lame in one leg and blind in one eye and thus "crooked"; she forces him to violate his *geis* and so weakens him, bringing about his death when his enemies overtake him. Perhaps it is for this battle that she warns him to "arm in battle-gear".

Line 17: *ar soegaul de an-tuaith* | "for the world of the great Túatha Dé" or "for the life from a great kingdom"

This line defies simple translation; Carmody gives two distinct readings of it. A keyword is *soegaul*, likely a variant of *saegul*, "lifetime, period of life, ending of life, world". This word has a great variety of uses and is highly contextual. If *de an-tuaith* is read as "of the great Túatha Dé", she could be speaking of their world or dominion—the Otherworld, to which he will go when her prophecy of his death comes to fruition. In the sense that *soegaul* may refer to his lifetime ending, much as we would say that someone's "time has come", she may also be speaking of his death directly. Alternately, we may have a verbal noun based on *saigid*, "attack", and *túaith* can also mean "witchcraft, sorcery"; so this line can be read entirely differently as "for an attack of sorcery"—perhaps the sorcery of the children of Calatín which will bring about his doom. The term for someone blind in the left eye and therefore magically dangerous, is *túathcháech*, "sinister-eyed";[58] a concept that the Y manuscript version alludes to in the preceding lines.

Line 18: *.i. cluas indairmgretha* | "hear the clash of arms"

She speaks not just of the noise of war-gear in general, but the phenom-

58 Borsje 2003 12

enon of *armgrith*, "clamor of arms". This phrase appears in many warrior tales, describing the practice of the warriors shaking and clashing their weapons and roaring—sounds intended to create terror in enemies on the field. Further, the *armgrith* is associated with the battle spirits. Enspirited weapons and armor are said to make such a clashing of their own accord. These phenomena are associated with visitations of the war Goddesses and with Cú Chulainn's "hero's shout". The line here thus refers to the spiritual phenomena as well as the noise and clamor of battle.

The Prophecy to the Black Bull

This poem is given by the Morrígan within the body of the *Táin*. The armies of Connacht and the four provinces have entered Ulster and are ravaging the plains of Brega and Muirtheimne on their way to capture the Donn Cúailnge; Cú Chulainn is on his way to meet them. The Morrígan appears to warn the Donn Cúailnge of his oncoming captors: "On the same day the Morrígu daughter of Ernmas came from the fairy-mounds and sat on the pillar-stone in Temair Cúailnge, warning the Donn Cúailnge against the men of Ireland..."[59] She is implied to be in bird form, perching on the pillar-stone; Recension 1 tells us so directly.[60] This is interesting in so far as it represents a unique case in which she gives a prophetic poem while in bird form.

The poem that follows is another archaic *rosc* in the terse, alliterative style so characteristic of the Morrígan's prophetic poems. Published translations vary dramatically on the interpretation of this poem, and most rearrange the order of phrases to create whole sentences, which erases the archaic quality of the *rosc* form. I have analyzed the poem using translations by Olmsted[61] and Henry,[62] producing an adaptation based on the two translations which attempts to replace the phrases in their original sequence and pattern. I reproduce Henry's translation here for comparison.

---

59 O'Rahilly 2010 174

60 O'Rahilly 2011 152

61 Olmsted 1982 167

62 Henry 1995 72. Note, both translations derive from supposed "archetype" poems reconstructed from manuscript variations. The Irish text reproduced here is from the LU manuscript and my commentary is based on that version. Punctuation and capitalization have been removed to preserve the feel of *rosc*.

Original

1 *in fitir in dub*
2 *dusáim can eirc (.i. cen bréic)*
3 *n-echdaig (.i. éca) dál*
4 *désnad fiacht*
5 *fíach nad eól*
6 *ceurtid namaib*
7 *ar túaith brega*
8 *bíth i ndaínib*
9 *tathum rún*
10 *rofíastar dub*
11 *día n-ísa maí*
12 *muin tonna fér*
13 *forglass for laich*
14 *lilestai áed*
15 *ág asa mag*
16 *meldait slóig*
17 *scoith nía boidb*
18 *bógeimnech feochair*
19 *fíach fir máirm*
20 *rád n-igir*
21 *cluiph Cúalgni*
22 *coigde (.i. cach die) día (.i. laa) bás*
23 *mórmacni iar féic*
24 *muintire do écaib*

My Adaptation

1 does the Black know
2 restless without deceit
3 the destructive meeting
4 the domain which has not fought
5 the raven not knowing
6 enemies impose
7 on the people of Brega
8 wounding of men
9 I have a secret
10 the Black will know
11 when he grazes in May
12 the bog-lands of grass
13 deep green becomes black
14 overpowered by fire
15 and battle from his plain
16 the armies crush
17 Badb's flower of champions
18 a bellowing fierce
19 the raven dead men
20 saying of sorrow
21 the shelter of Cúailnge
22 five days from his death
23 after the fight of the great youths
24 a people goes to death

Henry*

1 does the restless Black know
2 in good truth
3 of the encounter to the south
4 which the raven did not contest
5 not knowing
6 that enemies are circulating
7 in the outskirts of the land and in the hills
8 and that people are being killed
9 I have a secret

* Henry, P. L. 1995. "*Táin* Roscada: Discussion and Edition." *Zeitschrift Für Celtische Philologie* 47 (1). Reprinted with grateful permission.

which the Black will know
when he eats the May crop
the surfaces
of verdant grasses
that the warrior who owns the plain
will be attacked with fire and sword
the hosts overwhelm
the flower of champions is in the fray
lowing of cattle
fierce the raven; men dead
a grievous saying
about the cries of Cúailnge
after five days the death
of its great sons
after the death of Fiacc's kin

Notes:

Line 1: *in fitir in dub* | "does the Black know"

The name she uses for the Bull, *in dub*, is notable. *Dub* is "black, dark", but this can mean emotionally dark, "gloomy, melancholy, dire". The Bull's usual name at all other points in the tale is Donn Cúailnge; *donn* is "brown, dun". The Morrígan's choice of this name suggests that she is not referring just to his color: there is a hint of doom about it that aligns with the character of her warning to him.

Line 2: *dusáim can eirc* | "restless without deceit"

Dusáim is assumed by all translators to refer to the Bull; it is "uneasy, restless", his state at being hunted. Olmsted has presumed that *eirc* is intended *eric*, "compensation"; but in more than one version this is clarified with a gloss *bréic*, "falsehood". *Can eirc* then represents a stock phrase, "without deceit", the equivalent of saying "I tell you true."

Line 3: *n-echdaig dál* | "the destructive meeting"

Dál is properly "meeting", or "assembly". The translation "the destructive meeting" is suggested as an alternate by Olmsted, based on a form of *écht*, "slaughter, destruction", and presumed to reference to the *Táin* battles taking place elsewhere as the armies converge.

Line 4: *désnad fiacht* | "the domain which has not fought"

Désnad may be from *déis*, "land". More precisely, the clients of a chieftain's territory who would be expected to supply military service in time of conflict; so the term refers the martial force of a district. Olmsted translates "domain" in the military sense, the forces of that domain. Some translators have taken *fiacht* to intend *fiach*, "raven". More likely, it is a verbal term "fought", the phrase meaning forces which have not yet been brought to the battle, but which are, the poem would imply, an oncoming threat.

Line 5: *fiach nad eól* | "the raven not knowing"

Here *fiach* appears to be "raven" proper. Who might this raven be? Henry suggests it as a kenning for a warrior, tentatively identified with Cú Chulainn; this would fit her warning, in that help would not be coming from a warrior who was not aware of the Bull's position. Alternately, Olmsted reads *fiach* as "obligation, fine, penalty" suggesting an unanticipated penalty. Either reading tends to reinforce the sense of a warning to one unready for what is coming.

Line 7: *ar túaith brega* | "on the people of Brega"

Most interpret *brega* as a toponym, indicating the land around Mag Breg (Plains of Brega), and *túaith* as "people" or "tribes", yielding "the people of Brega". Alternately, *brega* can be read as a form of *bri*, "hill, hillfort", and *túaith* can refer to territory; thus "the land and the hills" is an alternate reading.

Line 9: *tathum rún* | "I have a secret"

Rún merits expansion; it is "secret", but especially something mysterious or occult, not just unknown. The secret she has for the Bull is not simply information he doesn't have, but hidden knowledge obtained through oracular means.

Line 11: *día n-ísa maí* | "when he grazes in May"

This speaks to the timing of the *Táin* narrative. The war takes place in springtime, and it is said that Cú Chulainn neither rested nor slept from Samhain till the day after the "festival of Spring" while he was guarding the province.[63] Tradition typically places this "festival of Spring" at Imbolc, when warrior-bands would return from winter hunting and raiding; this poem may point toward an alternate tradition relating this Spring activity to Beltaine.

Line 13: *forglass for laich* | "deep green becomes black"

Forglass is "very green" or "green-surfaced", the rich grasslands of the previous line. *For laich* may be a couple of things: Olmsted reads it as *loiche* "blackness, darkness" with *for* acting as an intensive or a verbal participle: what is green becomes black, implying that the lush green grassland hides ill-luck for the Bull. It may also allude to blackening

63 O'Rahilly 2011 184

from the attack of fire referenced in line 14.

Line 15: *ág asa mag* | "and battle from his plain"

Olmsted reads *ág*, "fight, battle, contest" as *ag*, "ox, cow". This tends to refer to a burden animal rather than a bull, and seems to me unlikely for the Donn Cúailnge. Following the previous line, I think "overpowered by fire and battle" makes more sense.

Line 16: *meldait slóig* | "the armies crush"

Two readings are possible from this line. *Meldait* may be from *mellaid*, "beguiles, seduces, deceives"; or may be from *meilid*, "crushes, grinds". Thus "the armies beguile" or "the armies crush"; translators vary on the interpretation of this line, and it is in part dependent on how one reads the following line as to what hero is referred to.

Line 17: *scoith nía boidb* | "Badb's flower of champions"

Key to this line is the phrase *scoith nía*, a phrase elsewhere used poetically to refer to a great warrior or champion; literally, "the flower of heroism" (*scoth*, "flower, blossom, pinnacle"; *nia*, "warrior, champion", alternately, "vigorous, spirited"). This is paired with *bodb*, the older form of the name we know as Badb. This champion is likely Cú Chulainn. He is well suited to carry the title "flower of heroism", and he is at this point in the story holding at bay the armies of all Ireland against Ulster. They will eventually overwhelm him and take the Bull, and it is to this future that the Morrígan points in her warning.

Translators differ widely here; Henry reads *boidb* as a reference to being "with the Badb", as a kenning for battle. Olmsted emends the line completely to read *scoith niab odib*, to fit a theory regarding the identity of the hero; however, I think we can dismiss that alteration, since it would interrupt the alliterative pattern of the poem, where the last word should alliterate with the first of the next line (*boidb* with *bógeimnech*).

Lines 18-19:

bógeimnech feochair | "a bellowing fierce"

fíach fir máirm | "the raven dead men"

As elsewhere, *feochair*, "fierce", can be descriptive of the bellowing—presumably this would be the Bull himself, or his cows, roaring as they are attacked, or possibly the roaring of the two bulls in their combat at the end of the *Táin*. If the lines are paired together, it may be descriptive of *fíach*, "raven". In either case, we have an image of ravens paired with dead men, the casualties of war.

Line 22: *coigde día bás* | "five days from his death"

Coigde is an obscure word which may be meant as *cóicde*, "a period of five days"; the glossators of the text have added notes to clarify this meaning: *.i. cach die*, "each day". Alternately, Corthals dismisses the glosses and reads it as a loanword from Latin *cocytia*, meaning "from the Underworld", a word used of the Goddess Alecto in the *Aeneid*, which he considers to have influenced the compilation of the *Táin*.[64] It is true that the Morrígan is called Alecto in this scene.

Line 23: *mórmacni iar féic* | "after the fight of the great youths"

This line speaks of the "mighty youths" in a collective as a troop or band, *mórmacni*. The phrase *iar féic* is obscure but may mean "after the assault/raid/fight". Some translators read the *bás*, "death", from the previous line as applying to these youths, "the death of the great youths". In either case, this likely points to the "Death of the Youths," a later episode in the *Táin* in which the boys of Ulster attack the Connacht army and all but one are slaughtered.

Line 24: *muintire do écaib* | "a people goes to death"

This line speaks of the death of a collective or family unit, *muinter*. The phrase *do écaib* is typically not used of violent death; it would usually refer to an individual, natural death. Here she seems to be speaking of the perishing of a tribe.

In this poem, again, we are not given much insight into the Morrígan's perspective. She speaks of herself once, "I have a secret"; apart from this, it is an impersonal delivery of prophetic warning. Her poem on the battlefield of *Mag Tuired* is the only poem in which we have heard her speak of her own experience in the poems. Indirectly, the poem still conveys her interest in the welfare of the Bull, for she is warning him of the armies coming to capture him.

The Poem to the Two Armies

The Morrígan speaks her last poem in the *Táin* on the eve of the final battle, when the two great armies—Ulster and the combined forces of the rest of Ireland under Connacht—have drawn close together. A truce has been declared from sundown until sunrise the next morning, and the two encampments are made together, with "scarcely a bare patch of earth between them".[65] At dusk, the Morrígan speaks in this space between the encampments, giving the poem below. The poem

64 Corthals 1996 24-25
65 O'Rahilly 2011 229

is followed by trance-speeches on the part of various warriors in the Ulster camp, and the attack of Némain with Badb and Bé Néit against the encampment of the allied Connacht forces.

O'Rahilly's edition of the *Táin* does not translate the poem, so I have analyzed the poem using two modern translations: Kinsella's[66] and Carson's.[67] Kinsella's translation seems to be the most direct, but alters some lines to create more complete statements. Carson's translation returns to the impressionistic feel of *rosc* as a series of images, but interprets the language rather freely. I have adapted elements from each of these two translations, in a few places proposing my own reading as close to the original language as possible.[68] I reproduce Kinsella's translation here for comparison.

	Original		My compilation
1	*crenaid brain*	1	ravens gnaw
2	*bráigde fer*	2	men's necks
3	*bruinded fuil*	3	blood gushes
4	*feochair cath*	4	fierce fray
5	*coinmid luind*	5	lances fed
6	*mesctuich tuind*	6	battle madness
7	*taib im thuill*	7	sides pierced
8	*im níthgalaib*	8	in war-frenzy
9	*iar luimnich*	9	black cloaked
10	*luud fianna*	10	warbands on the move
11	*fetal ferda*	11	heroic devices
12	*fir Crúachan*	12	men of Cruachan
13	*cotascrith imm ardbith*	13	destruction with great striking
14	*cuirither cath*	14	war is waged
15	*ar cosa alailiu*	15	each trampling each
16	*cénmair h-Ultaib*	16	long life to the Ulstermen
17	*mairc Iarnaib*	17	woe to the Irish
18	*mairc d' Ultaib immorro*	18	woe to the Ulstermen indeed
19	*cén mair Iarnaib*	19	long life to the Irish
20	*mairc h-Ultaib ol niscainedar a n-gle*	20	woe to the Ulstermen for they have not broken the battle

66 Kinsella 1969 238

67 Carson 2007 197

68 Punctuation and capitalization have been removed to preserve the feel of *rosc*.

Kinsella*

ravens gnawing
men's necks
blood spurting
in the fierce fray
hacked flesh
battle madness
blades in bodies
acts of war
after the cloaked one's
hero heat
in man's shape he shakes to pieces
the men of Cruachan
with hacking blows
war is waged
each trampling each
hail Ulster
woe men of Ireland
woe to Ulster
hail men of Ireland

Notes:

Line 5: *coinmid luind* | "lances fed" or "hacked flesh"

Kinsella and Carson both give "hacked flesh". Contextually, the verb *coinnmid* is used in reference to billeting—that is providing food and quarters as a matter of requirement, usually to soldiers. *Luind* may be a form either of *lúin*, "lance", or *lonn*, "fierce, violent, eager". A well-known instance of the term appears in the Luin of Celtchar, an enspirited lance identified with the Túatha Dé and which was said to be inherited by Dubthach, a character in the *Táin*; this lance was said to be ravenous for blood and would kill of its own accord if not appeased.[69] The poem here seems to suggest a lance being fed the blood which is its due.

Line 6: *mesctuich tuind* | "battle madness"

The phrase here is from the verb *mescaid*, to intoxicate; it is the same word used in the tale *Mesca Ulad*, the *Intoxication of the Ulstermen*. Its use

---

69 Stokes 1910 301

* Kinsella, Thomas. 1969. *The Táin: Translated from the Irish Epic Táin Bó Cúailnge*. Oxford: Oxford University Press. Reprinted with grateful permission.

here links to the concept of battle fury as a kind of intoxication—possibly reflective of a practice of using psychoactive substances such as alcohol, plant toxins, or other substances to encourage warlike ardor and courage. *Tuind* is from *tonn,* "wave", evoking the battle madness overcoming the warriors in waves.

Line 8: *im níthgalaib* | "in war-frenzy" or "acts of war"

The compound *níthgalaib* refers to *gal,* the "seething heat" associated with warriors in battle ardor; *níth* is "fighting, combat", or pertaining to warriorship. It describes the war-frenzy, but may also refer to the feats of valour achieved by warriors in that state, this latter meaning highlighted by Kinsella's translation of the line, "acts of war".

Line 9: *iar luimnich* | "black cloaked" or "after the cloaked one"

Here the meaning hinges on whether *iar* is read as a preposition, or as *íar,* "black". Kinsella's translation reads *luimnich,* "cloaked" as referring to Cú Chulainn, and attaches it to the series of lines following to create a complete sentence; however, this seems to rest on inserting a phrase "he shakes to pieces" (below, line 11). I prefer to retain the *rosc* pattern of raw sequences of images and have deferred to what seems like a more direct reading of the line.

Line 10: *luud fianna* | "warbands on the move" or "hero heat"

Luud is a form of *lúth,* which is motion or the power of movement. Kinsella reads this line metaphorically as internal motion, the movement of the "hero heat" or war-frenzy mentioned in previous lines. As *fianna* is a common term for groups of warriors, and as it falls between the line describing a cloaked warrior or warriors and the following line about the insignia of warriors, I tend to read this as descriptive of the movement of warrior bands in the action of the battle, rather than internal, metaphoric motion.

Line 11: *fetal ferda* | "heroic devices" or "in man's shape"

For *fetal,* DIL gives "that which indicates; a characteristic badge or emblem (of office or class), insignia (used both of dress and ornaments); a device or ornament on a shield."[70] *Ferda* is "male, manly", or a term for male genitalia. Here again Kinsella reads this line metaphorically, as describing Cú Chulainn returning to "man's shape" after his distortion. Another reading could take this more literally as descriptive of the battle displays of warriors with their insignia. It might not be too much to imagine warriors exposing their "manly devices" to insult and provoke one another, as part of pre-battle displays of bravado.

70 Royal Irish Academy 2013, entry *fethal.*

Lines 16-20:

In this sequence, it seems implied that the outcome of the battle has not been predetermined—that either side may yet reap victory or woe. The Morrígan appears to be both blessing and warning or cursing each camp in turn. The language used is interesting, as the terms for both are alliterative and resonant: *mair* and *mairc*. In the blessing, *mair* is from *maraid*, "lasts, persists", with *cén*, "enduring"; this is a blessing of longevity specifically applied to the collective—that the tribe will endure. The curse is *mairc*, "woe, sorrow", according to DIL an interjection which is particularly used in imprecations—"woe unto you."[71] She ends with a final warning or imprecation to the Ulster forces, which is not translated by Kinsella or Carson, but which O'Rahilly translates "Woe to the men of Ulster for they have not won(?) the battle".[72] The translation is uncertain; the term used is *níscainedar*, a negative from the verb *scaindrid*, to "disperse, shatter, break". The word translated for battle is *glé*, more precisely "dispute".

What are we to make of her blessing and cursing both sides at once in this poem? The poem can be read as the Morrígan stirring the two armies against each other; and certainly the language in much of the poem, evoking the action and bloodshed of battle, resembles language in her *Mag Tuired* battle poem, where the purpose of the poem and its impact is to incite the Túatha Dé to greater valor and to turn the battle into a rout in their favor. Here she seems to be inciting both sides against each other, rather than just encouraging one side. It also stands apart from the *Mag Tuired* battle poem in that she performs it not during the battle, when an act of incitement would be most effective, but the evening before. Thus while it can be read as containing elements of incitement, its timing may mark it as more an act of prophetic warning to each of the camps.

---

71 Royal Irish Academy 2013, entry *mairg*
72 O'Rahilly 2011 230

Part II
Cult

Having studied the Morrígan in some depth in the mythological context, in this second part of the book, we turn our attention to cults of worship, ancient and modern. Here, my aim is to provide at least the raw materials to engage the perennial questions about devotional practice: How was the Morrígan worshiped by ancient people? And: How can we create a devotional practice to honor her now?

This part of the book is organized into chapters according to distinct (though overlapping) areas of cult practice. The ways in which these areas of practice come to life for us in lived practice today, within the context of our own culture and society, will naturally diverge in important ways from the practices of the ancients. My intention here is to provide a survey of the source material from the ancient world from which we can draw inspiration for our own cults of worship, and then to suggest ways in which new traditions can be brought to life from these raw materials. For this reason, the remaining chapters will alternate between the ancient and modern contexts. Each chapter examines an area of cult practice first with respect to how it may have been enacted in ancient Celtic religions, followed by a "Living Practice" section which explores how we can bring this area into practice in a modern context.

Chapter 10 explores land veneration, sanctuaries, tombs and temples, and engagement with sacred places.

Chapter 11 looks at iconography and image worship, and explores devotional practices, including prayers, invocation, offerings, and votive practices.

Chapter 12 delves into sacrifice; its cosmological background, role in the cults of the Morrígna, specific forms and contexts for sacrifice, and ethical considerations.

Chapter 13 examines the functions of priesthood and sovereignty in relation to the Morrígna, the work of priesthood, forms of dedication and service, and the practice of sovereignty.

Chapter 14 explores oracular and divinatory practices, including the use of trance, intoxication, dreams, prophetic speech, oracular trance possession, and other modes of mantic knowledge.

Chapter 15 illuminates the various modes and techniques of sorcery and magical practice: incantation, binding, *geis*-prayers, cursing, and sexual magics.

Chapter 16 turns to forms of battle cultus, the action of the Morrígna in warfare, battle magics, and devotional aspects of working with a war divinity.

Chapter 17 focuses into the individual level of warrior cults, looking at warrior training and initiatory rites, the warband culture, as well as warriorship in the modern context.

Chapter 18 explores the roles of the Morrigna in death and funerary rites, and looks at ancestral cultus, heroic ancestor veneration, necromancy, and funerary priesthood as a form of service.

I wish to emphasize a few things. First, any representation of the past is an act of storytelling. We look at the evidence of literature, historiography, archaeology, linguistics, and the like, in an effort to draw together a picture of how the Morrígna may have figured into cults of worship in the ancient world. But this act of interpreting the evidence is always subjective, always bounded by the currently accessible information, and always influenced by the ideas and expectations of the culture from which we are looking into the past. The ideas I present here about the history of cult practices constitute my story, the story I draw from my studies. Other scholars, perhaps better scholars, may draw a different set of conclusions from the same evidence; may tell a different story altogether. You may wish to study the sources for yourself and develop your own story. Our stories may change over time as new evidence comes to light. In other words, I do not claim that the history I present here is authoritative. It represents my best understanding from the evidence.

Second, the "Living Practice" sections represent one set of examples as to how we might begin to build living modes of worship and religious practice honoring the Morrígan and Celtic traditions in our own time and present context. The practices shared here are reflections from a work in progress—they are the product of my experiences, training, and collaborations *up to this point*. The work of developing devotional cultus and traditions is the work of a lifetime and so the practices I share here are not presented as an endpoint, but as suggestions for you to work with and to build upon. They have been developed experientially, in collaborative practice with colleagues, co-priests, and teachers in the Coru Cathubodua Priesthood, the Anderson Feri Tradition, and with friends in other traditions. That is to say, the practices I share here are shaped by my particular background, environment, and life experience and may be of differing usefulness to readers depending on your own values and preferences in spiritual and religious practice.

Finally, it should be said that the "Living Practice" sections in this book each form just the beginning of an exploration into their topics. This is a necessity as the cults of the Morrígna touch on an enormous range and variety of practices—from devotional prayer and meditation all the way to sacrificial rites, spirit travel, necromancy, transgressive sorcery, warriorship and much more. It is not possible in the span of a single book to really teach each of these areas of practice or to do them justice—each merits a book of its own, and more. My intention for these sections is to illuminate how these forms of practice may fit together toward the development of cult and tradition for the Morrígna, and to provide some helpful direction and guidance for further study and practice.

10

Land, Sanctuary, Tomb, and Temple

Veneration at holy places in the landscape is among the most archaic and lasting forms of religious practice. We see this reflected in *Dindshenchas* traditions that embed names and stories into the forms of the landscape. The naming of land and the telling of stories embedded in landscape are acts of worship which enshrine numinous presences and meanings into the land. This sanctifying of landscape as living divinity is reinforced and honored in continued ritual practice. In many cases, these stories are all that remain and the lived ritual practice which may have accompanied them is lost. Traces can be found in the archaeological record, and bringing these evidences together we can begin to re-imagine what land veneration practices may have looked like.

Land as Living Body

In the chapters on the Morrígan and Anu, we touched on the landforms traditionally named and linked for the breasts of these Goddesses—the Paps of the Morrígan at Brúg na Bóinne, and the Paps of Anu in Kerry.[1] In each place the land itself has been sanctified as the body of a Goddess. In particular, the breasts of these Goddesses are enshrined into the landscape, highlighting their roles as land-mothers, tutelary mothers-of-the-tribe, and givers of wealth and sovereignty. The enshrining of the body of a divinity into the landform provides for a living landscape where the devotee can physically make contact with the body of their divinity, as well as a constant visual reminder of the embodied presence of the Gods.

This enshrining of the bodies of Goddesses into landforms, of course, is a folk practice seen worldwide, and is by no means unique to Ireland. Nor is it unique to the land-based veneration of the Morrígna; *Dindshenchas* texts and local folk traditions overflow with landforms named for the parts of bodies of divine and heroic figures. This mode of recognizing in the landscape the living body of a God is of course most pronounced with regard to tutelary and land divinities, of which both Morrígan and Anu are examples.

A possible further example of the landform as body may be seen in the place called Srúb Brain, the "raven's bill", a rocky crag on a coastal mountain in the far north of Ireland.[2] The extant stories in the *Dindshenchas* and Ulster Cycle texts (as well as a mention in the *Triads*) explain this name by an exploit of Cú Chulainn's, in which he killed a raven at the site, bathing his hands in its blood for apparently invocatory and/or divinatory ritual purposes. The stories here do not mention the Morrígan or Badb by name, but in view of Cú Chulainn's relationship with her, a connection linking her to the site seems at least plausible.[3] As with much

1 See above chapter 6, Anu.
2 Stokes 1894 450, Gwynn 2008a 257, Tymoczko 1981 24
3 Tymoczko argues for this in her analysis of the episode as appearing in *Aided Chon Roí* (Tymoczko 1981, 88 n).

of the *Dindshenchas* material, it is very likely that the place-name existed earlier and the explanatory story was later attached to the place. In this light, it is possible that Srúb Brain may in some ancient period have been seen as the "raven's bill" of the Morrígan in her corvid shape, and the extant piece of legend that remains is simply the explanatory tale.

Also relevant here, a thread within the tradition of identifying landforms with parts of divine bodies is the theme of sacrificial cosmogony seen woven throughout Celtic myth. A classic example of this is, of course, the two bulls whose epic combat both destroys and creates the landscape: the Donn Cúailnge and the Findbennach, the Brown Bull and the White-horned. This pair is the expression of a deep cosmological theme common to many Indo-European cultures, that of the creation of the world through the act of sacrifice, mythologically expressed within the framework of twins.[4] One brother is killed by the other, and from his dismembered body the world is created—a myth also likely expressed in the rituals of bull sacrifice such as the *tarb feis*.[5] The making of the landscape from the parts of the bulls' bodies embeds this mythic narrative into the land itself. A similar dynamic is expressed in the *Dindshenchas* stories about the landforms made from the bones and body of the monster Matha, as well as that of Méche, the Morrígan's son.[6] The mythologies surrounding both stories are redolent of sacrifice: a mighty creature, either heroic or monstrous but clearly placed in divine relation, is killed by another who creates the world and the landscape from the parts of its body. We do not tend to see landscapes named for the body parts of the Morrígan in this sacrificial context, because it is not the land Goddess who is sacrificed to remake the world; rather, she seems to be placed in relation to that sacrifice as the mother or guardian of the sacrificed one (i.e. mother of Méche and guardian of the Donn Cúailnge), as well as taking a hand in orchestrating the sacrificial combat (as in her role in bringing about the *Táin*).

Land as Territory

Many more places are named as belonging to the Morrígan or her sisters than those identified as her body. These are landscapes and land-

4 Meyer 1889 223, Lincoln 1991 34

5 This connection is reflected in a passage in the *Battle of Findchorad* in which the fight of the bulls is set in context of a divinatory sacrifice (Dobbs 1923 399).

6 See above, Chapter 3, for the possible connection between Matha and Méche.

forms claimed for, and by, a Goddess rather than embodying her being directly. These sites are reflective of another expression of the tutelary Goddess relation: the land is her land, the people her people, and she the protector of them. Examples of this type of land relation seem to cover all possible types of land-forms:

Forests: Ross, the "Wood of Badb"[7]

Plains and fields: Gort na Morrígna, the "Garden of the Morrígan";[8] Mag Macha, "Macha's Plain";[9] Mag Fea, "Fea's Plain"[10]

Mountains: Slíab Bodbgna, "Badb's Mountain"[11]

Caves: Síd Cruachan[12]

Islands: Inis Badhbha, aka Boa Island, "Badb's Island"[13]

Other landforms: Dún Sobairche, modern Dunseverick, a coastal promontory with the remains of an apparently Iron Age stone fort, is also said to belong to the Morrígan (and, incidentally, also to Cú Chulainn).[14]

Rivers

It is striking, in view of the strong tendency for Celtic peoples to name rivers and other water bodies by the names of Goddesses, that we do not find more watery sites carrying her name. In my research I have yet to discover a single case of a documentable water body named for the Morrígan herself. A river Nemnach may arguably trace its name to Némain (and possibly her consort, Néit).[15] Other water sites such as the coastal whirlpool of Coire Bhreacain (Corryvreckan, off the coast

---

7 Meyer 1888 231

8 Meyer 1888 231

9 Gwynn 1924 308

10 Stokes 1894 436

11 Gwynn 1924 196. This site's attachment to Badb herself is tentative, as the name may refer rather to Bodb Derg, a male deity and Síd king of the Túatha Dé.

12 Gwynn 1924 196. Not called by her name, but clearly thought of as hers, "her fit abode".

13 Wood-Martin 1902a 358

14 O'Rahilly 2011 217-218

15 The *Dindshenchas* name the river Nith, and say that it emerges from a well or spring called Nemnach located at one of the *síd*-mounds at Tara (Stokes 1894, 284). Carey, quoting a Leinster text, attributes both names to the river, calling it the Nith Nimannach, and identifies it as the Dee in County Louth (Carey 2004, 17n).

of Scotland) have been attributed to the Morrígan or Badb in popular materials, but so far as I can tell are more properly connected to the Cailleach Bheur, and not any of the Morrígna Goddesses per se.[16]

River and ford sites do feature prominently in the Morrígan's stories, but rather than being directly identified with her as her being or possession, they seem to be named for important events in her mythology. In this context stand sites such as the Bed of the Couple, a ford on the Unshin where tradition places her (possibly seasonal) mating with the Dagda; also called the Ford of Destruction, for her destruction of the king of the Fomoiri.[17] Similarly, the river ford where she attacks Cú Chulainn during his combat with Lóch by tradition is named the Ford of Combat.[18] A ford where Badb appears washing Cú Chulainn's bloody armor in the Early Modern version of his death-tale is called the Ford of Washing.[19]

In light of the Morrígan's strong associations with rivers and fords, and the Celtic habit of naming rivers for Goddesses, why this dearth of river sites named for the Morrígna? This apparent mystery becomes more sensible when we consider that the Goddesses whose names attach to rivers appear typically to be in the role of creatrix either as mother-of-the-tribe (such as the Welsh Dôn), as the source-stream of wisdom (such as Bóan and Sinann), or both (arguably *Danu).[20] It is also important to note that where Irish rivers are named for Goddesses, it is their deaths that release the rivers into which they become merged and which shape the landscape. We can discern that the Morrígan is not a mother-creatrix type, and that her relationship with rivers is a different one. She does not drown in the river, she straddles it (as woman), swims it (as eel), or fords it (as wolf and heifer). While she may sometimes act as a tutelary divinity and may be involved with land as wealth, territory, and even fertility, her relation with these aspects of land is emergent rather than generative. Her engagement is with rivers as liminal boundaries between worlds and between territories, and rivers as natural expressions of the life force and sovereignty of the land,

---

16 Beck 2009 246-247. The Cailleach is a mythic hag and creatrix with some interesting parallels to certain of the Morrígna in their hag forms, but on the evidence, I do not think they should be treated as the same entity.

17 Stokes 1891 85

18 O'Rahilly 1924 75

19 O'Grady 1898 247

20 See above, Chapter 6, for further examination of *Danu.

rather than herself being identified as a river Goddess.

The Breasts of Anu

At the Paps of Anu, the sanctified landscape of Anu's breasts has been augmented with a pair of stone cairns built near the peaks of the two hills, forming nipples on the naturally breast-curved mountains. The cairns are prehistoric and thought to date as far back as the Bronze Age at least.[21] The two cairns are not identical in size, but instead appear to be constructed proportionally so as to bring the slightly differing elevations of the two peaks to a close match in height at the tips of the cairns. Additionally, their siting is very deliberate—not quite at the peak of each hill, but instead *near* the peak, on the side of the hill yielding line-of-sight to the more inhabited region of valley below. As with many sacred sites, the Paps form one element of a broader ritual landscape including other sacred sites nearby, so that inhabitants of the area found their experience encircled and embedded within an enlivened, sacred landscape visible all about them.

In addition to their visual function as the landscape markers of the Goddess's breasts, the cairns may embed an ancestral function into the landscape as well. The construction of the cairns and their elevation and dating is thought to point toward the existence of ancient, pre-Celtic passage tombs underneath (dating to about 2500 BCE), which would have formed the first stage of ritual landscape enhancement at the site.[22] The likely presence of tombs within the cairns illustrates another mode by which ancient worshipers engaged with land veneration here and elsewhere. By embedding their own ancestry into the sacred landscape of the Paps, thus claiming identity with and descent from the tutelary Goddess of the land, they both legitimated and sanctified their presence and territorial right to the land.

Many sacred sites contain ancestral funerary monuments, but what distinguishes this type is that the ancestral monument has been inserted into a pre-existing, natural, sacred landform in order to heighten, emphasize and direct its sacred power.

21 Coyne 2006 29
22 Coyne 2006 52

The Cave of Cruachan

Another example of an enhanced natural site is the cave known as Oweynagat (Úaim na gCat, the Cave of Cats); this cave is referred to in the Irish literature as the Síd of Cruachan from which the Morrígan emerges and which is said to be her home.[23] Here, a pre-existing natural cave has been enhanced by the construction of a souterrain, or stone-lined tunnel through which the interior, natural cave is accessed from the ground surface. The natural cave likely was already in cult use in ancient times, prior to the medieval period when the souterrain entrance was added.[24] In this construction, lintel stones with *ogam* inscriptions have been inserted; one of which has the name of a legendary warrior Fráech, son of Queen Medb (VRAICCI MAQI MEDVVI) in common Celtic, an early precursor to Old Irish.[25] This identification of the cave with Fráech aligns with a story in the *Táin* in which Fráech is killed by Cu Chulainn and carried into the cave by a group of fairy women.[26]

According to John Waddell, these *ogam* stones appear to have been placed at key transition points in the cave/souterrain system, for protective or other ritual purposes. The cave site has a long-standing connection in both literary and folk tradition with the Morrígan and frightful Otherworldly powers, and its structure appears to be keyed to ritual usage in chthonic, initiatory, and warrior rites as we might expect for a cult of the Morrígan.[27] These rites will be explored in more depth in Chapter 17 and 18 below.

Circuits and Processional Ways

As part of the continued engagement with sacred landscapes, processions and circuits of the land appear to have been an important part of the practice in many places. Rathcroghan, a royal site with a constructed mound closely associated with the Síd of Cruachan, includes a marked ceremonial "avenue" or processional way featuring a carefully guided approach to the sacred enclosure, apparently conscious of the visibility, hiding, and revealing of important monuments along

23 See above, Chapter 3.
24 Waddell 2014 65
25 Beck 2009 491
26 O'Rahilly 2011 149
27 Waddell 2014 67

its route; a similar processional way is seen at Temair.[28] At the Paps of Anu, a series of stones set on edge traverse a line running down the "cleavage" between the two hills, and are thought to mark a ceremonial route between the two sacred mounds.[29]

Ceremonial processions and circuit-ridings are seen in the myths and may reflect the functions of these processional ways in ritual. For example, on the day that Cú Chulainn takes up arms, he rides a circuit round Emain Macha three times in his chariot before riding off to undertake his first combats.[30] This echoes Macha herself measuring the rath's sacred enclosure by drawing its circuit with her brooch-pin, in Emain's foundation legend. The riding of the circuit reinforces and re-enacts the origin stories, the link of the living with the ancestors, and their lived connection with the landscape. Rites of circumnavigation of sacred sites are mentioned in a number of sources and survive as folkloric custom into the modern period.[31] The custom seems all over Ireland to specify walking or riding "according to the course of the sun" or "right-hand-wise" (*deiseal*), as opposed to "left-hand-wise" (*tuathail*), which was considered unhallowed and ill-omened. *Deiseal* movement corresponds to what we now call "clockwise", *tuathail* to "counterclockwise".[32] Brunaux notes that Gaulish temples were usually built with a gallery surrounding the interior sanctuary, to facilitate similar ceremonial processions.[33]

A parallel process, writ large, may be in action in the ritual circuit-riding of kings around their territories. Brian Boru is said to have made a circuit expedition all round the circumference of Ireland when he established his kingship. His political purpose, of course, is to take hostages and establish alliances to cement his kingship. The details, however, suggest that it was also a ritual act with magical and religious purposes. This is shown in the careful orientation "keeping his left hand to the sea, and his right hand to the land", corresponding to the hallowing *deiseal* movement, and in the timing of the circuit, completing on Lughnasad.[34]

---

28 Waddell 2014 148
29 Coyne 2006 24
30 O'Rahilly 2010
31 Wood-Martin 1902 53-57
32 Wood-Martin 1902 56
33 Brunaux 1988 30
34 Todd 1867 135

Sanctuary, Tomb, and Temple

Passing from natural landscapes and landscape sites to constructed ones, we will examine sacred places of the built variety: sanctuaries, constructed groves, temples, and funerary monuments, as they may have figured into worship and cult practice of the Morrígna.

The Nemeton

In contemporary Classical writings about the Celts in Britain and the Continent, we read much of their practice of worshiping in sacred groves called *nemetona*. Traces of a related practice can be seen in Ireland, too. The *nemeton* as described in Celtic Gaul and Britain (and common to the Belgic and Germanic tribes) seems to have been a sanctuary clearing within a forest or grove of trees, within which were altars, and where religious rituals took place in association with druidic priestly work.[35] These sacred groves seem to have been perceived, by outsiders at least, as holy centers of dread spiritual power so potent as to present a danger to the uninitiated, as "nobody dared enter this grove except the priest."[36] In part these comments may simply reflect the authors' sensationalizing their subject particularly around the topic of human and animal sacrifice said to be performed in the groves. However, the simple element of an enclosed sanctum dedicated to one or more Gods and held separate and sacred tallies well with the evidence of archaeology, including both groves and temple precincts.

In Ireland, there is some evidence suggesting wooded groves as ritual centers. A term *fiodhneimeidh*, meaning "sacred tree" or "sacred grove" is referenced in early glosses as a place where "seers used to perform their rituals."[37] A place called Fid Némain, "wood of Némain", is mentioned in the *Táin*; a very suggestive reference given her links with sacred groves.[38] Among the *Triads* is found this: "Three dead ones that are paid for with living things: an apple-tree, a hazel-bush, a sacred grove," suggesting not only that sacred groves were known in Irish tradition, but

35 Aldhouse-Green 2010 37, 126; Suetonius 2006 337

36 Aldhouse-Green 2010 126, quoting Lucan, and parallel comments from Tacitus and others.

37 Ó hÓgáin 1999 71

38 O'Rahilly 2011 231

that they too may have been sanctified with sacrifices.[39]

A shrine structure buried beneath Navan mound at Emain Macha may represent something like a constructed grove—its circular plan, built of concentric rings of wooden pillars, according to John Waddell, may represent the "creation of a *nemeton* or sanctified stand of wood" surrounding a huge central post which may have served as a focus of worship.[40] If so, this timber *nemeton* might well have been a locus of the cult of Macha, whose roots as the tutelary Goddess associated with Emain Macha go deep. Perhaps relevant to this connection, in some of the *nemetona* on the Continent, wild white horses were let to roam and given divine status; this is a practice that would seem easily at home in a cult of Macha.[41] These unbroken sacred horses were also for ritual purposes yoked to sacred chariots, showing strong parallels to the horse and chariot elements in Irish rites of kingship.[42]

Némain, too, may have been worshiped in a timber or wooded sacred grove, as was Nemetona, her cognate in Britain and Gaul. As we have seen, Némain's name is related to the same root that gives *nemeton*, indicating sacred, privileged and holy status. Her nature as a terrible, death-bringing presence that appears (in the literature, at least) only when invoked against enemies in war also accords well with the attitude of holy dread that seems to have surrounded such sacred groves elsewhere.[43]

In the Celtic-Germanic border areas of northern Gaul, a war Goddess called Baduhenna (a likely cognate of Badb, as we have seen in the above chapter on Badb) had a sacred grove dedicated to her, according to Tacitus.[44] If timber or wooded groves were in fact used in Ireland as places of worship, such places could have been dedicated to the Irish war Goddesses such as Badb as well. We may imagine, though we cannot confirm, that a grove or *nemeton* might be indicated in the reference to the "Wood of Badb", also identified with the Morrígan, in the early Ulster text the *Wooing of Emer*.[45]

---

39 Meyer 1906 158
40 Waddell 2014 96
41 Waddell 2014 108
42 Macalister 1919 329
43 See Chapter 7 above.
44 Quoted in Donahue 1941 7.
45 Meyer 1888 231

Funerary Mounds

Another deeply ancient type of constructed sacred site traditionally linked to the Morrígna are the funerary mounds or megalithic tombs. Many of the important ritual centers of Ireland include such funerary mounds; they are prominent in the literature as the *síd* or "fairy mounds". These megalithic tombs are usually Neolithic to Bronze Age in origin—meaning they long predate the presence of Gaelic-speaking Celtic peoples we associate with the veneration of the Túatha Dé and divinities such as the Morrígan. It is clear that many of these sacred mounds were adopted or continued as ritual centers by peoples living around them long after their builders were gone. In a sense, to place the Gods of one's tribe into these pre-existing monuments is part of the way in which a culture claims a landscape; at the same time, the myths of the Celtic Gods also seem to encode fragments of remembrance about the origins of the monuments themselves.

Generally speaking, the funerary mounds may include stone-lined chambers and passages in a variety of configurations over which a great mound of earth has been raised. The base of the mound is sometimes reinforced by a cerb of large stones to prevent the mound slipping down. The chambers usually contain evidence of burial: traces of human ash, bone, or sometimes whole graves. In some cases, multiple separate chambers are built into the mounds with passages leading from different entrances. Sometimes other graves are found inserted at a later period. These earthen mounds, grown over by the grasses and herbs of the landscape, become in essence human-made hills—hills which contain the remnants of ancestral dead. They form a landscape which is ancestral on a physical level; both shaped by and containing the presence of ancestors. In many places, there is evidence that the tombs were not closed permanently, but were revisited again and again over long periods of time, to inter the remains of the dead and likely for other ritual purposes as well. In this sense, some of the largest of these may be more properly seen as funerary temples, rather than simply tombs, as the community seems to have continued to engage with them as ritual centers long after the construction and initial burial of the dead.[46] The Brúg na Bóinne (Newgrange) is a fine example of this blending of early pre-Celtic megalithic architecture into Irish Celtic

46 Ó hÓgáin 1999 14

myth. It is a great chambered tomb dating to about 3000 BCE, in the Neolithic era. The primary interior chamber contains four large hollowed stones which appear to have once contained cremated bone from multiple individuals.[47] The site is deeply connected in Irish myth to the Dagda; it is said to be his home, and bequeathed to his son Óengus, also known as Mac ind Óc. Stories and poems associate it with his marriage to both Bóann and the Morrígan.[48] In light of the Dagda's mythic association with the site, the carved basin stones might remind us of the mighty cauldron ascribed to him in the legends of the Túatha Dé.

The Morrígan, too, is said to have made her home at the Brúg, "after the battle of Mag Tuired."[49] We have little record of how she may have been venerated here, but evidence of continued votive offerings has been found at the site, dating well into the early centuries CE, including valuable goods such as coins and jewelry, as well as animal bones indicating food or sacrificial offerings.[50] A part of the Brúg na Bóinne landscape, likely a rath of some kind, was once called "the Rampart of the Morrígan", though we cannot say what if any ritual activity took place there. It appears from the evidence that rituals honoring the ancestors and enshrining the remains of newly dead took place in the great funerary temple, along with votive offerings of food and valuables. In her connection to the site, the Morrígan might have been among the deities honored in such rites during the Iron Age and later periods.

The Irish mythology records traces of a belief in a kind of recurring conflict between the Otherworldly beings such as the Túatha Dé and the human inhabitants of the land (or between the Túatha Dé and the Fomoiri), which results in the destruction of crops and fertility until it is settled either by battle or through a contract of peace. In one instance of this theme, as recorded in *Fingen's Night Watch*, the specific divinities involved in mediating this type of conflict are the Morrígan, Bodb, Midir, and Óengus Mac ind Óg (the son of the Dagda)—all of whom are associated with major *síd* mound sites in the Irish landscape, such as the Brúg.[51] It is very likely that rites would have been enacted and offerings made at these sites as part of a ritual cycle to protect the land and its resources for the human community. As the Morrígan stands in

47 Waddell 2014 15
48 Gwynn 2008 11, Stokes 1894 292
49 Gwynn 2008 11
50 Waddell 2014 31
51 Borsje 2009 186

clear relationship both as an inhabitant of the *síd* and as a protector of the land in these myths, we can expect that she could have been a focus of such cult activity.

Rath and Temple

Ireland's great royal centers, rather than single structures, represent sacred landscapes which include large ring enclosures, ceremonial routeways, funerary mounds, building remnants, and other structures linked together by ritual use. Centers of this type in Ireland linked to the Morrígna include Temair (Tara), Emain Macha (Navan), Brúg na Bóinne (Newgrange), and Cruachan (Rathcroghan), but there are many others. The ritual focus of these sites is often centered around kingship and sovereignty, as they tended to function as gathering-places for the periodic tribal gathering known as the *óenach*, at which event feasts, kingship rites and law-courts were held, along with horse-races, divinatory and devotional rituals, marriages, livestock trading, and merchant fairs.

Emain Macha has been discussed above, and was the major royal center for Ulster, deeply linked with the cult of Macha. The *Dindshenchas* stories giving Macha's tutelary connection with the site emphasize again and again that her tomb is the basis for the site's name and sacred history.[52] The great mound of Navan itself, however, is not actually a funerary mound but a large subterranean shrine, sanctuary, or royal hall of some sort.[53] Within the mound, a great central pillar is surrounded by concentric rings of vertical wooden posts (over 280 of them) set in the ground. Archaeological scholarship seems divided on whether this structure was a roofed and walled building, an open-sided roofed structure, or a constructed *nemeton* or sacred grove. The structure was very carefully laid out and raised, filled in with cairn stones and then the wooden structure inside burned, before the entire cairn was covered with earth to create the mound.[54] Given that this structure was raised at great effort and expense and never occupied, it clearly represents a ritual structure rather than a domestic one. We do not know just what its function was, nor whether it was ever used in ritual

52 Gwynn 1924 124, 308; Stokes 1893 481

53 Funerary interments are present elsewhere within the Navan complex, nearby the temple mound, however.

54 Lynn, McSparron & Moore 2002 9-10; Waddell 2014 96-102

before being burnt and buried. It is possible that its entire function represents an example of the sacrifice of valuable things to the Otherworld by destroying them, and that by building the temple and then burning and burying it, it was understood to then exist in the Otherworld for the use of the divinities there. The dates of its construction and burial accord very closely with the time-frame of Emain's myths, according to tradition set in the last centuries BCE to first century CE. These myths do record the building of a great house quite similar in description to the one inside the temple mound, and also contain tales of the burning of an important royal building.[55]

Surrounding the great temple mound is a rath. This is an earthwork fortification similar to those seen at many Iron Age Celtic sites in both Ireland and elsewhere, comprised of a ditch cut into the earth, with the rampart next to it built up using the earth cut from the ditch. Interestingly, at Emain Macha, as at other ritual sites of its kind, the ditch is internal and the bank outside it—the opposite configuration to that seen in the case of occupied domestic sites and military fortifications.[56] Here, rather than protecting from physical attack from outside, the intention seems to be containment of spiritual forces within the sacred enclosure. This pattern of reversal signals sacred, Otherworldly spaces and we will see it in a number of other temple sites. Nearby, stands a lake now known as Loughnashade, and this lake clearly featured in cult activity, as many deposited artifacts have been found in it.

Temair (Tara) as well is steeped in kingship mythologies, and this is reflected throughout its landscape. The Morrígna appear to be less centrally connected to Temair in the myths, but the presence of divine horse names and rites does link the site to a cult of the sovereignty Goddess in horse form, related to that seen at Emain Macha. A river Gabhra, "White Mare", flows between Temair's hills and near sacred monuments there.[57] The well and river named Nemnach and Nith, as mentioned above, appear to connect Némain and Néit to the site as well.[58] In mythology, the Mound of Hostages at Temair is used by the Morrígna as a place from which to cast their spells of battle sorcery against the Fir Bolg, suggesting that such a place may have been

55 Lynn, McSparron & Moore 2002 8
56 Lynn, McSparron & Moore 2002 7, Waddell 2014 72
57 Waddell 2014 124
58 Macalister 1919 236

thought to be a source for spiritual power. It, too, is a funerary mound containing a passage tomb.[59]

Temair also illuminates something profound about the nature of these sacred enclosures and temples. Waddell points out that its ancient name, Temair, comes from the Indo-European root **tem-*, "to cut", and is reflected in names for sacred enclosures throughout related cultures, such as the Greek *temenos*, and the Latin *templum*, from which our English word "temple" derives.[60] Thus, the original and primary act of defining a sacred space by setting it apart from the outside world may have been the cutting of the boundary ditch and the creation of the rath at sites such as Temair, Emain Macha, and elsewhere. The usage of the term *temair* to mean any prominent place may relate to this early meaning, the marking out of a sacred place by cutting its boundary.

Temples of Britain and Gaul

Though separated geographically and showing differences in use from the Irish model, the temples and sanctuaries of Britain and Gaul may have something to teach us about the cults of ancient Celtic divinities. They show elements of a dominant pattern seemingly common throughout the Celtic peoples in the siting and construction of shrines and temples, and are interesting both in their parallels and their differences from Irish sanctuaries. Fundamental to each is the sacred enclosure, marked out by a rath usually consisting of a ditch and bank, sometimes also with a wooden palisade. As with the Irish sanctuaries, this sacred enclosure is a primary and consistent feature; Brunaux marks it as Indo-European in origin and typical to the La Tène Celtic sanctuary.[61] Inside this sacred enclosure, the ritual structure of the shrine or temple is centered, and the whole tends to be sited on a topographically prominent place.

In particular, some of the Gaulish sanctuaries that appear to have been involved with cults of battle or of kingship are of special interest in understanding the cults of deities related to the Morrígna. As these sanctuaries generally did not include written inscriptions indicating the names of the deities worshiped within them, we cannot assume that

59 Fraser 1915 27
60 Waddell 2014 129
61 Brunaux 1988 25

they represent a cult of the Morrígna in any direct way. However, they may illuminate something of broader Celtic patterns of religion as pertaining to deities of war and sovereignty.

Roquepertuse

The Roquepertuse sanctuary was an Iron Age Celtic or Celto-Ligurian stone structure built on a raised platform against a steep cliff, and containing large statues of heroic warriors, along with carved stone heads and imagery of horses, birds, and snakes. Its most famous feature is a great, double stone portico of three uprights and two large lintels, into which were carved stone heads as well as niches for the display of actual severed heads. Above, a massive statue of a long-necked bird overlooked the portal—a carrion or predatory bird.[62] The bird's image is echoed by incised and painted carrion bird motifs on the pillars of the sanctuary. Prominent carvings and sculptures of horses, warriors, and heads also adorned the sanctuary. The display and curation of preserved heads and skulls seems to have been a major practice here, including heads showing evidence of physical injury. Archaeologists interpret the sanctuary's function as one relating to funerary honoring of elite warrior dead, heroic ancestors, and possibly kingship as well.[63]

Gournay

Some similar features are present at other Gaulish sanctuaries including one located at Gournay, in south-eastern France. Gournay, thought to be dedicated to Gods associated with war, dates from the early La Tène era and was in use until the time of the Roman conquest.[64] It featured the characteristic boundary ditch and palisade, defining the sacred enclosure and centering on an inner sanctum with a primary large central pillar and a series of sacrificial pits or "hollow altars" inside a shrine enclosure, which may also have been roofed.[65] At some points

62 Armit 2012 143. Earlier scholars sometimes interpreted it as a goose; with better reconstruction techniques, this view has generally been replaced by identification as a carnivorous bird such as a carrion bird or bird of prey, due to its hooked beak and long claws.

63 Armit 2012 145, Aldhouse-Green 2010 133, Waddell 2014 148

64 Brunaux 1988 13

65 Brunaux 1988 15

in its development, the shrine enclosure seems to have been rounded or ovoid, at others rectangular, possibly resulting from Greco-Roman influence. As at Emain Macha, it was nearby a large pool that likely became part of cult activity. The presence of great numbers of weapons and armor pieces, evidently war trophies, displayed on the palisade and then deposited into the ditch has been interpreted as evidence that the sanctuary was dedicated to deities and rituals of warfare.[66]

Ribemont

Related to the warrior and head cult functions, Ribemont sanctuary appears to have been a funerary temple in central France, roughly contemporary with the other Gaulish sanctuaries described above and near to Gournay. Along with the characteristic ditch and bank defining the sacred enclosure, it featured a huge ossuary—a shrine structure constructed entirely out of human bones, weapons and armor parts and, containing a central posthole filled with cremated human ash.[67] Along the bank of the sacred enclosure, hundreds of partly dismembered, headless skeletons were found, apparently in preparatory stages toward the bones being attached to the ossuary shrine. Here we appear to be seeing warrior excarnation, with the heads removed for display and curation somewhere (possibly similar to that seen at Roquepertuse), the bodies exposed to the Gods in carrion bird form, and the bones finally incorporated into the shrine itself. Brunaux suggests that rather than a grisly scene of mass sacrifice, this shrine represents a rite of funerary heroization.[68]

No inscriptions have been found to link these Gallic temples to any deity by name. Given the pervasive association among the Gauls as well as the Irish Celts of warfare, warrior rituals, and head cult activity with raven-form deities such as Cathubodua, Badb, and the Morrígan, and the presence of warrior iconography and the giant carrion bird, it is certainly plausible to imagine a Gaulish cognate such as Cathubodua, being among the Gods venerated in these shrines.

Interestingly, several of these Gaulish sanctuaries (including Gour-

66 Brunaux 2001 54-58
67 Brunaux 1988 17
68 Brunaux 1988 19

nay and Ribemont) were carefully destroyed and covered over by earthen mounds, in some ways paralleling the cairn covering at Emain Macha. The sacrificial pits were filled, cult pillars and structures burned. The walls of the bone shrine at Ribemont were gently leveled without damaging the bones and even leaving some of them still locked together in their original stacking pattern. Sanctuary enclosure ditches were filled in and the whole area covered over with soil.[69] Similar ritual destruction and burying of shrines is documented at a variety of Gaulish shrines at the Gallic War period. When Caesar wrote about the Gaulish religion, he described "constructed mounds" (*tumulos exstructos*) as objects of worship, and it is very likely that these constructed mounds were the very sanctuaries we have seen, ritually destroyed and buried in advance of his conquest, possibly to prevent desecration.[70] It would seem that the destruction and burial of the Gaulish shrines was undertaken for different reasons than the Irish; Emain Macha was not, to our knowledge, facing conquest and the temple structure may not even have seen any direct human use in the brief time between its construction and subsequent burial and burning. Nevertheless, the parallel remains striking and seems to indicate something in the cultural repertoire of Celtic religions—that ritual destruction and burial of a temple was a known method by which the sanctity of a place might be enshrined or protected.

The House of the Red God

In the early Irish text, *The Destruction of Dá Derga's Hostel*, the Hostel itself is characterized as a focal point for fateful, Otherworldly events and characters and is given numinous qualities of its own. This has led some scholars to speculate that it may allude to a folk memory of an Irish temple or cult house. Its description includes fantastical features such as seven doorways into the house, with seven rooms between each, "but there is only one door-valve on it, and that valve is turned to every doorway to which the wind blows," perhaps suggesting the circular plan seemingly typical for Irish temples.[71] The river Dodder is said to flow through the house, as does the road on which it sits, fea-

69 Brunaux 1988 33
70 Brunaux 1988 33
71 Stokes 1910 64

tures associated with ancient temples in literature.[72] Within the house, many rooms are described; these have been read by a few scholars as suggesting shrine compartments dedicated to different divinities. This interpretation is suggested by Ross and Macalister, though it should be noted that both authors are known to take liberties in imaginatively interpreting the material.[73]

Vivid pagan iconography with sacrifice themes emerge in descriptions of some of the rooms, most notably that of the triple Badb.[74] King Conaire's description of the gifts he has given to Dá Derga, the owner of the house, could read like a list of offerings, and closely matches in many respects the kinds of deposits that are actually found at Celtic sanctuary sites in both Ireland and elsewhere: "a hundred kine of the drove [cattle]... a hundred fatted swine... a hundred mantles made of close cloth... a hundred blue-coloured weapons of battle... ten red, gilded brooches... ten vats good and brown [of ale]... ten thralls [slaves]... ten querns... thrice nine hounds all-white in their silvern chains... a hundred racehorses..."[75]

Dá Derga himself would appear to be a God. The title *Dá* is "a god", and the name together translates as "Red God". Among the Dagda's bynames is Rúad Ro-fhessa, "Red One of Great Knowledge", and so red names and imagery are well established for him.[76] The text describes Dá Derga wearing a short, hooded cloak extending only to his rump and carrying a heavy club, as are his warriors with him—descriptors that are almost diagnostic for the Dagda in Irish literature.[77]

72 Stokes 1910 82 n. On rivers flowing through shrines, see Tech Mairisen, "House of Mairisiu", a purported ancient shrine at Tara similarly associated with the Níth and noted in Macalister 1939 261. The flowing of a stream through such a temple may be linked to its sovereignty function, as the river in *Dá Derga's Hostel* dries up when Conaire is facing his loss of kingship and his doom. See Chapter 13 discussions on sovereignty for further exploration of waters, kings, and magically induced thirst.

73 Ross 1996 85 and Macalister 1939 261. Macalister's interpretation of one-leggedness and grotesque appearance as indicating idols carved of wood is fanciful, but the points about the arrangement of shrine compartments and magical, Otherworldly qualities of the Hostel are intriguing.

74 Stokes 1910 87

75 Stokes 1910 62. For a full exploration of Celtic sacrificial practice, see Chapter 12.

76 Stokes 1897 150

77 Stokes 1910 69

Dá Derga is also said to keep a great cauldron in the Hostel which feeds all the men of Ireland, reminiscent of the Dagda's cauldron.[78] The related story *Dá Choca's Hostel,* following a closely parallel narrative to *Dá Derga's Hostel,* also gives a magical food-distributing cauldron as one of the features of that hostel.[79] It may also be relevant that the Brúg na Bóinne (Newgrange), the Dagda's home in Irish myth, is often called the "Hostel of the Boyne", or sometimes the "Mound of the Hostel", as the very concept of a hostel as a place of plenty and hospitality is deeply connected to the Dagda.[80]

Thus if the Hostel of Dá Derga is possibly a survival of the image of an ancient temple named for and dedicated as the house of the Dagda, it will not surprise us to find the triple Badb (whom as we have seen, the Ulster cycle tradition identifies with the Morrígan herself as the Dagda's wife) occupying it along with a host of Otherworldly beings and spirits who would have received offerings and sacrifices in the temple. Incidentally, the Hostel, as we have seen with several of the historic Gaulish sanctuaries and the one at Emain Macha, is finally destroyed by burning, though no mention of burial or mound-building is recorded for it.

Living Practice: Engaging with Land and Place

We have seen how deeply tied the families of Celtic Gods are to land, territory, tribe, and place. We have seen how the Morrígna and their relations often manifest as tutelary Goddesses tied to the landscapes and ancient peoples of Ireland. We see how landscape shapes story, and myth frames landscape. For a great many of us, entering into a practice of Celtic polytheism brings paradox. I write this, a dedicant of an Irish Goddess, living on the West Coast of the North American continent. At the time of this writing, I have not yet had the opportunity even to visit Ireland. If we ourselves are not of and in the landscapes of the Gods, how do we engage in practice with them with honesty and authenticity?

78 Stokes 1910 69
79 Stokes 1900a 315
80 Ó hÓgáin 1999 109

The Sovereignty of Spirits

Polytheism, as I understand it, is a practice rooted in relationality. It is, at its heart, the practice of being in relationship with Gods, spirits and other kinds of divine and spiritual beings. The experience of polytheist practice leads to a worldview that tends toward both animism and localism.

Practicing relationship with any group of deities or spirits hones the senses and opens us to the awareness of just how many other living spirits surround us everywhere. This experience is animism: the recognition that the world is alive with beings, that everything around us, including that which may appear inanimate, partakes of that life, and is possessed of a spirit with which we can engage in relationship. Spirits emerge from everywhere, the deeper we delve into our practices. We may be introduced by our Gods to other Gods, to spirit allies they wish us to know. Ancestors we didn't know how to hear before may begin to speak to us. The senses and skills we train to hear the voices of our Gods reveal spirits haunting the places we go, emerging from the landscapes where we live. Voices whispering from the hills. Someone stirring in the lake. I hear a voice—did someone die here?

Polytheist practice leads to the experience of animism, if we are paying attention: a world full of Gods, spirits, ancestors, living creatures, living places. Soon, that experience in turn leads to a kind of localism—an awareness of the shaping importance of context. Nature spirits aren't just nature spirits, and fairies aren't just fairies. They are this spirit here, and that one there. The reluctant fairy we keep seeing peering from the shadows of that thorn hedge. That mountain we visited has an old, watchful spirit in it. This valley that holds the memories of everything that has happened, has lived and died within it. Gods and spirit beings may not be bound in bodies, but they still emerge from *somewhere,* and not vaguely everywhere. Beings of land and nature emerge from landscapes, or landscape features in a particular place. Spirit beings and fairies emerge from Otherworld gateways in the spiritual landscape. Ancestors and animal spirits emerge from beings who lived and died, or from populations of beings in a particular ecology or culture. Gods emerge from cultural flowerings that took place in a particular region at a particular period in history, shaped by both the land and the people who named and worshiped them. This becomes part of who they are, just as the family, landscape, place, and culture that we each grow in is part of who we are. When we begin to engage in relationship with spiritual beings, agency is key. To enter into genuine relationship as one being speaking with another is to recognize that that being has its own history, context, and agenda, independent of our own. It has agency, in other words. Polytheism, as a religious practice of relationship, can only begin when we recognize and honor the agency and sovereignty of spiritual beings. Their lives and life force are not ours to command; their homes, landscapes, gateways, contexts, and histories are not there for our pleasure or even for our teaching. They live in the world as we do, existing for their own purposes, pursuing their own destinies, in sovereign relationship to their landscapes and contexts.

Begin Where You Are

To enter into relationship with any being in a polytheist practice demands an awareness of context. We have to begin where we are, by recognizing our own context. I am not a native Irish person—I did not grow up eating from the soil of the land where the Morrígan was born, watching the sun rise over the hills of her breasts, or walking the roads where the poets who recorded her words walked. I will always experience her from the position of non-locality, from the diaspora of devotion. That is my context.

As soon as we make the shift to awareness of spiritual agency and sovereignty, the need to begin with relationship to our own context and locality makes itself clear. This is where we begin: in relationship to our own lived context, our own landscapes, with their histories and spirits. We all live somewhere. This means our lives are intersecting, right now, with the lives and sovereign spaces of spiritual beings inhabiting and embodying our landscapes and places. It means every time we engage in devotional or magical practice, we are affecting everything that lives around us. If I invoke an ancient war Goddess from Ireland in my backyard, I have invited her also into the lives of the land spirits, fairy folk, local ancestors, and every other spirit who shares the area with me. Have I engaged these local spirits, introduced myself and my practice to them? Have I given them the courtesy of an offering, the hand of friendship and the invitation to be an ally? Asked them if there is anything they need from me?

We begin in relationship to our own local spirits. The first thing we should do in any place, whether it is our home or simply a place we will be working, is to address the spirits. Speak directly to the spirits of the land, to the ancestors of place, and to any other spirits who live here. Greet them, honor them. Introduce yourself, who you are, any lineage you represent, and what the nature of your work is. Acknowledge you are sharing the space with them. Make offerings. Ask for their consent and support in the work you have to do. And listen: listen for communication about what is needed to align your practice with the needs of your local spirits. Seek to understand how you can feed the land in reciprocity for its hospitality to you.

Be willing to make this a regular practice; relationships develop over time. In my practice, I begin every major ritual with a greeting and offering to local and land spirits, and I maintain a practice of periodically checking-in with them to learn what needs they have, how my practice is impacting or benefiting them, how I can be an ally to them. Over time these friendships with local spirits grow, and you can find them to be great allies who will help protect and support you in your work. It is always better to have friends in the Otherworld.

Sacred Landscapes

Every landscape has its sacred places, its power centers, its Otherworldly gateways. Some sacred sites are naturally occurring in the shape of the land and the visible and hidden forces within it. In other places, sacred sites develop from the embedding of human stories, religious practices, and ancestors into the landscape. While those of us living outside the Celtic homelands may not have access to the sacred landscapes associated with the Morrígna in antiquity, in practice we will find that our landscapes have their own places of power where presence and devotion are strongest.

High Places: As we saw in the ancient tales, the Morrígna are often drawn to high places—crags, hilltops, high rock outcrops. Where in Ireland, many of the hills and heights associated with them are not natural hills but constructed tomb-mounds, in my experience here in North America, naturally occurring heights still function as powerful sites for veneration.

Hollow Places: Just as they are seen in high places, so they also haunt the hollow places in the landscape. We have seen that *geniti glinne* "spectral women of the glens" is a term for Otherworldly females closely associated with the Morrígna.[81] And, of course, caves and underground places of all kinds can be sacred to the Morrígna, most especially to the Morrígan herself. In addition to naturally occurring caves, I have also found Otherworldly spiritual forces to be especially present in hollows, ravines, and such sites in the land where we can begin to feel the land over us. These places often harbor natural gateways into the subterranean Otherworld.

Waters: Lakes and springs also harbor natural Otherworld gateways and will often become places we can more readily contact spirit allies and Gods. Springs often carry flows of power within the land that upwell along with the water, so that where these waters break the surface, there is also an upwelling of spiritual force. Many naturally occurring lakes contain such springs in their depths, bringing this gateway function into the lake. Other lakes may be glacial in origin, which generally means they are carved very deeply into the land, also opening gateways in their depths. The Morrígna themselves do not have direct folkloric ties to lakes, but experience has shown that as strong gateway sites to Otherworld forces, they serve well as places of devotional contact.

Historic Places: It has been my experience that, having been brought into different lands by devotees, the Morrígna are present in places which carry embedded histories of conflict or death. Although in places such as North America, these sites do not carry the weight of Celtic ancestral tradition, nonetheless they seem to be readily adopted. I have experienced theophanies of the Morrígna dwelling in graveyards here, and others have spoken of old battle sites carrying their presences. Soil from any battlefield site carries a special charge sacred to the Morrígna and can be brought to other sites to sanctify them.

Sacred sites are also created by our continued devotion. All the ancient tomb mounds, standing stones, constructed souterrains, shrine sites, and the like were created and embedded into the landscape by human devotion. Any place where we pour out devotion or perform spiritual work for long enough can become saturated with these forces and begin to take on its own spiritual gravity as a place of power. The land remembers everything we do, everything it receives. This process can occur surprisingly quickly: in only a few years of people gathering and making offerings in a place, it can become a place of great power.

---

81 See Chapter 4, above.

Histories of Place

Just as the ancient stories are embedded in the landscapes of the Celts, stories are embedded in your landscape, wherever you are. Places retain memory. Landscapes absorb the lives and histories of all who live and die within them and this becomes part of the fabric of the living world around us. For me, life as a white Euro-American polytheist on the North American continent is never absent from the context and history of violence and colonialism. I want to say a few words about this, as I think many of my readers may live in similar contexts.

When we talk about engaging local spirits and entering into relationship with the beings who inhabit your landscape, this means coming into relationship with the history of place, too. Histories of place here in North America are interwoven with the histories of the Native peoples who lived here first, and whose traditions, ancestors, spirits, and divinities are also part of the land. The theft of their territorial homelands, genocidal warfare and forced relocation, destruction of their cultures and traditions, and a deep legacy of brutality and continuing cultural hegemony are also part of these histories. In this continent, we live on a great reeking battlefield. Even in places where this specific legacy is not relevant, similar dynamics can occur: histories of environmental destruction, great social trauma or depopulation and the like—any great change leaves its mark in the spirit world.

Our approach to relationship with the spiritual landscape has to take account of these histories and of our place relative to them. We need to tread carefully around this, with awareness that the land and spirit world may harbor wounds, traumas, hostilities, and damage remaining from these histories. It may or may *not* be our place to attempt to heal these wounds. In some cases this might be what the spirits ask for, but in other cases they may want nothing more than to be left alone by us—especially in places where we represent the lineage and heritage of a historic oppressor. Thus when I speak of engaging in relationship with local spirits, ancestors, and land, what I *don't* mean is white people appointing ourselves Great White Guardians of the Land and presuming to be able to undo any damage that may be present. What I *don't* mean is appropriating Native traditions of practice, or Native sacred sites, into our own practices, without being invited to do so by members of those cultures. Living in a landscape does not grant us the authority to adopt and appropriate cultural traditions belonging to other people within that landscape.

What I do mean is asking how we can be in right relationship to our local spirit world and to other cultures and traditions, and being willing to listen to the answers we receive. We are, no matter where we are, always an ambassador of our lineage and traditions with respect to other beings.

The Diaspora of Devotion

Histories of invasion, population movement, conquest, and subjugation are not unique to North America, of course. The history and mythic narratives of the Celts are in many respects stories of invasion and social movement. Whether it occurs through violent conquest or gradual absorption, populations shift and move and their Gods and spirits follow them. Populations adopt new Gods, too, and new centers of worship grow. Diaspora and migration is written into the story of Celtic religion. We who worship Celtic Gods now are a chapter in a long migration story. The Morrígan and her sisters may have been born in the western countries of the Iron Age Celtic world, but they have traversed the globe.

This is not to say that there is no difference between the religious practice of a worshiper born to the Celtic homelands for whom these really are the Gods of their landscape and their family lineage, and the practice of someone like myself living as the descendant of immigrants on another continent. The Gods have non-local agency, and can manifest where they choose and in relationship to people anywhere, without regard to ancestry or place. But our devotions and traditions of practice will always be shaped by our specific local contexts. This is the meaning of local cultus—a phenomenon that was profoundly important in the ancient world. Gods manifest themselves in different ways to different people and in different places, and our local cults of worship will not be uniform, nor should we expect them to be.

For the devotional polytheist, authenticity comes through relationship and through committed study and practice. To be authentic in our practice means being truthful to who we are and where we come from, and bringing honest devotion to our Gods from that place. We should seek to study and understand the deep history of the hearth cultures of our Gods, but not pretend to be anyone other than who and where we are. We can and should develop local cults of devotion that are adapted to the contexts we live and work within, whether that context is the doorstep of your ancestors within the Celtic homelands, or the broad, diverse horizons of the Celtic diaspora.

Hospitality and the Spirit World

Many of us will travel, at some time in our lives, to visit the homelands of the Túatha Dé. When we do, principles of guesting and hospitality apply—as in fact they apply any time we travel and engage with new landscapes and spirit ecologies anywhere in the world.

As travelers to any place, before we even leave our doorstep, we should seek to learn something about the customs, culture, and spiritual traditions of the place we will be visiting. In visiting, our first duty is to be authentic to our position as guests, which means first honoring the sovereignty of local beings within their landscape. On entering a place, our first practices should be to greet the land and the local spirit world—the Gods, ancestors, spirits of place, and other beings present. To introduce ourselves and speak to who we are, the traditions or lineages we represent. To make a friendship offering. To convey who or what has brought us to that place, and what we hope to do while there. Before assuming we are entitled to anything in our travels, and especially if we plan to be doing any kind of ritual or spirit work in a place, we should be asking for safe passage and guest-right, for hospitality, and for permission to engage in whatever our work there is. We should be asking for guidance on how to conduct our work, and how to give back to the place and spirits who are hosting us. We should be continually renewing our reverencing and extension of friendship with offerings and communication, and we should give thorough thanks-offerings upon leaving.

Dedicating Space

A few words are needed here about worship spaces. The terminologies in use by many people in current Pagan practice are muddied. When we come to creating worship spaces in our homes or other places, it will help to clarify meanings and approaches to this work.

Altars and Shrines: An altar is a place for operative spiritual workings. Traditionally, in ancient times, the primary use of an altar was for the preparing of offerings, typically sacrifices. A shrine is something different: a home for a spiritual being, such as a God.[82] We say that our Gods are "housed" in shrines. Shrine space is dedicated to the divinity who lives there. Their presence is ritually invoked and seated in the shrine, usually in an image such as a statue. Offerings may be placed in or before the shrine when they are offered to the divinity within it. A great many modern practitioners simply have one hybrid space—an altar, which may have devotional images on it, but is also used for ritual workings, to house one's magical tools, etc. We may find it helpful to develop greater discernment about how we dedicate and use these spaces. It is respectful, and greatly more effective in a devotional relationship, to give the Gods dedicated shrine spaces. This is not only a beautiful devotional gift, it also helps to more effectively seat their presences, by creating a well-defined "container" which can be filled by their presence.

Temples: As the cults of the old Gods are still gradually recovering from long centuries of loss and erasure under Christianity and modernism, few practitioners now have or have access to temples. To create and maintain a temple demands a very great deal of religious dedication and skill, as well as enormous labor commitment. It is not simply a matter of having a shrine in our bedroom and calling it a temple. Temples are intentionally established and dedicated as devotional spaces and are, generally speaking, not hybridized with other uses. In the Celtic traditions, their physical structure was established in distinct ways (e.g. through reversal of the ordinary protective structures) in order to create a space that is not only sanctified, but itself stands in the Otherworld and can contain numinous forces and presences.

Care and Protection: All devotional and spiritual working spaces need a commitment to care and protection. This is especially true of shrines and temples. The houses of the Gods need to be maintained in good spiritual condition if we hope for the Gods to remain in them and be present with us. Purifications, cleansings, and banishings are needed before establishing a shrine to ensure it is spiritually clear and free of other presences. Cleansings should be renewed often—at least once per lunar cycle is often a good rhythm, unless we have been given other specifics by the individual deity. Protective spiritual wards to maintain the sanctity of the space and control what kinds of presences can enter are especially important in temple spaces; shrines may need them too,

82 My thanks to Theanos Thrax for improving my articulation of these terms.

depending on the nature of the room or space the shrine is within and whether it has its own protections.

Sacred Enclosure: The Rath

Here I will share the practice I use for defining and consecrating the sacred enclosure. This method has been conceived and developed within the ritual practice of the Coru Cathubodua Priesthood. We refer to this as the creation of the rath: a system for preparing, defining, consecrating, and protecting the ritual and worship spaces we work within. The rath method attempts to reach beyond the more modern, Wiccan and ceremonialist modes of "circle casting", variants of which are used in many Pagan ritual contexts. With this system, we seek draw on the physical and spiritual structures of ancient Celtic shrines and sacred enclosures for our model, and to situate our ritual space fully within the local spiritual landscape in collaboration with local spirits.

Initial Offerings & Saining: We begin with offerings to the land spirits and a request for support in establishing the space and in the work to be done within it. Other local spirits in addition to land spirits can be included as appropriate (e.g. house spirits if indoors, etc.) Since the rath will be raised by cutting into the spiritual body of the land, we make a request for the land spirits to guide our hands in the construction process—to ensure we delve deep enough but not too deep, and that we build the rath strongly. Here the space is also cleansed; this is called "saining". Blessed water is our preferred method. Water can be blessed with prayer and the addition of salt, alcoholic spirits such as whiskey, a blessed oil, purifying herbs, or a piece of silver in the water. An effective method of space cleansing is to sprinkle the blessed water with a sprig of protective or cleansing herbs, but sprinkling with the hand works as well.

Rath Construction: Having prepared the space and gained the backing and support of the local spirits, we now raise the rath. Its structure follows the Celtic sacred enclosure system: the space is set apart by a ditch cut into the land surrounded by a raised bank and palisade. In most cases, absent the ability to build a permanent enclosure, the rath is a purely spiritual structure rather than a physical one. It is created by cutting into the spiritual body of the land, delving into the subterranean Otherworld to form an enclosing ditch. The land-forces released by this cutting are shaped outward and upward to raise the bank and palisade surrounding the ditch. How does this work? The ditch, since it is cut into the subterranean level, places the ritual space in contact with the Otherworld; the bank and palisade draw upon those powers to create a protective barrier. Together, the ditch and bank work to contain spiritual forces within, while shielding and separating the space from the outside world. A gate would usually be created so that the ritual space has an entry and exit point. This gate is shaped from the same land-forces raised to build the bank and palisade.

Apotropaic Guardian Spirits: Our practice relies on collaboration with spirit allies to act as guardians, protecting and watching over the sacred enclosure, just as in the ancient temples, apotropaic guardians were placed in the enclosure ditches, palisades, and gates. Your guardian spirits may be totemic animal spirits, familiar spirits, fairy beings, ancestral spirits, heroic spirits, divinities, or any of many other kinds of spirits. Each practitioner or group will have their own relationships with spirit allies who may be of help; what works best is to consult your own spiritual allies and ask for those who wish to work with you in this regard. In the rath sequence, once having cut the ditch and raised the palisade and gate, we call upon our spirit allies who have agreed to serve as guardians, invoking them into their positions in the rath. It is important to position guardian spirits in each dimension: in the ditch to protect from below, on the palisade to protect from above and outside, and on the gateway to guard the entry.

Activation: Finally, the whole system is activated by pouring an offering into the ditch at the gateway. This offering is to feed the guardian spirits in their work, and at the same time, its release into the ditch at the key access point serves to charge up and activate the entire system with spiritual power. When this practice is undertaken indoors and an offering can't be poured on the ground, a bowl can be placed on the floor to receive poured offerings.

Deconstructing: When it becomes necessary to close a ritual space, the process moves in reverse. First, another offering is poured for the apotropaic guardians, to thank them for their work and support. The rath is then brought down, beginning at its gate; the spiritual forces raised to shape gate, palisade and bank are released and redirected back down into the subterranean space opened by the ditch. A final saining is done to cleanse the space of any spiritual residues from our work. The effort here is to restore the space and land-forces toward their undisturbed condition. Finally, to thank the spirits of land and place, and to make amends for the disturbance created by the construction, a final offering is made. In our practice, this final offering is always of milk, cream, or butter, since these hold healing and restorative qualities in Irish tradition.

This system brings together the central elements I have sought to highlight in this chapter: in it, we engage with land and spirits of place, and we seek to respect the hospitality and sovereignty of the spirit world, while practicing good spiritual cleanliness and responsible safeguarding. In a permanent or long-term sanctuary context, it would likely be necessary to reinforce the rath and renew the offerings on a regular basis. It is, as I have said, a work in progress, and your practice may vary from our own as engagement with land and place bring you into relationship with the spiritual ecology around you. Each practitioner and cult group represents another unique nexus of tradition, experience, and locality.

11

Iconography and Devotion

We turn now to the subject of devotion. Within their sacred spaces and practices, how did the ancients worship the Gods? What might devotional practice have looked like for those who venerated the Morrígna?

Sacred Images

It has been often said that the Celts did not make images of their Gods. Greek historian Diodorus Siculus tells of the Gaulish king Brennus who laughed at the Greeks for venerating great lifelike stone statues of their Gods at Delphi.[1] This, and similar accounts, have been taken to indicate a general Celtic disdain for representational sacred iconography. And while this is not entirely true, it is certainly the case that images of the Gods from the ancient Celtic societies are relatively rare in comparison to Mediterranean contemporaries such as the Greeks and

1 Beck 2009 27

Romans. What imagery does exist of Celtic divinities from the ancient world is often either impossible to to clearly identify with a specific deity, or is late and heavily influenced by Roman or Christian models.

There are no statues, sculptures, or paintings made by the ancient pagan Celts which can be securely identified as the Morrígan or any member of the Morrígna group. However, rich artistic traditions did thrive among the pagan Irish as well as the other Celtic societies, and these have yielded many images which, while they may or may not actually represent the Morrígna, still enliven our understanding of how they would have been imagined and worshiped.

The Irish word *arracht* may shed some light on how the early Irish viewed spirits and their relationship to iconography. *Arracht* (usually in the plural, *arrachta*) often appears in the context of the group of battle spirits associated with appearances of the Morrígan and especially Badb. In some instances, Badb herself is called an *arracht*.[2] The word means "apparition, spectre, monster or demon", and it also means "idol, idolatrous image". It seems to have been used in the former sense more frequently in the heroic literature, and to be used in reference to idolatry primarily in the early Christian literature. This reflects Christian attitudes toward the pagan use of images to house and instantiate divinities. At the same time, it may also reflect something of the pagan usage it judges: that a spirit or divinity might be recognized both as a presence occupying a physical idol, as well as appearing elsewhere as a spectral presence which the Christian writers would identify as monstrous or demonic.

Pillars of Wood

The wooden pillar is a form of icon used in Irish cult practice from very ancient times, as well as elsewhere in many Indo-European societies. In some instances, this may have been a simple unadorned post. However, we know that in many cases it was the practice to carve simple humanoid images into wood pillars. Carved wooden figures have been found preserved from the Bronze and Iron Ages in Ireland, Britain, and the Continent.[3] These are usually iconographic rather than life-like in style, with simplified facial features (often called "crude" in earlier

2 O'Curry 1855 119
3 Ross 1996 460, Aldhouse-Green 2010 226

archaeological literature), often with large, staring eyes or an exaggerated mouth and a distinctive triangular head shape.

An example of such an icon is the wooden female figure excavated from Argyll, in the Irish-influenced Dál Riata area of Scotland. It was found surrounded by the remains of a wickerwork hut within which it seems to have been displayed and which may have been its shrine housing.[4] Such wooden images with human or animal features have also been found in Ireland, generally preserved in bogs. Scholars have suggested that the great central pillars at sites such as the Navan mound temple at Emain Macha may have similarly been carved into devotional images.[5] Central posts feature in several Gaulish sanctuaries as well and may have held devotional images.[6] As most such wooden pillar icons never survive the ages, just a few have been found, and none that can be identified with the Morrígna directly. We may reasonably imagine that such icons might have been in use in their worship, and such an image may be alluded to in *Dá Derga's Hostel,* where the triple Badb is seen "on the ridge-pole of the house,"[7] possibly describing a wooden image built high in the shrine structure.

Images in Stone

Unworked stones appear to have been venerated as living, sacred entities from a very early period. *Dindshenchas* lore and local Irish folklore speak of "talking stones", in which spirits were believed to dwell and which were given worship.[8] Folklore preserving a belief in the Otherworldly powers dwelling in stones and their ability to speak oracles appears to be quite ancient.[9] The Stone of Fál, at Tara, is a classic example of a talking stone, and was apparently at some time one of a triad of sacred stones there which were named, worshiped, and believed to have power to speak and act with special reference to rites of kingship.[10]

Such stone worship may stand behind the association of the Morrígan and Badb with pillar stones. Both are said on to perch in bird form

4 Ross 1996 460
5 Waddell 2014 96
6 Brunaux 1988 12, 25
7 Stokes 1910 87, O'Connor 2013 217
8 Gwynn 1924 297, Wood-Martin 1902 86
9 Ó hÓgáin 1999 22
10 Macalister 1919 329

on a pillar stone,[11] and the Morrígan comes "from the edge of a pillar" when she appears to a warrior before his death.[12] The association of spiritual entities with pillar stones may also be related to their funerary function; among other uses, pillar stones were raised as funerary monuments for the deaths of important individuals.[13] The *ogam*-carved stones used as lintels in the cave of Cruachan, the Morrígan's traditional home in Connacht, are thought to have originally been funerary pillar-stones.[14] We may be seeing the remnant of a belief that ancestral and Otherworldly spirits as well as Gods and Goddesses might dwell in stones, making them the focus of cult activity without the need for a likeness being carved into the stone.

Carved stone images do seem to have also been used by the ancient Celtic peoples. While the bulk of such sculpture is found in Britain and the Continent in post-Roman periods, there is some evidence for native Celtic use of carved stone images in pagan devotional cults, including in Ireland.

The Boa Island statues may represent examples of this tradition. This small island in Lough Erne, Ulster, is named after Badb, according to tradition (its older name Inis Badhbha having been Anglicized to become Boa Island.) A group of carved stones found in an old cemetery on the island appear to be pagan in nature, although they have not been scientifically dated and could belong to the Christian era. Two statues in particular are of interest and may possibly depict Badb herself or related deities. The larger, known as the Boa Island figure, is a double statue depicting two anthropomorphic entities back-to-back, each with arms crossed and with the distinctive triangular heads, wide, staring eyes and open mouths typical of Celtic devotional images.[15] Some scholars, though not all, have interpreted this couple as a male and female pair, noting a vertical protrusion on one that may suggest a

---

11 O'Rahilly 2010 174, Tymoczko 1981 61

12 Meyer 1910 16

13 An example in the literature, from the Destruction of Dind Rig: "'Come tomorrow', says Cobthach, 'that my tomb be raised by thee, and that my pillar-stone be planted, my assembly of mourning be held, and my burial-paean be performed; for I shall die swiftly,'" (Stokes 1901a 9).

14 Waddell 2014 63

15 Lowry-Corry 1932 202, Warner 2003 25. It is often incorrectly called a "Janus figure". Since the statue clearly shows two entities each with a pair of arms, and not a single entity with two faces, this designation is incorrect.

phallus, and what appears to be a vulval cleft, often seen on Iron Age Goddess statues, on the other. The supposedly female side of the statue also appears to have a protruding tongue within the wide mouth. Between the two, ornamental patterns possibly representing hair weave down the sides. A deep groove or channel is carved in the top between the two heads; its purpose is unknown, but it may represent a socket for attachment of something, or a channel for receiving sacrificial blood or other liquid offerings.[16] In the present day, a folk practice of leaving small offerings such as coins in the channel has developed.

Along with this double statue is another stone figure called the Lustymore figure, as it was originally found on the neighboring Lustymore Island and then later brought into the Boa Island group. Carved in a similar style, its gender is indeterminate, but its hands reach down and appear to grasp something.[17] The left eye of this statue is either incompletely carved or damaged, a feature which has led some to interpret it as Badb in the shape of a one-eyed crone. We cannot, however, know for certain.

Another statue containing two related entities back-to-back was found in the vicinity of Armagh, in Ulster. It appears to portray a warrior, with a helmet on the head, and the typical wide, staring eyes and prominent open mouth. Lines incised above the helm appear to radiate upward like a corona. The figure carved into the back of the idol is a beast, looking most like a wolf or dog, with large paws, a prominent muzzle raised and parted in an attitude of ferocity, and the radiating lines from the opposite figure forming spines or standing hair on the ridge of its back.[18] Again, the statue cannot be directly tied to any specific mythological figure. But it is difficult to suppress the thought of Cú Chulainn with his warrior's light, totemic dog/wolf imagery, and transformation into a beast-like form, just as the snarling beast appears to emerge from the warrior in the statue.

Related figures found near the origin of the Armagh idol include several more "beast" figures and a helmeted warrior who seems to grip his left arm, suggesting Nuada, the king of the Túatha Dé who lost his arm

16 Warner 2003 25

17 This posture has provoked comparisons to the "Sheela-Na-Gig" type, ancient carvings of female figures grasping prominently displayed vulvas; however, this comparison is probably not accurate as there is no indication of a vulva, let alone the prominence shown to that feature in Sheela-Na-Gigs.

18 Warner 2003 26

in battle and was given a silver arm to replace it. As with all the others, no concrete information exists to tie these statues to the mythological figures we are familiar with. It is clear, however, that the region must have held a cult center in the vicinity in which these idols figured.[19] It is possible that worship patterns at such a cult center focused on groups of statues such as these could have included veneration of the Morrígna, perhaps remembered in the name Inis Badhbha; though, as we have said, there is little direct evidence of it.

The Irish literature also records the veneration of statues in stone. A *Dindshenchas* story, versions of which are also found in some of the Annals, describes a great statue of a God called Crom Cruach (also spelled Crom Cróich or Cenn Crúaich), the chief idol in a cult center including twelve additional deities together at a place called Magh Slecht, and which is condemned and destroyed by Saint Patrick.[20] The twelve surrounding statues are said to be made of stone, but the central statue of Crom Cruach is said to be of gold, or of stone and covered in gold. The account has been contested as to the accuracy of the gruesome human sacrifice it portrays, and is very likely based on Biblical tales.[21] However, the core element of the veneration of a group of statues is not controversial, and may reflect actual pagan Irish practice.

Other Imagery

Outside Ireland, a few examples of cultic imagery exist which may be relevant to the cults of the Morrígna Goddesses and their British and Continental cognates.

We have touched on the sanctuary of Roquepertuse in Chapter 10 above on sanctuaries and temples. Here, a large sculpture of a carrion bird carved in stone dominates the sanctuary, presiding over the great double portico with its carved heads and skull niches. This sculpture would appear to represent the figure of a divinity related to death, excarnation, and the ritual veneration of heroic warrior dead—all themes that align closely with the Morrígna as known in Ireland. Similar imagery is found in Celtiberian funerary art depicting fallen warriors pre-

19 Warner 2003 26

20 *Dindshenchas*, quoted in Borsje 2007a 33; O'Donovan 2002 43.

21 Borsje 2007a 41

sided over and devoured by great carrion birds.[22] These images appear to form a common current across many ancient Celtic societies of a Goddess associated with war and warriors, appearing in carrion bird form and venerated in association with heroic, funerary, and ancestral cults.

Also possibly related, a small bronze votive figure of a bull with three unusual birds was found at Maiden Castle, England. The bull itself has three horns, and on its back are three small figures which appear to be birds with female heads or bird-like women.[23] Scholars parallel this figurine to the iconography of the Morrígan, who appears in triad and bird form, and has a special relationship with the great bull Donn Cúailnge, a semi-divine figure in bull form. It also suggests imagery found on Gallo-Roman altars depicting bulls with three cranes and titled Tarvos Trigaranus.[24]

Prayer and Invocation

The practice of prayer, that is, verbal supplication to a divinity, was another feature of Celtic religion. Little remains to show us the form of such prayers, but indications are that prayer would have been employed in the cult of the Morrígan. The *Dindshenchas* tell us that a druid, Tulchine, prayed to the Morrígan for help to marry a certain *síd* woman, Dil.[25] We read that "the Morrígan was good unto him", suggesting an ongoing devotional relationship within which Tulchine was able to ask for help and expect to receive it.

Other instances of prayer to the Gods are recorded in contexts that suggest prayer to the Morrígna could have been used in similar circumstances. In Ireland, Britain, and Gaul we see instances of Celtic tribes praying to war or tutelary Goddesses for aid before the start of battle. In the early medieval battles of Allen and Dun Bolg the Leinster forces are said to have "fervently prayed to St. Brighit that they might kill their enemies", and the specter of Brigit was seen over the battlefield terrifying the adversaries of the Leinstermen.[26] Similarly, before her final confrontation with the Roman forces, the British Queen Boudicca prayed to a

22 Armit 2012 143, 146, Aldhouse-Green 2010 240
23 Ross 1996 278, Olmsted 1994 270
24 Olmsted 1994 269
25 Stokes 1892 471
26 Stokes 1903 53, Mac Firbisigh 1860 41, 191

Goddess of battle and victory Andrasta ("the Unconquered"), imploring her "as one woman to another" for aid and victory. Here we read that in her prayer "Boudicca raised a hand to sky to speak to Andrasta", giving us a suggestion of a ritual gesture that might accompany such prayer.[27] We can imagine the Morrígna receiving prayer in similar circumstances before battles, and in fact this is suggested by Cú Chulainn's "warrior's shout", which is immediately followed by the appearance of the battle spirits and Némain attacking his enemies.[28]

Prayers before battles exemplify a special form of prayer: invocatory prayer. This type of prayer endeavors to call down the presence of the deity into manifestation in a specific time and place—in these examples, war and tutelary Goddesses are invoked into the battle for the benefit of the invoking groups. We also see invocatory prayer described in the divination rite *imbas forosnai,* in which the seer makes offerings to idols of his Gods and then "calls his idols to him" using a chanted invocation.[29] Language in the same text refers to "invoking" of idols, suggesting that prayer and invocation were used to call down and seat the presence of a deity within an image.

Such invocations appear to be distinct from the type of prayer employed by Tulchine for personal wish fulfillment, in which invocation of the presence of the Morrígan is not suggested, but instead a request for influence over a situation. Another form of prayer may be indicated by descriptions of divinatory prayer among the Gauls and Germans. Before divinations are cast, a prayer is offered to the Gods; presumably the prayer is for blessing of the divination lots, and a request for oracular messages to be received.[30]

A genre of prayer closely associated with the Morrígna and especially Badb is cursing and binding prayer. The word for Tulchine's praying is *rogaid,* from the verb *guidid,* "to beg, pray to, or entreat."[31] Etymology links the meaning of this word to a complex of ideas associating prayer with magical binding and verbal enchantment. The term *geis,* a magical binding or prohibition (sometimes translated as "taboo"), is derived from *guidid,* "to pray"; early sources speak of *ailgeis,* a type of "prayer

27 Diodorus Siculus, quoted in Koch & Carey 2003 12.

28 O'Rahilly 2011 182, O'Rahilly 2010 197

29 O'Donovan 1868 94

30 Tacitus quoted in Waddell 2014 27.

31 Stokes 1892 471

or request, the refusal of which brings reproach or ill-luck."[32] *Ail* itself means "satire, verbal insult, or reproach", as well as "weapon". Thus we have a tradition in which prayer may be employed as a weapon to create the magical binding known as the *geis*. According to Bernard Mees, the earlier meaning of *geis* may have simply been "a prayer". As Christian prayer came into prominence in Ireland, the usage of the various terms began to diverge. *Guide* came to be associated with Christian prayer, and *geis* came to refer distinctly to a more native, pagan form of prayer and particularly to the magical binding effected by such prayer.[33] As we see the Morrígna and particularly Badb actively involving herself in the enforcement of *gessi* in the myths, we can reasonably imagine that she might have been invoked in the *geis*-prayer when it was deployed.

Few texts reflecting such *geis*-prayers have been recorded. What we do have is a rich body of poetic and magical texts in both Irish and Gallo-Brittonic which show the rhythmic, incantatory and poetic nature of verbal prayer in the Celtic world. The central relationship between metrical poetry, prayer, and magic is demonstrated by many stories of the Morrígna in which they enact sorcery through the chanting of poems, as do many prominent poets and druids in the Irish lore. We will explore the features of magical practice, cursing, and its relation to poetics in more detail in Chapter 15 on sorcery.

Offerings

A worshiper brings gifts of value to a sacred place and deposits them with prayers to the holy powers at the shrine. This ritual, or some similar version of it, can be found in virtually every culture worldwide and throughout the historical record. The act of offering gifts to the object of worship is among the most fundamental of human religious acts.

Extensive evidence of offering practice can be seen across the Celtic world, pertaining to the Morrígna as well as the other Gods, spirits of the dead and Otherworldly beings. Offerings given in various contexts may include food and drink, natural objects such as flowers, valuables either produced or captured, symbolic ritual objects, as well as sacrificial offerings of living beings. In many cases, we may never see evi-

32 Royal Irish Academy 2013
33 Mees 2009 154

dence of this practice; if devotees ever brought gifts of food to the wood of Ross, or poured out libations at the crag of Srúb Brain, or laid flowers at the Bed of the Couple by the Unshin's waters, we would know only if archaeology had preserved it, or if literature or folk memory held a glimpse of it.

Much of ritual and religious practice never leaves a trace. However, a few elements of ancient offering practice can be found. Offerings such as food, drink and flowers seem to have been common, and in a few cases evidence of such offerings has survived, protected by being underground. At a wedge tomb in Altar, West Cork, ritual offerings and particularly food, continued to be added well after the building of the mound and the placing of the original funerary remains.[34] At Brúg na Bóinne (Newgrange), traces of votive offerings can be detected going back to the earliest times prior to Celtic presence, and align with veneration practices seen elsewhere, examples include food offerings, valuable objects, and in later times, coins as well.[35] We may imagine similar offerings involved in the cults of worship at other locations where evidence of offerings is less apt to survive through time. At the Paps of Anu, a folk tradition still brings small votive offerings to be placed at the cairns on the peaks, traditionally in May and generally by women, "for the health and fertility of family and livestock."[36] An apparent survival of Beltaine customs relating to fertility, this folk practice cannot reliably be dated to the period in which Anu emerges as a mythic entity, but it is no stretch to imagine that ancient people would have carried out such simple, heartfelt ritual here and at other sites connected to the worship of the Morrígna, such as perhaps the Paps of the Morrígan and other sites dedicated to her.

Ritual Deposits

Another source of evidence about devotional offerings is the widespread Celtic practice often called "ritual deposition", the burying of offerings in underground and underwater sites. This is seen throughout the Celtic world, including Ireland, Britain, and Gaul, and reflects the Celtic cosmological paradigm that the Otherworld is accessed ei-

34 Waddell 2014 28
35 Waddell 2014 31
36 Cronin, quoted in Coyne 2006 13.

ther through liminal boundaries at watery places, or through entry into the chthonic realm underground. These deposition sites take the form of ritual pits or "hollow altars", boundary ditches at sanctuaries, bog, lake and river depositions, grave depositions, and temple depositions.

Ritual deposits in wet places go back well beyond Iron Age Celtic cultures into the Bronze Age and perhaps earlier. In Ireland and Britain, evolutions of the practice have been found showing that earlier offerings consisted primarily of weapons. Later, personal ornaments, musical instruments, jewelry, cauldrons and horse trappings also show up in addition to continued offerings of weapons.[37] Weaponry seems to have been the dominant offering deposited into rivers, whereas ceremonial items such as cauldrons, gold ornaments and the like are more predominant in bog deposits. This may reflect the role of rivers as territorial boundaries, where needed protection would be sought by offering weapons to Otherworldly spirits at these boundary zones.

Hollow altars are found at many of the Celtic temple sites, including those in Gaul as well as Britain. In the British and Gaulish temples, a series of pits are generally found near the central sanctum; here sacrifices were enacted and the remains placed in the pits. The grouping of pits may suggest that in some cases one was dedicated to each of several Gods; the war sanctuary of Gournay held a circle of nine ritual pits.[38] Massive amounts of war-gear have been found in such ritual pits at some Gaulish sanctuaries.[39] At others, such as the British hillfort of Danebury, grain storage pits also received ritual offering deposits, including animal and human remains.[40] Such hollow altars seem to have been less the practice in Ireland, where instead, the grave mounds may have served as preferred underground deposition sites (such as the deposits of coins and other valuables found at Brúg na Bóinne and other funerary mound sites).[41]

Boundary ditch deposition of offerings is consistently seen across Ireland, Britain and Gaul. The practice appears to be protective. Offerings, especially of sacrificed animals but also including weapons and armor, were given to the Gods and then deposited into the boundary ditches surrounding the sanctuary precincts, where the spirits of the

37 O'Sullivan, referenced in Beck 2009 335, 339.
38 Brunaux 1988 15, 24
39 Aldhouse-Green 2010 62
40 Waddell 2014 65
41 Waddell 2014 31

offerings could serve as apotropaic guardians protecting the sanctuaries. At Emain Macha and Temair, evidence of ritual deposits spanning several centuries were found in the boundary ditches, including animal and human bones.[42] In Britain and Gaul, boundary ditch deposits also include weapons and armor along with bones of animals and humans.[43]

Caves were also used as locations for ritual deposition, seemingly due to their natural function as entrances to the world underground. The cave of Cruachan, identified as the home of the Morrígan, is thought to have been used for underground ritual offering deposition, as were several other cave/souterrain systems in Ireland, including Dunalis, County Antrim and Ballybarrack, County Louth.[44] Similar systems are also found at caves in Orkney and the Isle of Skye.[45]

Votive Dedications

"Votive offerings" or "votive deposits" are often described in the archaeological literature. This term is widely used to refer to any ritual offering, but the origin of the term "votive" is from *votum*, the Latin for a vow or oath. Thus in its more specific meaning, a votive offering is one dedicated in fulfillment of a vow or obligation to a holy power.[46] In this stricter sense, votive dedications represent a specific subset of offering practice, and where the dedications are recorded, they convey significant insight into religious practice and ideology.

Many of the votive dedications found to date are from the post-conquest periods in Britain and Gaul. It appears that the practice of votive dedication existed in the Celtic regions prior to conquest, but was simply better documented in the post-conquest period due to the widespread adoption of Latin writing. In the Latin inscriptions, the formula often used and which clearly signals a votive dedications is VSLM: *votum solvit libens merito*, which means the dedicator "willingly and deservedly fulfilled [his/her] vow."[47] The use of this particular votive formula indicates that the dedication was made by someone using Roman customs and language, but many of these dedications are

42 Waddell 2014 129
43 Brunaux 1988 15
44 Waddell 2014 65
45 Aldhouse-Green 2010 199
46 Beck 2009 23
47 Beck 2009 262

to Celtic deities. Similar dedication formulae in native Celtic language have also been found, indicating that the custom of votive dedication was not solely practiced by Roman folk.[48]

Votive dedications were usually the fulfillment of a vow undertaken earlier. In a typical case, a person in need prays to a deity for aid, vowing to make a votive dedication in their honor in thanks for that divine aid. Well-off patrons might have such dedications inscribed into stone altars; the less wealthy employed small votive tablets or plaques. For the wealthiest, entire temples were sometimes offered as votive gifts. Whatever the form of the offering, these votive inscriptions are evidence of a devotional pact that someone entered into with their Gods.[49] In most cases, the nature of the request is never described, and we see only the evidence of the vow's fulfillment in the votive formula. In the case of altar dedications, the altars would have then been used as sanctified places for the dedication of further offerings and sacrifices to that same deity, often inside a shrine or temple.[50] In this way, they serve to venerate and bring honor to the deity not just in the act of dedication, but each time further offerings are made there.

Altars to several cognates of the Morrígna on the continent have been found. These include Cathubodua, Baduhenna, Victoria Cassibodua, and Rigani[51] (see Chapter 8 above for discussion of these divinities and their relationship to the Irish Morrígna). Interestingly, some of these dedications were made by women. This was the case for the votive altar dedicated to Cathubodua, which reads (when the shorthand formulae are expanded) *Cathubodua Augustae Servilia Terentia votum solvit libens merito*, "To the honored Cathubodua, Servilia Terentia paid her vow willingly and deservedly".[52] Here, a woman named Servilia Terentia, a wealthy Gallo-Roman citizen, made a devotional vow to the native Celtic war Goddess Cathubodua, and in fulfillment of her vow commissioned the creation and dedication of this stone altar. In a related example from Britain, a woman named Cingetissa, "Warrioress", dedicated an altar to the tutelary Goddess Brigantia.[53]

48 For example, this dedication to Taranus: *Vebrumaros dede Taranu bratoude kantem*, "Vebrumaros dedicated first-fruits to Taranus by (divine) decree" (Rhŷs 1906 17-19).

49 Beck 2009 23

50 Beck 2009 27

51 Beck 2009 252-253, 262

52 Beck 2009 252

53 Beck 2009 221

It was the habit of Celtic warriors to enact votive dedications to their Gods in warfare. This was attested by Caesar and other contemporary observers of the Gaulish and British tribes: "Before battle, a large proportion of spoils to come are dedicated. After a successful battle, the promised spoils are burned or placed in consecrated treasuries or depositories."[54] Often, prisoners to be captured would also be dedicated before the battle, as reported by Caesar, Sopater and others.[55] These prisoners, along with captured animals (e.g. war horses) would then be sacrificed following the battle in fulfillment of the vow. The treasuries mentioned by Caesar are the Gaulish sanctuaries mentioned above in Chapter 10, where archaeology attests to the votive practices described here. The captured weapons, armor, wealth, and valuables deposited in consecrated temples in fulfillment of battle vows remain visible in the archaeological record.[56] We will explore the topic of war and Celtic battle cultus in greater depth in Chapter 16 below.

Ritual Destruction

A persistent—though not universal—feature of offerings to the Gods in Celtic religion is the ritual destruction or "killing" of devoted objects. Many of the weapons, tools, and other valuables found in ritual deposits in temples, subterranean sites and water sites have been ritually destroyed before being deposited. This can be readily seen as an intentional act. For example, swords in otherwise fine condition are found bent back on themselves to render them unusable. Other objects are found cut in half or carefully disassembled.[57] The belief seems to have been that objects broken or killed in this world would come into being in the Otherworld.

This belief seems to be the cosmological underpinning beneath a great range of Celtic practice, including ritual destruction of offerings, sacrifice, as well as the persistent association of woundedness with Otherworldly power or insight. Votive objects might be burned or broken to convey them to the Otherworld; this is seen in the form of broken grave goods as well as ritual deposits in natural and sanctu-

54 Caesar, quoted in Koch & Carey 2003 22.

55 Koch & Carey 2003 7

56 Brunaux 1988 25-33, Aldhouse-Green 2010 61

57 Aldhouse-Green 2010 61

ary sites. I see this practice as connected with the Otherworldly nature of living beings who have a part of the body "broken", as in the perennial presence of the lame and one-eyed hag, a shape often adopted by the Morrígna. The eye that is blind to this world is sighted in the Otherworld, giving the one-eyed the power of visionary magical sight beyond ordinary reality. The leg that is lame or broken in this world is strong in the Otherworld, giving the lamed person the power to walk and travel between realms. The same belief may underlie the practice of lethal sacrifice: animals and people killed in this world come alive to the Otherworld and are then able to serve the needs of the community on the other side. I believe these patterns suggest that ritual destruction of objects was itself viewed as a form of sacrifice, in which the spirit residing in the object was being ritually killed to send it into the Otherworld.

As sacrifice in Celtic traditions is a deep, complex and debated subject, and one which is centrally relevant to the cult of the Morrígna, we will explore it in full in Chapter 12.

Living Practice: Devotion and Daily Practice

In this section, we explore prayer and devotion in the context of living practice in our own time. Devotion is, of course, the work of a lifetime. A library of books could be written on the subject of devotional practice—and have been written. Here, we have not the space to delve into all aspects of devotional practice from first steps to the most complete practice. My intention instead is to share the core elements of devotional practice that I and fellow priests have come to find most effective. Further resources on devotional practice as a topic can be found in the recommended readings.

Fundamentals of Devotion

Devotional practices fulfill several distinct and related functions. Each of these functions integrates and overlaps with the others, so in some respects the order I share them in here is arbitrary.

The first function is honorary: the giving of worship, in the form of focused honorary attention to the Gods because we hold them worthy of it. Devotion here is an act of love. In a sense, devotion springs from the same place that moves us to adoration and praise of a loved one, or to show respect for an honored elder. Devotion is first an expression of the worth and importance of the one we are venerating. Service as devotion falls into this realm; doing work on behalf of our Gods in order to do them honor.

Another function of devotion is reciprocity. Reciprocity sees our relationships with the Gods as characterized by flow, and engages us as active participants within that cycle. From the Gods, we recognize a flow of blessings, protection, power, inspiration—whatever the specific gifts of a given deity may be. In gratitude for those gifts, reciprocity demands that gifts and thanks be offered in return, to ensure that the flow of blessings be continuous. Devotion of this kind can become transactional, and we see this as a strong theme in historical religious practice. The vast number of votive offerings and sacrifices attest to the practice of transactional devotion.

A third function of devotion is intimacy. We value a deity's presence and influence in our lives, so we seek to strengthen that presence. Devotional practices here recognize that although the Gods can be anywhere, their presence and attention is not constant everywhere, and we seek to draw them to us, or bring ourselves closer to them. Experientially, the giving of devotion opens a bond between the devotee and the deity, and this devotional bond functions as a channel for communication; through it our Gods begin to take up residence within us.

In all forms of devotion, a crucial feature is consistency and continuity. Devotional practice is about establishing relationship; relationships grow and strengthen from continued and consistent connection. Depending on the nature of a relationship, this may or may not mean daily—we can have devotional relationships that are less intimate and still valuable, just as we can have friends we talk with only now and again. To the extent that we wish for a deep, intimate, or personally transformative relationship, we need to cultivate devotional practice of that depth. This is particularly important when it comes to transactional devotion; if we are only bringing devotion at times when we have a request, then we are not contributing much to the deepening of the devotional relationship.

Daily Spiritual Practice

Personal spiritual practice underlies and supports devotion. Spiritual skills function like muscles; they atrophy when they are not used and they strengthen with use. The ability to direct and control attention, to sustain concentration, to modulate breath, internal energy, and life force, and the ability to detect and illuminate divine communications—all of these are skills crucial to devotional work which require regular practice to develop. Spiritual practice is like an internal martial art; as with any learned discipline, it is most useful when it can flow automatically at need, as a natural response to the present moment. This cannot happen without practice.

I recommend developing two forms of practice: core practice, and full practice. Core practice is our minimum daily practice for those days when we lack the time or energy for anything more. It can be as little as 5-10 minutes a day, but it should be completed daily. This core practice can be expanded for days when we have more time and energy, or when we have something important to prepare for. This approach allows for both flexibility and consistency in daily practice.

Core Elements

Spiritual practices can be built from many elements, and again, volumes have been written on this. Those that I see as core elements of spiritual practice, and which I also find integrate well into a Celtic devotional polytheist framework, are purification, soul alignment, and meditation. Here, for reasons of space, I will simply cover the methods I use for these elements of practice, fully recognizing that there are a great many other methods of value.

Purification: We need to cleanse or purify ourselves and our working spaces of spiritual influences which interfere with practice or bring spiritual harm. We have a great many methods which have seen use both within Celtic traditions and beyond: burning or "smudging" with herbs or incenses, saining with blessed liquids, banishing rituals to send away unwanted spirits, and the like. It is important to apply discernment here about the specifics of what is being done. *Purification* does not remove, but neutralizes or transforms harmful forces to restore a state of wellness. *Cleansing* disposes of unwanted influences by washing them away. *Banishing* specifically addresses spirit beings, sending them away from a place. A crucial distinction I apply in my own practice is that in most cases, I use purification rather than cleansing on myself, based on the principle that we never want to cleanse away parts of our own being, nor send away our own life force.[58] Cleansing and banishing are methods I usually apply for clearing and preparing a space.

Soul alignment: Simply put, most spiritual systems recognize that we have spiritual anatomy composed of multiple souls or soul-parts. We need periodically to align and integrate these centers of our spiritual being, to remain attuned to practice, strong within ourselves, and operating with all our inner resources. This is, again, a substantial topic unto itself. Here, I will simply note the frameworks I employ for this practice, drawn both from Celtic tradition and in combination with elements of other traditions in modern practice.

I employ a tripartite soul alignment practice, drawn from a fusion of sources. For the Irish tradition, a tripartite soul work system has been articulated by poet and scholar Erynn Rowan Laurie in her *Cauldron of Poesy*, based on early Irish poetic texts which speak of human beings containing three cauldrons or soul centers.[59] I also draw on compatible teachings from the Anderson Feri Tradition of witchcraft, which teaches a somewhat related tripartite soul alignment. In essence, as I work with them, the three soul centers are recognized in the belly, as the home of primal life force and the animal soul; the chest, as the home of the heart, emotions and human spirit; and the head, as the home of wisdom and the divine part of our nature. These three centers, cauldrons, or souls need to be kept in alignment with one another so that they support each other's functioning and unify us into a being of integrity. In my own practice, I begin all my meditative or ritual work with an alignment of these three souls. In its simplest form, my practice is to feed three breaths into each cauldron in turn, directing life force and vitality into each. This can be further expanded to include focused meditation into each cauldron, guiding flows of life force between them for balancing purposes, visualizations to build up the strength and functioning of each one, and more.

58 This principle was taught to me via the Anderson Feri Tradition of witchcraft; I apply it to the practice of Celtic polytheism as I find it very effective and useful.

59 Laurie 2010

Meditation: In many traditions, the breath is the vehicle for both magic and meditative focus, and this finds a home in the Celtic traditions as well. The essentials of meditation are sustained control of attention, breath, and stillness or positioning of the body. A diversity of meditation schools teach practices where the attention is focused on an image or thought, a repeated element such as a chant or "mantra", or centering on having no object of attention, but on emptiness instead. The core of the practice is simply to sustain attention—when the mind wanders from this, we bring it back.

In my own practice, I employ a meditation chant as a tool of meditative focus. The meditation I most often use consists of the first lines from the Morrígan's peace prophecy from the *Second Battle of Mag Tuired* in Old Irish: *síd co nem, nem co doman.* ("Peace to the sky, sky to the earth.") As a meditation chant, the *rosc* pattern provides a naturally trance-inducing rhythm. I usually chant the prayer internally, with the breath: inhaling *síd co nem*, exhaling *nem co doman.* I also engage vision with this meditation: on the inhalation, I focus on the expansion of the breath into my spirit, rising up to the heavens as the breath lifts my body, "peace to the sky". With the exhalation, I focus on blessing descending back down from heavens to earth, as the breath cascades out and my ribcage descends, "sky to the earth".

Prayer beads can be a helpful tool for meditation, providing several benefits: one, the prayer beads become a talisman, sanctified and attuned to the practice, so that just holding them can help us shift into a meditative state. Two, they give the hand something to do, and this small, gentle activity provides an outlet for any physical restlessness in the body. And three, the prayer beads can be used to set the rhythm and duration of meditation practice, which frees us from the distraction of wondering how long we've been at it. Any set of beads can be prayer beads, even a necklace, rosary or Buddhist mala. I have a set designed for my devotional practice: a set of 27 beads (3 sets of 9) with a small pendant at the endpoint. Every 9th bead is a different shape, so I can feel when I've completed each count of 9, and I can feel when I've completed a full count of 27. My usual daily meditation is to complete the full bead set three times, which then comprises 9 times 9 repetitions of the peace prayer.

Rites of Devotion

For many practitioners, devotions are also a daily element of practice. The frequency and intensity of devotions we need will be relative to the demands of the individual devotional relationship we have with a deity. Dedicants of the Morrígna and those who serve as priests will likely find daily devotions to be a necessity. For those just beginning a devotional relationship, daily devotions may help to fully establish the devotional bond more effectively than a casual practice will allow.

The core elements of devotional practice as I see them are simple. A basic devotion consists of a prayer or liturgy to address the deity and establish the devotional communion, and an offering. If there are requests or petitions to be made, or questions to be asked, these can be added. A period of listening for communications from the deity is a good practice to add on a regular basis as well, along with divination practices to verify that messages are being received and understood correctly. Following this basic pattern, core devotions in my daily practice consist of lighting the candles, speaking a devotional prayer to the Morrígan, and pouring out a liquid offering for her. I follow this with my daily spiritual practice and meditation, during which time I listen for insights and guidance.

For larger or more intensive rites than the daily devotions, a range of different kinds of invocations and liturgies may come into use, and our creativity and passion are our allies here.

Prayers, Chants and Songs

The simplest form of prayer, and the one I use most often in daily practice, is to speak her name. Speaking it aloud adds more power and life force to it than saying it silently, because speaking engages the breath and the muscles of the body. Names can be intoned as a chant, which becomes a vehicle for the heartfelt outpouring of devotion. That outpouring is the heart of devotion and brings as much power as the form of the liturgy that we use.

Invocatory chants have great power both for drawing the presence of the Gods, and for strengthening the devotional bond. For group devotions, they provide a means for all present to participate in devotion together. Here I share a few chants I use in devotions with the Morrígna. Most of these have been developed in practice with the Coru Cathubodua Priesthood.

Cathubodua Gaulish Invocation Chant

Words by Morpheus Ravenna. Music by Morpheus Ravenna, Rynn Fox and Amelia Hogan (of the Coru Cathubodua Priesthood). It should be noted that the words of this chant were received and arranged by me based on oracular inspiration and using a reconstructed version of Gaulish I was studying at the time. It is understood that the linguistics of this chant are not accurate for the historical Gaulish language; we have continued to use it as it has turned out to be very powerful and effective for invocation. This chant is sung in multiple harmonic parts, with the first and second lines interwoven.[60]

Cathubodua, Canu ni risu
Cathurigan, Cingethrigan, Marethrigan, Taran cruach

Battle raven, We sing to you
Queen of battle, Queen of warriors, Queen of the slain, Bloody storm

Morrígan Invocation Chant

Words by Morpheus Ravenna. Music by Morpheus Ravenna, Rynn Fox and Amelia Hogan (of the Coru Cathubodua Priesthood). This chant is sung in multiple parts, using the same melodic and harmonic structure written for the Gaulish invocation chant above.

Mórrígan mórda Nobered búaid
Ban a sídib, Ban-cháinti, Ban-túaithech, Día sóach

Mighty Great Queen, Bringer of victory
Woman of the fairy mound, Poetess, Sorceress, Shapeshifting Goddess

Badb Catha Invocation Chant

Words by Morpheus Ravenna. This chant is intoned rhythmically, or with spontaneous melody as inspired.

Badb catha, Bean sidhe, Lamia, Bean nighe

Battle crow, fairy woman, fury, washer at the ford[61]

---

60 A recording demonstrating the music of the chant is available online at the time of publication from my website at www.bookofthegreatqueen.com.

61 Strictly speaking, the Furies are distinct from the *lamiae* in Classical mythology;

Macha Invocation Chant

Words by Morpheus Ravenna. This chant is designed as a call and response; each line is given as a call, with a repeating response line. It is is intoned rhythmically or with spontaneous melody.

Macha, great Sun of womanhood | *Macha, mighty Queen, Macha, mighty Queen*
Macha, greatness of wealth | *Macha, mighty Queen, Macha, mighty Queen*
Macha greatness of pride | *Macha, mighty Queen, Macha, mighty Queen*

Macha, white shining royal mare | *Macha, mighty Queen, Macha, mighty Queen*
Macha who calls forth horses to the race | *Macha, mighty Queen, Macha, mighty Queen*
Macha, warhorse of the hero's chariot | *Macha, mighty Queen, Macha, mighty Queen*

Macha, swelling breasts of the rich land | *Macha, mighty Queen, Macha, mighty Queen*
Macha, shaper of fortress heights | *Macha, mighty Queen, Macha, mighty Queen*
Macha, bright plain defended by warriors | *Macha, mighty Queen, Macha, mighty Queen*

Macha first ancestor's daughter | *Macha, mighty Queen, Macha, mighty Queen*
Macha of the birthing pangs | *Macha, mighty Queen, Macha, mighty Queen*
Macha mother of heralded twins | *Macha, mighty Queen, Macha, mighty Queen*

Macha, red-maned warrior | *Macha, mighty Queen, Macha, mighty Queen*
Macha who revels in red slaughter | *Macha, mighty Queen, Macha, mighty Queen*
Macha, your harvest the heads of the slain | *Macha, mighty Queen, Macha, mighty Queen*

Macha sister of the dreaded three | *Macha, mighty Queen, Macha, mighty Queen*
Macha red-painted sorceress | *Macha, mighty Queen, Macha, mighty Queen*
Macha whose rage is the curse of tribes | *Macha, mighty Queen, Macha, mighty Queen*

---

we use the term "fury" here in a more general sense of a war-fury, as seen in some of the early Irish texts.

Macha who gives battle for sovereignty | *Macha, mighty Queen, Macha, mighty Queen*
Macha seven years reigning | *Macha, mighty Queen, Macha, mighty Queen*
Macha, bride of Sovereignty | *Macha, mighty Queen, Macha, mighty Queen*

Macha whose memory stands among Kings | *Macha, mighty Queen, Macha, mighty Queen*
Macha whose name is the battlefield | *Macha, mighty Queen, Macha, mighty Queen*
Macha the name of the place of assembly | *Macha, mighty Queen, Macha, mighty Queen*

Macha, greatness of wealth | *Macha, mighty Queen, Macha, mighty Queen*
Macha greatness of pride | *Macha, mighty Queen, Macha, mighty Queen*
Macha, great Sun of womanhood | *Macha, mighty Queen, Macha, mighty Queen*

Prayer of Long Life

This prayer is adapted from the medieval Irish prayer *Cétnad nAíse*, "Prayer for Long Life".[62] I have freely altered it into a devotional prayer to the Morrígna for protection and strength. The "seven daughters of Ernmas" refers to texts which speak of Ernmas as the mother of Badb, Macha, Morrígan, Anu, as well as the land Goddesses Ériu, Fotla and Banba. There are two versions of this prayer—a long form version and a short form version for easier memorization.

Prayer of Long Life (Long Form)

I call on the seven daughters of Ernmas,
who shape the fates of long life.
Three deaths be taken from me,
three lives given to me,
seven waves of plenty poured for me.
May phantoms not injure me on my journey
in my radiant armor of the spirit.
May my name not be pledged without truth;
may death not come to me before my time.

62 Tonsing 2014

I call on the radiant warrior,
to whom death is no terror;
may courage be granted to me as bright as bronze.
May my form be exalted,
may my will be ennobled,
may my strength be increased,
may my grave not be opened,
may I complete my journey,
may my destiny be ensured to me.
May the serpent in the heart not attack me,
nor the grey worming doubt,
nor the senseless fear.
May no thief attack me,
nor a hostile company,
without my company of warriors.
May I have richness of time from the Mighty Ones.

I call on Scáthach of the seven teachings,
who suckled heroes at sword point.
May my seven lights burn brightly.
I am an invincible fortress,
I am an unshakable cliff,
I am a mighty stone,
I am the bull of seven battles
May I know hundreds of truths,
hundreds of joys, each hundred after another.
I summon my good fortune to me;
may the fire of the Hero's Light be on me.
Your blessings, Queen, upon your people.

Prayer of Long Life (Short Form)

I call on the Mighty Great Queen,
who shapes the fates of her people.
May courage be granted to us as bright as bronze.
May our forms be exalted,
may our wills be ennobled,
may our strength be increased,
may our graves not be opened,

may we complete our journeys,
may our destinies be ensured to us.
May the serpent in the heart not attack,
nor the grey worming doubt,
nor the senseless fear.
May no hostile company attack us,
without our company of warriors.
May we have richness of time from the Mighty Ones.
May we know hundreds of truths,
hundreds of joys, each hundred after another.
I pray your great blessings;
may the fire of the Hero's Light strengthen us.
Your blessings, Queen, upon your people.

Offerings

Offerings are among the most ancient and pervasive of human religious acts. In my experience, the most important aspect of an offering is the life force contained within it. This may be why blood sacrifice was so popular and so pervasive in the ancient world as a form of devotional offering. This is also why, then and now, spirits and food are among the most highly regarded and common of offerings. Both contain potent and valuable life force which is readily received by the Gods. Life force is also directed into effort; so undertakings of dedicated work, and things we make by our own effort, also represent a dedication of life force in a more indirect way.

The life force contained in our offerings feeds the Gods. That is to say, the Gods are not dependent on offerings from us to exist; they are beings that live and have agency independent of ourselves, in my understanding. But the manifestation of Gods into the physical realm we inhabit, where they can become perceptible to our senses, requires power. This power is what we provide when we feed the Gods. Thus, we are not so much feeding them, as we are feeding their presences and giving life to the devotional bond by which we commune with them.

The offerings we give can be quite personal to the specific nature of our relationships with the Gods, so here I cannot give prescriptions so much as suggestions. Here I share examples of offerings I have given in my own devotions to the Morrígna, and those of priests I work with:

Liquid offerings—
Whiskey
Milk, cream, or butter
Irish Cream
Beer (dark, Irish-style seems to be preferred)
Mead or wine
Athelbrose (a traditional Scottish oat & milk drink)
Apple cider
Blessed water
Sexual fluids
Blood

Incenses: I have often been asked for recipes for devotional incenses. I do use incense as an offering, but I have no specific recipe to share. The tendency of modern Pagan spellbooks to create lists of herbs and ingredients that "correspond" to the Morrígan does not fit my theology. Instead, I gather ingredients for incenses on an ad-hoc basis as materials present themselves in a devotional context. For example, here are some ingredients my incenses have included: rose petals, mugwort, cedar, elder flowers, oak leaves, consecrated earth, dragon's blood resin. However, I have used these not based on a belief that they "correspond" with or are specially sacred to the Morrígan, but instead based on their situational meaning in my own devotional life. The roses were won in a combat tournament; the mugwort was used to preserve raven parts given by an ally; the cedar, elder flowers, oak leaves, and consecrated earth were gathered at sacred places where I and cohorts had done important devotional rites in her honor; and the resin was added just to increase potency and help the other materials burn well. Certainly another could adopt this list of ingredients, but greater devotional value might be found in a different set of materials within the context of their own lived devotion.

Solid offerings: These can take the shape of many things. Traditionally, food offerings such as a portion of one's meal, especially at feasts, are a common offering. Raw or prepared meat, bread or cakes, fruits, flowers, anything that contains life force, especially if it is fresh or made with care is a suitable offering. Any object of value may become an offering, as in the ancient practice of depositing weapons, jewelry, tools, and other valuables. Traditionally, offerings to the Gods in all sorts of ancient polytheisms would include the best of whatever people had to give—from harvest, from resources, from craft. The first fruits of harvest have often been a traditional offering. In Ireland, cattle would likely have been a primary offering to the Morrígan.

Dedicated objects: Situationally, objects that might otherwise not be considered valuable may become personally meaningful as offerings to the Morrígna. For example, in my armored combat practice, during my first fighting session in armor, I broke the buckle of my sparring partner's shield-strap. I brought that broken buckle back as an offering, representing a dedication of my effort toward warriorship. This provides one illustration of the highly personal nature of devotional gifts.

We should remember to exercise intelligence about offerings being deposited in natural places. Food offerings left out will often be consumed by animals; this may be seen as the Gods' way of taking them in, but we need to consider the health of those creatures. When possible, it may be better to bury food offerings if they would present a health impact to animals who will find and eat them. Similarly, anything non-biodegradable given outdoors as an offering should be thought through carefully; in terms of the impact to an environment, if we are not thoughtful we may essentially be littering. Consider what the fate of that object will be when left.

Dedicated Acts

Physical offerings are traditional and deeply satisfying to give, but equally so are offerings of effort. When we dedicate an act as an offering to the Gods, we are offering our life force, attention, effort, and time. In a sense, this can be the most intimate of offerings—it is an offering of self. We make this kind of offering by choosing a devotional act, giving a prayer of offering before undertaking the act, and keeping focused attention flowing toward the deity during the entirety of the act. This is a highly personal kind of offering and may be distinct for everyone. Here are some examples of devotional acts I have seen or participated in as offerings for the Morrígna:

Martial practice and acts of warriorship
Acts of service to warriors and veterans
Land cleanup at military sites or areas impacted by war

Acts of service for the welfare of animals sacred to the Morrígna
Wildlife rehabilitation for corvids or wolves
Horse rescue or veterinary service for horses and cattle
Habitat protection and care for wolves, corvids, or eels.
Devotional sex
Death and hospice service
Gravesite and cemetery care

Here, the possibilities for meaningful acts of service as devotion are likely endless and our imagination and passion can be our guides.

12

Sacrifice

As we noted in the previous chapter, sacrifice represents a specific and specially potent form of devotional offering which occupies a centrally important place in Celtic religious traditions. This chapter examines the historical context, meaning, and function of sacrifice, and its relation to the cults of the Morrígna.

A great deal of ink has been spilled about the practice of sacrifice in Celtic religion. Debates have raged over whether or not the druids and other Celtic priestly folk did in fact practice human sacrifice, as well as arguments about the moral value of sacrifice relative to the modern ethos. At the current state of scholarship on ancient Celtic civilizations, it is fairly well established that sacrifice, predominantly animal but also human, was in fact practiced by most, if not all, ancient Celtic peoples. What is more, it has become clear that sacrifice was in fact central to the cosmology and ritual life of Celtic religions. In this chapter, I endeavor to give as clear and comprehensive a picture of sacrificial customs and their cosmological underpinnings among the ancient Celts as possible, with special emphasis on elements of the practice that relate more directly to the cults of the Morrígna and cognate Goddesses. To understand the sacrificial practices of the ancients, we must reserve judgment in the present chapter, laying aside modern moral positions about the perceived brutality or savagery of the practice in order to first understand, as best we can, what it meant to people of the period. I take up the subject of sacrifice in a modern polytheist practice and its moral and ethical dimensions for us in the present time, in the section on Living Practice, at the end of this chapter.

The Cosmology of Sacrifice

> "Masters of healing arts as much as of sacrifice, the Druids thus emerge as a priestly group possessed of an esoteric knowledge: a knowledge centered on physiological lore, that is, the science of homologic connections between the bodily microcosm and the macrocosm beyond. This knowledge was encoded and transmitted in myths of creation (cosmogony and anthropogony), and enacted in such rituals as healing and human sacrifice. It should thus be obvious that the latter rite was not just barbaric slaughter, but was also a serious intellectual exercise, presided over by priests who considered themselves to have mastered the very secrets of the universe, secrets which they employed for the wellbeing — indeed, for the continued existence — of the universe.[1]"

At the root of the practice of life sacrifice (including both animal and human sacrifice) is the cosmological principle of the identity between the body and the world. This principle of microcosm/macrocosm referenced by Bruce Lincoln in the quote above is also expressed in the familiar Hermetic maxim "as above, so below"; or in its earliest version, "That which is above is from that which is below, and that which is below is from that which is above."[2] Irish notions of sacred kingship reflect this principle as well: what befalls the body of the king befalls the land. It is also refracted into the large number of creation myths found throughout Europe and elsewhere describing the creation of the world from the dismembered body parts of a primordial individual.[3] In Irish mythology, this sacrificial creation myth emerges in the stories of the Donn Cúailnge, the Brown Bull of the Táin cycle, who destroys

1 Lincoln 1988 389
2 Hughes 2005 238
3 Lincoln 1988 386

and dismembers the White Bull Findbennach in a primordial combat, shaping the landscape of Ireland from the parts of his body, before himself dying and merging with the landscape.[4] Sacrificial cosmogony is also reflected in the story of the healer Míach. Killed by his father, the healing God Dían Cécht, "three hundred and sixty-five herbs grew through the grave, corresponding to the number of his joints and sinews"—making explicit the connection between body and world.[5] Similar narratives in many cultures link these themes to the broader Indo-European background of Celtic culture.

Stories such as these clearly illuminate the cosmological relationship between healing, sacrifice and creation. For as sacrifice on a cosmological scale was responsible for the creation of the universe, so each act of sacrifice re-enacted that creation and served to feed, revivify and renew the world so created. Healing is thus the complementary practice to that of sacrifice. In Lincoln's words, "Thus, while a sacrificer employed matter taken from a victim's dismembered body to restore the cosmos, the healer used matter from the universe to restore a damaged body."[6]

In short, for the ancient Celts, sacrifice was understood as a fundamentally creative, rather than destructive, act. It was part and parcel of the entire system of druidic learning, in which the nature of the cosmos and its workings, both exteriorly in the natural world and interiorly in the realm of healing and esoteric knowledge, were one field of inquiry. Where the druids "claim that they themselves created heaven and earth and sea, etc., the sun and the moon, etc.," this is a description of cosmological creation being re-enacted in their ritual practice.[7] Fundamental to the Celtic attitude toward sacrifice as a creative and restorative act was the understanding that death was not a final end, and that the soul continued in an afterlife and might be reborn again. Contemporary Classical observers emphasize the strength of belief held by Celtic peoples in the impermanence of death, giving them less fear of facing death and less reservation about dealing it out.[8]

4 Lincoln 1991 34
5 Gray 1982 33
6 Lincoln 1988 387
7 Lincoln 1988 388
8 Caesar and Pomponius Mela quoted in Lincoln 1988 384.

The Morrígna and Sacrifice

Evidence for sacrifices offered to the Morrígna is, as with many other cult functions, primarily circumstantial—but it is also quite pervasive. When we bring together the hints and glimpses suggested by the mythic literature with the evidence of archaeology and history, a strong picture emerges of devotional sacrifice as deeply integral to their worship. We can also identify several functionally specific types of sacrifice, including totemic, apotropaic, and divinatory sacrifice. Here we will examine each of these forms of sacrifice in turn.

Three Chosen for Slaughter

The description of the ominous triple Badb in *Dá Derga's Hostel* provides one of the strongest literary references to sacrifice with respect to the Morrígna. We have discussed the suggestive status of the Hostel itself as a possible sanctuary or temple of the Gods to which Conaire is brought for sacrificial death.[9] In the section of the text describing each of the rooms or compartments, we find the following passage, "The Room of the Badbs":

> "I saw three naked ones on the ridge-pole of the house, gushes of their blood coming through them, and the ropes of their slaughter around their necks."
> "I know those, he said, three chosen *ernbaid*. Those are the three who are destroyed every time."[10]

Certainly the images in this passage, and the entire circumstance of Conaire's death at the Hostel, suggest sacrifice. Naked, pierced so as to bleed, and with ropes around them is a description that perfectly matches several actual human bodies that have been found in bog and lake sites in Ireland and elsewhere, so there is nothing at all fanciful about seeing this description as a reference to actual human sacrifice.[11] It also accords closely with descriptions of sacrifices to the Gaulish Esus, in glosses on the text of Lucan. These victims were said to be hung from trees and stabbed to allow blood to flow for divinatory purposes.[12]

---

9 See Chapter 10 above, and Chapter 13 below.
10 O'Connor 2013 217
11 Aldhouse-Green 2010 70, 74
12 Green 2011

Commentaries on this passage often focus on the auto-sacrificial terms of the description; it seems to be implied that the naked trio are at once the triple Badb, and also sacrificial victims offered to the Badb.[13] Anne Ross compares the imagery to that of the Norse Odinn, hung from a tree, wounded and bleeding, said to be "himself sacrificed to himself". Ralph O'Connor points out the parallel auto-sacrificial imagery also present in the Hostel in the form of the "Three Reds"—three red horsemen from the Otherworld who are also killed three times, returning each time in a cyclical sacrificial pattern similar to these "three who are destroyed every time."[14] Thus we may be seeing hints of a mythology of the triple Badb in which she may have been seen as cyclically sacrificed to herself; and perhaps a sacrificial rite in which three victims were first ritually identified with the Goddess before being sacrificed to her.

The obscure word *ernbaid* left untranslated by O'Connor is given by Stokes as "slaughterers".[15] The first element *ern* appears to be from *íarn*, "iron"; all related constructions seem to refer to this. The second element *baid* can be found as a form of *bás*, "to die". What is striking to me here is the resemblance between this obscure word *ernbaid* and the name Ernmas, the mother of the Morrígna triad of Badb, Morrígan and Macha, whose name is translated as "Violent Death" or "Iron-Death". Might these "three chosen *ernbaid*" thus be read as something like "three chosen for violent death", "three chosen iron-dead"? If the phrase would have been understood to refer to Ernmas herself, we might also have "three chosen of/for Ernmas". Given that the room is identified as the space dedicated to the triple Badb, and given her familial relationship with Ernmas, a connection is not out of the question and might suggest that Ernmas herself also had, at some point, an association with these sacrificial traditions.

The Bloody Garden

A passage in the early Ulster tale the *Wooing of Emer* tells of a place called Gort na Morrigna, the Garden of the Morrígan, a field dedicated to her and said to be her gift from the Dagda. There "after a year", she killed

13 Ross 1996 317

14 O'Connor 2013 217

15 Stokes 1875 491

a character named Ibor Boiclid, son of Garb, who is a relation to her, and in that year the plants that grew in her garden were "reddened".[16] *Ibor* appears to be a variant on *ibar*, "yew"; the second name Boiclid is a compound for which I cannot produce a translation, but the first element may be *boc*, a goat. This character thus seems to have agrarian associations and is killed by the Morrígan in her field, with a subsequent effect on what was seen to grow there. Twice, the passage references *an bliadain*, "the year", also implying a seasonal agrarian cycle.

What I see here is the suggestion of an annual agrarian sacrifice, perhaps of a goat, which was intended to fertilize the fields. Folklore retains hints of something similar; Irish peasants in some districts preserved a custom until comparatively modern times of bleeding the cattle on May eve and mixing the blood into the soil.[17] This custom as described apparently did not involve slaughter, though in earlier times it may have.

Devotional and Votive Sacrifice

As mentioned in the above chapter on offerings, votive and devotional offerings in the Celtic world often included lethal sacrifice, both animal and human. An oft-cited example of devotional sacrifice in Ireland is the story of sacrifices given to the God Crom Cruach at Mag Slecht, every year at Samhain. Variations of this story appear in the *Dindshenchas*, various Annals, and the lore of Saint Patrick who is said to have ended the sacrifices. The story is highly sensationalized and clearly based on Biblical morality tales, and so it may be fiction. Yet the core description—an idol venerated and fed blood from sacrifices—accords with other contemporary descriptions of Celtic devotional sacrifice. Jacqueline Borsje notes that the function of the Crom Cruach sacrifices seems to have been propitiation for the assurance of "corn and milk"; in other words, fertility and food production.[18] We also find accounts of holy wells, such as one called Slán ("Health"), to which devotional sacrifices were supposedly offered.[19]

Votive sacrifice is perhaps best documented in the practice of war-

16 Meyer 1888 153
17 Wood-Martin 1902 6
18 Borsje 2007a 47, 53
19 Wood-Martin 1902 47

fare. Sopater, writing in the 3rd century BCE, says of the Gauls, "Among them is the custom, whenever they win victory in battle, to sacrifice their prisoners to the Gods."[20] Similar observations were made by many contemporary authors writing about Celtic cultures, including those who were relatively sympathetic. These prisoner sacrifices would have usually been dedicated to the divinities of war prior to the battle, so that the post-battle sacrifice was in fulfillment of the votive obligation. The British Queen Boudicca (or her priests) reportedly performed such sacrifices to her Goddess of war and victory during the Iceni uprising against the Romans, where in this case quite vicious sacrificial deaths were meted out to prisoners, including women.[21]

Three Deaths of a King

In Ireland, the best documented context for sacrifice may be of kings. Sacral kingship seems to have been deeply tied to sacrificial customs. As the king was bodily identified with the land, required to be whole in body and just in his actions to guarantee the well-being of the land, so when that integrity and justice were compromised, his death might be required in order that his body might restore the land.

Deaths of kings are everywhere in Irish literature surrounded with omens and indicators of ritual, and attended by the presence of a sovereignty Goddess, in the form of the mysterious Otherworldly woman or the malevolent cursing hag, depending on the king's status relative to *fír flathemon*, kingly justice, at his death.[22] This sovereignty figure is sometimes a form of the Morrígan herself, particularly in the case of kings who have fallen into violation of *fír flathemon* and their attendant *gessi*—such as Conaire Mór, met by the Badb in *Dá Derga's Hostel* mentioned above.

Conaire's death exemplifies another persistent theme in the sacrificial deaths of kings: the triple death. A fatal druidic thirst afflicts Conaire, he is slain by sword, and he is a victim of a burnt house (and so at least by proxy suffers death by burning).[23] His death also takes place at the charged time of Samhain, and is surrounded by tripling of numerous

20 In Koch & Carey 2003 7
21 Aldhouse-Green 2010 126
22 Bhreathnach 1982 244
23 O'Connor 2013 216

other omens (the appearance of the triple Badb, the three doomed and sacrificed Red Riders, the three burnings of the house, etc.). Another example concerns a king Muirchertach mac Erca, a descendant of Niall of the Nine Hostages, who dies a triple death on Samhain night as well—burned, wounded, and finally drowned in a vat of wine. His death is attended by a mysterious and ominous Otherworldly woman named Sín, who shares some of her epithets with the hag Cailb, who is also the Badb.[24]

That this triple death is not simply mythological is amply demonstrated by the archaeological record. Bodies have been recovered from bog and marsh sites in Ireland as elsewhere in Europe showing clear evidence of ritual killing, including tripled forms of death and "overkilling". The celebrated British Lindow body exemplifies this pattern: he was garotted, his throat cut, and hit by a blunt killing blow to the back of the head.[25] Irish bog bodies such as Clonycavan and Oldcroghan also instantiate the pattern, both hung or strangled along with cutting of the nipples and dismemberment or other forms of violence.[26] The high status of these ritually killed men is shown by features such as valuable arm-rings, expensive imported hair resins and manicured condition of the nails.[27]

Ritual king sacrifice can be viewed as a specific form of devotional sacrifice. As the role of the sacral king is marriage to the Goddess of sovereignty, it is through her benevolence and the attendant spiritual backing of the Otherworld that the prosperity of his reign is achieved. The king's responsibility in this sacral contract is to effect *fír flathemon*, truth of sovereigns, and so ensure the continued benevolence of the Goddess and the Otherworld powers. Historically, these king sacrifices may have sometimes occurred at times of famine or hardship, conditions that would point to the king failing in his role as sovereign and consort, breaking the Otherworldly contract, as manifest in the loss of the land's prosperity. Thus his reign would be ended, and his life offered as a sacrifice to appease the Otherworldly powers in the hope of restoring the land.[28]

There is some evidence to suggest that an alternative practice of sub-

24 Macalister 1956361
25 van der Sanden 2013 407
26 Kelly 2012 237
27 Iping-Petterson 2012 24
28 Kelly 2012 238

stitute sacrifice developed in lieu of the death of a king. William Sayers notes that, in the final battle in the *Táin*, both the cosmological battle of the Brown and White-Horned Bulls and the combat between Fergus and King Conchobor of Ulster display signs thematic of sacrificial ritual.[29] Just before entering the battle, Fergus swears an oath to the tribal God in which he lists all the parts of men's bodies he will strike and sever, from head down to toes, in a ritualistic anatomical litany that strongly recalls similar litanies in tales of the creation of the world from the parts of a victim's body. Swearing this oath, Fergus calls for his sword, "the sword that cuts men's flesh," which is described in cosmological and talismanic terms.[30] In the ensuing combat with King Conchobor, he undertakes a ritualized sword strike: this begins with the sword point touching the ground on its backswing, intending to arc across the sky "as a rainbow in the air" and strike three killing blows against the Ulster king. He is stayed by another warrior, Cormac Cond Longas, and instead of slaying Conchobor, Fergus turns the sword, sweeping it over the heads of the hosts, and cuts the crests of three hills nearby. Sayers suggests that this altercation is a mythologized representation of sacrificial substitution, followed as it is by the combat of the Bulls which ends in the sacrificial dismemberment of the White Bull and rebuilding of the world with the parts of his body. It may suggest that the very ancient practice of ritual king sacrifice might have been at some stage replaced by bull sacrifice—a practice we also know to be closely associated with rites of kingship.[31] Substitution of cattle for human beings in sacrificial contexts is alluded to in a few other texts as well.[32]

Totemic Animal Sacrifice

In quantity, animal sacrifices have represented by far the greatest share of sacrificial practice among Celtic peoples. We see a variety of forms of animal sacrifice, representing different religious and magical functions aligned to the mythical qualities associated with the different animals.

29 Sayers 1985 33
30 O'Rahilly 2010 267
31 Sayers 1985 54
32 Ó hÓgáin refers us to a late medieval story of Conn Céadcathach in which a cow is substituted for the "son of a sinless couple" in a druidically prescribed sacrifice to protect the fertility of the land (Ó hÓgáin 1999 48).

Celtic belief around sacrifice and consumption of totemic animals is complex. There is substantial literary and historic evidence of taboos prohibiting or controlling the consumption of animals when a given person or tribal group is identified with them—as, for instance, Cú Chulainn's *geis* against eating dog meat, as his namesake and personal totemic animal, or the *geis* of Conaire Mór against killing birds, as a kinsman of the Otherworldly bird people. Multiple instances of such taboos exist with respect to different animals. Yet, evidence of sacrifice and even consumption of these same animals is often also present within a given cultural context. It appears that these taboos are not always absolute prohibitions, but rather are specific to individuals, or restrict sacrificial use and consumption of the totemic animal to specific ritual occasions. Animals may also be treated as totemic to a specific function—such as kingship, warriorship, druidry, or prophecy—and cultural norms controlling the sacrifice and consumption of animals are often oriented around these functions as much as individual totemic identities, and are often not simple, absolute prohibitions. We will examine these kinds of taboos with respect to individual animals below.

Feast of Champions

Most animal sacrifices in Celtic societies would have taken place in the context of collective gatherings involving communal acts of feasting as part of the sacral rites. Royal ceremonial gatherings at sacred centers of Ireland such as Emain Macha, Temair, Cruachan and others clearly included communal feasts as a central part of the ceremonial activity. At these feasts, meat from animal sacrifices would have been shared with the community. Similar traditions are seen outside Ireland in Britain and Gaul.

The central place of feasting as a communal rite in Celtic culture is attested by the many chieftain burials which include feasting equipment. The institution of the Champion's Portion seems to date back to very ancient times, as reflected in the heroic sagas of Ireland as well as accounts of Gaulish culture. This is a status-oriented feasting ritual in which the finest cut of the animal and other valuable gifts was contested by various heroic warriors through boasting and tale-telling of their high lineage and valorous deeds.[33]Pigs were a favored animal for

33 Waddell 2014 3, Leahy 1905 33

feasting in Ireland as well as Britain, having strong connotations of Otherworldly power and association with forces of fecundity as well as warriorship (as attested by the prevalence of boar-headed helmets and war trumpets). Remains of pigs slaughtered for food and likely also as sacrificial offerings have been found in numerous hillfort locations, along with evidence of ceremonial feasting and other valuable offerings. Pigs are also a frequent sacrificial meat offering found in high-status graves.[34] Royal sites such as Temair, Emain Macha, and Cruachan yield abundant animal bone deposits showing evidence of butchery, indicating the slaughter and consumption of pigs, cattle, sheep, goats, horses, and even occasionally dogs.[35] Of these, pigs were by far the most common, followed by cattle; the others are found in much lower quantities, suggesting that the ritual slaughter and consumption of animals such as horses and dogs was likely an infrequent, highly ritualized occasion. The Champion's Portion itself would usually have been a boar.[36]

The Bull Feast

Cattle were a major meat source in the Irish diet as well as among other Celtic peoples. The bones of cattle figure prominently in feast deposits, showing regular consumption as well as ceremonial use. As a common domestic food animal, specific taboos restricting the consumption or use of cattle are not prominent in the literature. However, cattle, both heifers and bulls, had their sacred status and specific cultic usage.

The *tarb feis*, "bull feast", is the best-known example of cattle sacrifice in the Irish context. It is described in several texts from the Irish heroic literature, in remarkably consistent terms. A bull is sacrificed to the Gods by druids; one among them then eats a full meal of its meat and drinks the broth in which it was cooked. He then lies down wrapped in the fresh bull-hide. The other druids chant a "spell of truth" over him, and he sleeps. Dreams that come during this enchanted bull-sleep are considered prophetic and will be interpreted for omens.[37] This ritual was deadly serious; the seer was bound to tell the truth of his vision

34 Aldhouse-Green 2010 60, 62
35 Waddell 2014 101, 129
36 Henderson 1899 9
37 Stokes 1910

and would be expected to die if he did not. Omen-taking for this ritual is associated with the identification of future kings and the outcome of important battles, such as the *Táin*.[38] Several texts specify that the bull should be white; this associates the ritual both with the cosmogonic sacrifice myth of the Brown and White Bulls, as well as reports of very similar druidic sacrificial rites involving white bulls among the Gauls.[39]

Cattle were invested with magical potency as a result of their role in the creation cosmology, and this magical potency was inherited into the bodily remains of the cattle after sacrifice. A sacrificial cattle ritual related to the *tarb feis* may be hinted at in the case of the warrior Fráech, who is wounded and placed in a curative bath of the meat of cattle and restored by it.[40] Other stories tell of marrow mash made from cattle bones that was believed to have curative properties for warriors.[41] Bull hides seem to have been a favored cloak used by druids, a fact that is likely related to the association of bulls with sacrificial cosmology as also reflected in the *tarb feis*.[42] Partaking of the bull by consumption, bathing, or wrapping oneself in the hide would seem to bring one into contact with a deeper level of the cosmos, where one might see the patterns of reality unfolding and access the creative, restorative and prophetic powers arising there.

The Horse Sacrifice

A notorious account of an Ulster kingship ritual centering on horse sacrifice is recorded in the histories of Giraldus Cambrensis. Many have dismissed this account as fictional due to its salacious and sensationalizing tone; it was clearly intended to portray the Irish as backward and savage. However, in its details the ritual it describes aligns strongly with other textual accounts within Ireland,[43] evidence from across several other Indo-European cultures,[44] as well as archaeological evidence from within Ireland, including at Emain Macha, the ancient center of

38 Dobbs 1923 399
39 Waddell 2014 137
40 Waddell 2014 137
41 Sayers 1985 32
42 O'Curry 1873 213
43 Accounts in *Betha Mholaise Daiminse* and the *Dindshenchas* regarding Loch Gabor, as pointed out by Fickett-Wilbar 2012 333.
44 Fickett-Wilbar 2012 318, Waddell 2014 108, Sayers 1985 40

the Ulster cult of Macha. Excavations at the fort of Emain Macha have demonstrated that horse sacrifice and consumption were at least occasionally practiced here. Horse bones displaying evidence of butchery and roasting are among the remains of ritual bone assemblages found at the site.[45] Related evidence of ritual horse consumption, interpreted by archaeologists as evidence of kingship inauguration rites, has also been found at Rathcroghan and Temair.[46]

It seems clear that horsemeat was not an ordinary domestic food staple, for taboos surround its consumption, as would be expected for an animal with such elite sacred status in Celtic societies.[47] Horses are ever linked to kingship, sovereignty, and war, as the animal of chariot warfare and a defining element of the elite mounted warrior class.[48] Symbolisms conveying the power of the horse are deeply interwoven into Macha's mythology, and also attested in the title carried by many mythic kings and chieftains, *Eochaid*, "horseman" or "horse-lord". The sacrifice and consumption of horses seems to be generally reserved for funerary and sovereignty contexts.

A taboo relating to the consumption of horsemeat is mentioned in the archaic *Wooing of Emer* text, where Cú Chulainn mentions having been served horsemeat as a guest in an Otherworld house: "The ruin of a chariot was cooked for us there," says Cú Chulainn. He later explains, "A foal is the ruin of a chariot to the end of three weeks ... And there is a *gess* on a chariot to the end of three weeks for any man to enter it after having last eaten horse-flesh. For it is the horse that sustains the chariot."[49] This quote at once demonstrates the deep totemic association between horses and elite warriorship, while also showing that warriors were understood to engage in consumption of horse meat under specified and ritually controlled circumstances; e.g. not within three weeks of riding a chariot. This would appear to be a separate context from the more well-known kingship rituals involving horse sacrifice and consumption. Perhaps related, there is a story of the Gaulish war chieftain Vercingetorix sending thousands of horses out from the citadel during the siege of Alesia, believed to be on account of a taboo

45 Waddell 2014 101
46 Waddell 2014 129, McCormick 2007 91
47 McCormick 2007 92
48 O'Hagan 2013, part 1
49 Meyer 1888 72, 152

that the Gauls held against eating horsemeat.[50] This prohibition held in such sacred importance that the Gaulish warriors would choose death by starvation before eating their horses, at least outside of the proper ritual context.

Warrior Bands and Dog Sacrifice

Dogs and the consumption of dog meat are the subject of another prohibition in the Irish lore, specific to Cú Chulainn as a dog-identified warrior. This *geis* features in his death-tale: "It was also *geis* to him to eat the flesh of the animal he was named for."[51] The identification of warrior with dog or wolf belongs not just to Cu Chulainn personally, but to the collective identity of the warrior in Irish society, and beyond. Cú Chulainn's rival is also named for the dog: Cú Roí, "Hound of the Battlefield".[52] The activity of warrior bands operating on the margins of Celtic society was referred to as *faelad*, "wolfing", and these warrior bands are deeply and pervasively linked with wolf and dog identities.[53] As a totemic animal belonging to warriors, the *geis* against eating dog or wolf meat is a natural one for Cú Chulainn to carry, and likely would apply to warriors of his class in general.

And yet, we do find evidence of dog sacrifice occurring, and in some cases with the implication of consumption. Dog sacrifice is mentioned among the rites practiced by the druids as offerings to the Gods, and in order to access oracular knowledge about the outcome of a coming battle. "They demanded advice as to how they should give battle. They were telling their druids to find out for them what would be the consequences of the battle and which of them would be defeated... These are the sacrifices they offered; the flesh of dogs, pigs and cats."[54] A sacrifice of a puppy is alluded to in the *Wooing of Étaín* as part of the opening of *síd*-mounds in the search for Étaín.[55] Remains of butchered dogs have been found in the boundary ditch at Temair among the other sacrificial remains, showing evidence of cultic use and possible consumption.[56]

50 Reinach 1906 4
51 Tymoczko 1981 176
52 Stokes 1901a 41
53 O'Connor 2013 83, Wood-Martin 1902 118
54 Dobbs 1923 399
55 Bergin & Best 2011 185
56 Waddell 2014 72

In Britain, dog sacrifices repeatedly show up in connection with warrior associations: a ritual offering pit containing a dog buried with a war-helmet,[57] and dogs or puppies are found deposited with remains of ravens and crows in a large number of cases, often also paired with weapons or other war gear.[58]

It seems that dogs were used in cultic sacrifice in association with warrior rites across a wide range of ancient Indo-European groups. Patterns appear in folklore across Irish, Germanic, Vedic, Scandinavian and Greek cultures outlining traditions in which young men left their families for a time to enter warrior societies where they were trained to a life of seasonal hunting, fighting, and raiding; an Irish example of this institution is the Fianna.[59] We will explore these warrior societies and their relation to the cults of the war Goddesses in a later chapter. Here what is important is that sacrifice and consumption of dogs or wolves, along with the wearing of the skins, attaches to the initiatory rites of these warrior societies. Evidence of such an initiatory rite, closely paralleling these myths, has been found at the Late Bronze Age Russian site of Krasnosamarskoe, where over a long period of years, a series of rituals left bone deposits from dogs and wolves showing evidence of dismemberment, roasting, consumption, and ritual deposition. These rites repeatedly took place in the winter season and included evidence of oracular ritual as well as dog and wolf sacrifices.[60] Scholars Brown and Anthony link the site's evidence to the broad Indo-European tradition of wolf-identified warrior bands, pointing out that "eating dogs and wolves was a transgressive act of liminality, ...a taboo-violating behavior of a kind often associated with rites of passage. In this case the passage was a transition to a status symbolized by becoming a dog/wolf through the consumption of its flesh."[61]

Cú Chulainn's *geis* against eating dog meat is, paradoxically, compatible with a culture in which warriors did partake in such sacrificial rites. If a form of this initiatory ritual was in use among the Irish war bands—and most scholars consider it highly likely that it was—then young warriors following the model of Cú Chulainn may have undertaken such sacrificial rites, partaking of dog meat as they were ritually

57 Aldhouse-Green 2010 60
58 Serjeantson & Morris 2011 96-97
59 Powell 2013
60 Brown & Anthony 2012 8, 12
61 Brown & Anthony 2012 1

inducted into the company of warriors. It is precisely the sacredness and liminality of these initiatory rites that underscores the importance of the *geis*: during initiation, while entering into the identity and status of the warrior-dog, and at no other time in his life, he would consume the flesh of this totemic animal. Once having undergone this initiation, he now partakes of the nature of the animal, and consumption of it becomes *geis* to him.

The Raven's Bill

A curious episode of raven sacrifice performed by Cú Chulainn is recorded in several different Irish texts. Narratively, it is placed within the story of the *Death of Cú Roí,* when Cú Chulainn has been defeated and shamed by rival warrior Cú Roí. After this, Cú Chulainn follows a flock of ravens, killing one in each district they pass through until reaching a place called Srub Brain, "Raven's Bill". The text suggests that the killing of the final bird here gives Cú Chulainn knowledge of who has humiliated him.[62] The story in this text lacks detail, but it does convey a divinatory function to the bird's death. The episode is expanded in the *Dindshenchas* versions, where we find the full ritual: Cú Chulainn kills the raven, severs its head, bathes his hands in its blood, weaving "mystic signs", and then places the raven's head upon the rock of the mountain; thus giving the name Raven's Bill to the place.[63] Here we can see plainly that this is no wanton killing, but a sacrificial ritual. Tymoczko associates this ritual act to the "fatal and supernatural" nature of ravens, their connection to battle, prophecy, fate, and the agents of these powers, the Morrígna, suggesting that Cú Chulainn's raven sacrifice could be viewed as an invocation of these prophetic powers under the tutelage of the war Goddesses.[64]

Were sacrifices with ravens or crows actually practiced in Ireland? I have not yet seen direct evidence of it, but a substantial archaeological record of raven and crow sacrifice has turned up in Iron Age Celtic hillforts in Britain, and may demonstrate related cultic activity. At Danebury and at least a dozen other Iron Age sites, corvid (crow, raven, and rook) remains were found in many ritual offering pits and

62 Tymoczko 1981 24
63 Stokes 1894 450, Gwynn 2008a 257
64 Tymoczko 1981 88

boundary ditches, representing over 80 percent of bird remains, including fully articulated skeletons, separated wings, and disarticulated bones.[65] The remains are often carefully placed, as one example from Rooksdown where a raven was placed with a formation of three upright horse skulls and a puppy skeleton in the base of a ritual pit.[66] In other cases, heads of ravens were found, just as in Cú Chulainn's ritual. Some birds' wings had been removed, leading researchers to suggest that the wings were taken to attach to helmets, transferring the sacral power of the sacrificed animal to the warrior.[67]

Several ravens showed evidence of advanced age and may have been kept as companions or oracular birds by druids or other priests; these may not have been sacrifices at all.[68] At several of these sites, most notably Danebury, funerary excarnation was practiced, the bodies of the dead were laid on platform structures for exposure to carrion birds before the cleaned skulls and bones were collected for sacral curation elsewhere in the settlement. As this funerary tradition would attract many corvids, researchers at the sites suggest that priests may have developed ongoing relationships with these birds, even "calling" them to funerary excarnation rituals, which could have led to companion relationships with the birds as well as their involvement in sacrificial rites.[69]

Corvid sacrifices are distinct from that of other animals in that we do not find evidence of these birds ever being eaten. Scholars note that this separates them from all other sacrificial animal remains seen in the archaeological record.[70] This is likely the result of the carrion-feeding habits of these birds, making them, in the minds of Iron Age people, unsound and deadly for humans to consume. It is of course true that animals such as dogs, wolves, and wild pigs will at times also eat carrion, but it is not usually their primary sustenance, and so they do not carry the cultural connotation of feeding on death that marks the corvid species apart as birds of deathly omen. This status, of course, is precisely what gives them their association with prophecy, war, Otherworldly magic, and the battle Goddesses, and thus is the reason for their particular role in sacrificial practices.

---

65 Serjeantson & Morris 2011 85-87
66 Powell and Clark cited in Serjeantson & Morris 2011 93.
67 Serjeantson & Morris 2011 99
68 Serjeantson & Morris 2011 100
69 Serjeantson & Morris 2011 102
70 Serjeantson & Morris 2011 89

Apotropaic Sacrifice

A distinctive pattern shown in the archaeological record is the deployment of sacrificial remains into boundaries, foundations, and other arrangements where they serve a protective function. In many places, the bones from sacrificed animals (and sometimes people) were placed into intentional arrangements in rath ditches defining sacred enclosures, to act as guardian spirits for the sanctuaries. Brunaux, writing of this phenomenon in the context of Gaulish sanctuaries, calls this deployment of animal remains in the boundary ditches the "apotropaic cordon"—a continuous boundary formed by the skulls and bones of sacrificed animals, including cattle, horses, and others, whose spirits were understood to serve an apotropaic role following sacrifice.[71] Similar phenomena are seen in Ireland at sites such as Temair, Emain Macha, Cruachan and the like. Skeletal remains of sacrificial animals including cattle, sheep, pig, horses, and dogs, along with human bone, and in one case even an infant, were placed into the boundary ditches, apparently to serve a protective function in the sacred enclosure.[72]

A striking example of apotropaic sacrifice is the "Ghost Cavalry". At the Gaulish hillfort of Gondole in what is now France, a group of eight horsemen were buried with their horses just outside the gates of the fortress. This was no ordinary funerary rite, as no grave goods were included, but the careful positioning and lack of any skeletal trauma suggests a sacrificial death and ritual deposition for a protective purpose. Each warrior's arm was placed over the shoulder of another warrior, each horse's foreleg positioned similarly, so that the group of horsemen hold together as a warrior band.[73] This apotropaic burial was placed at about the time of Caesar's conquest of the region and may have been undertaken in an effort to establish an especially strong level of spiritual protection at a time when the tribes of the region felt themselves to be under threat.

In Ireland, apotropaic sacrifice is seen in the placement of bog bodies. New research into the deployment of bog sacrifices has identified that a significant number of them are found along important tribal boundaries. In some places whole bodies were deposited, and in others

71 Brunaux 1988 25

72 Waddell 2014 72, 101, 129

73 Aldhouse-Green 2010 63

only parts such as heads or severed limbs. This phenomenon is linked to the prevalence of high-status individuals among the bog sacrifices, and suggests that the practice of king sacrifice (discussed above) may have been accompanied, in some cases, by the dismemberment of the king's body and its distribution along the borders, so that he would continue to guard the kingdom in death.[74] Many other valuable objects of kingly or elite status, along with anthropomorphic statues in wood, are also found in border depositions, possibly placed for an apotropaic guarding function.[75] We can see a reflection of this in the Welsh legend of Brân ("Raven"), whose head is said to be buried at London, its presence protecting the island of Britain from invasion, recorded in the Welsh *Triads*.[76]

The related practice of foundation sacrifice seems to have been common in the ancient world, reflected in the lore of Emain Macha. *Cormac's Glossary* records a folk etymology interpreting Emain from *ema* "blood" (in Greek) and *uin* "one": "Or *Em-* is from *ema* that is: from blood, because *ema* is blood. *Uin* that is: one, because the blood of one man was shed at the time of its founding."[77] The folk etymology no longer aligns with how modern linguistics traces the origin of the name, but it reflects a belief on the part of the early Irish in the notion that a human sacrifice needed to be entombed into the foundations of the fortress in order to ensure its strength and protective function.

Divinatory Sacrifice

Divination presents another major context of sacrificial ritual. This has been seen above in the *tarb feis*, or bull feast, in which the bull is sacrificed and its parts used in divination to seek foreknowledge of kingship and battles. We have also seen it in the divinatory raven sacrifice performed by Cú Chulainn, and linked to traditions of warriorship. Another instance occurs in a visionary divination ritual called *imbas forosnai*, practiced by a number of prominent poets in the literature, including the warrior-woman Scáthach who taught Cú Chulainn in the arts of war. *Imbas forosnai* seems to have involved the same group of ani-

74 Kelly 2012 237
75 Iping-Petterson 2012 35
76 Skene 1868 Triad 34
77 Borsje 2007a 46

mals mentioned earlier—the sacrifice of a pig, dog, or cat, whose raw flesh was chewed and offered to the Gods with an incantation, followed by an enchanted sleep in which dreams would reveal the knowledge being sought.[78]

In addition to these accounts, we also see numerous references to the practice of divinatory human sacrifice. Arrangements of entrails, the movement of the victim's limbs in their death throes, or the patterns of blood shed by the victim in the sacrificial rite, were read for patterns that could reveal the future. This practice was reportedly performed upon prisoners of war, with the intent to draw prophecies about the outcome of future battles.[79]

The crucial point to understand about divinatory sacrifice is its reflection of the very same sacrificial cosmology that placed sacrifice at the center of Celtic devotional ritual. That is, the cosmological myth "describing the creation of the physical universe from the dismembered body of a primordial victim."[80] As the body of the universe itself was spiritually identified with the body of the sacrificial victim, that same identity which allowed the world to be restored and renewed in the act of sacrifice also provided that all the macro-patterns of the created world could in turn be observed within the body of the victim. Thus, in the act of sacrifice, as the world was re-made with the substance of the sacrificial victim, knowledge of the unfolding of those cosmological patterns in the time to come could be observed. It is for this reason that divination as well as healing were so deeply tied to sacrifice in Celtic religious practice.

The Blood and Blades of Offering

Sacrifice was seen as so crucial and indispensable to Celtic religion that, in the Continent, even when sacrifice itself was abolished under Roman rule, altered versions of the practice were continued. Partial dismemberment was practiced instead, in the form of offering pieces of flesh cut from the body in such a way as to not kill.[81] Blood could also be offered at will without requiring the full lethal sacrifice of a per-

78 Meyer 1888 302. These practices are explored in further depth in Chapter 14.
79 Aldhouse-Green 2010 213
80 Lincoln 1988 386
81 Lincoln 1988 385

son, as reported by Pomponius Mela just after the conquest.[82] A similar practice of bleeding both people and cattle, to provide an offering without killing, is recorded in Ireland into historic times.[83]

Indeed, the blood itself seems always to have been significant to the rite of sacrifice. Accounts of sacrificial ritual among the Celto-Germanic Cimbri describe the throats of victims being cut and the blood collected in great vessels, over which priestesses would draw prophecy.[84] Cult regalia matching these descriptions have been found in gravesites. The famous Gaulish burial at Vix may reflect this: here, a high-status woman, a priestess, princess, or queen, was buried with wealthy grave-goods including an enormous vessel which could have been used for such a purpose, though it may instead have been related to the serving of mead or wine in the context of warrior or sovereignty rites.[85] Votive representations such as the Strettweg "cult-wagon" sculpture may also be related; this example depicts a woman surrounded by stags and hunters, bearing a large bowl upon her head. This central figure is interpreted by some scholars as a priestess holding up a vessel of sacrificial blood.[86]

Among the sacrificial regalia found in Iron Age deposits, knives have been recovered from several Gaulish tombs, sometimes deposited alongside the sacrificed animals that were likely last killed with them. Some such collections of sacrificial regalia also include bowls apparently for sacrificial blood, and pairs of spoons, usually in bronze, apparently used for divination.[87] Their frequent association with sacrificial knives in grave collections suggest that sacrificial blood may have been among the sacred materials used in this divinatory rite.

82 Koch & Carey 2003 31
83 Wood-Martin 1902 6
84 Aldhouse-Green 2010 213
85 Aldhouse-Green 2010 225
86 Aldhouse-Green 2010 225
87 Aldhouse-Green 2010 162-163

Living Practice: Gifts of Life

From examining the remnants of sacrifice as practiced by the ancients, we now turn to look at sacrifice in living traditions today. Sacrifice has disappeared from the practices of a great many modern Pagan traditions and communities, though not all. Modern Pagans often say that it is no longer relevant or morally acceptable as a practice; that it is among the things we should be proud to leave in the dust of history on the path of progress. Many would prefer to dissociate themselves even from acknowledging that sacrifice was historically practiced within their traditions, out of fear of being vilified by mainstream Judeo-Christian cultures. But I think we can be more courageous than this. Instead of reacting from fear and horror to dismiss sacrificial practice, I think we need to re-examine it intelligently with respect to our values and the way we practice today.

The Ethics of Animal Sacrifice

The cosmological fundamentals which made sacrifice relevant in ancient Celtic traditions, as an expression of Indo-European cultural patterns, have not changed. Devotional principles of gifting, reciprocity, and feeding our connections with divinities have not changed. It remains relevant in polytheist religious practice to offer the best to our Gods; and there is no higher value than life itself. It remains true that the shared flow of life force between Gods and devotees is central to devotional relationship; and there is no more potent form of life force we can give than an actual life. It is biological fact that we are animals who live by consuming other living things, and to make that killing and consumption a sacred act is still an effective way to honor that which has died to feed us, and the powers that continue to make that life possible.

Ethical objections to animal sacrifice often center around the idea of cruelty, the suffering of the animal who is being killed. Yet many people are willing to overlook and numbly accept the cruel, painful and degrading conditions animals in our meat supply suffer in modern industrial farming: the overcrowding, filthy conditions, caging and restriction, painful industrial-style killing, and panic-inducing exposure of animals to the slaughter of other animals. When we examine the conditions under which religious animal sacrifice occurs in a modern and ancient context, as a rule it is far more compassionate than industrial farming, because it is highly personal and intentional. And it should not surprise us that this would be so. A person killing in a priestly capacity and for sacred purposes is deeply invested in and sensitive to the sanctity of the entire process. That practitioner understands that the entire religious value of the offering will be tainted by a failure to uphold these rigorous standards.

I am personally acquainted with several priests who practice animal sacrifice; without exception, they are rigorous in their commitment to compassionate treatment of sacrificial animals, both in their raising and in the slaughter experience.[88] These sacrificial practitioners are usually either raising their own animals with care, or obtaining them from small farms within their communities. They visit their farmers and investigate how animals are being raised, and will only work with farmers whose practices provide a high standard of living for the animals. They deeply commit to the dignity of the animals they work with at all points in the process. When the time comes for a sacrifice, they expend great effort to ensure that the animals do not experience stress, fear, or pain, and they employ rigorously practiced techniques to ensure that animal has a gentle, pain-free, and dignified death. Most of these practitioners employ humane slaughter methods similar to accepted Kosher and Halal practices. And just as in the ancient world, most sacrificed animals are shared with the community as sanctified food.

Another objection raised about animal sacrifice is the concern for killing a sentient being who presumably, if given the choice, would want to continue living. In my view, this is a valid ethical question—one which applies to the killing of animals for any purpose, not just religious sacrifice. If we believe individual autonomy and consent important for human beings, we have to at least consider them as meaningful for animals who we know to be capable of complex thought and feeling. For this reason, some people find the entire idea of killing and eating animals abhorrent and choose vegetarianism or veganism. This is a valid personal choice and one I respect. However, it doesn't solve the ethical problem of killing sentient living things who didn't ask to die. The further we delve into research on sentience, sensitivity, and responsiveness in living things, the more we find that all the life around us shows signs of awareness and the ability to feel. We now know that

88 Acknowledgements and thanks to my colleague Theanos Thrax, who has provided invaluable education to myself and many others on these matters.

these qualities are not simply the domain of mammals, nor even vertebrate animals, nor are they even restricted to animals at all. We are now beginning to be able to observe the consciousness and sensitivities of plants, too. Yet we must eat to live.

What is now dawning to our understanding is a truth that the ancients always knew: participation in life is participation in death. As living beings who need to eat other living beings in order to survive, we cannot opt out of participation in the ecology of life and death. We are part of a deeply interwoven system of beings who live through consumption of other life. The best ethical position available to us is to participate in this ecology of life and death compassionately, intelligently, and unapologetically, in an active commitment to respecting other beings.

Animal Sacrifice in Practice

In my view, all this makes animal sacrifice a valid and ethically sound religious practice, when performed according to high standards of dignity, compassion, and respect for the animal. In practice, though, these standards represent a barrier for many people. Since sacrifice has been eliminated from many of our traditions, and since we have a largely urban population of practitioners who lack any experience of humane animal slaughter techniques, in practice very few modern Pagan groups have been able to re-integrate sacrifice into their traditions.

This is as it should be, for now—bringing sacrifice back into our traditions will take time. To be ethically and religiously sound, the sacrifice of living animals requires specialists. Historically, there is every indication that sacrifice was always the domain of highly trained specialists. Among the Celts, these specialists would have been the druidic priests we have read so much of, and who underwent many years of training. Ritual sacrifice has never been, and never should be, a congregational skill that any and all Pagans should expect to perform. It employs a variety of crucial skills that require expert training: compassionate animal handling and care; techniques of killing without inducing pain, stress, or fear; butchering and preparation of meat; handling and preservation of other parts such as hides, bones, and the like. Ritually and in religious terms, every element of the process requires a high standard—failures of skill which cause animals to suffer stress, panic, and pain introduce spiritual harm that can render the sacrifice into an insult to the Gods as well as the animal. Sacrificial practice also relies on crucial priestly skills for specialized ritual preparation and purification; divination, to determine the nature of a needed sacrifice; and finely honed animal communication methods to ensure that only willing animals are killed. All these skills depend upon access to experienced, expert individuals to provide training and oversight. The practice also necessitates some system of accountability within one's tradition, to exercise control over who is authorized to perform sacrifices, and how training and skill are measured.

In essence, ethically sound religious sacrifice depends upon a well-established and structured tradition within a strong community. Few modern Pagan traditions have these safeguards in place. Where we lack them, we can look to certain other polytheistic communities as models of how tradition, structure, and community around sacrifice need to work: some African traditional religions, Diaspora traditions, reconstructionist polytheisms, and others.

In some communities who lack sacrifice specialists, people have instead connected with local family farmers who slaughter their own animals humanely, arranging for an animal to be ritually consecrated, with the actual killing completed by this skilled person. It is better to forgo sacrifice than to perform it wrongly, and it is better to outsource sacrifice to an expert specialist than to do it ourselves without training. In the absence of the right specialists, it is better to simply make other substitute offerings.

Human Sacrifice

There is now no real question as to whether or not ancient Celtic peoples practiced human sacrifice. That they did, of course, does not mean we should. Our societies today place a different value on human life and especially the autonomy and self-determination of individual people. For the same reasons that we now categorically reject and abhor slavery—the subjugation of a person's life and liberty to another—most people also now reject human sacrifice on principle. We understand personal autonomy and the individual merit of human life differently than our ancestors did. I feel it is important to be willing to look at the truth of history and understand why ancient peoples did practice human sacrifice, and in particular how deeply it is tied in to the cultic traditions of the Morrígna, but I certainly do not advocate for a restoration of human sacrifice in our traditions today.

But this is not the end of the conversation. Many people have made the observation that in truth we do still practice human sacrifice today. In the United States, many states apply the death penalty for certain crimes, some states more actively than others. The death penalty is applied despite the demonstrated fact that criminal justice systems contain enormous distortions due to racism, socio-economic oppression, and other factors that result in innocents being punished. We also know that in many cases the death penalty does not actually work to deter crime, but is applied as a form of moral retribution imbued with religious ideology. Our death penalty is in fact a direct inheritance from Judeo-Christian religious culture, and so in a very real and historic sense it does represent a form of state-sanctioned prisoner sacrifice.

Military deaths can also be viewed as a form of human sacrifice. A great many wars in my short lifetime have been pursued by the military-industrial political elite without any real achievable objectives, but rather toward vague metaphysical ends such as "ending terrorism", or a battle against "evil". Millions of people, both soldiers and civilians, have been killed in pursuit of these metaphysical goals. It might sound like a stretch to call such deaths human sacrifices, were it not for the fact that people dying in this context have recognized and named themselves as victims of human sacrifice. In a letter to the political authors of the 2003 Iraq war, maimed veteran Tomas Young on his deathbed wrote these words: "Hundreds of thousands of human beings, including children, including myself, were sacrificed by you for... your insane visions of empire."[89] Tomas Young believed he was sacrificed to greed. Who among us is willing to dismiss his authority to speak about the meaning of his own imminent death?

It is my belief that we especially, as devotees of a war Goddess, bear an obligation to contemplate these things. What we categorically reject we often are ignoring and repressing within our own society. In our desire to distance ourselves from the perceived barbarity of ancient practices such as druidic human sacrifice, we may easily make the mistake of ignoring real human sacrifice that is ongoing and sanctioned by our societies today in the absence of our gaze. Each of us needs to look deeply at the dynamics and systems that underlie these modern manifestations of warfare, justice, and state-sanctioned killing, and consider what they mean for us both personally and spiritually.

89 Young 2013

Non-Lethal Blood Sacrifice

Many devotees of the Morrígan and related Goddesses share an experiential understanding that they do still want blood offerings from us. In my own practice, I have found this to be true, and in my work as a public priest of the Morrígan I hear from people all over the world. Commonly, she asks for blood.

The value of non-lethal blood offerings—and whether or not they should be considered a form of sacrifice—varies within different Pagan and polytheist traditions. For some traditions of sacrifice, the crucial element of the gift being offered to the Gods is not just the life force within the blood, but the entirety of the life itself. That is, for these practitioners and traditions, full lethal sacrifice is the only recognized form of sacrifice. Other kinds of offerings, such as bloodletting, are valued but not termed sacrifice.

In my view, Celtic tradition offers flexibility on this point. As we have seen in the chapter above on the history of sacrifice in the cults of the Morrígna, the literature and historical record point toward substitution of non-lethal bloodletting for lethal sacrifice, as well as substitution of animal for human sacrifice, placing all these acts within a common religious continuum. Thus in my own practice, I recognize bloodletting and other blood offerings as forms of lesser, non-lethal sacrifice.

For those who wish to offer their own blood, here are some considerations based on my own practice. It should be noted that practices such as bloodletting and tattooing should be considered for adults only, and only for people who are healthy enough to do these practices safely.

Bloodletting: A direct offering of one's own blood may be a beautiful personal offering. About this, a few words on safety and approach are warranted. Any time blood is being exposed, especially in group situations, an awareness of the potential for bloodborne illness is paramount. Tools used in bloodletting should be single-use and never, ever shared between people. Small medical lancets used for blood testing are the safest option; they produce just a droplet. If more than a drop is needed, sterile disposable blades can be used; employ these with great caution as it is easy to cut too deeply. Women who menstruate can offer that blood as an alternative. In a modern devotional context, a blood offering is usually not needed on a frequent basis and is not the default offering. It will usually be a small amount, taken from a small cut which does not need to be deep and should be done with safety foremost in mind. I strongly recommend inexperienced practitioners seek more experienced people for training or mentoring around this practice.

Tattooing: As being tattooed involves the release of small amounts of blood, tattooing represents a very effective form of non-lethal blood offering. It also presents the lovely ability to weave embodied devotional art into the sacrifice, opening the door to endless possibilities for creative use of this form as a devotional offering. The permanence of a tattoo itself represents a devotional act; in a sense, that part of one's skin has been dedicated. For the same reason, of course, it should be taken seriously and with consideration for safety and health risks. As a professional tattoo artist myself, I strongly recommend only working with licensed professional tattoo artists who have health and safety training and work in a professional manner with regard to bloodborne pathogen safety. Most in-home tattoos are not legal and should be avoided. Your tattoo artist may be willing to work with you to adapt ritual elements into the tattooing process, such as prayers or consecration of the inks and equipment. You can also bring back something with a bit of your blood on it from the tattooing process to offer at your home shrine or altar.

Blood donation: I recognize blood donation as an effective modern form of voluntary sacrifice. This operates on the same principle that allows a sacrificed animal to be given to the Gods, and the sanctified meat afterwards shared with the community. Similarly, in this form of offering, the blood is offered and sanctified to the Gods, and then shared with the community via the blood bank.[90] Blood donation provides the benefit of giving life not only to the Gods, but to our community at the same time. Blood banks are often in great need of blood donations which are used quite literally to save lives. It should also be said that some people are excluded from giving blood—including, at the time of writing, a highly offensive ban preventing gay men and those connected to them from donating in the United States. For this reason, and for the theological reasons noted above, blood donation will not be a suitable sacrificial practice for everyone.

90 It is worth noting that some practitioners believe that offerings must be given entirely to the Gods, and cannot be shared with the community afterward, so this mode of sacrifice does not work for all practitioners and traditions. The non-sanctified and unritualized handling of the blood by the blood bank also presents a religious problem for some practitioners.

In exploring these modes of practice, I wish to emphasize that offering blood is not necessary or appropriate for everyone. I believe no one should feel compelled to the practice against their own judgment. Many people have specific agreements with their Gods or spirits not to ever intentionally shed their own blood, or may have other agreements or conditions that make this practice inappropriate for them. It is a highly personal matter between the individual practitioner, their Gods, and their own lived understanding of their religious traditions.

Offering one's blood to a divinity also may have profound connective effects that the practitioner needs to be aware of. Sharing blood can engender a binding between the offerer and the recipient, in a manner somewhat analogous to the common idea of a "blood bond" between people who have mingled their blood. In my experience, when we offer our blood to the Morrígan, this does engender a real and significant binding. She may receive the blood offering as granting her a claim upon the life of the offerer. The nature and extent of this claim may be different for any individual, but in any case is not something to be entered into lightly or spontaneously. For any practitioner considering making such an offering, I strongly recommend that agreements be negotiated around what is being offered, what claims and impacts it may entail, and when such offerings can be expected in the future.

This leads us into the subject of dedication, and its connected realms of priesthood, sovereignty, oaths, and personal service. In the next chapter we look at how priesthood, service and sovereignty figured into ancient cults of the Morrígna, and how we engage with them today.

13 Priesthood and Sovereignty

The previous chapters on devotional practices, offerings, and sacrifices have brought us to the subject of priesthood. For ancient peoples who venerated the Morrígna, what might priesthood have looked like in practice? What was the nature of the relationship between priests and the Morrígna, between priests and sovereigns, of priesthoods within the structure of societies? These relationships bring a central dynamic of the Celtic paradigm into clear view: the functions of sovereignty and sacral kingship as mediated by priesthood.

Priests & Kings

In ancient Ireland, the sacral king served as the vessel and embodiment of relationship between the community and the Otherworld. The role of the priesthood was to orient, illuminate, and shape that relationship. The priestly classes seem to have held great power during the pre-Christian period in Ireland, a dynamic which continued well into the Christian era. In many respects, poets are portrayed by the surviving sources as wielding as much power as the king himself, perhaps more. It was the priesthood of druids and poets who performed the divinatory rites to identify and select a candidate for kingship, and who prescribed and performed the rites to confer kingship upon him. It was the priesthood who managed the communication between society and the Gods, determining what rites and sacrifices were needed. While the king was responsible for giving judgments, poets are also described as having specific judiciary functions as well; and they were likely active advisers on most matters of state and important judgments.[1] In the end, it would have been the priesthood also who performed the rites and divinations that might determine the need for an end to a king's rule.

The structure of the Celtic priesthood in pre-Christian times is difficult to clearly articulate, as the data that survives is fragmentary. In the case of Ireland's priestly classes, information about their roles and functions in pagan society is obscured by the evolution of their functions into the Christian period, as the druidic schools continued to exist in altered form within the monastic system. We must condense a subject that merits entire books of study here to a brief overview. In short, common to descriptions of the priesthoods in Ireland, Britain and Gaul are a tripartite division of functions, with the specifics of these functions varying over time and region. In Gaul, the primary branches of the priesthood seem to have been, roughly speaking, poetic priestcraft (encompassing prophetic and magical speech), ritual priestcraft (including augury, divination and sacrifices), and judicial priestcraft (including theology, cosmology, and their application to justice).[2] The tripartite division of priesthood in Ireland seems to have placed a greater emphasis on poetic priestcraft, with the poets serving as the pre-emi-

1 Ó hÓgáin 1999 81
2 Koch & Carey 2003 13 quoting Diodorus Siculus; 18, quoting Strabo; Olmsted 1994 17.

nent priests, fulfilling judicial and diplomatic roles as well as prophecy, while the druids were primarily concerned with sorcery and sacrifices.[3]

Nonetheless, the titles of the various priestly classes, while used differently across regions, derive from common roots. The title for a poetic priest was *fili* in Irish (Gaulish *velets*), a name which derives directly from a Celtic root **vel-* "to see" and indicates that poetic functions were never separate from seership.[4] Another type of poetic priest was *bard* (Gaulish *bardos*), from the root **gwerh-* "to chant" or "to sing".[5] Another title is *fáith* in Irish (Gaulish *vatis*); likely from a root **uet-* "to say", with a connotation of speaking with the Gods, or in an inspired or possessed state.[6] In Ireland the *fáith* was predominantly an oracle or diviner; in Gaul *vatis* seems to have held a connotation of sacrificial and divinatory priesthood. The title druid, *druí* in Irish (Gaulish *druis*) traces from **derwo-* "firm" or "strong" with **uid-* "to know", giving a meaning of "strong in knowledge".[7] It should also be noted that the word "druid" is used generically in some texts to refer to any of these priestly classes without specificity, which confuses the matter.

Kingship is closely coupled with priesthood in early Celtic societies, as we would expect for a group of cultures built so strongly around religious ideologies. In many Irish tales of kings, their poets and druids accompany them. In the post-Christian form in which these tales were recorded, these characters are often reduced in status to be described as "jugglers", "conjurers" or the like, possibly through confusion between the word *drúth*, "buffoon, jester" and *druí* for "druid". Nonetheless, the sacral functions of these characters can still be observed within their actions, as will be demonstrated through a few examples.

Friend of the War-Goddess

Tulchine provides an illustrative example of the functions of priesthood for our interests. A companion of King Conaire in the *Destruction of Dá Derga's Hostel*, Tulchine is called a juggler and conjurer in this text. Hints of his status are present, however: he wears a "speckled mantle" similar to those described among the accoutrements of a druid; his

---

3 Mac Cana 1970 14
4 Delamarre 2003 311
5 Delamarre 2003 67
6 Delamarre 2003 308
7 Olmsted 1994 381, 391

"juggling" is a highly symbolic act involving the balancing in motion of symbols related to the different aspects of a king's rule (apples, swords, and shields); and during this action, Tulchine enters a trance state in which he gives an oracular prophetic poem.[8] Of course, we have met this character before: in the *Dindshenchas* text of Mag mBreg, where Tulchine is directly identified as Conaire's druid. Here his tale is a personal one—he prays to the Morrígan for help in gaining a *síd* woman's hand in marriage, and the Morrígan is "good unto him" and grants his prayer.[9] Tulchine thus presents a portrait of a druidic priest and poet who serves in an official capacity as spiritual adviser and guide to a sovereign, and also maintains a private, personal devotional relationship with an individual Goddess. Ralph O'Connor calls him "a friend of the war-goddess".[10]

Tulchine's character also raises questions on the nature of relationships between priests and individual deities. Were these priests in any sense dedicants of specific deities, or did their roles require them to serve more broadly as priests to a range of deities? Was there such a thing as a "priest of the Morrígan" in antiquity? We cannot answer this question with certainty. Toward illuminating it, we can note that Ireland and other Celtic realms share a pattern of both priests and sovereigns taking names identifying them with a divinity. Jacqueline Borsje notes that in the Mag Slecht stories, centering on the worship of the God Crom Cruach, the king's druid is named Cromdes, suggesting a naming based on the deity.[11] *Des* is "order, arrangement", with the sense of "rightful order"; alternately it could be a variant of *dess*, "right hand". The name may yield something like "Rule of Crom" or "Right Hand of Crom" perhaps. Like Tulchine, Cromdes appears to be someone who both serves the role of public priest to a sovereign, likely requiring priestly service to a collective of tribal Gods, while also holding a special relationship to a particular God. Similarly, we have a character named Mug Nuadat, "Slave of Nuada", perhaps suggesting dedicated service.[12] A related practice may be reflected in Gaul and Britain where the records show tribal leaders, who may have been priest-kings or priest-queens, named for deities: such as Boduognatus

8 Stokes 1910 286-287, O'Connor 2013 187
9 Stokes 1892 471
10 O'Connor 2013 187
11 Borsje 2007a 47
12 Macalister 1956 469

"Born of Bodua"[13] and Boduogenus "Son of Bodua";[14] the British Boudicca appears to have taken the name of a Goddess Boudiga.[15]

These priests in Celtic priestly systems seem to have usually served in public religious functions related to sovereignty, kingship, warfare, justice, and more. We can imagine they must have therefore maintained devotional practice toward any Gods of their people involved in those functions. But the evidence seems to show that in at least some cases they might also have held personal dedications or special devotional relationships with favored deities.

Sovereignty & Sacral Kingship

Kingship in early Ireland cannot be decoupled from religious and spiritual functions. It was understood, at its root, as a contract with the Otherworld. The king represented the combined and balanced aspects of the whole society, encompassing its three functions or estates (martial, priestly, and productive). Standing beyond and embodying all three functions, the sovereign mediated between them and the Otherworldly forces through which prosperity was believed to be obtained.[16]

Kings in early Irish society, as in other ancient Celtic societies, were drawn from the warrior elite and were measured for fitness by their martial capacities. Yet the identity of a king was not solely martial. Accession to kingship involved taking on a new, highly sacralized and liminal status embodying all parts of society. As Bruce Lincoln puts it, speaking of Indo-European societies inclusively, "kings were forced to pass through elaborate coronation ceremonies which had as their chief goal the creation of a new social identity for the future king, not as a warrior but as one who integrated within himself the essence of all three social classes."[17] The obligations of the sovereign incorporate all three functions: the martial function in providing military force and serving as a war-leader; the priestly function in upholding *gessi*, observing religious rites and customs, and giving true judgments; and the productive function in feast-giving, generosity, and the taking and redistribution of tribute, as well as the crucial function of maintaining the

13 Delamarre 2003 81
14 Olmsted 1994 411
15 Beck 2009 139, Olmsted 1994 411
16 Bray 1999 109, Borsje 2009 176
17 Lincoln 1991 4

fertility of the land through right relations with the Otherworld.[18]

Above all, the central requirement of kings fuses all three functions: the obligation to embody and enact justice through speaking truth and giving true judgements, called *fír flathemon*, "truth of sovereigns". This concept encompasses the whole relationship of the king to land, people, and Otherworld, through which prosperity was understood to be secured. As the king was identified bodily with both land and people, failure of right action or personal integrity on the part of the king was believed to manifest itself in the loss of fertility and well-being in land and people: cows would lose their milk, grain would not grow, defeats in battle would occur, and people would suffer famine.[19] These occurrences themselves would be signs that the spiritual force of sovereignty had withdrawn itself from the king because he was no longer worthy of it.

Sovereignty in the Irish paradigm is thus a spiritual force which arises in the Otherworld and is channeled or mediated through the person of the king, and which should flow toward land and people to sustain their well-being. His primary function was the maintenance of that relationship with Otherworldly forces which allowed him to preserve that flow of blessing and sovereignty. That sovereignty itself was conceived of as a fluid force is demonstrated by the many myths in which it is conferred upon the sovereign in the form of a Goddess or Otherworldly woman offering him liquid from a cup, or from a well.[20] These Otherworldly females embody the Celtic pattern of identifying divine power with waters, as seen in the many river Goddesses. Rivers and wells rise from the land, just as the force of sovereignty and its blessings are seen to flow from an Otherworld centered beneath the land.

Sovereignty and the Morrígna

Details pertaining to rites of sovereignty could, again, fill volumes; here we will restrict ourselves to aspects of sovereignty practice relating to cults of the Morrígna. We find the Morrígna present in several distinct aspects of sovereignty: in relation to the rites of accession to kingship; in relation to protection of sovereignty and especially the binding and enforcement of *gessi*; and in relation to the sacrificial death of kings. In

18 Bray 1999 109-110
19 Bray 1999 111
20 Beck 2009 523, O'Connor 2013 211

the mythology underlying the cult practices, the relationships of the Morrígna to sovereignty are complex and seem distinct from the classic "lady with a cup" archetype of the Goddess of the land who confers sovereignty. The Morrígan displays an active interest and relationship with sovereignty, yet rarely herself acts directly as the lady of sovereignty. Macha does present many of the features of the sovereignty Goddess, yet her relationship to that role is complex and transgressive. Badb appears most strongly in relation to the failure of sovereignty, often presenting herself as the hostile face of sovereignty. As we examine each of them in turn here, we will find that while the Morrígna clearly hold important positions in the ritual life of sovereignty, their roles are never simple.

Ban-Feis: the Sacred Marriage

Macha is perhaps the clearest example among the Morrígna of a sovereignty Goddess, relating as she does to a complex of ritual and mythology surrounding the sacred marriage rite of kingship. As we saw in Chapter 5, above, Macha in her various myths displays characteristic features of the bride of sovereignty: identification with the land as tutelary Goddess, granting kingship through marriage, and manifestation as a mare.

The ritual of kingship through marriage to the Goddess in horse form has been mentioned already in the discussion of sacrifice. As noted, the account of Giraldus Cambrensis is a hostile and sensationalized one, clearly intended to justify the subjugation of the Irish as "savages".[21] Yet its details accord remarkably well with a trans-cultural genre of kingship and status rituals also seen in the ancient Vedic, Hittite, Roman, Rus, and Norse cultures, strongly suggesting very archaic Indo-European roots to this form of ritual.[22] Further evidence within Ireland itself corroborates many elements of the ritual, including textual evidence, the preponderance of place-names associated with horses at royal sites, as well as physical evidence of horse sacrifice at these sites, as already noted in Chapter 12 on sacrifice.

Aligning the parallel details found in various texts, David Fickett-Wilbar has identified the core outlines of the Irish ritual as follows: At an

21 O'Hagan 2013, part 2
22 Fickett-Wilbar 2012 318, Waddell 2014 102, Sayers 1985 40

assembly with a sacred fire, a white mare (or a pair of horses) is brought forward; there is a chariot race to or around a sacred tree; the king professes himself a beast and has intercourse with the mare;[23] there is a proclamation of kingship by vassals; the mare (or pair of horses) is drowned, butchered and its meat boiled; the king is bathed in the broth; and the king and his people eat the meat and drink the broth.[24] It is likely that prior to this rite, the mare would also have been consecrated as the living vessel of the Goddess herself through some form of blessing or invocation. Cambrensis's account details the new king declaring himself "a beast" like the mare; John Waddell suggests that this declaration was the profession of sacred marriage with the Goddess, using such words as *I am horse, thou art mare,* following the known Vedic marriage formula *I am he, thou art she.*[25] I think it is likely that Macha would have been invoked in rites of kingship such as this one in at least some times and places—perhaps at sovereignty rites of the Ulster kingship in the prehistoric period, centered at Emain Macha.

Conflict and Protection

Turning to the Morrígan, her nearest approach to the action of a Goddess conferring sovereignty appears to be her tryst with the Dagda on the eve of the *Second Battle of Mag Tuiredh.* Yet here, what she confers on him is victory more directly than sovereignty. The battle is being fought for the sovereignty of Ireland, and she gives aid to win it, but the Dagda does not take up the kingship in this story.[26] Rather, she offers him help as a war-leader, rather than the kingship itself.[27] Her prophecies in this tale hinge around the future of the sovereignty, but her action here is in her role as prophetic seer.[28] The cognate Goddess Rhiannon (whose name, like the Morrígan's, and several Continental Queen-Goddesses, likely derive from an ancient antecedent *Rigantona) displays strong characteristics of the sovereignty Goddess in horse

23 The sexual intercourse is reported as literal bestiality by Giraldus Cambrensis, but this may well have been politically motivated, and the sexual element of the ritual may have been symbolic.

24 Wright, Hoare & Forester 1863 138, Fickett-Wilbar 2012 338

25 Waddell 2014 104

26 He will later be a king over the Túatha Dé in another part of the myth cycle.

27 Stokes 1891 85

28 Stokes 1891 109

form, intimately involved with rites of kingship, and this may implicate the Morrígan as at least descended from an ancient sovereignty Goddess.[29] However, as we see her in the surviving tales, the Morrígan never acts directly in the role of granting sovereignty.

The Morrígan's actions relative to sovereignty are in closer alignment with the works that would be performed by a poet or druid in support of a king: sorcery to help bring victory in battle, and recitation of prophetic poetry about the fate of sovereignty in the battle. Thus we should not look to locate her directly in the rites of kingship such as the sacred marriage, but in rites and practices related to the warrior and priestly functions—both of which are inextricably involved in the contestation and protection of sovereignty. For this reason, although the Morrígan clearly has a distinct interest in sovereignty, the identifiable aspects of cult practice involving her are found primarily in practices relating to battle, prophecy, sorcery, and related traditions. These cult practices will be explored in greater detail in chapters 14, 15, 16, and 17.

The Hostility of the Otherworld

In the stories of sovereignty and sacral kingship, Badb emerges clearly as an agent of the downfall and removal of kings. Her role is well illustrated in *Dá Derga's Hostel*. After the tragic King Conaire has already started down the path toward his doom by giving false judgment and breaking some of his *gessi*, Badb appears in the shape of the malevolent crone Cailb and seals his fate by entrapping him to break another *geis*, and by verbally cursing him with a death prophecy. She occupies a very similar role in the related story *Dá Choca's Hostel*.[30] In other narratives not centering around kingship, similar malevolent crones appear as agents of destruction or the prophecy of destruction, often by way of triggering the breaking of heroic *gessi*, as in the case of Cú Chulainn.[31]

Badb's relationship to *gessi* and her role in the downfall of kings illustrate an important aspect of sovereignty in early Irish belief. That is, sovereignty was understood to be established and maintained by means of a crucial contract between king and Otherworld. This Otherworldly contract might predate the inauguration, as it does in Conaire's

29 Waddell 2014 89
30 Stokes 1900a 315
31 O'Grady 1898, O'Curry 1855 119-127

case, where he has been selected for kingship through familial relations with the Otherworld from before his birth. A bond of mutual obligation between king and Otherworld is established in this contract. The king gains the power and right to rule through the aid and support of these Otherworldly forces (often personified as *síd* beings; in Conaire's case, bird-men). But this support is maintained only as long as he upholds his reciprocal obligations to them. These reciprocal obligations are embodied in the *gessi*.

Gessi are not simply "taboos", in the sense of "things to avoid". They are, in Bernard Mees's phrase, "curse-enhanced oaths" or contracts with Otherworld forces.[32] They represent active bonds with spiritual forces, in which the binding of the *geis* itself grants an accompanying power. In the case of some champions, the accompanying powers are identified as heroic "gifts" (*búaida*), granted to the hero by virtue of the same binding that gives him the accompanying *geis*.[33] So long as the terms of the *geis* contract are observed, the relationship is an essentially positive one which benefits and strengthens. When the *geis* is undone, it unleashes itself as a curse, while also withdrawing the power it had granted.[34]

There is a living, volitional quality of *gessi* conveyed in the literature—they seem to partake of the spiritual agency of the Otherworld as a living force. Conaire describes this evocatively when he says, despairing, "All my *gessa* have seized me tonight."[35] In the narrative of downfall, once one of the *gessi* has been violated, the rest do not wait, but seem to take on a life of their own, entrapping him into situations where he will break them. This spiritual agency becomes progressively more personified, appearing first in the form of mysterious animals who are *geis* for Conaire to hunt, then in the form of the "red riders" who are *geis* to Conaire to follow on the road, and finally appearing in the ominous person of Cailb, who is none other than Badb, and who personifies a *geis* against receiving a solitary woman to his company at night.[36] Badb emerges from these tales as the active force of the Otherworld in its malevolent stance. She is, essentially, the agent of the hostile Otherworld; when power granted to a hero or sovereign has been misused, as measured by the violation of *gessi*, she arrives to retract that

32 Mees 2009 152
33 Mees 2009 145
34 O'Connor 2013 111
35 Stokes 1910 65
36 Stokes 1910 36, 70, O'Connor 2013 111, 138

power. She appears when the Otherworld contract has been breached, as part of the cascading series of *gessi* unbinding themselves into curses, becoming the force which then binds the failed king to his doom. The relationship of Badb to the sovereignty is inextricably tied to her role as the face of the hostile Otherworld. In acting as the agent of the kingly *gessi* and bringing about the king's downfall, she is protecting the sovereignty by withdrawing it from a man no longer considered worthy of it. And here she is also protecting the land: his actions in giving false judgment and breaking *gessi* violate his *fír flathemon*, and will destroy the prosperity of the realm if he is allowed to retain the sovereignty.[37]

The *Dá Derga's Hostel* text vividly highlights this role of Badb as the malevolent face of sovereignty. Ralph O'Connor argues persuasively that the text intentionally contrasts Cailb with Étaín. At the beginning of the text, Étaín is positioned as the classic Lady of Sovereignty—glowing with Otherworldly beauty, meeting the king at a well to grant him marriage and the favor of the spiritual realm for the founding of his dynasty. Étaín's description dwells on brightness in a descriptive sequence likening her to sun, moon, wealth, and the land flowering in summer. At the point of downfall, Cailb arises in stark contrast; her description following a similar literary pattern, but highlighting blackness instead of brightness, and harsh, frightful, and gloomy imagery in place of natural fertility and beauty. Cailb's name sequence highlights these contrasts as well:

> "fine weather turns stormy (Sinand), beauty turns ugly (Díchoem), sweetness and music turn harsh and noisy (Blosc), a gentle, dignified voice becomes an outcry (Égem), cheerfulness becomes gloom (Mod), neighbourly love becomes the fury of battle (Níth, Noenden, Némain), and nature's fertility withers to a wasteland (Seiscleand)."[38]

Remembering that these names are delivered in the form of a curse, they convey a clear message of the smiling benevolence of the Otherworld turning to dark hostility as the sovereignty is withdrawn from Conaire.

37 O'Connor 2013 9
38 O'Connor 2013 150

Sovereignty as Death Goddess

It is often observed that sovereignty tales resolve themselves into death tales. In the death tales of kings and heroes, a "mysterious woman" often appears, typically with a fusion of both ominous and erotic themes, involving herself in the downfall and death of the king.[39] Badb, as we have seen, exemplifies this—soon after her encounter with Conaire (in the form of Cailb), the Hostel is attacked and he is killed in the battle. Another characteristic death tale of this type is that of Murchertach mac Erca, mentioned in the *Roll of Kings* and described in more detail in his death tale.[40] Murchertach had married an Otherworldly woman called Sín or Sinann (among Cailb's names, incidentally); the text calls her "a goddess of great power".[41] She involves herself in his death in a ritualistic fashion on Samhain night.[42] Notably, the deaths of both Conaire and Murchertach are triple ones. Murchertach drowns in a vat of cursed wine after being wounded and burned inside a burning house.[43] Conaire dies of wounding, thirst induced by a druidic curse, and in a burning house.[44] The involvement of magically charged drink or thirst for drink in both tales is a key element, signaling that the death is in relation to sovereignty, which presents itself as a spiritually potent liquid.[45]

It seems intuitive that these tales of ritually-induced triple deaths of kings may contain the remnants of a tradition in which kings were ritually sacrificed. As we have seen in the chapter on sacrifice, there is abundant evidence in Ireland and elsewhere pointing to a tradition of king sacrifice, the details of which have been already discussed. Here, we add that that the presence of a hostile sovereignty Goddess in these tales—exemplified by Cailb, Badb, Sín or Sinann[46]—strongly suggests that such Goddesses would have been part of the proceedings when such sacrifices were carried out. To my mind, the description of the triple Badb inside Dá Derga's Hostel, in language evocative of triple sacrifice, points to her as a Goddess to whom such a death would be

39 Bhreathnach 1982 citing Rees, Mac Cana 244-245.
40 Macalister 1956 361, Stokes 1902 395
41 Stokes 1902 408
42 Macalister 1956 363, Stokes 1902 425
43 Macalister 1956 533
44 O'Connor 2013 216
45 O'Connor 2013 213
46 O'Connor 2013 148, Bhreathnach 1982 244

consecrated.[47] In her role as the agent of the Otherworld vengefully reclaiming the sovereignty from a king who has failed it, she protects land, sovereignty and people, as we have seen. The sacrificial death might be offered to her in the hope of further protection. The protective qualities of king sacrifice have also been highlighted by the deployment of kings' bodies or body parts as bog deposits along territorial borders.

We should also note that in each of these cases, the sacrificial king death occurs at a house which is burned. In both *Dá Derga's Hostel* and *Dá Choca's Hostel* the kings have come to stay at a hostel, each associated with Otherworldly qualities and with a name suggestive of a divinity: *Dá* meaning a God, as we have seen in Chapter 10. Murchertach's death is in a place called the House of Cletech, a royal house over the Boyne river.[48] In each case, as part of the triple death the house burns down around the king—with Murchertach, it is the hostile Goddess Sín herself who sets the fire.[49] As fire is often an element of the triple deaths, and the element of the burning house is so consistent in the tales, it may be a reflection of a custom related to king sacrifice in which the house or shrine in which the sacrifice took place was burned as an element of the rites.

Living Practice: Personal Sovereignty, Dedication and Priesthood

For us today, the world occupied by the druids, priests and kings of the ancient world can seem very far away. How do we integrate these wisdoms into living practice? What might sovereignty mean for us now?

Sovereignty, Then and Now

We have talked much of sovereignty in its historical context, as the numinous power within the land, vested in the person of the ruler through the Otherworldly contract, mediated and protected by Goddesses of sovereignty. We who read this now, of course, have a different rela-

47 Stokes 1910 87, O'Connor 2013 218
48 Stokes 1902 401
49 Stokes 1902 423

tionship to the concept and power of sovereignty. We do not live under sacral kings who embody the ritual heart of our society. We are ruled through different governing systems. We concern ourselves with notions of self-determination, democratic ideals, civil liberties. Our processes are very different from those of the Irish kings. At root, however, the lore of sovereignty expresses a fundamental concern all societies must address: How shall our land and our people be rightly governed? The central question of sovereignty is the question of fitness to hold power, and of right relationship to the source of our power.

This fundamental concern is partly reflected in the modern political notion of sovereignty, which in common usage has now come to mean the authority of a people or a nation to govern itself. We see this aspect of sovereignty being discussed with regard to the treaty rights of Native American tribes as sovereign nations, for example. Political conversations about sovereignty tend to be secularized, however, and so often lack the spiritual dimension that underlies sovereignty in its ancient Celtic context. The political dimension of sovereignty is important, but for us forms just part of a picture within which individual, collective, and spiritual sovereignty are woven together.

The gendered dynamics of sovereignty change in modern practice, too. Throughout this book, when speaking of antiquity, I write often of kings in the masculine gender, because that is what is contained in the source material. Though there were powerful queens in Celtic societies, they are historical exceptions, and certainly the literature of sovereignty is highly gendered and consistently refers to a male sovereign and female sovereignty Goddess. I have preserved this gendered language when speaking of history and lore, but of course, when it comes to sovereignty as a spiritual practice, we adapt this model to be spiritually suitable for all sexes and genders of people.

Personal Sovereignty and Justice

In some modern Pagan and polytheist practice, sovereignty has been redefined in personal terms, as an individual spiritual practice or goal. Popular ideas around personal sovereignty tend to reflect cultural values of empowerment, autonomy, and self-possession. Practitioners speak about seeking full ownership of our own lives, becoming fully self-possessed, developing inner authority through practicing honor, integrity, justice, and spiritual authenticity. Yet there is more to sovereignty than personal autonomy.

The principle of personal sovereignty shares the same fundamental concerns as that of collective sovereignty: it is the principle of right rulership, sustained by binding relationships both to what we serve and to the source of our power. So while sovereignty is centered in autonomy, it does not mean being answerable to no one, just as wielding kingship in the Irish paradigm did not make a king answerable to no one. We are, in both cases, answerable to the very power that we wield, and to the source of that power. Personal sovereignty is not equivalent to freedom or autonomy, for to be a sovereign is to be bound, just as the king was bound by the Otherworldly contract that granted him his power. The one who claims the sovereignty is at the same time claimed by it.

To understand sovereignty in its full dimension, we need to look beyond the notion of personal autonomy that is so attractive to our modern cultural values. We need to look at the central concern of sovereigns: the obligation to enact justice. Justice is the defining act of a sovereign—the one thing the sovereign must embody and enact in order to be a sovereign. This obligation is expressed in the term *fír flathemon,* "truth of sovereignty", and it speaks of both political and spiritual truths.

The spiritual dimension of *fír flathemon* is the principle of integrity—being in wholeness, spiritual authenticity and alignment with one's values. This is as crucial in the practice of personal sovereignty as it was in the old paradigm of kingship. Kings were bound by *gessi,* oaths and ritual requirements that kept them in alignment with the spiritual forces which supported their community's thriving. We, to be sovereign, must similarly bind ourselves to standing in integrity and alignment with the spiritual forces which support us and our communities.

This spiritual dimension of integrity is the centerpoint from which the social and political dimensions of sovereignty flow. That is, integrity extended into the collective becomes justice; the role of the sovereign is to be a servant of that justice. Here we begin to see more fully the relational nature of sovereignty. The service of a sovereign is to give justice to their community—to all those with whom they are in relationship. I frame this in the language of service intentionally; the lore of sovereignty teaches that it is a living spiritual force, and so in truth the sovereign's role is as a servant of that force, to channel sovereignty from its source within the land outward into their community in the form of acts of justice that bless that community.

Personal sovereignty is thus always relational. It begins in our relationship to ourselves and to the spiritual world, and it flows into relationship with community and landscape at every level. It also is not something we achieve at any point; it is an ongoing practice of commitment to integrity, justice and right relationship with everything that sustains and surrounds us. This will sometimes require fighting to protect our sovereignty from those who would take it away, or from our own ingrained habits of giving it away. As often, it will require standing for the needs and rights of others. It will require also a commitment to recognizing and honoring the personal sovereignty of all beings, an awareness of their own inherent inner worth, their right to self-possession, their boundaries and their needs.

Nine Streams of Sovereignty

Sovereignty being relational, we can recognize it as flows of power operating on three social levels:

- the power flowing in the land which arises from the life of the land
- the flow of that power within us, as personal sovereignty
- the flow of that power between us, our people, and our leadership, as collective sovereignty

Each dimension is integral to the whole. Within and between each dimension, a restriction or severing of these flows of power subverts and destroys sovereignty. Without relationship to the life of the land, we weaken and starve physically or spiritually; we require access to its resources in order to live, and it requires us to give back to it. To control a person's access to the resources of the land is to control their sovereignty. Within ourselves, to the extent that we are able to direct own inner resources in alignment with our values, to be in a state of integrity, we have personal sovereignty. In relationship with others and with the collective level of our group, society, nation, this flow is also preserved—to the extent that justice is enacted in the relationship between individual and group, we are participants in collective sovereignty. Notice that if we are imprisoned or enslaved at the personal level, if our personal sovereignty has been stolen or given away, we are compromised in our ability to delegate it into the hands of leaders who represent us. Personal and political sovereignty are never fully separate.

Intersecting with these three social levels we can also recognize sovereignty in action within the three functional divisions that run through the Celtic worldview—the sustaining, spiritual, and martial functions, embodied by the productive, priestly, and warrior groups. Just as in the ancient model of kingship, a king had obligations representing each of these functions, so we should examine our embodiment of sovereignty in these terms as well. The flow of sovereignty into the sustaining function manifests as hospitality; its flow into the spiritual function manifests as truth, or justice; and its flow into the martial function manifests as protection. What are our gifts and obligations with respect to hospitality, in relationship to land, self, and collective? How do we offer truth and justice to land, self, and collective? Who can claim our protection, or whose protection can we claim? What must we fight for?

It is important to recognize that sovereignty is not an abstract. It is a living power, rooted in the life of the land and the body. The nexus through which these flows move is the body of the individual. When the individual within this set of relations is not in possession of the sovereignty of their own body and life force, the entire set of relations breaks down. Thus the fundamental ground of sovereignty is the sanctity and integrity of the body. This has profound implications for our relationship to sex, gender and power, and illustrates why, throughout history, rape has been used as a tool of oppressors everywhere. Sovereignty begins, for the individual, with the sanctity and integrity of the body. It is the realm in which we must first be sovereign.

There are a few tools I employ toward developing the inner practice of sovereignty. Much of this material has been developed in collaborative ritual and spiritual exploration of sovereignty within the Coru Cathubodua Priesthood.

Power, Agency and Justice

The simplest practice and the one I have found most profound is simply the asking of questions. We can examine our internal world, our relationships with others on the personal and political levels. Looking at each dimension, we ask: How is power flowing? Where is the agency in this relationship? Does justice emerge from it? These questions will help illuminate how the flow of life force or personal power is being directed, and therefore whether sovereignty is being maintained or subverted in a given relationship.

- In our relationship to the land, the resources that sustain us: How is power flowing between the land and our being? Where do we hold agency in our relationship with the land, and where does it hold agency with respect to us? Are we in integrity in this relationship? Are we giving back to the land in reciprocity for its flow of resources to sustain us? How do we relate to the sovereignty model of marriage to the land?

- Within our own being and life: How is power flowing through the body? Where do we hold agency in how and when we commit our bodies, time, energy, and life force? Is this relationship in alignment with our values, and is justice embodied within it? Do we fully embody and enact the commitments we have made?
- In our relationships, interpersonal, social, and political: How is power flowing between us and our close kin? Our social and spiritual groups? Our political bodies? Who exerts agency within these relationships and in what contexts? Are we sharing power with others through agreements we make, and are those flows of power manifesting as justice? If we are delegating power to others, how does that flow of power return to us? If others have delegated power to us, how are we returning that flow of power to them? What is our relationship to our political collective, and is justice embodied in that relationship?

The revelations that come with these exercises can be quite challenging and sometimes painful. It has been my experience that once we become aware of sovereignty, of its flows within us and between us and others, we cannot un-see it. Deep awareness of sovereignty can bring seismic changes to relationships, to political consciousness. Yet it is important work, especially so for anyone who seeks to integrate the powers and wisdoms of the Goddesses of sovereignty and battle.

Rite of Sovereignty

This ritual is one that was created within the Coru Cathubodua Priesthood as an experiential way of integrating the teachings of sovereignty and committing to its practice. It should be emphasized that we do not develop sovereignty through ritual alone—much more important is the constant examination, exploration, and practice of sovereignty within the dynamics of our lives. Ritual can help embed this awareness and practice within our body and life force, can sanctify our commitment to the practice, but it does not stand alone.

Preparations: We use blessed water as the physical conduit of sovereignty in this ritual. Mead would also be traditional and suitable. If water, it should be clean and drinkable. To embody the life of the land in the water, it can be infused with honey, essences from fruit, herbs or flowers, or other things as inspiration suggests. We have a large bowl filled with this water in the working space, with a cup or chalice we can dip into it to drink from (or a dipper to fill cups).

Invocation/Meditation:[50] This rite is done under the auspices of the Sovereignty Goddess—who may take many forms. The ancients seem to have recognized sovereignty Goddesses in the form of many different Goddesses we know, and this ritual can be done in relationship to Macha as a Goddess of sovereignty, the Morrígan as herself a sovereign, and a guardian of sovereignty, or with others you may have a relationship with. So for this ritual, we invoke and offer prayers to our sovereignty Goddess, and then using meditative trance, we undertake a trance journey to greet her, asking for a blessing as we step into relationship with sovereignty. The journey will likely culminate in her offering us the cup of sovereignty, though she may show us many other things.

Chalice Rite: Emerging from the trance journey, we raise up the bowl filled with the infused water. We ask our sovereign Goddess to bless and charge the waters with the power of sovereignty, and ask her blessing on us in our commitment to sovereignty. Then we draw three cups from the water, for the three realms of sovereignty.

- Once for affirming personal sovereignty. Each participant fills their own cup and drinks, making a commitment to personal sovereignty.
- Once for affirming collective shared sovereignty. Each participant fills a cup for the person to their left, and each drink, making a commitment to collective sovereignty.
- Once for the returning flow of sovereignty to its source within the land. Each participant fills a cup and pours it out onto the earth nearby (or if absolutely necessary, a potted plant can stand in.)

50 This ritual assumes some knowledge of how to undertake a meditative trance journey. For reasons of space, I elect not to spell out all the details of the journey, as most practitioners with basic experience will not need this level of detail provided for them. For beginning resources for practices like this, please see recommended reading lists.

Dedication

Many people, when they begin a devotional relationship with the Morrígan, feel drawn to undertake dedication to her. A substantial amount of confusion exists within devotional communities as to what it even means to be "dedicated" to a God. People often speak of being devoted or dedicated to the Morrígan, without discernment as to what these terms actually mean and how they are different from devotion in a more general sense. So, first, some clarifications of these modes of devotion and the way in which I use these terms.

Devotion: A devotee is someone who is in an active devotional relationship with a deity (or other spiritual being). Participation in that relationship is devotion. The term devotion comes from the root *votum*, which in the ancient world did mean "vow". In modern usage, however, it does not have this connotation of a binding commitment. When we speak of someone who is devoted to a cause, for instance, what we really mean is that they are passionate about it and willing to put a significant amount of effort into it. Similarly, when we speak of a devotee of the Morrígan, or someone who is devoted to her, this can include commitments, but not necessarily so; it simply means they are pursuing a devotional relationship. Its primary connotation in the context of polytheism is *intimacy*.

Dedication: Dedication is a specific mode of devotion, within which we undertake binding spiritual commitments, typically in the form of oaths. An oath represents a submitting of one's life force toward the target or recipient of the oath. In a spiritual context, this is not simply a promise which we need to uphold at risk of our honor. An oath creates a magical binding which changes and impacts our spiritual nature, tying part of our soul and life force to the recipient of the oath. In other words, it does not just impact our honor as someone who fulfills their word—an oath alters our destiny, tying it to that of the oath's target or recipient. The primary connotation of dedication in polytheism is as a *binding*. In the Irish context, this takes the form of the *geis*, the lore of which amply demonstrates the life-altering and fating impacts of an oath.

Distinctions are not always as clear as these, however, and there are as many potential variations on these modes of engagement as there are people. It should be clear from this discussion that dedication is not necessary for everyone and should not be entered into lightly or spontaneously. Dedicating oneself to a Goddess, particularly one who embodies such potent forces as warfare, sovereignty, death, and the potentially fatal power of the *geis*, is a serious and life-changing action. There are many reasons to undertake dedication—personal, situational, transactional, service-based—far too many to cover here. What I do want to point out is that I often see people look to dedication when what they are actually seeking is intimacy with their Goddess, to draw closer to her and bring her power more fully into their lives. When intimacy is what we are seeking, other forms of devotion serve perfectly well and often better than dedication.

Dedication and Sovereignty

Dedication entails, as I have said, binding. It need not remove our agency in the relationship, however. The Morrígan can and often does insist on relationship with individuals, and her call can sometimes be impossible to ignore. However, when we enter into relationship with her, we are not necessarily required to surrender our personal sovereignty to her, even in situations of dedication. We should also remember that the central function of sovereignty is service, and we may likely be asked for commitments that will bind us to being in service.

When any of us do consider undertaking oaths of dedication to the Morrígan, we must bring our practiced awareness of sovereignty to the table. Dedication can and should be approached as an intentional commitment, undertaken from a negotiated position. We should look on dedication as what it is—a binding of a portion of our life force, and therefore our sovereignty, within an oathbound commitment. This does not mean giving away personal sovereignty, but rather binding it into relationship with something larger, intentionally committing it to her service, as an act of conscious agency.

The boundaries defining that offering need to be given deep consideration, for the result of the binding will be that to the extent we have dedicated ourselves, we align our destiny with her interests. This can have profound impact on everyone around us. We should be willing to consider how much of our being and life we are willing to dedicate, for how long, in what manner, and what we need guaranteed to us or protected in the exchange. Not every dedication must be a permanent, irrevocable one. Some oaths can be undone, and others cannot. Oaths of dedication should consider at least the following:

- what we are specifically offering
- what she wants our dedication for (and what, therefore, we may be transformed into in service of that)
- what we are expecting to receive from her
- what we wish to exclude or protect from the effects of the binding
- under what terms we are making the commitment (the form of the oath)
- what manner of binding we are undertaking in the dedication (the nature of the *geis* and its impacts)
- for how long the binding will be in effect
- whether it can be renegotiated if our situation changes
- how the impacts of the binding may ripple beyond us through our relationships and community

Finally, it is wise to remember the relationship of the Morrígna with *gessi*, and of *gessi* and heroic valor. Obviously, as Goddesses deeply connected to the delivery of *geis*-curses for those who break their oaths, it is unwise to swear anything we have reservations about being able to fulfill. However, we do not need to be fearful about this. We should remember that each *geis* brings with it its own gift—the *búaid*. That is, it brings with it the special strengths and resources we need to rise to the fulfillment of it. This is her gift to us.

Priesthood

The first thing that needs to be said about priesthood is that it is a path of service. Priesthood is in the doing; it is not an identity but a mode of action that is primarily outward-directed. To be a priest is to be committed to religious service in connecting the Gods and one's community. It is this service orientation that makes priesthood distinct from personal devotion and dedication, though of course one can be practicing all three.

In Pagan devotional circles it is common to hear people talk about being "called" to become a priest or priestess, and people offering priesthood training in weekend workshops, or online groups. Most of what is being presented in these contexts is not in fact priesthood, but simply devotional practice. The core question we should be asking with regard to priesthood is who benefits from our religious practice. If a person's practice consists primarily of private devotions and seeking personal guidance for their own life path, that is not priesthood.

Solitary practice is not priesthood. If we are performing religious ritual services for others, providing and maintaining ritual spaces, shrines, or temples others can benefit from, this is priesthood work. If we are providing teachings and training to others, providing insight, guidance, divination on spiritual matters and life problems, these are the hallmarks of priesthood. If we are developing traditions, reconstructing or building modes of practice, theologies, ritual tools and modes others can employ, this is priesthood work.

This community service function is crucial. One cannot be a priest without a community to be in service to. In most cases, the existence of the community comes first. Communities call forth priests because a need exists, and that need draws people to step forward and be of service. We become priests by finding our place within the web of community and providing something of value to that community. We first commit to developing and deepening our own devotional practice, learning as much as we can about both the Gods and how to understand them, and also about our community and understanding its needs and functioning. We develop community relationships. We continually ask, "how can I help?" and "what is needed here?" In time, people who hold a commitment to depth of practice and to being of service emerge as religious leaders in their communities.

In some communities, organizational structures exist for the training of priests. We need to foster these priesthoods, fellowships, and orders, not just because they provide better training than the organic, boot-strap method of landing in priesthood. Perhaps more importantly, because what these fellowships provide is peers. Priests need to be in relationship with one another as peers at least as much as they need to be in relationship with communities they serve. Peer relationships are crucial because they allow us to support one another: every priest has their special skills, and equally their blind spots or areas where they lack expertise. We need to have priestly peers and allies we can call in to help us be of service to community members who may need something we aren't qualified to help with. Peer relationships are also crucial in keeping standards of service high. We need to hold each other accountable. Leaders of any kind who only relate to students or congregational community members, can end up not seeing any critique or challenge to their work, and this leads to poorer service and occasionally to abuse. Any priest, no matter how experienced, can always learn from their peers. We need a collegiate culture of priesthood that places effective service as the highest value.

Priesthood, Service, and Sacrifice

It is wise to remember that all leadership paths involve sacrifice. In the Celtic paradigm of sovereignty we have been exploring, priests and sovereigns are closely tied together; in some ancient expressions, we see the two roles fused into the person of a priest-king or priestess-queen. Together, priests and sovereigns carry the burdens of service, of embodying and enacting justice, knowledge, and spiritual integrity for and within their communities.

The paths they tread move toward sacrifice. We have seen this in the literature of sovereignty and kingship, with its mythic pattern of marriage to the land leading toward king-sacrifice. We have seen this in the mythology of divine kings such as Nuada, in his relationship to wounding, sacrifice, and leadership. We have seen the bodies of priests or kings drawn from the belly of the bogs where they were preserved. Those who are called to service as leaders, sovereigns, and priests eventually come into relationship with sacrifice as part of their path.

In modern priesthood work, we would not usually expect to see someone being physically sacrificed into a bog. Yet sacrifice is quite real as a dimension of service and it manifests in profound ways. In making the commitments that bring us into sovereign leadership roles, in dedicating ourselves in service, in marrying the land or the Gods—in all the many shapes such commitments may take, the common thread is a binding of one's destiny to the forces that we commit to serving. That binding brings us into the sphere of sacrifice. For in undertaking that binding, we may be asked to sacrifice the person that we were, allowing the Gods to shape us into a new being in their service. In rare instances, this sacrifice is physical: I have known several priests who have undergone near-death or full clinical death and returned to life as part of their entry into service as dedicated priests. These experiences impact a person profoundly, changing the landscape of their being and destiny irrevocably.

The centrality of service in the work of priesthood as a function of sovereignty can bring sacrifice to manifest in subtler ways too. Here, we may also speak of sacrifice in the metaphorical sense—something we are asked to give up. In the commitment to service, priests will find themselves sacrificing sleep, comfort, convenience, personal interests and pastimes, wealth, and all manner of things. We may find ourselves sacrificing cherished personal goals, the life we might otherwise have had, accepting a new destiny bound to the Gods.

A final form of sacrifice, and perhaps for some the hardest, is to step down from leadership when the time comes to hand it onward to others. The commitment to integrity required of a sovereign is irrevocable, but most communities are better served by a change of leadership from time to time. For priests in leadership positions in spiritual communities, it is crucial that one's personal identity is not allowed to merge with the role one is fulfilling as sovereign. It is crucial that attachment to the idea of leadership is never allowed to eclipse the commitment to service and the needs of the community. When the time comes that the community and the Gods are best served by our stepping down, we must be willing to make that sacrifice with a light heart—it should, in truth, not feel like a sacrifice. Our model for this is Nuada, who voluntarily stepped down in favor of Lugh when the needs of his tribe called for it. As sovereign, his commitment to the well-being of his tribe was greater than his desire even to be in the role of sovereign. Our commitment to service as priests should be no less.

14

Oracles and Divinations

In previous chapters we have glimpsed many instances of prophecy in the cults of the Morrígna and in Celtic religion more broadly. We have seen that prophecy is among the core functions of the Morrígan and her sisters. We have also seen that the seeking of prophetic knowledge, and its deployment in the service of public ritual, in acts of sovereignty, warfare, and justice, were key practices of the priests in the traditions embodied by the Morrígna. In this chapter, my intention is to illuminate what we can learn about divinatory and oracular practices that may have been employed within these traditions. We will examine a range of practices, including the use of dreams, intoxication and other mantic trance practices, oracular prophecy, gazing and other omen-taking methods, and lot-casting.

Dream Incubation

Prophetic dream cultivation is pervasive in Celtic practice. The *tarb feis* exemplifies this in Ireland; a rite in which druids sought prophetic knowledge about kingship, or the outcome of a battle, by dreaming after partaking of a ritual bull feast. We glimpse a related practice in Gaul, where a Greek of the 2nd century BCE reported that people would seek prophetic dreams by sleeping at the tombs of ancestors or heroes.[1] The central insight driving practices such as these is that in dreams, the dreamer slips beyond the temporal realm to contact the Otherworld, and can bring back meaningful knowledge of future events or unseen realities.

The Gaulish dream incubation practice gives no specifics about the practice, other than its employment at tombs of important ancestral figures. Parallel Irish practices are described in some detail and in a handful of variations within the texts. Common to all versions of these Irish dream incubation practices seem to be the sacrifice of animals to the Gods, a chanted spell, and a prophetic vision obtained in dream. Gathering together details from all the variants, we can construct a fairly comprehensive ritual.

According to *Dá Derga's Hostel* and the *Wasting Sickness of Cú Chulainn*, in the ritual called *tarb feis*, "bull feast", a white or hornless bull is sacrificed to the Gods, skinned and butchered. The meat is cooked; likely in a stew, as texts mention both meat and broth. This meat and broth are consumed by the druid undertaking the vision; he eats and drinks his fill of both, enough to induce a heavy sleep.[2] He lies down in a ritually prepared bed, covered or wrapped with the hide of the slaughtered bull. Over him, a group of four druids now chant a "spell of truth". The chanted spell has not been recorded, but it seems clearly intended to bind the dreamer to speaking the truth of his vision; one version tells us that "the sleeper would perish if he uttered a falsehood."[3] The chanted spell also likely contained elements to evoke the power of prophecy so that the dreams to come would be true ones.

An apparently related visionary dream incubation ritual appears in the *Battle of Findchorad*. The central elements of *tarb feis*—the sacrifice, sleeping on a bull hide, and visionary dream—are all present. Here, however, the sacrifice is different: the flesh of dogs, pigs and cats are offered; all Otherworldly animals said to emerge from the *síd*.[4] Four

1 Koch & Carey 2003 10
2 O'Curry 1858, Stokes 1910 22
3 Stokes 1910 22
4 Dobbs 1923 399

Gods are named, to whom the offerings are made: Mars, Osiris, Jove, and Apollo; possibly pointing to Irish Gods who have been syncretized or interpreted through a Classical lens in this text.[5] The ritual suggests that sacrifices in this context would be offered to a group of Gods; in at least this case, these may have been deities involved in the realms of war, death and ancestral lineage, rulership and judgment, knowledge and healing. We also find details on ritual preparation of the visionary bed in this text: it is woven out of rowan staves (a wood imbued with magical properties which often appears in Irish magic), and it should face north, "towards Hell". As the ritual is taking place at Cruachan, this reference may well be to the Cave of Cruachan, Oweynagat, called the "Irish entrance to Hell",[6] or the subterranean Otherworld realm, more broadly.

Another seemingly related divination rite is called *imbas forosnai,* and attributed to Scáthach, Fedelm, and other seers in Irish tradition. The details of the ritual are described in *Cormac's Glossary*: the seer seeking a vision chews a piece of raw flesh of pig, dog, or cat, "then places it on a flagstone behind the door," offering it to the Gods, with a series of sung incantations apparently intended to consecrate the offering and invoke the Gods.[7] He then goes to sleep (with "his two palms on his two cheeks"), and is watched over by others to ensure that his visionary sleep is not disturbed until the prophetic dream comes. The text also mentions that the ritual might be conducted for as long as nine days.[8]

The variations in these rituals may represent regional or tribal forms of dream incubation custom, as the *Dá Derga's Hostel* and *Wasting Sickness* texts describe rites performed for the Tara kingship, whereas the *Findchorad* ritual is undertaken for the forces of Connacht and Munster. Additionally, the purpose of the rituals differ: the Tara *tarb feis* rituals

---

5 Phillip Bernhardt-House discusses this subject, but does not propose that these represent any form of Irish deities (Bernhardt-House 2007 54). A speculative listing might include Néit (a war God often syncretized with Mars); Donn (an ancestral God and lord of death, who may be connected with the dismemberment myth of Donn Cúailnge); Dagda (as a father God and wielder of a mighty weapon in some ways similar to Jove); and Lugh (as Lugus is sometimes syncretized with Apollo on the Continent). However, it is possible that the inclusion of these deities was simply meant to connect an Irish ritual to Roman and Greek traditions.

6 Waddell 1983 22

7 O'Donovan 1868 94

8 Meyer 1888 302

are performed to identify a new king, whereas the *Findchorad* ritual is a to divine a coming battle. The *Cormac's Glossary* description mentions no specific purpose for *imbas forosnai* other than divination generally, but Scáthach employs the associated prophetic ability to foretell Cú Chulainn's personal destiny as a warrior,[9] and the seeress Fedelm employs it to give Medb a prophecy of the fate of her army.[10] These differences might also suggest that while the *tarb feis* as such is identified with rites of kingship specifically, it was likely part of a fuller genre of visionary dream incubation rites which could be applied in a variety of contexts, with accompanying changes to the details of the rite.

Intoxication and Trance

To cultivate visionary states, in addition to the heavy enchanted sleep of the dream rituals, we can also discern traditions of ingesting consciousness-altering alcoholic and herbal compounds. Evidence for this practice seems to be more substantial among the Continental Celts than the Irish, but the prominence of intoxication and trance as sources of visionary inspiration, and the presence of characters such as Medb, whose name refers to mead and means "Intoxicating", suggests that it may have been part of visionary trance practice in Ireland as well.

Alcohol, primarily mead, was a favored intoxicant among many Celtic groups in the ancient period. Herbal additives increased potency and the range of intoxicating effects. Evidence in Scotland, Gaul and Germany indicates the use of henbane as an additive in mead or beer, probably for its psychoactive effects.[11] Brewing vessels may have been a means of delivering additives. Vessels made of yew wood were sometimes used for brewing, and Beck suggests (based on a claim in Pliny) that small amounts of the toxic yew alkaloids, leaching into the drink, might have added psychoactive effects. Many of these yew vessels have been found in offering wells and other sacred places, indicating that the brewing process, and likely the drinking of the intoxicating brew, held a sacred function and were used in religious rites.[12]

Classical authors such as Lucan and Pliny the Elder record other

9 Meyer 1888 302
10 O'Rahilly 2011 126
11 Nelson 2005 12
12 Beck 2009 481

plant materials used by the Gaulish druids for divination. Vervain and "pigeon plant" are mentioned in divinatory rites; ingestion is not specified, so they may have been burned for smoke or used in another way.[13] A British burial thought to be of a druid, the Stanway "doctor", contained a strainer bowl with residues of an unspecified *Artemisia*; a family of herbs with intoxicant properties and a long history of use in European trance practices, which includes mugwort, wormwood and related plants.[14] Lucan records that the Gaulish druids ingested a preparation of acorns, and under its effects would practice divination.[15] Beck suggests that the Irish belief in hazelnuts as containing wisdom may refer to a practice similar to that of the Gaulish druids and the acorns.[16] Acorns and hazelnuts do not, to my knowledge, have known psychoactive properties, so these may have been components of a visionary preparation that were included for another reason.

Oracular Trance-Speech

Oracular speech often comes when emerging from sleep or trance in the Irish tales. We have observed this in the trance-speeches of heroes, kings and warriors on the eve of battles, as in the trance-speeches of Dubthach, Láegaire, Amargin, and Conchobor in war-camps during the *Táin*,[17] and the trance-speech of Conaire in *Dá Derga's Hostel*.[18] In each of these cases, the seer speaks "in his trance", or arises from sleep to chant. This practice forms part of a continuum of Celtic spiritual techniques for obtaining prophetic knowledge through inspired speech, best articulated within Irish tradition. A similar practice is described among the Welsh where *awenyddion*, "inspired people" would give prophetic speeches, emerging from a deep trance or ecstatic state "as from a deep sleep", as in the Irish cases.[19] The central insight of this stream of practice seems to be that altered states of dream, intoxication, and trance, within a specific sanctified context, place the practi-

13 Beck 2009 476
14 Aldhouse-Green 2010 107
15 Beck 2009 476
16 Beck 2009 480
17 O'Rahilly 2011 130, 231
18 Stokes 1910 82
19 In Giraldus Cambrensis, where he spells the term *awenydhyon*. Wright, Hoare and Forester 1863 501.

tioner in contact with spiritual forces or presences which may speak truth through them via the state of divine inspiration or possession. The Welsh example strongly suggests that possession by spirits is the mechanism of these trance-speeches.[20]

The lore describing oracular trance-speech tells us little about the methods by which these inspired trances were induced. The *Táin* and *Dá Derga's Hostel* instances of pre-battle trance speeches tell us only that the warriors rose from a "sleep" (*chodlad*), or that they spoke in a "trance" (*búadris*). We may note that the word *búadris* (literally, "victory-tale") is specifically linked to trance by intoxication—DIL cites a reference for the word describing the intoxication of the senses experienced after drinking "streams of old mead."[21] Beck and Brunaux point to a widespread Celtic practice documented on the Continent of "armed councils" before war, which included a ritual drinking component "aimed at making contact with the gods so as to be protected, helped and possessed by the supernatural forces."[22] Something similar may well have been practiced in Ireland, and is likely reflected in the association of warriors, female warrior-sovereignty figures, and mead, exemplified by Medb herself. Thus the trance-speeches in the camps appear to reflect a practice of imbibing sacred mead, likely infused with trance-inducing herbs, to engender an inspired state within which the warrior contacted the Gods and spiritual forces, gained their protection in the coming battle, and accessed divinely inspired knowledge expressed in poetic trance-speech.

Prophecy and the Morrígna

It is notable that in almost every instance of *búadris*, trance-speech, one of the Morrígna is either present or appears immediately following the poetic performance. In the case of *Dá Derga's Hostel*, the triple Badb is present in the Hostel.[23] In the instances of *búadris* in the *Táin*, each time the trance-speeches are performed, war Goddesses appear: first Némain alone, then Némain with Badb and Bé Néit (likely referring to the Morrígan here). In the latter triple instance, the Morrígan has

20 Wright, Hoare & Forester 1863 501.
21 Royal Irish Academy 2013, entry búadris.
22 Brunaux quoted in Beck 2009 516.
23 Stokes 1910 82

also been seen just prior to the trance-speeches.[24] Viewing this pattern, it seems likely that in these traditions of ritual intoxication and trance-speech, particularly those occurring in war camps, the Morrígna would have been among the deities contacted, and from whom inspired and prophetic speech was sought. In other words, it may well have been the Morrígna who possessed the warriors rising in their trances to speak prophecies of the coming battles.

The Morrígan herself is strongly associated with poetic prophecy in general, as we have seen. She is called upon by the Túatha Dé to serve as an oracle for poetic prophecies in the Second Battle of Mag Tuired. In the Táin cycle, she identifies herself as a poet and seer, giving poetic prophecy to Cú Chulainn and to the Brown Bull.[25] Her visitation as prophetic poet in the *Cattle Raid of Regamna* encounter with Cú Chulainn encounter is particularly interesting in its parallels to another seer, Fedelm. We meet Fedelm early in the Táin; she identifies herself as *banfili*, "poetess", and appears in wealthy clothing, armed, and standing in a chariot.[26] Similarly, when she meets Cú Chulainn, the Morrígan identifies herself as *banchháinti*, poetess or satirist, also dressed in fine clothing and in a chariot. Both proceed to offer oracular poems about the fate of Cú Chulainn and the armies he will fight against in the *Táin*—though the details of the visions in the two poems are different.

These parallels suggest that the authors of these stories recognized a recurrent role: the high-status female poet-seer who employed oracular powers and poetic art to give prophecy about the fortunes of warriors and war, and who was to some degree identified with the image of the war Goddess herself. Fedelm exemplifies this role and archetype. She is clearly identified as a person with Otherworldly status or powers, having "three pupils in each of her eyes."[27] Her name is etymologically derived from the Celtic root **uid-* "to know", with a connotation of knowledge gained by visionary sight. The Gaulish cognate to the name Fedelm (also spelled Fedelma) is the title *uidlua*, attested as a title for a female enchanter in a Gaulish curse-text.[28] Fedelm is also identified, by Medb, as a *banfaíth*, the term for a female practitioner of the art of prophecy, and cognate to the Gaulish *vates*, diviners and sacrificers.

24 O'Rahilly 2011 130, 231
25 See Chapters 3 and 9 for citations and details.
26 O'Rahilly 2011 126
27 O'Rahilly 2011 126
28 Mees 2009 163

Fedelm's prophetic poem bears the hallmarks of the same tradition of visionary, oracular insight delivered in poetic form that we see again and again performed by the Morrígan. Her oracular speech also makes use of the key prophetic formula *atchíu*, "I see", a phrase used in other instances of prophecy by both the Morrígan and Badb, here repeated again and again.[29] The exchange with Medb takes on a rhythm that suggests the words are ritual cues:

Feidelm banfaíth, co acca ar slúag?	"O Feidelm prophetess, how do you see our host?"
Atchíu forderg, atchíu rúad.	"I see it bloody, I see it red."[30]

The use of signal words for red color in the recitation *atchíu forderg, atchíu rúad,* as we have seen, also appears in the Morrígan's prophetic poetry. Also among the ritual cues is the request to Fedelm to "look once more for us, and tell us the truth". We can imagine a divinatory practice in which the prophetess, having accessed the divine powers through trance, and perhaps positioned in a chariot, is asked by a war-leader for visionary insight using this series of ritualized phrases, answering in inspired mantic verse.

Gazing into the Otherworld

Prophetic knowledge gained through the power of visionary sight is evoked again and again in these tales. Some of the sources also imply that scrying (divination by gazing) may have been in use. In the *Siege of Knocklong,* several druids employ a method of divination about the fortunes of war and the movement of war-bands through gazing at the sky and clouds.[31]

The practice of gazing into water or other liquids has some attestation in early Celtic and Celto-Germanic contexts. Vessels contained in graves associated with other ritual implements have sometimes been interpreted by archaeologists as potentially used in scrying or related divination practices. For example, the bronze bowl found in the grave of a Gaulish woman at La Chaussée-sur-Marne, France, together with a set of what may be divination spoons, is suggested by Aldhouse-Green

29 O'Connor 2013 141
30 O'Rahilly 2011 126-127
31 Ó Duinn 2014 38-39

as a bowl for containing divinatory and/or sacrificial liquids, such as oil or blood.[32] Among the Cimbri, Celto-Germanic neighbors to the Gauls, seer-priestesses were described scrying for prophecy by gazing into the blood from sacrifices contained within a large bronze vessel. This description, incidentally, closely matches that of vessels found in graves such as the Gaulish Vix burial, also of a woman indicated by her grave goods to be a priestess of some kind, though the Vix vessel may rather have been for serving sacred drink.[33]

Viscous Fluids

Divination by casting liquids over a surface also appears to have been in use in some places. The paired divination spoons mentioned above are found in several Celtic priestly graves in Gaulish and British contexts. They are, according to Aldhouse-Green, always paired, with short handles which fit together; one spoon of the pair usually has a drilled hole in its bowl, and the other is typically marked with lines dividing it into quadrants.[34] These lines may represent symbolic divisions of the world by cardinal points, representing a map onto which divinatory materials could be cast. The proposed method of use is this: the spoons were cupped together bowl-to-bowl, and a viscous liquid was blown through the hole to cast it against the quadrant map, where its distribution could be read for divinatory information. Material used for this might be fine powders such as crushed ochre or woad mixed into a fluid, or other viscous liquids such as oils or blood.

This method is not, to my knowledge, seen in Ireland. We do have an interesting case of divination by the use of blood, attributed to Cú Chulainn in several texts. This is the story of his raven sacrifice, which appears in the *Death of Cú Roí* as well as the *Dindshenchas*. The *Cú Roí* text only tells us that he kills ravens, and thereby learns the whereabouts of his enemy Cú Roí. The *Dindshenchas* version elaborates on the details of the ritual: Cú Chulainn kills the ravens, and taking the last one, he cuts off its head and bathes his hands in its blood. Then, according to the text, "the cunning hero wove each mystic sign", before placing the

32 Aldhouse-Green 2010 162
33 Aldhouse-Green 2010 213, 223
34 Aldhouse-Green 2010 162

raven's head on the crag.[35] Our texts do not explain how these ritual elements constitute divination or deliver prophetic knowledge. Speculatively, the text could support a reading of the blood itself being cast against the rock and its distribution read as in the spoon divination, and the "mystic signs" a reference either to those castings, or to ritual actions undertaken to invoke the power of divination. Alternately, the ritual could be oracular rather than divinatory, and its intent focused on asking the raven's spirit directly for information. Ross suggests that bathing his hands in the blood is meant to imbue Cú Chulainn with the prophetic Otherworldly powers of the raven.[36] Of course, some of these elements may simply be poetic invention by the medieval author—we simply do not know.

Raven Knowledge and Animal Omens

Cú Chulainn's divination by ravens has also been interpreted as augury—the practice of reading omens in the behavior of birds. This is based on reading the *Cú Roí* version alone, without the details provided by the *Dindshenchas* text. Certainly, augury is very well documented as a divinatory practice employed in a variety of Celtic contexts. The practice of bird augury, and particularly focusing on the voices of birds, was condemned by early Irish monastics, again suggesting that it had a place in Pagan practice.[37]

For the early Irish, the link between divination and the raven was so close that a branch of divinatory knowledge was called *fiachairecht*, "raven-lore". Remnants of this school of divination were recorded in a medieval tract by that name, with another on related divinations from the behavior of wrens.[38] In the *Raven-Lore,* along with classic auguries based on wild flight behaviors and calls, detailed interpretations are also specified for the behavior of ravens inside houses and other domestic spaces. This points toward a tradition of keeping ravens as partner animals for divinatory work. As has been noted, archaeological evidence suggests a similar practice in Iron Age Britain.[39] The practice of *fiachairecht* in Ireland seems to have been part of a broad Celtic tradi-

35 Gwynn 2008a 251, Tymoczko 1981 329
36 Ross 1996 325
37 Attributed to Columcille; Best 1916 120
38 Best 1916
39 See Chapter 12.

tion within which birds, and especially ravens and crows, were treated as prophetic oracles. The Gaulish stronghold of Lugudunum carries a legend attributing its founding to the appearance of a flock of crows as an omen.[40]

Other animals appear also to have held divinatory meaning within the cults of the Celtic war Goddesses. We have seen how Queen Boudicca, as part of her pre-battle prayer and address to her army, reportedly also released a hare and its movement was read by her and her troops as a battle omen.[41] The belief appears to have been that the army toward which it ran was the one favored for victory. According to Tacitus, Germanic tribes kept sacred white horses for kingship rites at protected sanctuaries, a practice that resonates with the Irish traditions of kingship at Tara and Emain Macha. These sacred horses were also ascribed divinatory powers, and their movements were read for omens as well.[42] Similarly, in Ireland the actions of the sacred horses in the Tara kingship ritual were read as omens reflecting on the virtue of the king and the prospects for his reign.

Casting in Wood

Many accounts, speaking of both Irish and other Celtic societies, describe a divinatory casting method using signs inscribed on lots, typically of wood. For example, in a version of the *Wooing of Étaíne*, the druid Dallan uses a set of four wands of yew inscribed with *ogam* signs to discover the whereabouts of the bride Étaíne.[43] The word for this druid's "keys of knowledge" is *crandchur*, literally "casting in wood". A similar term *fídlanna* "wood-divination" is mentioned among the practices of druids and pagans in the *Second Vision of Adomnán*.[44]

The reference to *ogam* as the specific symbolic system used for divination is questionable; the dating of known *ogam* inscriptions places its earliest documented use in about the 4th century CE, just before the Christian period.[45] However, the existence of this term *crandchur* in the language suggests a pre-existing cultural link between divinatory

40 Clitophon quoted in Beck 2009 131.
41 Dio Cassius, quoted in Koch & Carey 2003 46.
42 Aldhouse-Green 2010 126
43 O'Curry 1873 193
44 Volmering 2014 662
45 Olmsted 1994 14

knowledge, wood, and the practice of casting lots. This link is found in other Celtic languages as well; a Welsh term *coelbren* is attested with the literal meaning of "omen stick."[46] So whether the magical signs in use were *ogam*, an ancestor to the *ogam* script, or another symbol set, the practice of casting inscribed wooden lots for divination seems well-attested in prehistory.

Tacitus describes a rite seen among Celto-Germanic tribes for casting divinatory lots:

> "They cut off the branch of a nut-bearing tree and slice it into strips; these they mark with different signs and throw them completely at random onto a white cloth. Then the priest of the state, if the consultation is a public one, or the father of the family if it is private, offers a prayer to the gods, and looking up at the sky picks up three strips, one at a time, and reads their meaning from the signs previously scored on them."[47]

The nut-bearing wood here likely parallels the Irish belief in the hazel as the tree bearing knowledge.

In fact some artifacts have been found which may represent examples of Celtic divinatory casting sets. At a megalithic site at Loughcrew, Ireland, a great many small well-polished slips made from cattle ribs surfaced, some unadorned and some showing La Tène Celtic inscribed art; archaeologists have suggested that they may be divinatory lots, although another cultic purpose is possible.[48] Another proposed divination set, found in what is thought to be a British druid's grave at Stanway, consists of long slender rods of copper-alloy and iron with flattened ends, two larger and two smaller of each metal.[49] It should not surprise us too much that wooden casting sets have not been found, as wood survives the ages poorly compared to more durable materials such as bone and metal. The Stanway set, we may note, included groups of four staves, matching the number used by the druid in the Irish example.

The numbers of staves used in divination are significant and point to distinct methods of casting and reading. The examples of sets com-

46 Mees 2009 162

47 Tacitus, quoted in Waddell 2014 27.

48 Waddell 2014 27

49 Aldhouse-Green 2010 151. It should be noted that these rods alternately may have had a medical rather than divinatory use.

prised of four staves might suggest a binary divination system, where all four are cast together and the number falling marked-side upward or downward represents a variation within a binary spectrum of answers. The example from Tacitus may suggest a symbolic divination system, whereby a semantic message is read from the symbols on the three selected staves.

Living Practice: Prophecy, Possession & Divination

Mantic practices such as divination, oracular trance, and trance possession remain vibrant in a number of living Pagan and polytheist traditions, including some forms of Celtic polytheism. In this section, I will explore methods for working with these traditions in lived practice, concentrating on oracular trance possession, since this is central to my own work with the Morrígna. I will also briefly explore the use of divination to support oracular and devotional work.

First, some defining of the way in which I use terms. Trance states are altered states of consciousness that may be accessed in order to achieve communication with Otherworldly forces and spiritual beings, using a variety of methods including (as we have seen) meditation, breath control, rhythmic activity, chanting and poetic recitation, ingesting intoxicants, and more. Within this broad stream of trance practices is trance possession: the use of trance specifically toward possession by a deity or spirit. In trance possession, the presence and voice of a deity or spirit is channeled through or embodied into the person of a priest, who may be said to "carry" the deity. It is understood by practitioners that in trance possession, the deity enters into and seizes control of the priest, so that for the duration of possession, the speech and actions on the part of the priest are essentially those of the deity. This oracular channeling is often done for divinatory ends—to receive knowledge directly from the divinity through possessed speech—but it may also be done for devotional or other reasons. The word "oracle" itself comes from Latin *orare* "to speak", so when we speak of oracular practices, this refers to any work in which a spiritual being is speaking through a priest, whether for divinatory or other purposes.

It has sometimes been said among practitioners of polytheist faiths that trance possession is a modern innovation. I think from the evidence of this chapter, it seems clear that oracular trance, and likely trance possession, was used by the ancients. To the forms of trance and oracular practices described here for Celtic practitioners, such as *búadris*, we could add any number of other ancient examples, such as the *seiðhkona* of the early Norse, the *sybilla* of the Romans, the *Pythia* and *prophetai* of Delphi, and so many others. Trance and oracular practices do have a very ancient pedigree. The form in which these practices unfold today among Celtic polytheists may differ in various respects from their ancient contexts, but they stand as part of a continuum of practices from antiquity.

Trance Possession: Why

Why do we practice trance possession? In part, for the same reasons the ancients did: there is great value in accessing direct communication with the Gods. Prophecy is highlighted as a purpose of oracular trance among the ancients, and the value of this kind of knowledge remains relevant now. Trance possession places us in conference with beings operating on a different level of reality with respect to time, space, vision, and predestination. With Gods such as the Morrígan, so deeply tied to prophetic speech and vision, the opportunity to gain direct guidance is invaluable. This is especially needed from the perspective of priesthood and service. As priests seeking to be of service to her, it is crucially important that we keep an open channel of communication with her voice in as direct a manner as possible, to ensure that we are being guided by her in our work.

There is another reason we practice trance possession: it represents the most intimate of gifts to her that we can give, the gift of our own body's sensate experience for a time. The Gods do not live in physical bodies, and outside of this kind of practice, their experiences are not sensory. They have, of course, a range of powers and abilities we do not, but in being non-incarnate, what they do not have is our lived experience of the world through the body's senses. For some Gods—and in my experience the Morrígan is among them—the embodied sensate experience seems to be fascinating. When I invite her to enter my body in trance possession, I am offering her the gift of a moment in the human sensate experience, and at the same time the ultimate expression of trust and deep intimacy.

That intimacy also is a gift to other devotees. For most of our devotional lives, we will be experiencing her in much more subtle, discarnate ways: as a voice within our psyche, as visions in meditation or dream, as shimmering or shadowy presence, as omens appearing in our path. The oracular moment is unique in offering us a chance to touch her hands, be touched by them, look into her eyes, let her speech wash over us; to experience and connect with her presence in our own living bodily experience.

It should be said, however, that not everyone is or should become an oracular priest. For some, the skills simply come too hard to learn. For others, it is not a matter of skill but of choice—some priests do not choose to engage in possessory work for reasons of spiritual integrity, oaths that prevent them, or any number of other reasons. These are valid choices too.

Risks and Consequences

Any powerful practice brings risks, and possession has many hazards. It is not a practice to be entered into lightly and without thought for consequence. The very thing that makes trance possession so meaningful—its intimacy—is also the source of a significant risk. The presence of a deity in trance possession is always being filtered through an individual human personality. This puts enormous psychic and psychological pressure on that human being. When this is done by someone without enough preparation and training, or who is not emotionally and psychologically stable and resilient, it can result in trauma, psychological damage, and the triggering of latent mental or emotional disorders. Even absent any notable traumas or triggers, gradual effects over time can be problematic as well. We often see a blurring of identity, experience, and perception. To a certain extent, this is the natural result of the intimacy of the relationship; just as married people begin to take on each other's habits and perceptions, oracular priests tend to internalize some of the energy and presence of their deity, coming to "feel" more like them. This in itself is not necessarily problematic, but it can easily become so. The oracular priest, if not practicing good spiritual discipline around possession work, can easily lose track of whose perceptions are whose and begin to identify with the possessory presence, experiencing their own identity and perceptions as those of the deity.

This becomes a social and spiritual hazard for the community as well. If priests are not practicing good spiritual discipline, and projecting their own perceptions and identity into their possessory work, the community will be receiving distorted messages which can center the priest's ideologies in the life of the community in unacknowledged and damaging ways. This can lead to severely unhealthy community dynamics. Even in the absence of a priest making this mistake, social projection can still occur in ways that are harmful to both priest and community. Community members can come to identify the persona and face of the priest too closely with the deity, treating them as an avatar or embodiment of the deity. This, of course, is not healthy for anyone—priests are not Gods and should never be treated as such.

Skills and Safeguards

To safeguard against these risks, trance possession practice should be taking place in the context of structured community and with training and precautionary practices in place. While the practice can employ natural channeling abilities, these talents are not enough in and of themselves to establish a solid trance possession practice—natural talents need to be trained, honed, and paired with other skills for safe practice. These are not skills that can be learned from a book. Oracular possession is not and never has been a solitary practice; its context and function is social. Thus, I am not attempting to teach the practice here. Instead, I will simply outline the needed skills that underlie it and point the reader to the necessity of finding experienced people to practice and learn with if this work is new to you.[50]

Rotating the Oracle: Within a given group, the preferred situation is to have more than one oracular priest who can serve. This situation provides for the work of doing trance possession to be shared and rotated among multiple priests for different occasions. Selection of the priest to serve as oracle on any given occasion can be done through drawing lots or another divinatory method. This accomplishes several things: the use of a randomizing method for selecting who will be doing oracular work allows the Gods themselves to choose, and minimizes

50 For some who may not live near communities with experience in these practices, this may be difficult. In the absence of local resources, I would encourage anyone working in this realm to at least seek out an experienced mentor via online communities.

any risk of priests using the opportunity for personal "grandstanding". Rotating the work between different priests also greatly helps minimize identity blurring between priest and deity, both internally and socially. Communities who see more than one visage embodying a given deity are healthier for it.

Personal Shadow Work: Aspects of the personality that are unacknowledged, repressed or sublimated are the most likely to surface as projections within oracular work, and the least obviously to be recognized as such. Trance possession can provide a vehicle for these un-integrated personality aspects to act independently and present themselves as the voice and presence of a spirit or deity. To safeguard against this, priests doing oracular work should also have undertaken work to recognize and integrate these aspects of their psyche. Various traditions provide useful methodologies, such as Jungian shadow work, "demon work" as taught in some witchcraft traditions, and the like. This also is not something we do and are done with, but needs to be integrated into our practice.

Trance Practices: Facility with trance practices is, of course, a crucial skill. For the oracular priest, the ability to readily slip into deep trance is central to their work. This is built upon deeply ingrained practice in breath, meditative, and consciousness-altering ritual techniques. Effective trance for possession usually relies on the development of personal trance keys: objects and experiential triggers which are attuned and consecrated to the deity, and to which the priest has also developed an ingrained trance response. For example, priests may have certain regalia they wear or carry; specific drum rhythms, sounds, chants or incantations; scents or tastes; or any number of other specific keys can be developed and linked to that deity's possessory presence. Skills for returning and re-grounding in the body after possession are of course equally important.

Surrender and Control: When we speak of possession, we are speaking of the most complete level of embodied presence. But this exists on a spectrum from light presence (called "aspecting" in some circles) to deep uncontrolled possession and intermediate points between, depending on the depth and totality of the invoked presence and the level of control surrendered to the deity invoked. This spectrum is sometimes spoken of in terms of how "heavily" the deity is riding the priest. The oracular priest, to be of service in doing this work, needs to have the ability to exercise control over when, how, and how deeply they will surrender to possession. In other words, the value of trance possession in religious life is contextual; as priests, we will sometimes be called upon to do ritual work within which it may be inappropriate and even damaging to invite full possessory presence of the deity. We need to have the ability to control and target the depth of invocation and the "weight" of the presence. This ability rests on practice, on well-developed psychic and trance skills, and most importantly on having negotiated agreements with the deity as to when we will give them full surrender and when we can choose not to.

Specificity of Aspects: With a deity such as the Morrígan who herself represents a constellation of different faces and aspects, or (depending on your view) a closely related sisterhood of Goddesses, and who emerges in many forms, it also becomes important to develop discernment about which aspect or identity is being invoked into possession. This means developing specificity in how we address our invocations, which in turn will be based on deeply studying and understanding her different aspects, their functions, and how they relate to each other. We might sometimes be willing to let her choose who will speak with us and how, but we need to also have the ability to exercise this discernment and discretion.

Verification: A responsible group also needs to develop methods for verification of the deity's presence. This will help protect the group from confusion and harm arising from mis-targeted invocations (someone other than the intended deity entering), as well as from priests succumbing to the temptation to falsify or "perform" oracular possession. We can learn much from traditions that have more continuous histories with these possession practices. Verification can take the form of behavioral signs such as changes in voice, characteristic involuntary movements, changes in eye color or other physical indicators; the ability to tolerate normally intolerable things; speaking in languages or revealing knowledge the priest could not know, and many other methods. Divination can also be used to verify the presence of the deity.

Support Priesting: One of the keys to effective oracular possession lies not in the oracular priest but in the support priests who work with them. Their roles include purifications and other protections to assure the safety of the oracular priest by preventing unwanted spirits and malevolent influences from accessing the oracular priest while they are in a spiritually open state. Support priests are usually the primary agents of invocation, calling the deity into the oracular priest; this allows the oracular priest to focus on entering trance and surrendering. They also provide crucial support by feeding the deity's presence using offerings and other devotional methods; this allows the presence to be sustained without draining and exhausting the oracular priest. Finally, these support priests are also needed to bring about the end of the possession trance, devoking the deity when the time comes, assisting the oracular priest in returning, re-grounding into their body, and recovering from the experience.

The Oracular Experience

I have noted above that people can sometimes undergo spontaneous possession—by deities, or by other spiritual beings. It is not uncommon for people entering into relationship with the Morrígan to have these experiences as she seeks points of entry into their life and practice. This can sometimes be confusing and overwhelming, so I think this experiential aspect bears addressing. The first thing that should be said is that none of the experiences I describe here is a guarantee that it is in fact the Morrígan whose presence we are experiencing. Before agreeing to let a spiritual being ride us, it is best to verify its identity.

People experience the presence of and possession by the Morrígan in distinct and personal ways. A common experience, however, is a feeling of being overshadowed from behind and above, as if a cloak or hood of shadows were being drawn over one's head. Others have described the experience as being swallowed, as if by the mouth of a giant raven; or of disappearing into the darkness of her vast cloak or enfolding wings. This can also be accompanied by experiences of gripping or shuddering sensations in the body, strange and intense appetites, someone else looking out through one's eyes, thoughts and words not one's own rising in the throat, or a range of other sensations. In full possession trance, these experiences will become more and more overwhelming and one may feel as if they were dissolving into her as she takes over. Others experience the element of surrender as if they are traveling away from their body into some Otherworldly place while she enters in.

Within the possession trance, people may find that they have a natural level or "weight" of possession they can go to, and no further. For some people, this means they never fully disappear into possession, but are always to some degree conscious. They may even surrender control fully, but may remain aware as if watching from a long way off or in a dream. Others will black out completely and remember nothing for the duration of the possession trance. This variation is quite normal. What matters most for the purposes of oracular possession is the ability to let the consciousness and especially the voice of the deity come through.

Giving voice to the deity is sometimes more challenging than practitioners expect. Experientially, I have observed that the language functions of our minds, which the deity needs to employ in order to speak through us, are the hardest for their presence to integrate fully into. Priests who are learning oracular possession often find that they are able to be ridden by a deity for some time before they manage to be able to bring forth oracular speech. I note that in the druidic schools, priests extensively studied the arts of poetry and speech, including skills specific to the ability to speak spontaneous poetry while in an inspired state. This skill would be useful, of course, when it comes to oracular possession.

Divination Tools

A few further notes on divination, which was, as we have seen, widely in use alongside oracular methods of prophecy. Modern practitioners will find many uses for divination to verify insights in almost all aspects of spiritual practice. While some divination methods have a stronger ancient pedigree than others, the truth is that almost anything can be made effective in divination. Many of the ancients readily adopted tools and methods from different cultures they contacted, and we need not be more rigid than they. In my own practice and in collaboration with other practitioners, I have seen effective use of scrying, dreaming, Norse/Germanic runes, Irish *ogam*, bone casting, card reading, pendulum work, Ephesia Grammata, bibliomancy—and likely a hundred more could be added to this list. The Gods and spirits can speak through most anything we give them, if we develop the skill of reading it.

I will not attempt, in the space we have here, to teach the use of various divination tools. Each merits its own focus and resources can be found elsewhere. Instead I will just share these principles about the use of divination.

Visionary vs Symbolic: Broadly speaking, I look at divination systems as falling into one of two kinds. Open-ended, visionary modes rely on entering a meditative or altered state and seeing or receiving visions—such as in scrying and dreaming. Symbolic divination systems are based on a predetermined symbol set, from which messages are drawn—such as runic or *ogam* alphabets, and the image sets in card reading decks. Both groups are very effective, and both appear to be represented in the Celtic traditions. Each type tends to convey different kinds of messages. Practitioners may find it helpful, as I have, to be working with at least one method from each type, providing a complementarity and a broader scope for extracting divinatory knowledge.

Binary: Binary divination is the use of a system which can produce a direct yes-no answer. These too can be very useful for clarity in answering direct questions. We find them especially useful for confirming knowledge from other sources. Most symbol-based divination systems can be adapted to also function in a binary capacity. The symbols of the set—the runes, *ogam* ciphers, or whatever—can be assigned positive/negative semantic values so as to yield binary answers. Alternately, direct binary divination methods also exist, such as the four-shell binary divination methods seen in some African Traditional and related practices. Binary divination seems to have less currency in European traditions, but modern practitioners may find it useful to incorporate this into their practice.

Mantic practices like those we have discussed here form a continuum with more aggressive varieties of magic. The Morrígan herself moves within the ambiguous space between prophecy and magic, speaking prophecies which become charms or curses in the act of vocalizing. Many of the same or related techniques for prophecy and divination come into play in the realm of sorcery as well. This is the topic we take up in the next chapter.

15
Sorcery

"Nemain, Danand, Bodb and Macha, Morrigu who brings victory, impetuous and swift Etain, Be Chuilli of the north country, were the sorceresses of the Tuatha De. It is I who sing of them with severity."[1]

The identity of the Morrígna as sorceresses is not in doubt: again and again we see them embody this role in the poems and tales. They haunt the stories, chanting spells of sleep, of attack, calling fire and bloody rain against enemies, altering their shape, laying *geis*-traps, binding, cursing, confusing. Here, we will explore the practice of sorcery as an element of the cults of the Morrígna and related Goddesses. Sorceries employed in the theater of warfare in particular will be covered separately in Chapter 16 on battle cultus.

The Poetics of Sorcery

It is clear that the Morrígan's poetry serves as her primary mode of accomplishing sorcery. Her action in this realm falls within a broad Celtic tradition of metrical verbal magic for which there is abundant evidence

1 Dobbs 1930 318

of use by ancient peoples. This tradition sees the practice of rhythmic ritual poetry as divinely inspired, possessed of an Otherworldly force, and thus effective in both vocalizing numinous truth (as prophecy), and in weaving magical effects (as sorcery).

The Morrígan identifies herself as a poet in the encounter with Cú Chulainn: "I am a female satirist in truth."[2] The title she uses is *banchháinti*, from the verb *cáinid*, which typically means "reviles, rails at, reproaches", but also "laments, bewails" and may be related to the practice of funerary keening.[3] As a title, *banchháinti* refers to the school of poetry known as *cáintecht*, satire. This is the Irish tradition whereby poets, usually acting in a judicial capacity, were credited with the ability of using harshly aggressive poetry to cause wounding and blemishing upon a person who had committed a wrong or unjust act. Satire presented a particularly significant threat toward kings, since according to tradition a blemished king could not continue to rule. Thus, the poets in this system represented a very real check against the power of kings.[4] It is this tradition of weaponized, political poetry the Morrígan claims when she identifies herself as a satirist—in addition to her identity as a prophetic poet, demonstrated elsewhere.

The forms of satire poetry in Irish lore place it within a broader Celtic tradition of metrical cursing and charming. In Irish, the term *bricht* is often used in poetry; it can refer to a particular eight-syllable poetic meter, but also means "incantation, charm, or magic spell."[5] The cognate term *brictom* in Gaulish refers to an incantatory poetic magical text.[6] This word, and the poetic charms which it describes, appear in Gaulish and British curse texts, representing a Celtic adaptation of the Classical tradition of inscribing written curses and spells on tablets and other objects and depositing them in magical places. And while the practice of writing curses on tablets, called in Latin *defixiones*, may be Mediterranean in origin, the distinctive language and poetics of the Celtic curse texts link them firmly into the tradition of poetic sorcery

2 Leahy 1906 132
3 Note, there may be a further association between keening the dead and necromantic divination; such connections seem to be suggested in related Indo-European cultures such as ancient Greece. Credit to C. Lee Vermeers for suggesting this connection.
4 Kelly 2003 44, 138
5 Mees 2009 172
6 Mees 2008 128

so well articulated in Ireland. Bernard Mees characterizes the evidence as demonstrating "an indigenous Celtic tradition in which spells were primarily intended to be sung," and which was adapted to the Mediterranean practice of tablet inscription.[7]

Rosc poetry, the metrical form in which most of the Morrígan's poetry is delivered, emerges as an Irish expression of this common tradition of rhythmic magical poetry which also articulates itself in the form of magical texts. Many of the Irish *rosc* poems, including the Morrígan's, are composed in a meter characterized by triplicity—word-foot trimeter, meaning lines of three words each, and in the *conachlonn* alliterative linking pattern.[8] Key structural elements of these *roscada* are also seen in Gaulish and British spell tablets, including metrical triplicity and related magical formulae in the language.[9] Scholars trace these archaic metrical patterns to the deep past, deriving them from ancient Indo-European ritual custom, reflected in related poetic forms in Welsh, Icelandic, and Roman poetry.[10]

The language of Celtic verbal sorcery, as reflected in Irish poetics and in various Celtic curse texts, contains notable patterns and key phrases. We have seen how the practitioner of the art of poetic magic or prophecy is called *uidlua*, "seer", in both the Gaulish texts and Fedelm or Fedelma in the Irish literature.[11] Among the magical formulae employed in this tradition of Celtic verbal sorcery we also find the practice of breath control, the concept of fate, turning, binding, and "destining a destiny"; imagery of piercing and wounding; and a particular genre of sorcery referred to as "the magic of women". We will look at each of these aspects of sorcery in turn.

Druidic Breath

In the Irish literature, druids engaged in magical conflicts employ something called "druidic breath". This breath is used by Mogh Ruith and other druids in the *Siege of Knocklong* to generate and to dispel illusions, to alter the clouds and weather, creating darkness and confusion,

7 Mees 2009 77

8 See Chapter 9 on the poetry of the Morrígan, above, for more detailed descriptions of these forms.

9 Mees 2009 184

10 Corthals 1996 28, Olmsted 1994 24

11 Mees 2009 163. The Gaulish text cited here is the Larzac *defixio*.

to generate forceful winds, to stir up wildfires, to cause blemishes or turn enemies to stone.[12] While some of these effects may be fanciful elaborations on the part of the medieval authors, what emerges clearly is a druidic fixation on magic accomplished through the use of the breath. This emerges in the language used; Mogh Ruith's charm says "I blast...", *seidim-si*, meaning at once a blast of wind, and also blasting as in cursing.[13]

The use of both breath and chanted poetry in magic are not incidental. Standing behind this nexus of ideas about magic is the notion that "the breath used to incant magical spells could itself be seen as magical."[14] Ancient practitioners of poetic sorcery undoubtedly noticed that breath was the medium by which incantations were vocalized. Further, in developing the ability to intone verbal poetry effectively, practitioners would need to master control of the breath—to time the breath to the rhythm of poetry, to modulate it for tone and vocal force. That is, the practice of poetic sorcery presupposes the practice of breath control. In particular, the mantic trance practice that is indicated by so much of this poetic magic would also have relied upon breath control. Based on patterns common to the many Indo-European traditions of poetic incantation, Olmsted suggests that at the early, pre-Celtic phase, priests of these arts would have already been employing breath control to induce trance states and altered perceptions.[15]

Examples of such magical breath control are visible within the Irish literature. Badb herself, in the form of the hag Cailb, intones her incantation against Conaire while "breathing one breath."[16] This reflects a belief that anything intoned all within one breath would be given the force of truth; Cú Chulainn is granted wishes by an Otherworldly giant in *Bricriu's Feast*, so long as he can speak all his wishes within one breath.[17] Breath and voice feats on the part of warriors are also mentioned in hero-tales, implying a practice of breath control.[18]

Breath techniques such as these can, of course, be found in almost any tradition espousing mantic, magical, or meditative practices. In the

12 Ó Duinn 2014
13 Mees 2009 138
14 Mees 2009 138
15 Olmsted 1994 25
16 Stokes 1910 70
17 Henderson 1899 109
18 Meyer 1888 302, Sayers 1983 63

Celtic traditions, centered as they are on the use of the voice and verbal enchantment, the practice of magic arises out of breath, shaped by language and rhythm toward its ends.

Binding Spells

Binding spells are prominent in the literature, constituting a genre of magic oriented around tying or fating the object of the spell. One particular form of binding is the *sithcura*. The word appears in the *First Battle of Moytura*, translated by Fraser as "a magic spell."[19] Etymologically, it is derived from *cor*, "putting, placing or casting" and *síth*, "peace". Mees calls this a "peace-binding" and places it among the class of binding charms alongside the more baneful type exemplified by Mogh Ruith.[20] We might wonder if the Morrígan's poem, with its metric repetition of phrases about peace, ending with the line *bidsirnae síth*, "it will be eternal peace", may present an example of an incantation that might be used in such a *sithcura*, binding its targets (the Túatha Dé and Fomoiri tribes, in the *Mag Tuired* case) into a compact of peace.

Binding charms more often employ language and imagery of constriction with cords, or of winding or turning under the effects of binding. Language used in Irish binding charms includes forms derived from the verb *rigid*;[21] its direct meaning is to subdue, control, or rule, but it is also used in constructions related to tying and binding, as "to tie a calf."[22] Mees suggests that a binding curse is alluded to in the *Wasting Sickness of Cú Chulainn* as well. The text as it remains to us refers to Otherworldly women striking or lashing Cú Chulainn with a horsewhip, but Mees points to similar tales in related Indo-European mythologies and suggests that the original meaning may have been closer to "lashing" in the sense of binding with a thong or cord.[23] Certainly the effects of the lashing on Cú Chulainn—his immobility, silence and debility—are characteristic of the traditional effects of binding curses.

Perhaps the most vivid language of binding is that of Mogh Ruith in the *Siege of Knocklong*. Here the imagery of the binding spell weaves together the binding coils of an eel's body, and both fiery and watery

19 Fraser 1915 19
20 Mees 2009 138
21 Carey 2004 19
22 Royal Irish Academy 2013, entry 2 rigid.
23 Mees 2009 150

forces. Mogh Ruith sings a poetic incantation over a special druidic stone and summons a mighty eel, *eascann*, described so: "a red water-snake", "a sea eel", a "fiery, stout, powerful dragon" arising from the waves.[24] The eel binds itself in nine coils around his adversary. Mogh Ruith's invocation refers directly to binding, saying "the bonds which it binds on" will be deadly. This magical eel is female gendered, and is named Mongach Maoth Ramhar, names which mean Long-haired, Sleek, Thick. Her behavior in the story evokes the actions of the Morrígan in eel form in the *Táin*: at combat of two warriors in the ford of a river, the dangerous female eel binds her coils round the feet and body of the adversary, hindering his movement and knocking him down so that the other warrior is able to slay him with the thrust of a magic spear.[25] Mongach is so fierce in her attacks that after helping to kill a second adversary she takes off after a third warrior who is not an intended target, and the druid must hold her back and calm her rage.

While we cannot assume that this eel is the Morrígan herself, it seems clear that both tales draw on a common tradition about Otherworldly female powers who could be invoked in eel form, and whose mode of action was the deployment of disabling, deadly binding curses. We have noted the possible etymological relationship between the word for "eel", *eascann* (or *escong*), and the verb *escainid*, to curse. Here we have a deep-rooted association of cursing and binding power with eels, employing a poetic mode of summoning reflective of Celtic spell texts.

Destining a Destiny

Irish binding spells like Mogh Ruith's often employ an emphatic ritual formula that links them to a deep tradition of Celtic binding magic, common to Continental and British curse tablets and the like. Mogh Ruith's invocation of the mighty she-eel and direction of her binding power contains the line "the bonds which it binds on."[26] The word Mogh Ruith invokes in his spell is *nascad*, "to bind or make fast", a term that also appears in the usage of binding to a contract or promise.[27] Parallel language following an emphatic pattern similar to "binding

24 Ó Duinn 2014 77
25 Ó Duinn 2014 82
26 Ó Duinn 2014 79
27 Mees 2009 141

a bond", and incurring contractual language, occurs in a great many other Celtic contexts of binding and fating.

We see a similar construction in the Gaulish Chamalières spell tablet, found carved on lead and deposited in a spring: *Etic segoui toncnaman toncsiiontio*, translated either as "it is the destiny of the victor to which they shall be destined" or alternately "it is the oath of the victor which they shall swear."[28] The key phrase is *toncnaman toncsiiontio* and the ambiguity as to whether the words refer to "destining a destiny" or "swearing an oath" is crucial. This phrase is etymologically cognate to the parallel phrases also attested in other early Celtic-language texts;[29] the Welsh *tynghaf tynghet*, "I destine a destiny", or "I swear an oath"; and its cognate in early Irish, *tongu a toingend*, typically occurring within the oath-formula "I swear by the Gods my people swear by." This formula is spoken by Cú Chulainn to the Morrígan in the form *fortongu dol día toingthe Ulaid*, "I swear by the god by which the Ulstermen swear". These ritual phrases all trace back to an ancient Celtic semantic complex based on the Indo-European root **tenk-*, "'to become solid, manifest, fixed."[30] Within the various Celtic languages, this root developed into words for destiny, the magical fixing of a destiny, along with the ritual process by which such a destiny might be fixed—the swearing of an oath or the laying of a binding curse.

In short, when a person takes a fateful binding upon themselves, we might say that they have sworn an oath; when a person lays a destiny upon someone else, we would call it a binding spell. Koch suggests "I doom a destiny on you" as an alternate translation for the language used in such predestining oaths.[31] The intimacy of the terms for both oath-swearing and fate-fixing, and the antiquity of this relationship in Celtic languages, attests to a fundamental truth in the Celtic conception of destiny: oaths and binding spells are two sides of the same coin. They represent two ritual modes by which one's destiny may be fixed or made manifest, and the difference between them is a matter of the agency by which the destiny is fixed. Our primary example of this relationship between binding, cursing, and oaths is, of course, the *geis*.

---

28 Koch & Carey 2003 2

29 Schumacher 1995, Mees 2009 155

30 Schumacher 1995

31 Koch 1992 250 n.

Geis-Prayers

We have discussed above how the *geis* is the mechanism by which a contract with Otherworldly forces or divine beings is bound and enforced. Mees summarizes this when he describes *gessi* as "fateful personal contracts."[32] In the Irish lore, we encounter them primarily in a literary context, and some scholars have dismissed them as plot devices created by the compilers of the tales. Patterns in their use and structure, the language surrounding them, and their relation to traditions of binding, cursing, and oath-taking practices in Celtic antiquity suggest that they are more than just literary devices, and in fact reflect an ancient religious practice.

In some places, *gessi* are associated with heroic gifts or *búaida*, along with the *geis* come special heroic powers, such as the warrior feats. This connection between kings and warriors, special powers, and binding *gessi* suggests, according to Mees, that "they may have originally been connected with rites undergone by young nobles in early Irish society."[33] He points to the fact that *gessi* are conferred by someone, rather than undertaken voluntarily. They appear to be ritual prohibitions which would have been laid upon the young warrior as part of rites of accession to a new status (such as at naming, taking up arms, warrior initiation, kingship, and the like). In many cases these *gessi* are directly given by Otherworldly entities, such as the bird-kinsmen of Conaire Mór,[34] or they may be prescribed by druidic priests using divination. Cú Chulainn's dog-meat *geis* accompanies his taking of a new name as a warrior and here again, the agency of a priest is suggested; the druid Cathbad pronounces Cú Chulainn's new name from the hound he has killed, and we can infer that the *geis* likely would come to him with a naming rite.[35]

The linguistics of *gessi* show their relationship to ritual and religious custom. The word *geis* derives from the same root as *guidid*, "to pray", and alternate usages of the word *geis* in early texts include "spell" and "incantation".[36] The cognate Gaulish verb *uediiumi*, "I pray" or "I in-

32 Mees 2009 145
33 Mees 2009 145
34 Stokes 2009
35 O'Rahilly 2011 142
36 Royal Irish Academy 2013 entry: *geis*.

voke" appears in spell tablets such as the Chamalieres *defixio*.[37] This semantic complex of related words for prayer, invocation, binding, oaths, and spells illustrates the position of these practices within the ancient pan-Celtic tradition of verbal ritual magic. Thus a *geis* is not just a contract with the Otherworld, with its prohibitions and requirements—it is also a binding ritual by which the contract is enacted, and the incantation or prayer used to invoke that binding.

The metrical forms and patterns common to Irish mantic poetry and Gaulish and British curse texts likely reflect remnants of the kinds of *geis*-prayers which would have been used in binding rites to invoke and seal these Otherworldly contracts. We can expect that such invocations would have partaken of similar rhythmic patterns, circular and alliterative elements, and in particular the use of language such as "destining a destiny" or "binding a bond".

Death-Songs

Another domain of Celtic verbal sorcery is that of cursing. These magics tend to employ similar poetics and rhythms, with imagery of blemishing, piercing, wounding, and death-enchantment. We have spoken above about satire as a genre of weaponized poetry. Beyond the content and metrical form of such poetic attacks, there are several interesting ritual elements that characterize their use. A form of satire called *glám dícenn* appears in several sources. Described as "a particularly dire form of satire", it seems to be a poetic curse associated with intense or loud vocal performance. The name is composed from *glám*, "noise, din, outcry", and *dícenn*, "end, extreme limit"; Stokes translates *glám* directly as a "curse", but also refers to it as a poem. The extremity referred to in its name may also mean that it was considered especially severe in its impact and would have been reserved for extreme situations. The poet Cairbre indicates its use in battle sorcery in the *Second Battle of Mag Tuired*, intended to weaken the Fomoiri "so that through the spell of my art they will not resist warriors,"[38] a *geis*-like binding effect.[39]

A specific ritual posture is associated with the performance of *glám dícenn*—the one-legged "cursing posture" which we have seen Badb

37 Mees 2009 154
38 Stokes 1891 93
39 Mees 2009 195

adopt. Usually, this is described as standing on one leg, closing one eye, and holding up one hand (or with one arm behind the back.) As discussed above, the posture seems to be intended to mimic the condition of woundedness on one side, with the belief that the missing or damaged part was active in the Otherworld. The one-legged posture often involves the speaking of magical incantations within a single breath. Lugh adopts this posture when he performs battle sorcery in the *Second Battle of Mag Tuired,*[40] as does the hag Badb (as Cailb) in *Dá Derga's Hostel,*[41] and Cú Chulainn in the *Táin.*[42]

This posture is called *corrguinecht* in *O'Davoren's Glossary* and several other Irish texts.[43] The name is a colorful poetic pun: *corr* is "pointed, peaked", and also means a water-bird such as a crane or heron; and *guinecht* is "wounding". Thus, the name may be read "pointed wounding" or as "crane-wounding". This double-entendre describes both the sorcerer's pose, balanced on one leg like a wading bird, and also the action of the spell, its piercing power and wounding ability, perhaps also conjuring the lightning-fast stabbing action of a crane's bill while it hunts. Another name associated with this practice and employing similar imagery is *congain comail,* "conjuror's wounding" (alternately translated "binding wounding".)[44] One text describes an operative spell using staves of whitethorn, the thorns of which would be made to pierce and wound a clay effigy of the spell's target.[45]

In each of these modes of sorcery, the vocal incantation is a central component—in these Irish examples, the *glám dícenn* or another form of poetic attack. Common to many instances are images of piercing, wounding, and binding. Similar imagery and language as well as metrical devices connect these magics to a particular class of poetic sorcery referenced in several Celtic curse texts: death songs. Variations on this term appear in early Gaulish and Gallo-Latin curse texts. In one example, a hybridized Greco-Latin term *necracantum,* "death song", appears along with distinctly Celtic words such as *masitlatida* "breaking and diminishing curse"; their association in the curse text indicates "a baleful ritual of 'breaking and diminishing'" using rhythmic, sung incanta-

40 Stokes 1891 99
41 Stokes 1910 70
42 O'Rahilly 2010 150
43 Stokes 1901 257
44 Mees 2009 190
45 Stokes 1891 284, appendix to the manuscript.

tion.[46] The mixed Greco-Latin context of this particular curse disguises what is actually a native Celtic form, as we find a parallel term in the Gaulish *duscelinata* "evil death song" in an inscription from Larzac, and *ison canti* "curse song" from Chamalières.[47] Mees interprets these various death-songs and curse-songs as expressions of a related, and quite ancient, Celtic tradition of sung curses, featuring rhythmic incantatory metrics and emphatic language patterning, also manifest in the Irish poetic tradition of the *glám dícenn* and other poetic sorceries.

Cursing and Transgression

As we have seen, the hag Cailb, an identity of the Badb, employs many of these ritual practices in her curse-prophecy against Conaire Mór in *Dá Derga's Hostel*: she adopts *corrguinecht* pose, she employs the druidic breath technique of speaking the curse within one breath, and her sung incantation employs the same rhythmic, emphatic and alliterative qualities common to many Celtic curse texts.[48] In addition to these qualities, her curse also illustrates another domain of Celtic sorcery—its use of transgressive magics.

Everything about Cailb bespeaks liminality, the condition of being on the border between two realms. Her *corrguinecht* pose positions her as having one foot, one eye, and one hand in the Otherworld. She arrives just after sundown, between day and night. She stands at the doorway of the house. She is not only a liminal presence, she manifests an actively transgressive relationship towards established order and these borders between realms. She is there as a result of Conaire's transgression of his *geis*-bonds to the Otherworld, and her very presence invites further transgression. She violates sexual norms about female decorum in her disturbing, grotesque sexuality ("Her lower hair used to reach as far as her knee. Her lips were on one side of her head.")[49] Her veiled sexual proposition to the king insults his royal status while inviting him to violate another *geis*.

Even her name is a curse, and after she has delivered that curse by

46 Mees 2009 71. *Masi-* is cognate to Irish *maidid* "breaks"; *-tlati-* connected to Welsh *-dlawd* "diminished".

47 Mees 2009 195. Note, the translation of the Chamalières curse is a matter of scholarly debate.

48 O'Connor 2013 138

49 Stokes 1910 70

singing all her names at him in the curse posture, Conaire responds as though it represents another invitation to transgression that he must refuse, he swears that as long as he might be there, he will not call her by these names. Perhaps he believes that to agree to call her by any of these names would in some sense implicate him in her transgressive incitements, which he still hopes to avoid. Among Cailb's list of names she includes the name Nóenden. Given that Macha's name is also among the list, we can interpret this as a reference to the *nóinden* of Macha—her curse upon the Ulstermen.

Macha's curse is itself another highly illustrative case of transgressive magic. As Toner points out, Macha's very being is transgressive: she has crossed over from the Otherworld, and as a pregnant woman from the agrarian class who has overcome the king's royal chariot horses, she represents a usurpation of the social order. Her curse is transgressive as well. The *nóinden* violates the divisions of gender identity by inflicting the inherently female birthing pangs onto the male warriors of Ulster, and it violates the social order by stripping the elite warrior class of their martial strength—in effect, their defining powers.[50] These effects are in turn the manifestation of the king's transgression against natural justice in dishonoring Macha, which in itself may be viewed as a violation of his *fír flathemon* and thereby his kingship.

The mode of action of this curse, according to some versions of the tale, is shame, the social cost of transgression. Implied in some of the narratives is the idea that the curse comes into effect on the warriors as a result of their exposure to Macha's shame while she is humiliated, dying in childbirth before everyone's eyes at the race-course.[51] The exposure of women's bodies plays a role in several Irish tales as a transgression of social order which causes shame and results in weakening or debility to warrior powers, such as the Ulster women baring their breasts to reduce Cú Chulainn's battle ardor,[52] and the *Ces Ulad* alternate tale of the Ulster debility in which Fedelm causes it by exposing her naked body to the Ulstermen.[53] In each of these stories, women draw power from the deliberate transgressing of social norms about control of the female body and sexuality, and this power is directed into

50 Toner 2010 93-96
51 Toner 2010 94
52 O'Rahilly 2011 147-148
53 Carey 2004 18

a curse or limitation impacting the exercise of martial power.

Macha's case is particularly detailed and interesting. Some versions imply that the mechanism by which the *nóinden* curse is deployed is actually the sound of her scream, instead of (or in addition to) her shame and outrage. Toner suggests that the transgressive shame is the motive force behind the curse, and the scream its agent—a vocal element of the deployment of the curse, along with her verbal invocation of the terms of the *nóinden*.[54] We might, in Macha's cursing scream, hear an echo of the "cry of extremity" of *glám dícenn*. As well, we might recall the triad which tells of three oaths that do not require counter-oaths (e.g. which can stand as legal testimony on their own): "the oath of a woman in birth-pangs, the oath of a dead man, the oath of a landless man."[55] Each of these classes of people has a liminal or Otherworldly status. In other words, while she is in childbirth, a condition which crosses the boundary between life and death, the speech and voice of a woman carry a numinous force, and it is this too that Macha calls upon in her curse.

The Magics of Women

Many early Celtic sources attest to a genre of sorcery intrinsically linked to the agency of women. A medieval Irish prayer, the *Lorica of St. Patrick*, contains a devotional charm to protect "against the spells of women and smiths and druids."[56] The language of the phrase "spells of women" is significant: *brichtu ban*. A similar phrase appears in the *Adventures of Connla*: *brechtaib ban*, "spells of women". Attesting to its common origins in Celtic antiquity, a precisely cognate phrase also appears in the Larzac Gaulish spell text: *bnanom brictom*, "spells of women". What we have is not simply a convention of language but a tradition of practice—for the Gaulish text containing the phrase is itself a spell, displaying the key elements of Celtic poetic magical texts, in a *rosc*-like incantation referencing a group of female practitioners.[57]

54 Toner 2010 95

55 Meyer 1906 23

56 Mees 2009 56

57 Mees 2008 134. It may be worth noting also that the gender identities of the women named in the text appear to be fluid, with some names contextualized in both male and female forms; possibly suggesting a less biologically deterministic meaning for the term *bnanom brictom*.

What might this magic of women be? There are many examples of acts of sorcery and magic tied specifically to female agency. In the above examples of transgressive magic, all are performed by women and with the female body as the implement of magical force. These are each, in a sense, "spells of women". The presence of Fedelm in this group is interesting. She is already known to us as a seer from her prophecy to Medb; this use of the power of the female body as an agency of magic may mark her out as a practitioner of female sorcery as well. Indeed, it is in the same Larzac spell text invoking *bnanom brictom* that the title *uidlua* also appears, which is itself directly cognate to Fedelm's name.[58] Fedelm may represent an example of a female seeress and sorceress, recognized across the spectrum of Celtic cultures, who in addition to being prophetic, wields mysterious and dangerous magical powers intrinsic to her female sexuality.

The Larzac text employs these spells of women for a binding curse against another group of women. In Irish sources, binding magical effects are often associated with women's sexuality, as well as with water. An early Irish charm apparently written as a binding curse upon a man's sexual potency employs similar poetic devices, along with images of female sexuality and flooding water:

I bind your vigour,
I bind your passion,
I bind your strength,
I bind your force.
A wanton woman binds
a stag of flood in a ford.[59]

The phrase describing the "wanton woman", *ben drúth*, is telling: *drúth* means both "wanton, harlot, courtesan", and "satirist, jester, or vagrant".

The poem makes a subtle connection between uncontrolled female sexuality, uncontrolled water, and binding magic. Carey has noted the preponderance of tales which identify waters and floods with female sexuality and present threats to men or warrior characters. A Gaelic folktale called *The Knife Against the Wave* echoes these themes: "Here a man saves himself by casting his knife at a great wave of the sea as it threatens to engulf him, and subsequently learns that he has struck a

58 Mees 2009 163
59 Carey 2004 19. Note, where Carey's translation gives "stag of flood", the phrase dam díli may be stag or ox. See Bernhardt-House 2007a for further exploration.

fairy woman, who was seeking to take him as her mate."[60] In this nexus Carey also includes the interaction of the Morrígan with Cú Chulainn in the *Táin*, beginning with her sexual offer and leading to the combat at the ford.[61] In a similar vein, the tale of the *Wasting Sickness of Cú Chulainn* follows a similar pattern: an approach of an Otherworldly woman (Fand, with her sister Lí Ban), a threat or an attack, an offer of a sexual liaison, and an incitement to a battle.[62] Interestingly in this regard, Fand's poem of sexual desire is accompanied by a poem in the margin of the manuscript about the Badb's bloodthirsty desire for violence; the Badb poem has no referent in the story, but seems to have been added to emphasize the threatening, dangerous nature of female sexuality.

It may be tempting to dismiss this association of female sexuality with threatening forces as the moralistic overlay of Christian scribes, but I think this is a mistake. The use of the key phrase "spells of women" in the context of sexual magics, threats and binding curses, the consistency of this complex of ideas across Celtic cultural hearths, and its expression through archaic native poetic devices, suggest that it is of very ancient origin.

Living Practice: Blessing, Binding and Boundary-Crossing

The foregoing chapter has shown us a great many vivid examples of sorcery at work within the ancient traditions surrounding the Morrígna. In this section, we will explore additional techniques and methods for integrating these modes of magical work into living practice. To begin, a discussion about the ethics of sorcery is needed.

Ethics, Justice and Transgression

A great many modern Pagans reject the use of cursing and baneful magic outright, following the Wiccan model based on the "harm none" principle. This is clearly a great departure from the ethical orientation of the ancient practice of Celtic magical traditions. Neither should we expect the ethical posture of the ancients to apply to us completely—these were,

60 Carey 2004 16
61 Carey 2004 16
62 Borsje 2007 86-87

after all, the same people who also participated in a vibrant slave economy. It is my belief that binding and cursing are important tools to keep in our arsenal. To assume that we will always find ourselves in a position of safety, comfort and well-being, without the need for methods of aggressive defense, magical counter-attack, binding of dangerous people; this is an assumption that arises from a position of relative privilege. Not everyone has the privilege of assuming such safety. As devotees and priests of a Goddess of war, who stands for the protection of sovereignty and the warrior ethos, we should expect that our work will at some point call upon us to stand behind our values, to protect the defenseless, to fight against injustices, or to do what is needed to prevent harm to our communities from dangerous individuals. Sorcery, binding, and cursing are among our tools to rise to this calling, though non-magical modes of care and protection are equally important.

This being said, it has also been my observation that the most experienced, effective and powerful people seldom find need to resort to baneful sorcery; they have so many other well-developed tools in their repertoire that rarely do problems escalate to the level of calling for a curse. In my view, baneful magic should never be our first resort to solve a problem. We should reserve it for necessity. Cursing can be spiritually costly; my experience has shown me that whatever we do in sorcery, we do first to ourselves. We are ourselves bound when we bind someone. Thus, when we do use baneful magics, we need to be careful to avoid simple retribution or vengeance. Instead, we target the harm we are working against, rather than simply casting a curse at someone broadside. In this way, so long as we are not guilty of the same wrongs, we can be safe from personal impacts of our cursing. For example, when a friend of mine was sexually assaulted, I helped her with a binding and banishing curse against her attacker; but rather than simply hit him with retribution, we targeted his violent misogyny, so that any instance of that behavior would engage the curse to tighten like a noose and bring him suffering. That is a noose I willingly accept around my own neck, as it only binds me more strongly to principles I already espouse. In this way, cursing can actually support, rather than degrade, our honor.

This brings up another point: the best use of baneful magic is for redress against misuse of power. Cursing is transgressive by nature. It draws its power from boundary-crossing, both in the sense of calling on Otherworld power and in the violation of social norms. This transgressive force is at its strongest when it is used to right another transgression or redress a violation—to restore balance. If we look at the use of cursing by the Morrígna, it is used in this way in several important instances: Badb's cursing of Conaire, who has already violated his kingly oaths; Macha's curse against the Ulstermen, who have already violated the principles of social justice. The use of satire against oppressive kings, such as Cairbre's satire of Bres, represents a similar use of cursing. In other words, the best use of baneful magic is in the context of "punching up"—using our sorcery to redress injustices, abuses of power, and transgressions perpetrated by the powerful against the less powerful, rather than for purely personal ends. In this, the natural dynamics of transgressive magic work with us rather than against us and we more readily find the powers of the divinities and the Otherworld supporting us.

The Support of the Otherworld

Sorcery is liminal and transgressive, as we have said; it gains its power through crossing the boundary with the Otherworld. Many of the features of Celtic sorcery exemplify this, the use of ritual postures to imitate woundedness or blindness on one side, positioning the practitioner in a liminal state which draws power from the Otherworld to deploy into this world; the calling up of Otherworldly beings as magical allies, such as the druid's she-eel ally; the skills of traveling in the Otherworld and changing forms. Our ability to accomplish sorcery is built on our relationship with Otherworldly forces and beings. It begins with the cultivation of these relationships.

So, in addition to devotional practice toward the Morrígan, most practitioners find that they need to cultivate relationships with a range of other spiritual allies, and with the Otherworld itself as well as its gateways and paths. Toward this end, several practices become useful; each of these are practices that merit deeper study than we have space to explore here, so I will mention them and point the reader to resources elsewhere and listed in the appendix.

Otherworld Alliances: We benefit from having friends who will look out for us, aid us, and stand at our backs in need—this is as true in the spiritual realms as in daily life. We may find allies among the human and ancestral dead, among the fairy or *síd* folk, animal spirits, heroes and demi-Gods, and others. All of these can be observed in action both in the lore and in the experiences of practitioners now. There are a variety of ways that we can find or be introduced to Otherworld allies: most effectively, we can ask the Morrígan to introduce us to potential allies, and we can undertake spirit journeying to seek them. In my experience, people who are focused and consistent in their devotional work do not go long before such allies begin to appear. We can cultivate these relationships using similar devotional techniques to those we use for religious devotion to our Gods: offerings, prayer, and mutual aid and service.

Spirit Travel/Hedgecrossing: This represents a suite of time-honored shamanic techniques for leaving the body in spirit-form and traveling the paths and landscapes of the Otherworld. We find reflections of this practice in a huge range of cultures. It is certainly represented in Celtic tradition by spirit-travelers who take animal shape, leaving their bodies behind (often in wolf or bird shape). In later European and modern witchcraft traditions practices of this kind are sometimes called "hedgecrossing", where the "hedge" is the Otherworld boundary. Some modern practitioners have adopted New Age terminology such as "astral projection". Not all these practices are identical. Each tradition of spirit travel should include certain safeguards and protections to make this practice spiritually safe, and these are of course important to incorporate into our practice. Again, space here is far too short to teach this practice, but I refer the reader to resources for learning this important practice.

Shapeshifting: Related to spirit travel is the practice of shapeshifting. In this practice, we develop an animal or Otherworldly form which we can shift our spirit into. This shape often takes the form of a totemic animal with which we identify, although people often have more than one spirit form—as does the Morrígan, of course. Otherworld allies can be of great help in teaching this practice and helping us to identify our spirit forms. In my experience, we can benefit from practicing the ability to shift into multiple forms; different forms will aid us in travel in various realms such as the chthonic underground, watery places, terrestrial spaces, airy realms, realms of the dead, dream spaces, and the like. We find it valuable to be able to adopt one kind of form for casual exploration, and a more protective form—what I have come to call a "battle form"—for instances where we may find ourselves under threat in the spirit world. Again, deep bodies of teaching exist for learning shapeshifting, and I encourage the reader to seek out those resources.

Talismanic Tools: As Mogh Ruith has his favored druidic "hand-stone" which he uses to conjure his eel spirit ally to help him in battle, I have found talismanic stones to be an especially useful tool in sorcery and Otherworld work. The type of stone I favor is a special kind commonly called "hagstones", "holy stones", "adder stones" or "witch stones" in folk magic: a stone which has a naturally occurring hole through it. A hagstone may or may not be what a druid such as Mogh Ruith would have used, but regardless, a deep and well-attested folk tradition attaches to them within Ireland and Britain as well as many other places. Large holed stones set in the ground have been centers of cult activity; for sorcery, we typically use one that is palm-sized or smaller and can be carried on the person. The hole through the stone represents a channel or entry between this world and the Otherworld, a traditional belief whose veracity I can attest through extensive practice of my own. The hagstone provides a talismanic contact which can be used to help in spirit travel and safe return from travel, in making more immediate contact with Otherworld allies to call on their aid, and in all manner of spiritual operations. Hagstones can often be found at beaches or rivers, as the holes are most commonly made by the natural action of water. I recommend giving offerings before taking a hagstone. Your stone can then be consecrated ritually, including keying it to any spiritual allies or the members of your spiritual group.

Blessing and Binding Charms

Here we have not the space to share a full exploration of all the elements of a practice in sorcery, so I will share a few charms and incantations I have found useful in my own practice and those of priesthood colleagues.

Corn and Milk Blessing

This blessing prayer is drawn from the Irish *Dindshenchas* texts.[63] Since it comes from a metrical text, it preserves some of the flowing, alliterative qualities that make a good incantation. It builds on a phrase common in Irish tradition, *ith ocus blicht*, "corn and milk", a folk saying along the lines of "milk and honey" in Biblical culture, meaning richness and plenty.

Ith, blicht,	Corn, milk,

63 Gwynn 2008a 18

síth, sáma sona,	peace, wellness,
lína lóna,	full nets,
lerthola,	ocean's plenty,
fir ríglaich,	wise guidance,[64]
co combáid cind.	strong allies.[65]

Short form blessing:
Ith, blicht, síth, sáma sona.

Healing Incantation

This is a healing charm drawn from the healing of Nuada's arm by Miach, son of the healing God Dían Cecht, in the *Second Battle of Mag Tuired*.[66] The formula itself follows a very ancient pattern seen in liturgies related to both healing and sacrifice, identifying the body with the material of the cosmos and so effecting healing.

Alt fri alt ocus féith fri féith	Joint to joint and sinew to sinew

Variations on this incantation can be elaborated at will using the poetic imagination.

Sithcura: Peace Binding

Poetic lines from the Morrígan's peace prophecy, also in the *Second Battle of Magh Tuiredh*, lend themselves well to deployment as a spell for peace, a charm to seal agreements, or a benediction to seal any work of magic. The poem itself in its entirety represents a *sithcura* or peace-binding, and can be incanted as such.[67] Its extracted opening and closing lines also work well as chanted incantations:

sith co nem	peace to the heavens
nem co doman	heaven to the earth
sith co nemh	peace to the sky,
bidsirnae sith	be it nine times eternal (literally, "it will be eternal peace")

64 literally "grey-bearded men"; a phrase referring to old veteran warriors.
65 literally "alliances with chiefs"
66 Gray 1982 33
67 Mees 2009 138

The *Geis*-Prayer

For the undertaking of an oath, or the binding of a *geis* onto someone, we have examples of ritual incantations from the literature, upon which imagination and ingenuity can expand. The core principle of the *geis*-prayer is its emphatic and binding qualities, typefied in the phrase, "I destine a destiny". The Irish form of this ritual phrase is *tongu a tongend*; the Gaulish form is *toncnaman toncsiiontio*. In the deployment of a *geis*-prayer to create an oath or binding, this construction will be followed by the litany of the terms of the *geis*. Absent the language skills to compose the rest of the *geis*-prayer in a Celtic tongue, practitioners may also just as well perform the work in their own native tongue.

Taking the example of a Gaulish binding prayer[68] and extracting the particulars from it, we have the following format:

[Petition to a deity for assistance]	"I beseech the great… by means of this spell"
[Invocation of Otherworld allies]	"Quicken us, by the magic of the Otherworld spirits"
[Identifying the practitioner, their lineage etc.]	"…the invoker, etc."
[*Geis*-prayer]	"And it is the destiny of… to which… shall be destined" or "It is the oath of… which… shall swear"
[Litany of terms]	(Here the specifics of the oath or *geis* binding are described—what is to befall its target; traditionally in poetic and evocative language.)
[Final invocation, calling on a deity]	"By… I prepare them, by… I prepare them, by … I prepare them, by …"

In the Chamalières text on which this is based, two deities are invoked. Maponos ("Divine Son", a Gaulish cognate to the Welsh Mabon and possibly the Irish Mac ind Óg), is petitioned in the opening, likely as an Otherworldly go-between. The final invocation and sealing

68 Koch & Carey 2003 2

of the spell is, in the original, dedicated to Lugus (a Gaulish cognate of Lugh and the Welsh Lleu), as a traditional God of oath-swearing.[69] Depending on one's relationship to these Gods and preference for tradition or inspiration, this pattern can be adopted or altered.

The important functional aspect of a *geis*-prayer as an incanted poetic prayer should be kept foremost; in other words, the ability to speak the charm effectively and give it mantic rhythm and power is more important than clinging slavishly to a specific formula.

This chapter necessarily only skims the surface of the realm of active sorcery. I have chosen not to delve too deeply into the mechanics of cursing and the more malevolent forms of sorcery, such as poetic cursing, piercing wounding, and death-songs. Those with an avid interest in such things will know how to adapt the examples from the early literature, and to create more of their own. In our next chapter, we will begin to explore the broader arena within which sorcery is often employed in the Celtic context: the arena of battle.

69 Koch 1992 255

16

Battle Cultus

War among all the Celtic peoples was a matter surrounded by ritual and charged with religious significance. As the Morrígna have battle among their primary functions, a significant body of war custom and battle-related ritual surrounds their lore. In this chapter, we will explore the evidence for ancient cult and rites related to the Morrígna in the context of warfare. We will look at invocations, prayers, and battle blessings; customs for intimidation; battlefield sorcery and weapon-charming; offering of spoils and sacrifices; and the cult of head-collecting.

Battle Blessings & Invocations

It seems to have been the practice among a wide range of Celtic peoples to offer prayers and invocations to their tutelary and battle Gods prior to entering battles. As we will see, the functions of these pre-battle rites included petitioning the deities for aid and victory, to attack the enemy on their behalf, votive pacts and exchanges by which their blessings might be secured, and seeking omens for strategic guidance and foreknowledge of the outcome of battle.

Historical and literary descriptions of pre-battle rites and prayers can be found across the range of Celtic societies. The Irish literature often shows us druids praying to or invoking their Gods for aid before battle. In the *Battle of Knocklong*, a druid Colpa gains victory by "gathering together the full force of his magic powers and invoking his god,"[1] and another druid resists attack by "placing his confidence in his gods" and employing druidic powers given by them.[2] We see hints of pre-battle invocatory prayers in the attacks by Némain and the Morrígna triad following invocations or trance-speeches by warriors on the eve of battle. Similarly, an account in the Annals tells that the warriors of Leinster "fervently prayed to St. Brighit that they might kill their enemies."[3] In Britain, Classical historians recorded that Queen Boudicca, when addressing her troops on the morning of battle, gave an invocatory prayer to her war Goddess Andraste, "Unconquered", raising hands to sky and imploring her for aid in the battle.[4] While this account may have been embroidered by the authors who recorded it, it seems to reflect a genuine native practice of invocatory prayer before battles. Caesar recorded a similar practice among the Continental Gauls, offering votive prayers to the Gods with promises of the spoils from battle to be offered afterwards, should the battle be successful.[5] That such spoils were in fact offered is attested by the archaeological record showing temples filled with captured arms and treasure.[6]

Two Handfuls of Blood

The *Second Battle of Mag Tuired* offers an intriguing hint of how a battle ritual might look, including pre-battle prayers and post-battle blessing rites. Following the Morrígan's sexual tryst with the Dagda before the battle, she relates prophetic information relating to battle strategy, and she promises to kill Indech, the king of their Fomoiri adversaries, and to take "the blood of his heart and the kidneys of his valour". Then

1 Ó Duinn 2014 46
2 Ó Duinn 2014 36
3 Mac Firbisigh 1860 191
4 Koch & Carey 2003 46
5 Koch & Carey 2003 22
6 Brunaux 1988 15, 19

she gives "her two handfuls of that blood to the hosts."[7] To my eye, this sequence has the look and feel of a battle ritual. In this ritual as I imagine it, the Morrígan is propitiated as war Goddess through prayer and symbolic sexual union with the war leader. She is then asked for victory, and her blessing given with the promise of destroying the enemy and oracular information on points of strategy in the battle. Then, following the battle, what appears to be a completion or blessing rite in which the slain adversary's blood, or possibly sacrificial blood as its stand-in, is given back to the warriors. The detail of the "two handfuls" of blood suggests to my mind a priest or priestess with hands dipped in blood, sprinkling the blood over the warriors or otherwise marking them with the blood as a victory blessing. If such a thing were to be done after battles or raids, perhaps such bloody marks might represent the "warrior's mark" referenced in warrior re-integration rites, something we will return to in Chapter 17 on the initiatory rites of warriors.

Another interesting reference to blessing rites and blood occurs in the later version of Cú Chulainn's death tale. Before setting out to the battle, his mother Dechtire greets him and offers him a drink drawn from a vat "from which to take a draught before journey or expedition undertaken was to him a certitude of victory."[8] This suggests a blessing practice where, before setting out to a raid or battle, a blessing cup was taken which would confer victory in the endeavor. In Cú Chulainn's death tale the blessing rite fails and the contents of the vessel turn to blood three times as Dechtire attempts to fill the cup for him; he reads this as a terrible omen. So, although to be marked or sprinkled with blood *after* battle might be taken as a blessing, its spontaneous appearance *before* battle is ill-omened, just as when the bloody apparition of the Washer at the Ford appears. Elsewhere we find Irish kennings for blood which call it *deog tonnaid*, the "drink of death", or *loimm tonnaid*, "milk of death."[9]

7 Stokes 1891 85. The sequence of these actions relative to the battle is somewhat obscured by the telling; the scene is before the battle, yet the giving of the two handfuls of blood is said to be done "aftewards", and Indech remains living until the height of the battle that follows.

8 O'Grady 1898 246

9 Arbuthnot 2010 134

The Clamor of War

Legends describe the sonorous chanting of the Irish Fianna war bands—the *dord fiannsa*.[10] The chant was made by the blending of many warriors' voices in a deep harmonic droning or booming chant, punctuated with sounds produced by the clashing of spear-shafts, a type of wooden gong and droning horns.[11] Warrior bands sang these chants in public assemblies as well as in the field, and likely also in battle array. Such practices are recorded for Celtic peoples on the Continent as well, likely reflecting a practice common throughout many Iron Age warrior cultures. Roman authors evocatively describe British and Germanic tribes employing vocal effects while gathering for battle: "The war-song of the men, and the shrill cries of the women, rose from the whole line…"[12] These scenes also evoke the shrieking women who, together with druids, were said to run among the warriors casting curses against the enemy during the Roman invasion of Britain, a practice we will return to shortly.[13]

War trumpets were also a favored element of battle paraphernalia for the creation of battle music and frightening sound. The Greek Polybius described an enormous, terrifying roaring noise created by the blowing of war trumpets and horns, the voices of the armies, and the clamor of weapons, together "so loud and piercing that the clamor didn't seem to come from trumpets and human voices, but from the whole countryside at once."[14] Irish literature describes similar uses of trumpets in war.[15] The trumpets themselves have been found right across the Celtic-speaking world including Ireland, Britain and Gaul. Examples include the Loughnashade trumpet from Ireland,[16] and animal-headed war-trumpets (*carnyx*, plural *carnyces*) from Tintignac, France and Leitchestown, Scotland—trumpets sculpted with the heads

---

10 Pennington 1930 102-102

11 O'Curry 1873a 380. The droning horns described in texts match closely with reconstructions of ancient instruments which have been found to produce a sound similar to the Australian didgeridoo. See Moriarty 2014.

12 Tacitus in Beck 2009 289; Epstein 1998 15.

13 Suetonius 2006 337

14 Koch & Carey 2003 9

15 Ó hÓgáin 1999 44

16 Moriarty 2014

of boars and serpents.[17] Reconstructions of such war trumpets have been sound-tested and found to produce a harsh, roaring sound very similar to that described by ancient observers. These would have been employed together with the droning, *didgeridoo*-like horns also used in association with the *dord fiannsa*, or war songs.[18]

The Irish tales also describe a practice called *armgrith*, "clamor of arms". Warriors are said to "shake their weapons in fury", clashing armor and weapons together, with vocalizations such as Cú Chulainn's hero's shout, to create a great furor and noise.[19] Visitations of the war Goddesses and the battle spirits are often associated with this phenomenon—such as when Cú Chulainn's *armgrith* invokes the appearance of these entities. At the same time, these attacks can also bring on the clamoring of arms in the camp that is under their attack, as though the presence of these frightful entities might stir up the weapons and armor to shudder and crash of their own accord.[20]

Demons in Weapons

The relationship of battle spirits to warriors often expresses itself in the physical gear of war. Beyond appearing following acts of warriorship, the battle spirits also attach themselves to the possessions of warriors and are seen to emerge and to speak from them. In Cú Chulainn's stories, the battle spirits shout, cry or scream from the peaks and angles of his war-helmet,[21] from the rim of his shield, his sword-hilt, and the butt of his spears.[22] Though described most fully with Cú Chulainn, similar phenomena surround other heroic warriors such as Congal Claen, Finn and Fer Diad as well.[23]

There is a notable specificity about the descriptions as to where these spirits located themselves in the heroes' war-gear: such as sword-hilts, shield-rims, and spear-butts. This suggests that we may be seeing the remnants of a ritual practice in which battle spirits were intentionally ensouled into weapons and war-gear. The prevalence of anthropoid

17 Aldhouse-Green 2010 62
18 Moriarty 2014
19 Borsje 1999 239
20 Borsje 1999 231
21 O'Rahilly 2011 186
22 O'Rahilly 2010 228
23 Borsje 1999 235

sword and dagger hilts among the Celts lends itself as evidence toward this possibility, shown in the archaeological record in Ireland, Britain and Gaul.[24] If warriors were in the practice of ritually ensouling their weapons with battle spirits to aid them in war, we might expect them to choose hilts shaped into human-like portraits as idols for these spirits to occupy. Vivid descriptions of weapon-cultus rituals emerge in the Irish literature, such as the sword of the Fomoire king, recovered by the Túatha Dé after the *Second Battle of Mag Tuired*. The text explains that "spells have been kept in swords", and that "the reason why demons used to speak from weapons then is that weapons used to be worshipped by men". After recovery, the warriors offer tribute to the sword by unsheathing it, cleaning it, and asking it to speak and recount its deeds in battle.[25]

Similar stories emerge of spears which are alive and surrounded by hints of cult behavior, including veneration and feeding the spirit in the weapon. The Luin of Celtchar, an ensouled spear described in greatest detail in *Dá Derga's Hostel,* is considered to be alive and would cry out and make *armgrith,* clatter and knock itself to the ground when it was agitated with the thirst for bloodshed. To quench its ardor it had to be plunged in a cauldron of poison to prevent it catching fire.[26] Similar ensouled spears appear in several other texts. Jacqueline Borsje notes several examples; many of the accounts describe tribute or offerings that were required by these spears, to keep the spirit appeased: "And whenever any one went past without leaving anything with it, a demon would move it, and it would leap among them and make a slaughter of them."[27] Just as with the sword, we have a practice wherein weapons were believed to possess an indwelling battle spirit, which was ritually fed and propitiated so that it could assist in the act of battle.

Swords also served as guarantees of truth; oaths were sworn on swords because the spirit ensouled in the sword was understood to be able to testify to the truth by means of oracular speech, and by battle ordeal. If a warrior gave false oath or boast about his deeds, it was expected that in the next battle his sword would turn against him.[28] Many texts attest to this practice of warrior oaths proved by the action

24 Ross 1996 101
25 Gray 1982 162
26 Stokes 1910 301
27 Borsje 1999 229
28 Borsje 1999 225

of spirit-ensouled swords. A typical example is this from *The Sick-Bed of Cú Chulainn*:

> "they laid their swords over their thighs when they declared the strifes, and their own swords used to turn against them when the strife that they declared was false; nor was this to be wondered at, for at that time it was customary for demon beings to scream from the weapons of men, so that for this cause their weapons might be the more able to guard them."[29]

Battle Sorceries

Many Irish tales paint visions of druidic sorcerers mustering with armies to battle, practicing their magical arts against the enemies from the edge of the fray. This image is deeply mythological, and we see the Morrígna acting in this role, as do several other deities. Yet it is also described innumerable times of human characters in the tales, sometimes in a historic context. And as we will see, there is evidence to suggest that members of the priestly classes did employ such practices in at least some contexts in the Celtic-speaking world.

A classic instance of battle sorcery is presented by the Morrígna in the *First Battle of Mag Tuired*. Badb, Macha and Morrígan attack their Fir Bolg adversaries with "magic showers of sorcery and compact clouds of mist and a furious rain of fire, with a downpour of red blood from the air on the warriors' heads," continuing for three days and nights.[30] This specific list of phenomena—attacks of druidic fire, obscuring clouds, and showers of blood, occur together in other tales, such as the sorcery of the druid Mogh Ruith. The parallel specificity suggests both accounts draw on a common tradition about this type of sorcery.[31] Mogh Ruith's story provides more detail about the conjuration. He makes a burning ball of wood from the rowan tree (also known as mountain ash, a sacred and very magical tree) which has been gathered by each of the men of the tribe, including the king. This wood is bundled together into a large ball with butter and shavings from the handle of a spear, and he chants a rhythmic incantation over

---

29 Leahy 1905 41
30 Fraser 1915 27
31 O'Curry 1873 213

it as it is lit afire. Mogh Ruith then employs "druidic breath" to conjure black clouds in the sky from the smoke of the druidic fire, and these clouds produce the showers of blood.[32]

Battle sorcery practices have a curious association with pillar stones; druids at battles frequently station themselves "on pillars and points of vantage, plying their sorcery."[33] Pillar stones are often grave markers and seem to have held powerful functions, both as locations of ancestral power, and as boundary-markers. It may be for this reason that at least two such stones were incorporated into the structure of the souterrain at the Cave of Cruachan, the Morrígan's mythic home (as seen in Chapter 10, above). Such associations of pillar stones with ancestral powers could provide part of the rationale for druids employing them as stations for sorcery; the tales do not elaborate, but we can imagine that those ancestral powers may have been felt to be accessible to the practitioner positioned upon the stone.

Cú Chulainn employs a pillar stone in a martial challenge, during the phase of the *Táin* narrative when he is engaging Ulster's enemies in guerrilla warfare. He issues his challenge in the form of a binding, which he deploys by inscribing it in *ogam* onto an oak sapling twisted into a ring, and pushing the ring down over the pillar stone.[34] His enemies read this as "a champion's bond", and they obey its terms out of fear of him—specifically, he binds them to stay where they are and encamp there, to prevent them leaving the area. This is reminiscent of an episode in the *First Battle of Mag Tuired*, in which the Túatha Dé sorcerers, including the Morrígna, "fixed their pillars in the ground to prevent any one fleeing till the stones should flee."[35] The fixity and permanence of pillar stones, together with their ancestral and liminal functions, magically directed using *ogam* or verbal incantation, may underlie their use in both contexts as magics for controlling the movement of an enemy in war.

Battle sorcery also manifests in the phantom army—a host of spectral creatures which may be illusions or may be actual spirits, sent against enemies to confuse and terrify them. The daughters of Calatín use sorcery to conjure a phantom army from leaves in Cú Chulainn's death

32 O'Curry 1873 213-215
33 Fraser 1915
34 O'Rahilly 2010 151
35 Fraser 1915 45

tale.[36] Similarly, two Túatha Dé sorceresses, Bé Chuille and Díanann, conjure a phantom host from "the trees and the stones and the sods of the earth", to create terror and scatter the Fomoiri in the *Second Battle of Mag Tuired*.[37] Ériu conjures phantom hosts from sods of the mountain peat against the Sons of Míl in the *Lebor Gabála Érenn*.[38] Accounts of this sort continue into the historic era, including an episode in the 12th century Norman invasion.[39]

Did druids or other priestly folk attend battles and practice sorcery against their martial adversaries? It seems likely that in many instances they did. Classical accounts of Roman battles with Celtic and Germanic peoples describe this, as in the well-known account by Tacitus of the invasion of Mona: "Among them were black-robed women with dishevelled hair like Furies, brandishing torches. Close by stood Druids, raising their hands to heaven and screaming dreadful curses."[40] While this account pertains to Britain rather than Ireland, and the description may have been creatively embroidered by the author, it does converge closely with several elements common to descriptions of Irish battle magic. In both genres we see fierce priests attending battles to support the armies with ritual attacks, the use of fire in battle magic, and vocal incantation as the means of cursing enemies. Aldhouse-Green suggests that a vengeful Fury-like war Goddess would likely have been called upon in battle sorcery such as Tacitus described of these black-cloaked women.[41] It seems likely that a tradition of invoking war deities such as the Morrígna for the aid of battle sorcery underlies the mythological accounts of their action in warfare.

Spoils and Sacrifices

As war was understood to be shaped by spiritual forces and its outcomes directed by the will of the Gods, battle would be followed by

36 O'Grady 1898 240. The later *Brislech Mór* version details phantom warriors conjured from "thistles, the light wee puff-balls and the wood's withered fluttering leaves". The earlier *Aided Con Culainn* version simply says that they "shaped hosts" to create the illusion of war (Tymoczko 1981 38).

37 Gray 1982 55

38 Macalister 1956 37

39 Mullally 1999 89

40 Aldhouse-Green 2010 215

41 Aldhouse-Green 2010 215

giving the Gods their due. This becomes particularly necessary in cases where votive dedications have been made prior to the battle; those dedications must be fulfilled. For this reason post-battle offerings are often shown in the literature and archaeological record, their details varying by region and cultural idiom. Captured wealth in the form of treasure, weapons and armor, war horses and domestic food animals, as well as prisoner sacrifice, were given in dedication.

Gaulish and British sanctuaries contained great heaps of treasures, often deposited inside sanctified temple buildings, with captured shields, weapons and armor displayed prominently along palisades and gates.[42] Many contemporary authors describe this practice of dedicating battle spoils into sacred treasuries; such depositions were treated with the utmost sacredness as belonging to the Gods. Observers remarked that these treasure hoards could be displayed openly without fear of theft, as everyone knew that a violation of the sanctuaries would bring on the most terrible of curses.[43] Temple deposition seems to have been more common in Britain and Gaul, less so in Ireland. On another hand, water deposits of dedicated spoils into lakes, rivers, and bogs are seen across the range of Celtic regions, including many in Ireland.[44] We cannot always establish that the hoards found represent battle spoils, but in many instances their contents argue for it, where the deposits are primarily made up of war gear such as weapons, armor, shields, chariot fittings, and war trumpets. Sometimes, especially in Gaul, portions of captured spoils were burned as a means of offering them to the Gods.[45] Prisoners were sometimes sacrificed as offerings in payment for the support of the Gods in war; described in Chapter 12 above.

Macha's Mast: The Head Cult

A special and very popular form of war trophy was the collection of heads of slain adversaries. This practice is so widely spread and so ubiquitous among Celtic peoples from Ireland across to the Continent, that it might almost be considered one of the markers of Celticity. Severed head motifs adorn Celtic art spanning across this same range, reflecting

42 Brunaux 1988 25, Brunaux 2001
43 Diodorus Siculus, Strabo in Koch & Carey 2003 12, 15.
44 Beck 2009
45 Caesar in Koch & Carey 2003 22.

a deep cultural preoccupation with the head. War customs pertaining to the collection of heads, and the rites and practices surrounding them, show remarkable parallels across the Celtic world.

The Irish literature describes warriors collecting the heads of adversaries they have killed, bringing them back as trophies to display. Cú Chulainn collects the heads of adversaries and displays them on his chariot, as well as using them in guerrilla warfare terror tactics by impaling them on poles for their friends to find.[46] In his own death tale, when his adversaries finally succeed in killing him, they cut off his head and right hand and take them as trophies.[47] Similar practices of head collecting and carrying them at the girdle or attached to the chariot are described in a great many texts, and accord closely with Classical accounts of head-collecting among the Gauls.[48] The practice of collecting heads was not only performed to display martial dominance over enemies—it also reveals a spiritual basis in head veneration. The belief seems to be that the spirit and valorous qualities of a warrior could be accessed through the collection and use of the head. This is apparent in the funerary rituals surrounding severed heads in tales such as the *Battle of Allen*, and in pervasive legends of such severed heads developing oracular powers of speech (discussed in greater detail in Chapter 18 below). The *Siege of Howth* records a peculiar practice of extracting the brains from a slain adversary's skull, mixing them with lime, and drying the mass into a hardened ball kept as a trophy, which could also be weaponized through use as a sling-stone.[49] Gaulish priests were said to make ornamented, gold-covered ritual libation cups from the captured skulls of enemies.[50]

Were head collecting solely a display of conquest or martial dominance, one might expect heads to be desecrated. Instead, heads were not only collected, but curated as devotional objects, incorporated into ritual and battle paraphernalia. This veneration and ritual appropriation of the power in the enemy's head likely springs from the same complex of belief that saw the head as the seat of the hero's light and the indwelling spirit of the warrior. For similar reasons, the heads of slain enemies likely would have been among the devotional and votive

46 O'Rahilly 2011 134, 146
47 Tymoczko 1981 61
48 Stokes 1887 63, Wood-Martin 1902a 327
49 Stokes 1887 63
50 Livy in Koch & Carey 2003 36.

offerings given to the deities of battle. The kenning for severed heads, *mesrad Macha*, "Macha's harvest" or "Macha's mast", reflects this.[51] The passage implies that "the heads of men that have been slaughtered" belong to the three Morrígna as their due. Indeed, the devotional offering of heads to Macha is implied again in several other texts, in the person of Macha Mongruad for whom the sons of Dithorba leave "a slaughter of heads before her"; a phrase that suggests devotional tribute.[52] A similar custom is likely reflected in the phrase *cuailli Badbhba*, "stakes of the Badb", referring to trophy heads displayed on stakes.[53] As the war Goddess is the motive spiritual force behind the emanation of the hero's light from the head of the warrior in battle ardor, the slain head of a respected and worthy adversary becomes a fitting offering to her.

Living Practice: Facing the War Goddess

As the preceding section has shown us, the Morrígna have a deep history in the theater of war and the practices and rites of battle cultus. Our task in this section is to examine how this aspect of cult practice can be brought into living practice today. This presents a problem as most living Pagans are not involved in warfare, and many experience a cognitive dissonance about integrating this aspect of Celtic culture and religion into our practices. Where the ancient Celtic societies centered war in the experience of their people, most Pagan practitioners today have no lived context for warfare. For this reason, instead of offering ritual theory about battle cultus for modern practitioners, in this section I will address this theological and moral dissonance so many experience when facing the war Goddess, seeking to offer a deeper level of engagement with her and the forces she embodies.

Devotees of the Morrígan everywhere are surely as familiar as I am with the incredulous question: "Why would you want to worship a war Goddess?" For many people, the aspects of the Morrígna relating to warfare, violence, bloodshed, carnage, and death seem horrific. Surely

51 Stokes 1900 271. The phrase has sometimes been translated "fruit crop", but the sense of *mesrad* is specifically "mast", a nut crop, such as acorn or hazelnut (Hennessy 1872 36).

52 Meyer 1888 151

53 Epstein 1998 132

if we value peace, we would not wish to worship war? By worshiping a Goddess who is said to revel in slaughter, are we not simply inviting those terrible forces into our lives, invoking them more fully into the world? These questions have a personal dimension for me. I was introduced to the worship of the Morrígan as part of the traditional practices of the witchcraft coven in which I received my early training. I did not seek her out and was not, at first, drawn to her. At the outset of the relationship, I was deeply disturbed and had to process through this same set of moral and theological questions for myself before I could progress in my devotional relationship with her.

As it should be clear from our explorations in this book, the Morrígan is far more complex a divinity than simply the embodiment of war and violence. Yet there is no denying that battle is fundamental to her identity and function, just as the ethos of warriorship and battle were fundamental to the ancient Celtic experience and worldview. How do we reconcile veneration of a bloody war Goddess and her warrior culture with a desire to live well, safely and in peace?

Deeper than Bloodlust

My first answer to this question is that we need to look more deeply at the roots of her relationship to war. The Morrígan's battle aspect arises from something deeper than bloodlust or glorification of violence. In its spiritual context, battle is *sovereignty in action*. It is this that the Morrígan embodies, and this is why she merits worship even for those who wish never to participate in violence of any kind. She embodies, activates, and empowers something that we need to survive: the willingness to protect what sustains us. This statement isn't a new-age revisionist view of her; it is borne out by her history, as we have seen. Among her earliest identities are forms arising as tutelary and territorial Goddesses. If sovereignty is the power flowing between land and people, personified in sovereignty Goddesses, then war is the character of that power when that unique bond between land and people is threatened. The Morrígan is the face that sovereignty takes on under threat: protective, fierce, martial, uncompromising.

Warriorship, too, is deeper than bloodlust. It is what naturally arises from deep commitment to something of value—the willingness to fight to protect it. At the most personal level, every parent understands this. Facing a survival threat to their family, almost all will find that they become warriors. Warriorship is the capacity for action we find within ourselves when we love and value something more than than we care about our own safety. In its essence, warriorship is love in action. These principles—the protection of sovereignty, the willingness to fight for what we love, and the instinct to survive—are what lie beneath the bloody face of the Morrígan. Worshiping a war Goddess does not mean worshiping violence for its own sake. It means embracing the meaning and value of warriorship, and the positive role that conflict can take.

Peace and Conflict

The Morrígan speaks to us of both war and peace in her poetry. Profound teachings on the nature of peace and conflict emerge from her vision. The peace she conjures in her poems is not characterized simply by the absence of conflict. She conjures a vision of peaceful plenty defended and upheld by strength, and both that strength and that peace flow from justice. The deeper truth contained at the heart of this vision is one modern activists know well—that there can be no peace without justice.

Peace is not defined by the absence of conflict. Peace is more rightly to be understood as the condition of being free to live well; freedom from violence is only one of its elements. That is to say, a situation where there is no active violence happening can be just as oppressive as open conflict—very far from any kind of peace we would value. Injustices may be enforced in the name of preserving "the peace", but often what we see being served in this context is not peace, but order. We see militarized security states, ethnic and cultural suppression, and police states; where people are kept pacified and controlled by fear, deprivation, or more subtle psychological coercion. In these situations there may be an absence of overt violence, yet still there is not peace. Where order comes at the expense of human dignity and safety, there is no peace, even if there is no violence yet. That is a condition that is neither war nor peace – and it is in that charged in-between space where we most often hear her voice inciting toward the conflict.

There are lessons to be found here about the costs of choosing order instead of peace. The desire to distance ourselves from conflict at all costs is a mark of privileged culture. Its unexamined assumption is that as participants in the wealthy dominant society, we can afford to reject the idea of conflict in favor of a better way. In fact, the assumption that all will be well and that what we love and value will be safeguarded without our needing to undertake risk or conflict is itself a reflection of a privileged society for whom order represents comfort. For less privileged peoples, for those directly suffering oppression, the established order does not safeguard peace, and the necessity of conflict toward liberation and as a prerequisite for true peace will already be understood.

This is what the Morrígan teaches: that conflict and violence are not always antithetical to peace. Peace and conflict do not exist in metaphysical opposition, but as coupled aspects of one dynamic. Conflict can be liberating, can be a necessary prerequisite to peace. Injustice represents a state of latent, unexpressed violence that must like a spring be uncoiled before conditions can come to rest in a true peace. She teaches that we sometimes have to fight for justice before the time will come when we can pray for peace.

War Goddess with a Conscience

Some may find it surprising that I speak of the Morrígan in terms of justice, privilege and liberation. As a Goddess who is deeply tied to both warfare and kingship, we might on the surface assume her to be more interested in glory, battle and conquest than social justice. Yet, a careful look at her lore reveals a deep social consciousness.

Her compassion comes through strongly in the second of the two *Mag Tuired* prophecies, the poem sometimes called the Dark Prophecy. It is among her most emotive poems, conjuring evocative images of the suffering of ordinary people in the absence of *fír flathemon,* justice of sovereigns or truthful leadership. She speaks of sad mouths, howling faces, terrible torments and sorrows. Of people betrayed by kings, judges, and their own kin. Of the sufferings brought by crime, unchecked hostility, the treachery of leaders. We can glimpse a sense of environmental justice too—the reflection of social justice in the life of the land—in her words about seasons coming without harvest, seas empty of fish, destructive floods, all the impacts of a failure of justice and sovereignty.

In other poems we also see her warn and bewail the costs of violence. She incites, but she also speaks of the grief and destruction of war, the terrible cost in blood, the counting of bodies. In her manifestations as an omen of death to warriors, she sometimes adopts a mourning stance, grieving the blood and carnage, wailing over the corpses as she washes them in preparation for the rites of death. In a sense, the gruesome-ness of these appearances, the visions of horrible bloody spoils, the red blood washing into the streams, serve in part to remind us of the terrible cost of war.

The Love of Violence

How do we reconcile this apparent social conscience with the other stories which tell of her bloodlust and delight in carnage? If she can display compassion and empathy toward the suffering that warfare and violence brings, why does she also seem to enjoy it so much?

My answer is that the love of peace does not preclude the love and incitement of violence. This may sound contradictory, but consider that warriors do not prevail in the arena of war by maintaining a distaste for bloodshed nor an ambivalence about violence. A warrior may love peace, but when the moment of conflict does arise, the necessity is to throw your whole being into the fight, leaving no room for hesitation or ambivalence. The warrior in that moment must love battle ardently, must desire nothing but the mad glory of the fight, the perfection of violence as martial art. This is what brings the greatness of heart, the madness required to charge forward into the waiting blades of an adversary against all the natural instincts of self-preservation. Hesitation and moral ambiguity in the moment do not lead to survival. This is what the Morrígan incites, when she is inciting warriors to battle. She is drawing them into their battle ardor, pushing them to a state of enhanced fury and power that will allow them to survive and to prevail.

I believe there is an ecological dimension to her complex relationship to war, also. As a Goddess whose most primal identities include a theophany as carrion bird devouring the slain, in a sense it can be said that she enjoys carnage because it is her job to do so. It is part of her eco-spiritual function as a Goddess presiding over death in battle. She, somewhat like the Norse *valkyrja*, plays a role in the transition of the souls of fallen between this world and the Otherworld. She is herself part of the gateway through which the war dead pass as the crows devour their bodies. Should we tell the mountain lion she ought not to revel in the death of the deer? Tell the carrion crow to shudder when she wets her bill with the blood of the dead? Perhaps, the Morrígan lusts for blood also because it is her role in the shape of things. All beings hunger for that which it is their nature to eat.

The Shadow of War

My years of devotion to the Morrígan have shown me that while she is identified with warfare and violence, our wars and our violence are our own responsibility. We cannot blame our war Gods for the continued existence of war and the suffering that it can bring. We are the product of our heritage, just as she is of hers: we are inheritors of the whole bloody river of history and all its ingrained cultural habits.

I do not believe the problems arising from Western civilization's relationship to warfare can be chalked up to violent Gods. It isn't as simple as the notion that violent Gods move us toward violent goals. I think perhaps the problem with our civilization is the opposite one: we have given up our war Gods, or at least pretend we have. We have persuaded ourselves that we don't need war Gods, that we are above venerating war. In doing this we have pushed war into our cultural shadow—into our collective unconscious, to use a psychological metaphor. We claim to be driven by principles of peaceful democracy, Christian kindness and forgiveness, the rule of law. This identity provides cover for ruthless hegemony, imperialistic conquest, and constant war driven by a seemingly endless, faceless military-industrial war machine. Forces unacknowledged and not faced take on a life of their own in the darkness of this shadow. War, for western civilization, has become part of our shadow. This is amply demonstrated by our society's treatment of its war veterans who, in the U.S. at least, come home from serving in our wars to find themselves discarded and disrespected. We do this, I think, because our military service people represent to us everything we seek to avoid facing—they embody the shadow of war, and we do not want to look at it.

What I propose is the possibly radical notion that we need war Gods, not to encourage us unthinkingly toward violence, but to be in right relationship with war as a society. We need to be in relationship with war Gods like the Morrígan so that we can be in a conscious relationship to conflict and war and their relationship to peace, justice, sovereignty and all the other things we value. We need war Gods to teach us how to integrate war into our value system in an intentional way. The Morrígan, at least, will insistently remind us to count the cost of war, will remind us of our honor, will demand of us to consider what exactly is worth fighting for.

Reclaiming War

To reclaim our relationship to both war and sovereignty, we must gather the courage to look these forces in the face. We must be willing to see the ways we participate in and benefit passively from violence, injustice, and imperialism. We must be willing to see the role conflict and violence play in our lives, including the ways we have pushed these forces into our cultural shadow and projected them onto others. We have to be willing to face the war monster we have created with our blindness, and to seek guidance from the war Goddess.

As war is the face of sovereignty in action, so sovereignty is the counterbalance to contain the unchecked drive for war. To a large degree, the development of the military-industrial war monster driving our civilization is paralleled by the steady erosion of sovereignty of individuals within the state. We have arrived at this current time where the democratic mandate of the individual—our delegation of sovereignty to our leadership—has become virtually meaningless, subsumed by the control of the state by the economic and military-industrial elite. This is profoundly about loss of sovereignty on the part of the people, and is directly linked to the uncontrolled making of war by Western nations, primarily the U.S.. Yes—this is a political contention—as questions of war, sovereignty, and justice always are.

For spiritual practitioners, the necessity is to become sovereignty itself, to reclaim it by ourselves embodying it. We must become inviolable. To do this, we need to internalize the teachings of the Goddess of war and sovereignty, the heart of warriorship that teaches us to value love and justice above personal comfort. The practice of warriorship, its rites and customs, and the role of the Morrígna in the lives of warriors, is the subject we take up in the next chapter.

17

The Warrior's Initiation

Warriorship is enacted collectively in the cultural practices of battle and warfare, but it begins with the training and experience of the individual. In this chapter, we examine Celtic beliefs and practices pertaining to warriorship and the relationship of warriors to the war Goddesses. The dynamic series of interactions between the hero Cú Chulainn and the Morrígan in the Ulster cycle can reveal much about this aspect of cult practice, as can the lore of Finn mac Cumhaill and the Fianna. We will draw on these sources as well as other literary, historical, and archaeological evidence to seek a glimpse of the cults of warriorship.

Popular interpretations of the relationship between Cú Chulainn and the Morrígan have tended to focus on the adversarial dynamic that can be seen in a surface reading of the stories, yet with deeper examination, a great deal more depth emerges. We will understand much more when we place the relationship between warrior and war Goddess in the broad cultural context of Celtic and Indo-European social, ritual, and religious patterns.

The Adversary

The relationship betweeen Cú Chulainn and the Morrígan is often interpreted in an adversarial light in popular materials. This reading tends to focus on the series of interactions within the *Táin*, beginning with the episode called *The Conversation of the Morrígan with Cú Chulainn*, in which the Morrígan offers him a sexual liaison and her aid in his battles to defend Ulster against the forces of Connacht. Cú Chulainn refuses the liaison, saying "it is not for a woman's body that I have come."[1] In response, she warns him that she will instead attack him when he is fighting his enemies, making his combats worse for him: in the forms of eel, wolf, and heifer she promises to attack, and he responds with equivalent threats to break her in each form. These actions proceed as promised: she attacks as eel, wolf, and heifer; he counterattacks, and both are wounded in the exchange.

The adversarial reading of this story frames Cú Chulainn as a prideful, arrogant warrior who spurns the Morrígan's help, and her actions are in turn read as arising from spite and rage at being refused by him. She attacks him and wounds him, and for the duration of the story their relationship is adversarial—she hinders him in his battles, and in the related tale of his death after the *Táin*, some read her as the agent of his undoing and death at the hands of his enemies. The related episode in the *Cattle Raid of Regamna*, a foretale containing an alternate version of the threat exchange, is also often read in this adversarial light. Cú Chulainn's story is often treated as a moral parable; its simple lesson being: don't insult the war Goddess, or she will destroy you.

The Irish heroic literature represents a much more complex and nuanced body of myth than this simple moral parable, however. If we look more closely, the character of Cú Chulainn and his interactions with the war Goddess stand within a rich constellation of lore about the ideology and practice of warriorship in Iron Age societies. These stories fall within a genre within which the identity and role of the heroic warrior is intimately tied to the patronage of the war Goddess.

The Dedicant

Gazing at the broad picture of Cú Chulainn's life, including the tales of

1 O'Rahilly 2011 177

his youth all the way through to his death-tale, what emerges is a warrior dedicant who is followed at every step by the shadowy presence of the war Goddess in her various forms. Her presence and attitude toward him are by no means always benevolent. Yet at the same time, her persistent interest in him is surely evidence of something beyond simple spite.

Cú Chulainn's story draws on elements from a deep history of warrior bands as a central institution in Celtic culture, and paralleled across the broad landscape of Indo-European societies. The somewhat later Irish warrior-poet Finn is another exemplar of these same themes. Their tales illuminate the life of the legendary warrior within the context of the warrior band. The warrior band was an initiatory and religious institution inasmuch as it was also a social and martial one, and in a great many respects its practices connect back to the worship of the Morrígna and cognate war Goddesses, as patrons of warriorship. Its outlines can be traced within a wide range of sources, including the Irish mythological and heroic literature, as well as the literatures of related cultures, and to some extent reflected in the archaeological record.

Heroic narratives hint at a sequence of stages and ritualized threshold moments in the life of a warrior within the context of the warrior band. Broadly speaking, these include youthful warriorship and the taking up of arms; the warrior's formal training, typically under female tutelage; initiatory dedication rites involving totemic identification and a sacrificial component; Otherworldly ordeals and combat challenges; entry into relationship with battle spirits, the warrior dead and the divinities of battle, especially tutelary relationship with the war Goddess; the accession to special heroic powers, feats, and forces resulting from these relationships; and finally heroic death and funerary rites under the auspices of the war Goddess, with entry into the ranks of the heroic warrior dead. Here we will trace each of these ritualized stages, up to the accession to heroic status. Heroic death and funerary rites will follow in the next chapter.

Early Combats, Fostering and Taking Up Arms

Cú Chulainn's boyhood combats are told in the *Boyhood Deeds*, an embedded story within the *Táin*. His initial testing comes when he leaves home to travel to Emain Macha and challenge the boys training there, in the form of a violent hurling match which turns into a brawl. This is his introduction to the household of King Conchobor, his uncle and foster-father.[2] His relationship with Conchobor reflects the Irish custom of fostering the children of relatives and clients in the households of more powerful families, which both provided training for the child and ensured loyalty between the families. The institution of fosterage is strongly linked to the training of young warriors—the "boy-troop" of Emain Macha which Cú Chulainn challenges is essentially a cohort of youths taken in fosterage to be trained toward warriorship in the king's household, and represents a preparatory stage toward entry into the warrior band. Cú Chulainn's challenge and entry into the boy-troop are marked by ritualized prohibitions; the new youth is required to undertake a binding guarantee of protection between himself and the troop. A parallel, but simpler narrative of the boyhood exploits of Finn begins with a similar hurling contest and combat challenge with a youth troop at his clan's stronghold.[3]

The war Goddess also makes her first appearance in Cú Chulainn's youth. Conchobor has been wounded and left on a battlefield, and Cú Chulainn must go out and retrieve him. On the battlefield he is attacked and thrown down by the lingering spirits of those slain in the battle. While he is down on the bloody earth he hears the voice of the Badb calling from among the corpses, mocking him for allowing himself to be bested by phantoms. Her incitement provokes him to rise up, overcome the terrible specters, and finish his gruesome task.[4] This episode does not show us any specific ritual features, but it suggests the beginning of a tutelary relationship. She has used incitement to push him past the panic of facing his first encounter with the horrors of war—the gruesome field of corpses. The interaction in this encounter establishes the pattern that will be borne out throughout their relationship: her attitude toward him is one of fierce tutelage, pushing him toward greatness through both supportive and challenging actions.

Cú Chulainn's taking of arms is highlighted with spiritual significance and ritualized actions. He chooses a fateful day when the druid Cathbad foretells that "he who takes up arms today will be famous and renowned, but he will, however, be short-lived".[5] In taking up arms, Cú

2 O'Rahilly 2011 137
3 Cross & Slover 1936 361
4 O'Rahilly 2011 138
5 O'Rahilly 2011 143

Chulainn is presented with his own set of weapons, and a chariot—after smashing a sequence of each for which he is too strong. Following this taking of arms and the pronouncement of the omens on his career as a warrior, he undertakes a series of feats which also suggest a ritual character to this event. First he circles Emain Macha three times in his chariot; then he goes to the boy-troop whose ranks he is leaving, and they pronounce blessings and well-wishes on him.[6] He then drives to the borders of Ulster to undertake a series of combats, including taking his first turn as the warrior guarding the border of the province, and a series of three fights with dangerous warriors who are enemies of Ulster, the sons of Nechtan Scéne. Finally, he completes a hunt and returns to Emain Macha bearing the deer and birds he has captured in the hunt, and the three severed heads of his first warrior's kills.[7] His return to the stronghold is also met in a ritual fashion; since he is returning from his warrior's circuit still possessed by the battle rage, he has to be met and ritually de-escalated from this state before he can re-integrate with his people. This is accomplished by sending the women out to bare their naked bodies to him, and by the warriors seizing him and plunging him in a series of water baths to cool the battle ardor. He is then dressed in a new garment and placed by the side of the king.

This sequence would appear to reflect a ritualized series of acts involved in a young warrior's taking of arms: omens are taken, gear of the warrior given to him, a procession and display is made around the stronghold, and blessings given. He then traverses the province to prove his warrior's skills in both hunting and fighting, returning to ritual re-integration and honors.

Feats Learned from a Warrior-Priestess

The warrior's formal training would begin after the taking up of arms, and one of its striking and consistent features is the tutelage of a female warrior-teacher. In most versions of Cú Chulainn's narrative, he is sent to train with the warrior woman Scáthach, or in some cases, Scáthach is part of a trio of warrior women who teach him.[8] The most

---

6 O'Rahilly 2011 143, O'Rahilly 2010 164-165. The circuits of Emain Macha are alluded to in the Recension 1 version, and spelled out more clearly in the *Book of Leinster* version. The well-wishing appears in both versions.

7 O'Rahilly 2011 147

8 Stokes 1908 115

familiar version of this story of his training is from the *Wooing of Emer*, in which he must go to Scáthach for training as an ordeal requirement before being allowed to marry. In this tale, Scáthach "who lived eastward of Alba" is the premier martial teacher, presiding over a training-school for warriors on an island off the coast of Britain.[9] Cú Chulainn trains with her for a year, also joining in the "friendship of the thighs" with her, her daughter Úathach, and her rival, another warrior woman named Aoife. In another version, *The Training of Cúchulainn,* he takes training under a series of woman warrior teachers, each of them for a year, beginning with Úathach of the Glen, in Munster; then Dordmair, the daughter of Domnall in Alba (Britain); and finally Scáthach, here the daughter of Buanuinne, the king of "Scythia".[10]

The exchange in the latter text that sends Cú Chulainn searching for Scáthach is illuminating. During his studies with Dordmair, an Otherworldly man appears and casts aspersions against the quality of training Cú Chulainn has learned. In response, Cú Chulainn asks him, "Is there in the world a woman-knight who is better than the woman-knight with whom I am now?" His question assumes that if there are mightier feats to be learned anywhere, it will be with a woman.[11] We do not know if such warrior schools led by women actually existed. Accounts of women warriors are not uncommon in the Irish literature, such as Creidne, who led three Fianna warrior bands of her own,[12] and Ness, the mother of King Conchobor, also a warrior with three warrior bands.[13] Historical evidence for women as warriors and war-leaders among the Iron Age Irish and other Celts suggests that they did exist, but may have been somewhat exceptional, rather than the norm. Yet a pervasive cultural framework is reflected in the surviving literature of both Ireland and Wales, conveying that even if warfare as a vocation was primarily male, it was women who taught the martial arts and es-

---

9 Meyer 1888 234

10 Stokes 1908a 115. "Scythia" is likely mythopoetic language for "the East" as a general idea, and may have arisen from the similarity of the Irish words for Scythia and the Isle of Skye, which is traditionally associated with Scáthach, and bears place-names attributed to her.

11 Stokes 1908a 115

12 Meyer 1910 xii

13 Stokes 1910a 23. In both cases, three bands of nine warriors are mentioned. Warrior bands are often organized in groups of nine; leadership of "three nines" may be a marker or threshold for status as a major warrior-leader.

pecially the specialized heroic feats.

It is possible that these warrior-women teachers are primarily mythological and reflect a tutelary relationship between warriors and martial Goddesses, rather than an actual historic practice of women teaching martial arts to young warriors. Certainly, the warrior women who teach Cú Chulainn and the other heroes of legend have mythic qualities. Scáthach means "Shadowy One",[14] and she shares many qualities with the Morrígan: warlike attributes, tutelary relationship to heroic warriors, associations with phantoms and specters, and the use of prophetic poetry. Epstein goes as far as to suggest that Scáthach may be viewed as an aspect of the Morrígan.[15] Úathach, the daughter of Scáthach, is equally suggestive of a mythological status. Her name means "Horror" and relates her to a class of terrible spirits associated with battle, called *úatha*, "horrors"; creatures that are closely associated with the Morrígan as well.[16]

Finn is also trained in the arts of war and hunting by a pair of warrior women with mythic qualities, his foster-mothers.[17] They are called Bodbmall *bandraí* and Liath Luachra.[18] The first, Bodbmall, is recognizable as a compound of *bodb*, "crow", obviously also one of the names of the war Goddess; and *mall* "slow, soft, or gentle". When applied to women the latter term usually refers to gentility, so this name might be best translated as "Gentle Crow".[19] Bodbmall's epithet *bandraí* is "sorceress" or "druidess"—a title that also applies to Scáthach, as well as the Morrígna. The second of Finn's foster-mothers, Liath Luachra, means "Gray One of Luachair"—a name that is reminiscent of Cú Chulainn's semi-divine horse, the Liath Macha, who itself is associated in legend with Macha of the Morrígna (see Chapter 5, above).

Early Welsh literature also yields an account of martial teaching by warrior women. The hero Peredur is trained in the warrior arts by a group of nine "sorceresses", beginning with an encounter in which he bests one of the sorceresses in combat, makes demands of her, and pledges her to train him. At the end of his training, she grants him arms

14 An alternate translation as "Shield" or "Protective" is proposed by Beck, deriving from a possible etymological relationship to *sciath*, "shield" (Beck 2009 331).

15 Epstein 1998 138

16 Borsje 2007 75

17 Cross & Slover 1936 361

18 Meyer 1881 198

19 Royal Irish Academy 2013, entry *mall*.

and a war-horse.[20] The parallels between this account and the encounter of Cú Chulainn with Scáthach are striking.

All these parallels amount to a pattern that may point to these women as mythological reflections of a fundamental intimacy between warriors and tutelary war Goddesses. Scáthach's prophetic poem to Cú Chulainn in which she prophesies his fate and the outcome of the *Táin* is structurally and thematically similar to the prophecy of the Morrígan to Cú Chulainn in the *Cattle Raid of Regamna* text.[21] This and the other similarities might suggest that if Scáthach had a cult in ancient times, its poetic liturgies may have been related to those used in connection with the Morrígan. Notably, souterrain/cavern structures on the Isle of Skye and other Scottish isles show notable similarities to some features of the cave of Cruachan, one of the Morrígan's centers of cult activity, and it is quite conceivable that Skye may have hosted a parallel cult involving tutelary divinities and warrior practices.[22] A later medieval text claims that the feats taught by Scáthach, Úathach and Aoife were learned "in the confines of Hell."[23] This reference to Hell may simply be Christian condemnation of pagan practices; but it may be something more. We know that the subterranean Otherworld was viewed as the home of chthonic powers we also know associated with cave sites such as those at Cruachan and Skye; and that the Cave of Cruachan itself was often called an entrance to Hell.[24] These warrior women may then be human representatives, *bandraí* or priestesses of the war Goddesses under whose tutelary care and leadership the warriors were trained in such places.

Combat Ordeals

Cú Chulainn must undergo ordeals and tests to enter training under Scáthach, including athletic feats he must complete to reach her stronghold and combat ordeals among the other warriors in her school. The warriors tell him directly that the reason for the combat ordeals is so that "although there be many armies and multitudes, and much hardship and hurt before thee, there would not be fury or excitement on

20 Guest 2014 Sec 1a
21 Olmsted 1982 165
22 Waddell 2014 68, Aldhouse-Green 2010 199
23 O'Rahilly 1924 23
24 Waddell 1983 22

thee before them, considering the hurt thou wilt receive in this house tonight."[25] In other words, they attack him to harden him up for war as part of his entry into elite training. This is accomplished in a series of three physical attacks, including the detail of making him bleed.

Cú Chulainn is also required to fight huge, imposing warriors with suggestive Otherworldly qualities. In the *Training of Cúchulainn* version, he is challenged by Scáthach's two giant sons Cuar "Crooked", and Cat "Cat", before he can fight her for the right to learn the secrets of the heroic feats.[26] In the *Wooing of Emer* version, he is sent to fight Aoife's three sons, Cuar, Cett, and Cruife. The similarity in names suggests that this combat with a series of formidable entities is an important detail preserved from an archaic version of the myth. It is also significant that one of these giants is named "Cat". At the Cave of Cruachan, another story tells of Cú Chulainn undergoing an ordeal there in which giant otherworldly cats attack him, and which he must overcome. Other tales tell of a triple-headed phantom monster Ellén emerging from the same cave, a being who also appears among the creatures the warrior-poet Finn has to combat before acceding to leadership of the Fianna.[27] There appears to be an archetypal myth relating to warrior ordeals at such sites involving combat with Otherworldly cat-like monsters. Waddell proposes that, given Cú Chulainn's ordeal at the cave along with its connection with heroic warriors such as Fráech, Nera, Amairgene, Loegaire, and Conall, the cave likely was the site of warrior initiatory ordeals, which he calls "rites of terror" and which may have included altered consciousness, isolation, sensory depivation, and ritualized combat ordeals. The presence of the Fráech inscription within the cave, he suggests, may indicate that introduction to the spirits of the warrior dead likely also played a role in these rites.[28] We may note also that tales associate wolf-like warriors and monsters emerging from this cave: the fearsome Olc Aí, whose name *olc* is related to "wolf"; and a band of female werewolves who come from the cave to attack and raid about the countryside.[29]

25 Stokes 1908 125
26 Stokes 1908 127
27 Ó hÓgáin 1999 181
28 Waddell 2014 67
29 Waddell 1983 22

Wolf Rites and the Warrior's Initiation

The initiation rites for warriors seem to have involved totemic animal identity and sacrifice. The warrior bands into which youths were inducted through these rites and ordeals are consistently associated with dog and wolf identities, both in Ireland as well as other Celtic societies and the Indo-European world generally. As noted earlier, warriors such as Cú Chulainn and Cú Roí take their names and identities from dogs. The mode of activity of the warrior bands was called *faelad*, "wolfing".[30] These warrior bands can be seen in Irish, Gaulish, Germanic, Greek, and Indo-Iranian cultures, and involved cohorts of young warriors leaving their families to run as "wolf packs", warrior societies operating in the open lands between kingships, and who derived their living by hunting, raiding and battle.[31] This represented a liminal period in the lives of these young warriors, during or after their training, but before marriage and accession to land-owning status; one of the Irish terms applied to them was *díthír*, "landless".[32]

The "wolfing" behavior of the warrior bands was not simply a symbolic representation of hunting and raiding as predatory activities. There are strong indications of warrior practices involving trance states of spiritual frenzy in which the warrior entered into the experience of wolf-nature, particularly in the context of combat or hunting. Speaking of the plundering warrior bands featured in *Dá Derga's Hostel*, O'Connor observes "the charged image of the wolf as an embodiment of social chaos echoes on throughout the saga; and a word later used of the plunderers, *dásachtach* ('frenzied'; line 398), may hint at the berserk-like trances associated with werewolves in mediaeval Europe."[33]" Medieval texts speak of wolves with human voices hunting among flocks and herds; this was attributed to people whose spirits could leave their bodies and travel in wolf shape, and who could be defeated by moving or interfering with their human bodies before their spirits returned—a clear enough description of the practice of spirit travel.[34] In addition to this type of somnolent trance where the spirit leaves the body in wolf shape, there is also a great deal of evidence pointing to a more active,

30 O'Connor 2013 83
31 Powell 2013
32 Brown & Anthony 2012 22
33 O'Connor 2013 83
34 Wood-Martin 1902 118

embodied wolf-trance, the battle ardor in which the warrior is possessed by wolf-frenzy during combat. The most spectacular example of this, of course, is Cú Chulainn's transformation. He is not explicitly described as taking wolf or dog shape, but the distortion is clearly an entry into a primal state, marked by bestial changes in anatomy. Similar distortions of the body with frenzied battle ardors and totemic qualities are seen among the Fianna as well as Norse and Germanic warrior groups such as the Einherjar and Berserkir groups, identified with wolves (or sometimes bears).[35]

The entry into this state of wolf-warrior identity, and the accession to its powers and abilities, was likely accomplished through an initiatory ritual. This rite appears to have involved the sacrificial killing and consumption of dogs or wolves by the young warrior initiates, as a means of ritually taking in and internalizing the spirit of the animal. We can see archaeological evidence of such rituals in a different early Indo-European society at the Bronze Age site in Russia, where deposits from a repeated series of sacrificial rites involving ritual killing, dismemberment, consumption, and ritual deposition of dogs and wolves have been found.[36] It is also likely that the event of Cú Chulainn's name-taking, by virtue of killing a dog at a feast and thereby taking on the role and identity of the dog, contains a distant reflection of this practice. Just so, another component of the warrior-wolf initiations may well have been the taking of a new name by the warrior initiate. The pelts of the wolves or dogs killed and eaten in these rites would likely have been worn by the warriors thereafter; this is suggested in the literature on the Fianna, and is certainly also reflected in many cultures where the wolf-warrior band institution is found.[37]

The activity of these warrior bands seems markedly seasonal. The seasonal pattern begins with the warrior initiation rites, which in most instances of the Indo-European warrior band pattern took place in the winter.[38] The transition points when these warrior bands would leave society to run as warrior wolf-packs on its margins, and when they would return to society, were marked by important rites of separation and re-entry. It seems to have been particularly crucial to ritualize the

35 Sjoestedt 1994 106
36 See Chapter 12 above, for greater detail on the evidence at this site.
37 Keating 2010 329, Brown & Anthony 2012 24
38 Brown & Anthony 2012 4

re-integration of warriors returning to society, in order to protect the society itself from the violence, terror, and battle spirits associated with the activity of warriors.

Encountering the War Goddess

For certain heroic warriors, a further initiatory stage is suggested, going beyond the cycle of the warrior band. This aspect of the warrior cultus appears more individual, rather than collective, and involved personal identification with the war Goddess as tutelary figure, including engagement with her or her human representative in the form of sexual liaison as well as combat challenges.

Cú Chulainn has parallel sexual relationships with each of the warrior women Scáthach, Úathach, and Aoife, and a sexual relationship is framed as being at least a possibility in his relationship with the Morrígan.[39] There are distinct parallels and ritual markers in the actions and exchanges that take place in Cú Chulainn's encounters with the Morrígan and Scáthach. The encounter with the Morrígan in the *Táin*[40] presents a simplified version of their encounter in which only the sexual offer and the exchange of combat threats is present. However, if we look at the *Cattle Raid of Regamna* version, the episode is much expanded. Cú Chulainn challenges her by leaping over her, setting his feet on her shoulders and his spear on her head, to make a request of her. This request leads to her delivery of a prophetic poem foretelling the outcome of the *Táin*, and his own fate and future, before the exchange of combat threats between them.[41] Similarly, when Cú Chulainn challenges Scáthach, it is a closely parallel series of actions; he leaps upon her practice platform, places his two feet on its edges and the point of his spear at her breast, and makes his request of her; a request that leads to her tutelage, their sexual liaison, and to Scáthach's closely parallel prophetic poem foretelling the *Táin* and Cú Chulainn's fate.[42] It seems very likely that each of these episodes hearken to an archetype myth, possibly reflecting of a practice in ancient warrior cultus wherein such a challenge, sexual liaison with the war Goddess through her human

39 Sjoestedt 1994 93
40 O'Rahilly 2011 177
41 Leahy 1906 136
42 Meyer 1888 300

representative, oracular prophecy concerning the warrior's future, and ritualized combat ordeals might have taken place.

It is also possible that the sexual offer from the Morrígan as King Buan's Daughter, and Cú Chulainn's refusal of it, reflect alternate initiatory pathways; that the warrior is making a choice between two dedicatory paths of king/chieftain, and heroic warrior. This may be reflective of different local traditions about the way in which heroes engaged with the tutelary war Goddess. In this regard, it may still be useful to compare with the Morrígan's tryst with the Dagda in the *Second Battle of Mag Tuired*. In the *Táin*, the offer to Cú Chulainn is not simply a sexual tryst; she has brought her cattle and wealth and is in fact offering him a form of royal marriage—conferring her wealth and status as well her help in his battles. To the the Dagda, she makes a somewhat similar offer: sexual union, help in the battle, and the achievement of kingship over Ireland. We know that as a heroic warrior, Cú Chulainn is not seeking kingship, nor is he eligible for it. He is seeking immortality through the greatness of his martial accomplishments, having said, from his first day in arms, that "provided I be famous, I am content to be only one day on earth."[43] Rulership, sovereignty, and wealth are neither his destiny nor his identity. His way is combat, and in each version of this encounter, it is he who chooses combat as the form of his engagement with the Morrígan. He makes his choice verbally plain: when she describes the combat ordeals she will pit him in, he responds, "I prefer that to the king's daughter."[44]

In either case, combat ordeals in which the hero must fight the war Goddess or her representative are prominent in warrior cultus. We have seen that Cú Chulainn must fight and best Scáthach to earn access to her most elite teachings—the heroic feats which she does not offer the other warriors in his cohort. It seems likely to me that the combat of the Morrígan and Cú Chulainn at the ford is a reflection of this type of warrior ordeal as well. These combats are no ordinary fights: in my view, they have taken on the ritualized character of a set of ordeals. The warrior dedicant is now undertaking a series of magical combats against each of the war Goddess's alternate animal forms, while at the same time maintaining his fight against a human adversary in the theater of live, consequential warfare. These encounters will test

43 O'Rahilly 2011 143
44 O'Rahilly 2011 176

his prowess to the utmost.

The ritual nature of these combats is notable: the *Book of Leinster* version has Cú Chulainn placed under magical bindings by the women of his people "not to let the Morrígan go from him without checking and destroying her."[45] Three ritualized combats take place at the ford of a river during Cú Chulainn's fight with a formidable warrior, Lóch. The Morrígan comes against him as the eel, the wolf, and the heifer. Each time, Cú Chulainn succeeds in wounding her and survives his ordeal; but each time, he is wounded. We catch a glimpse of a suggestion that the wounds may be paralleled: when the eel coils round his feet and throws him on his back, Lóch wounds him in the chest. When Cú Chulainn rises again, he deals a blow to the eel and breaks her ribs. This detail of parallel wounds is missing from the other two combats, but in each case, each wounds the other: the she-wolf attacks him, and he breaks her eye with a stone from his sling; the red hornless heifer attacks him along with a stampede of cattle, and he breaks the heifer's leg with another stone.[46]

The episode that immediately follows underscores the ritual nature of the combats, and the intimacy between warrior and war Goddess. Wounded and weary Cú Chulainn sings a poem of lament, saying that he is almost overcome from fighting so many enemies alone. Though he has survived his ordeals, he feels he is undone. It is at this time that the Morrígan appears again in the form of a hag milking a cow, and another ritualized exchange ensues—this time one of healing. Cú Chulainn and the Morrígan exchange three healings to mirror the three combats. She gives him three drinks of milk from the cow, healing his exhaustion and weariness, and in exchange he gives her three blessings which heal each of her three wounds.[47] In the Recension 1 version, the exchange of healing closes with a jibe from the Morrígan, reminding Cú Chulainn that he had said she would never be healed by him; to which he replies that if he'd known it was her, he would not have. In the *Book of Leinster* version, however, this sniping does not occur: we simply have the warrior initiate and the war Goddess exchange healing and blessing after the bloody combat ordeals are done.[48] Máire Herbert suggests that the

45 O'Rahilly 2010 194
46 O'Rahilly 2011 180
47 O'Rahilly 2011 181
48 O'Rahilly 2011 181, O'Rahilly 2010 196

adversarial slant of hero triumphing over Goddess has been added in to the narrative by the compiler, and that the original form of the tale would have simply shown an exchange of healing between the two.[49]

The War Goddess's Spirited Hero

We have seen a series of challenges, initiatory rites, and ritual ordeals, bringing the heroic warrior to an elite status which conferred special powers, feats, and unique weapons. First among these gifts are the *cles-sa*, or "feats". These are specialized feats of warrior prowess, taught by Scáthach and similar warrior-teachers. The most rare and specialized feats belonged to the most elite warriors such as Cú Chulainn, having proved himself with ordeals before Scáthach would grant the teachings. The feats have names, and we find lists of them occurring in the literature; some appear to be simple acts of athleticism and agility, such as rope-walking, long and high jumps, sprinting and rapid traversing of obstacles, and feats of strength. There are feats of breath and voice control, including using the voice as a kind of shock-weapon, and feats of precision weapon handling, such as the juggling of blades, maneuvering with sharpened shields, and the like. Others seem more esoteric, as with spectacular vaulting feats performed over the points of spears and on the frames of chariots.[50] The tales note daily practice of such feats by Cú Chulainn and other warriors of his cohort, and practicing in difficult places such as on stretched ropes in a hall, and in a "feat basket", a woven platform suspended in a tree so as to challenge the agility and equilibrium of the warriors in practice.[51] The *clessa*, once mastered, would be used primarily in ostentatious pre-battle displays for intimidation of enemies, a practice recorded by contemporary Classical authors about the ancient Celts. William Sayers points out that the hero-feats represent an honor-oriented sport as much as a true combat skill: "The exercise of the feats may also have had a ritualistic, hence magical dimension. The feats would complement the boasts, taunts and challenges, these too intended as self-fulfilling."[52] At the same time, however, the enhanced training they provided would also serve to sharpen

49 Herbert 1996 145
50 Sayers 1983 63
51 Sayers 1983 67
52 Sayers 1983 68

the skills of warriors for the more grueling demands of true battle.

Cú Chulainn's unique special feat, the one which he employs in extremis and which Scáthach teaches only to him, is a specialized weapon feat. This is the feat of the *gaí bulga*, a vicious many-barbed spear employed in an outlandish magical fashion by casting from between the toes to strike the enemy, filling the entire body with barbs.[53] The meaning of the name has been the subject of speculation; *bulga* has been attributed to *bolg*, "belly" or "sack", yielding "belly spear" or "disemboweling spear". Alternately, it has been read as a name reference to the Fir Bolg or Belgae, suggesting a model of spear originating with specific tribes; or to a purported lightning-God named Bolga. Sayers also points to evidence tracing it to an early Celtic word *balu-gaisos* which he translates "death-spear".[54]

Another notable ability of the heroic warrior is invocatory access to special powers, an ability that appears to emerge from his intimacy with the war Goddess. Shortly after his initiatory exchanges with the Morrígan, Cú Chulainn encounters the hosts of Connacht and the four provinces gathered against him, and in rage at the scale of the armies he faces alone, he utters "a hero's shout deep in his throat."[55] This hero's shout appears to be one of the special powers of the champion, for it functions as an invocation: in response, the host of battle spirits shriek in answer, "the goblins and sprites and spectres of the glen and demons of the air" who are so closely associated with the Morrígna. And Némain herself appears in response to the invocatory shout and attacks the hosts of his enemies, causing such terror that a hundred of them die from fright.[56] This, it seems to me, is the power that has come to Cú Chulainn through his initiatory ordeals: the war Goddess and her host of battle spirits are now his kin and come to his aid at his mighty invocatory shout.

Shortly after this, Cú Chulainn's famous *ríastrad*, "distortion" comes upon him; perhaps this, too, is among the transformations brought by the warrior's initiation. The *ríastrad* has been mentioned before among his stories, in the *Boyhood Deeds*, but the language in the *Book of Leinster* version of the *Táin* suggests that there is something new in the

53 O'Rahilly 2011 207
54 Sayers 1983 56
55 O'Rahilly 2011 182
56 O'Rahilly 2011 183

transformation that comes now: "Then his first distortion came upon Cú Chulainn so that he became horrible, many-shaped, strange and unrecognisable."[57] Also novel here are manifestations of fire and storm about him, with specific reference to the war Goddess.[58] This fiery phenomenon is called the *coinnle Bodba*, "torches of the war Goddess", and is accompanied by the *lúan láith*, "hero's light". Enrico Campanile compares the hero's light to similar phenomena in related Indo-European cultures and proposes that it is a very archaic aspect of warrior culture. In the Irish context, it often manifests in bird form, called *én gaile*, "bird of war-fury" or "bird of valor", highlighting its connection to the war Goddess in bird shape.[59] The hero's light is also associated with battle frenzy and transformation into wolf form, a pattern shared with its cognates in the Germanic literatures.[60]

The *ríastrad* illustrates a deep ambivalence within Irish culture toward the violence inherent in the warrior mode. It is said again and again that under the distortion he would not know friend from enemy, and would attack and kill indiscriminately, like a beast. Ralph O'Connor points out that Cú Chulainn himself embodies the duality of warriorship, being celebrated and adored for his youthful beauty, and at other times transforming into a grotesque, destructive monster, epitomizing "the warrior-hero's liminal status, not only poised between world and Otherworld, but also embodying at crucial moments (like Cailb and Etain) the Otherworld's two aspects of horrifying destructiveness and divine beauty."[61] The warrior in Celtic society occupied a privileged, elite status for the power they wielded against external threats, and the wealth they won for their people; yet the violence inherent in their role always presented an internal threat at the same time which required ritual and social controls to protect the stability and well-being of the people.[62]

Specters and Horrors

Participation in warfare, with its violence, killing, and carnage sets warriors apart from society and places them in contact with deadly Other-

57 O'Rahilly 2010 201
58 O'Rahilly 2011 187
59 Campanile 1988 91-93, Todd 1867 189
60 Henry 1982 240
61 O'Connor 2013 197
62 Lincoln 1991 4

worldly forces. The ancient Irish recognized these Otherworldly forces as a group of frightful spiritual entities—the battle spirits we have referred to previously. Spirits in this group include some that appear to be ghosts of the slain and other spiritual entities emanating from places of slaughter, such as *úatha* "horrors", *airdrecha* "ghosts, revenants", *urtrochta* "phantoms", *arrachta* "specters". Others are framed as demonic or fairy-like spiritual entities, such as *bánánaig* "pale creatures", *boccánaig* "horned creatures", *demna aieóir* "demons of the air", *síabra* "sprites". Otherworldly human-like beings, primarily female, also appear such as *ammaiti* "hags", *geilti glinne* "mad creatures of the glens" or *geniti glinne* "witches of the glens". These battle spirits are all closely identified with another primary type of battle spirit, the *badba*, "crows", which usually refer to war-furies in bird form who are seen as avatars or manifestations of the war Goddess, Badb.[63] All these spirits were believed to be active at battles, shrieking and fluttering over the heads of the combatants. They also haunted battlefields and other places of violent death afterwards. Many of them are specifically identified with or linked to the Morrígna.[64]

Cú Chulainn's encounter with the revenant corpse (an *airdrech*) in the *Boyhood Deeds* episode illustrates some aspects of this relationship between warriors and battle spirits. By entering the battlefield and walking among the slaughtered he exposes himself to these Otherworldly creatures and the deadly forces they personify. The *airdrech* attempts to attach itself to him and he must struggle to free himself of it.[65] A related corpse-carrying episode befalls Nera in the *Adventure of Nera* foretale, illustrating that contact with the violent dead (in Nera's case, the corpse of a hanged man) can confer a spiritual condition of being "taken" by the Otherworld, becoming drawn into it and belonging to it rather than to the world of the living.[66] Contact with these spirits could lead to their attachment to a person, particularly that of the warrior who spent so much time in their company; even to transform him into one of them.

This may be one reason Cú Chulainn is often called by the epithet *sirite*, another word meaning "sprite". This epithet has particular reference to his *ríastrad* distortion: Fergus barks at him *a serriti siabarda*, "you distorted sprite."[67] The distortion itself was seen as a manifesta-

63 Sayers 1991 49-50, Borsje 1999 234-235

64 Borsje 2007 82

65 O'Rahilly 2011 138

66 Meyer 1889 217

67 Sayers 1991 52

tion of Cú Chulainn's Otherworldly nature and supernatural qualities. His engagement with and partaking of the nature of deadly Otherworld forces is the source of his superhuman abilities—the battle distortion and supernatural strength that make him so mighty—yet this same Otherworldly nature is also what makes him a danger to his own society. This danger is expressed in the state of rage wherein he would not recognize friends from enemies and would destroy indiscriminately if not controlled. William Sayers refers to this as the "permeability between hero and supernatural opponents," a status which both grants him the power to combat such deadly foes, and also places him at risk of becoming one of them.[68]

Another risk arising from contact with the battlefield is the risk of becoming a *geilt*, a lunatic. The belief seems to have been that the violence and horror of battle and the presence of the battle spirits could send some people into an ecstasy of terror from which they never returned, but instead flew panic-stricken away to become like frightened birds haunting the wild places, or like spirits themselves. Suibhne Geilt is the classic example of this phenomenon, fleeing in terror from the Battle of Magh Rath "like any bird of the air.[69]" That such people might themselves become merged with the battle spirits is suggested by the inclusion of *geilti glinni* "mad creatures of the glens" among the lists of battle spirits.[70]

Rites of Purification

Because of these many associations of warriors with deadly forces and horrific battle spirits, rituals of re-entry for warriors into society were vitally important. The dangerously violent and Otherworldly powers that attached themselves to warriors required purification rites to render the warrior safe for contact with the rest of society. We find examples of these rituals both in the immediate context, in rites of purification after an individual battle, as well as the seasonal context, in rites of re-entry after a season of raiding and hunting with the warrior band.

In the case of individual battle, Cú Chulainn's lore provides an example: returning to the fort with the battle rage and distortion still on him,

68 Sayers 1991 54
69 O'Keeffe 1913 15
70 Borsje 1999 234-235

he must be "quenched" of his heat and ardor to render him safe. This is done in two ways: first, by exposing him to the sight of the naked bodies of women, and then by plunging him into a series of water baths or into a stream, to cool him.[71] The use of water as an agent of cooling and purification is classic and self-explanatory; water cleans and quenches fire. Women's nakedness as a counter to violence and rage is a more complex issue. The texts tend to present it as operating through sexual shame, as though the embarrassment of seeing women expose themselves caused the warrior to lose his rage. Gregory Toner reads it as representative of a gendered opposition whereby female nudity and the powers of fertility were seen as a control upon, or an emasculation of, male violence and the powers of warriorship.[72] Toward this notion, he points to the debility of the Ulstermen, for which an alternate myth attributes the debility to Fedelm showing herself naked to the Ulstermen. On another hand, the nakedness of women may have its effect because of the association of women's bodies with life-giving powers, nourishment, and fertility—that is, the nakedness of women may be rendering a kind of positive, life-affirming talismanic force that is able to counter the deadly, maddening influence of the battle spirits. Relevant to the latter interpretation, the milk-giving function of women's breasts may also be at play here.

Milk, and milk products such as butter, appear again and again as agents of both healing and purification, as in the Morrígan's healing of Cú Chulainn by giving him milk, and other folkloric and literary sources as noted by Phillip Bernhardt-House.[73] This function of milk is highlighted in the rituals that attended the seasonal re-integration of wolf-identified warrior bands into settled society, in the spring. The name of the early spring quarter-day celebrated in Ireland, Imbolc, is etymologically linked to milk purification, and possibly to wolves as well. The popular folk-etymology of *oi-melc* "ewe's milk" has been discredited. Its meaning is more likely derived from *imb-fholc* "washing oneself" or possibly *imb-olc* "milk-wolf" or "butter-wolf".[74] The holiday itself is surrounded with symbolism and fragments of ritual related to wolves, warriors, rites of purification, and milk products. These rites of

71 O'Rahilly 2011 147-148, O'Rahilly 1924 15

72 Toner 2010 94

73 Bernhardt-House 2002 58. Milk as a remedy to poison also occurs in the *Lebor Gabála Érenn* episode of the battle of Ard Lemnachta (Macalister 1956 175-177).

74 Bernhardt-House 2002 58-59

purification appear to have been conducted under the auspices of the Goddess Brigid (or a related antecedent to the divinity known from medieval times as St. Brigit). Folklore for Brigid speaks of a ritual in which she washed away the *signa diabolica* "diabolical sign", a warrior's mark apparently carried by those engaged in *dibergach*, raiding[75] (a mark likely connected to battle rituals, as described in Chapter 16). Bernhardt-House points out that this fragment of ritual may be illuminated by looking at the Roman Lupercalia, as another reflection of the Indo-European pattern of warrior band rituals: here, also in early February, the blood from a sacrificed dog and goat (perhaps representing predator and prey) are used to mark the foreheads of youthful warrior-priests, and the mark is then washed away with milk.

From these threads, we can imagine that there must have been parallel Celtic rites of warrior band reintegration, taking place in late winter or spring, with the purpose of purifying and blessing warriors, cleansing away the stain of violence, the specters of battle, and the wild winter life as wolves, and preparing them for re-integration into settled society. In Ireland, this would seem to have taken place at the time of Imbolc, and to have involved the blessing of Brigid or a similar Goddess, as well as the cleansing away of a warrior's mark, possibly made in blood, using milk or butter as the agent of purification. The rite likely included the "washing of hand and foot and head" referenced in an early Irish poem.[76] It may have also included fertility-related elements such as also appear in the Lupercalia.

Living Practice: Modern Warriorship

We have seen how warriorship among the ancients surrounded itself with rituals and social structures giving religious context, social control, and counterbalances upon the latent violence of warriorship. In this section, we explore how warriorship, warrior culture, and the lore of the warrior band can be brought into living practice.

When we come to speak of warriors, we approach a subject that can be divisive, and around which a great deal of misinformation and con-

75 Bernhardt-House 2002 64-65

76 Bernhardt-House 2002 58

fusion abounds. Warriorship, for the ancient Celts, was woven deeply into their culture, embedded in ideas of honor, gender, social order, and power. Many—perhaps most—of the characters we meet in the Irish tales are warriors, even if they are also poets, druids, hostellers, farmers, or many other kinds of folk. For members of the upper classes, warriorship was embedded into identity, even if they did not all undergo intensive training or membership in the warband. Many of us who read these stories have a different relationship to warriorship. Few of us are warriors in any direct or realistic sense. Most of us identify as something that would have been somewhat alien to most ancient warrior societies: the "civilian". For many of us, the warrior experience is something imaginary. Thus, we need to begin by first looking at what a warrior is, and who our warriors are today.

Finding Our Warriors

Our orientation towards warriors may be very different from the ancients, but the fundamentals of what makes a warrior are somewhat timeless. As I see it, a warrior is someone who faces personal risk to life and safety on behalf of their community, as a dedicated practice or vocation. A warrior is someone who moves toward danger in order to combat that danger on behalf of others. These are, for me, the defining elements of warriorship.

In this we can include members of the armed forces, members of paramilitary and police forces, and members of guerrilla, insurrectionary, and revolutionary armed forces. I would argue firefighters are warriors as well, regardless of the fact that the adversaries they combat are nonhuman. In some contexts, medics, activists and journalists may be appropriate to consider as warriors: where they are operating in war zones, hazardous disaster zones, or within violently charged or repressive situations in which they are placing themselves at risk for the sake of a people.

Practitioners of martial arts disciplines represent another orientation toward warriorship. In a sense, these people can be thought of as practicing for warriorship. Martial practice systems have always been part of the training and preparation of warriors for combat. Yet, to the extent that the actual risks to life and safety are minimized within the controlled context of a martial arts dojo or fighter training organization, we still need to recognize that there is a difference between this practice of warriorship and that of people who daily face the threat of death in combat. I count myself in this group: I practice an armored combat art based on medieval fighting. Certainly this experience has changed me and brought me into a more embodied understanding of warriorship; every time I practice, I have to face people violently attacking me with weapons. But at fighter practice, in a tournament, or in a martial arts studio, no one is seeking to kill, and that is a crucial difference. Martial practices teach us the skills of warriorship: courage, clarity under threat, physical skill and discipline. They constitute warriorship practice, if not the lived experience of full warriorship.

There are several more metaphorical forms of warriorship which to some degree draw upon the same reserves of character, courage, and willingness to face risk, but due to the less fatal nature of the risk involved, I think that these should be recognized as indirect forms of warriorship. In this realm we can recognize people who "fight" against difficult and challenging situations, facing spiritual, emotional, or economic adversity for the benefit of others. Dedicated activists outside of mortally dangerous contexts; whistle-blowers; intellectual subversives, "social justice warriors"; and the like. Here also, people who must summon courage as a condition of their lives such as those who are said to "battle" disability or bigotry on a daily basis.

In the most abstract sense, people sometimes speak of being warriors based on emotional strength or fortitude, even in the absence of real adversity. There is a sense that warriors are those who "do what is right", who are unafraid of interpersonal conflict, who will step forward and volunteer for the difficult work and have that uncomfortable conversation that needs to be had. For some, this can represent real courage; often this notion expresses itself in the tendency to seek conflict. In my view, if the primary arena in which one's "warriorship" is expressed is interpersonal communication, this usually points to a confusion between the idea of warriorship and simple honor—which is what "doing what is right" actually means.

Becoming Warriors

The most important thing about entering warriorship is that it is a lived practice. We do not become warriors by adopting the identity like a title. We don't become warriors by performing a ritual. We don't become warriors by taking an oath or even by making a commitment to be a warrior. We become warriors by taking up the practice of warriorship, making it part of our life's work, and placing ourselves in service as warriors. Practice and experience make us warriors, not intention or inner orientation. It is a path of action and service, not of identity.

I also feel it is important to recognize that while not everyone needs to be a warrior as their vocation, we can all practice warriorship. We can bring a martial component into our practice to the extent that our physical abilities allow, and welcome the changes in character that it brings. We can all integrate the warrior ethos into our embodiment of honor. I say that not everyone needs to be a warrior, but the Morrígan often does ask warriorship practice of her dedicants. In my own devotional relationship, she has demanded it of me; it was made clear to me that if I was going to be in a position of teaching people about her, I needed to gain a more experiential understanding of warriorship through physical and spiritual practice. I cannot speak for every practitioner, but I strongly encourage devotees of the Morrígan to consider developing a physical warriorship practice to the extent that our health and abilities allow.

Physical, embodied practice changes us in ways that contemplative practice alone cannot. As all practitioners of physical disciplines know, what we practice in the body, we cultivate in the inner world. When we practice the fighting arts, we become resilient, resolute, indefatigable, alive with survival instinct. Fighting teaches us to think instead of react, to keep clarity of mind while threats are coming at us. It teaches us, on a bodily, instinctive level, to shed our animal defensiveness, our inborn avoidance of pain and conflict and instead to love the sensation of being alive in the fight, the joyous freedom of motion of the body at its height of power. It teaches us to love and honor our worthy adversaries and companions in arms, without whom we cannot hone our skills. It teaches us to be powerful, not fragile. It brings us into a new relationship with sovereignty, where we ourselves become the body of sovereignty in action. We no longer fear pain and conflict, and this frees us to act from honor rather than self-preservation, to rise to the moment without hesitation. It teaches courage and freedom under fire.[77]

---

77 I recognize that my emphasis here on physical warriorship practice can read as prejudicial toward disability and those who experience it. I wish to affirm that there are many ways to serve the Gods, and physical warriorship is only one of them. I also recognize that other forms of warriorship and other forms of service are important and sacred as well. We each bring unique gifts to our practice and our service.

Heroic Ethos

What arises from practice in warriorship is the heroic ethos. "Little care I," said Cú Chulainn, "though I were but one day or one night in being, so long as after me the history of myself and my doings may endure." The heroic ethos insists that a life is best measured in meaning, not in length. It recognizes the highest values as honor and sacrifice in the service of what we love. It sets personal safety as the least of our concerns, and legacy and impact as the greatest.

Warriors are intimate with death, recognizing that willing or no, death will come to us. There is nothing to fear when the end of the story is known. Our blood will be spilled one day and will flow back into the land. The only question will be when, and whether we had yet given what we had to give. Being small will not make us safe. The battle that we each have before us—whatever that is—the birth struggle of that world that can not come to be except through our effort, will not be achieved without personal sacrifice. The heroic ethos recognizes that the price of destiny is our very life. To achieve the greatness that is in us requires us to give ourselves fully to that purpose, and this giving transforms us. This is how heroes are made, in the simple choice to give.

The heroes of saga are not always selfless. Their pursuit of greatness and heroic fame sometimes brings them into conflict with honor itself. Cú Chulainn's kin-slaughter exemplifies this: he kills his own son in battle as a result of strict adherence to his society's warrior code which required him to give battle to the stranger entering his borders. The heroic ethos can lead us astray, too. When we forget that there is a difference between personal glory and the honor achieved through contributing to something greater than ourselves, we can lose our way. The lessons that the heroes of saga have for us are contained both in their tales of glory and greatness, and their tales of downfall and mortal error. The heroic ethos we should strive to embody is not found through emulating the actions of any hero in a tale, but in distilling their teachings and seeking to embody them.

Destruction and Glory: The Hero's Light

This duality of warriorship and the heroic ethos comes to full expression in the hero's light. At one and the same time, this phenomenon embodies the divinely inspired glory of warriors, and their horrific destructiveness. The hero's light appears in the lore as a phenomenon of divine possession by the battle Goddess, in the form of the shining black bird of valor, with glowing, fiery emanations of heroic radiance. It comes with the towering excitation of warrior's ardor, sometimes described in terms of elevation of spirit and ardor for justice. Yet it also brings pure, brutal, mindless, destructive rage. It births the beast in the warrior, the ugliness of force personified in a terrible, unstoppable distortion. In the grip of its murderous rage the warrior slays without thought, ruthlessly killing even his own. It is the apotheosis of warriorship, its best and its worst.

Can we bring something forward into our own understanding and practice of warriorship from this? Can we seek to embody the beautiful hero's light without embodying the monstrous one? I think we can, but only by keeping foremost in our awareness the brutality and destructiveness that is always a latent potential within warriorship. It will be in forgetting its risks and too thoughtlessly glorifying warriorship and violence that we find ourselves falling prey to its darker side. We need to contemplate both the shining bird of valor and the grotesque monster that emerge from the hero. We need to never forget that these are two faces of the same divine, transformative power.

Kindling the Hero's Light

I have hesitated to attempt to teach a spiritual practice based on the hero's light, sensing that to be authentic, one needs first to experience it in the context of embodied warriorship. I had developed and spent some time working with such a practice, based on active engagement of the animal soul and the indwelling presence of the war Goddess. Yet it was not until I experienced my first transformative epiphany of battle ardor on the field in my own combat practice that I felt I had the beginnings of an experiential insight into the hero's light. The experience brought forth some of the phenomena familiar from the tales: a brilliant light breaking over my head; the Morrígan's presence seeming to burst out of me and hover over the field; a sudden, invulnerable sense of perfection in my fighting; a wild intensity for the combat that felt like both rage and lust at the same time. I know, however, that in so many ways this could be only the palest shadow of the hero's light we know from the tales.

I still believe that whether warriors or not, there is wisdom and power to be found in seeking the hero's light. It is clear to me that this is not something that can be learned from a book, but I will share some of the elements of practice I see as foundational to approaching the hero's light.

Martial Practice: For all the reasons I have shared above, and because combat is intrinsic to the hero's light as we know it in the Celtic tradition, developing a martial practice should be the beginning for anyone who is physically able to do so. I did not experience the beginnings of the hero's light until I had been fighting long enough to be comfortable in my practice and past the point of having to think about each move I made in a fight. I suspect most people will find similarly that a physical practice is where we need to begin.

Animal Soul: Intimacy with an animal form—the practice of shapeshifting, in fact—seems to be central to this phenomenon. I think it is through the practice of entering animal spirit possession or becoming animal form that we are able unleash the ferocity embodied in the hero's light. Thus, another foundational practice is the cultivation of the animal soul as a vehicle for embodied, active spiritual work, toward spirit possession, shapeshifting, or (in the language of modern witchcraft) the Fetch-beast.

Indwelling of the War Goddess: Central in the tales of the hero's light is a visitation of the war Goddess as Badb, one which emerges from within. This suggests to me that an indwelling of her presence has been established within the warrior. This is borne out by my own experience, as I had an indwelling of her for some years before my experience with the hero's light. An indwelling means that through dedicated devotional practice, a presence (a fragment, spark, or reflection) of the deity takes up permanent residence within one's being; experienced as a constant presence nested inside our own spiritual anatomy. This can occur organically through long devotional practice, especially when trance possession is part of the practice. An indwelling can also be embedded intentionally through invocation in a ritual dedication. Again, these are not practices I can teach through a book. They should be approached with sufficient support.

Calling the Bird of Valor: When the foundational elements are in place, the emergence of the hero's light can happen spontaneously.

It can also be summoned. This seems to be the function of Cú Chulainn's "hero's shout". Other instances focus on the warrior's excitation of breath and spirit just prior to the emergence of the hero's light. What we are looking at here is an invocation which can employ breath and vocalization to raise the warrior into a heightened state in which the animal soul is arisen and the indwelling bird of valor, the presence of the Badb, is unleashed. In my experience, the form this invocation takes will need to be quite individual, and will be discovered through practice building on the foundational elements above.

The Warrior Band

Warrior culture is largely not a solitary experience. The traditions of warriorship in Indo-European streams of culture are always embedded in the context of the warrior band, the wolf pack, the *fian*. Warriors need the intense bonding and kinship of the warrior band; in contexts of real warfare, the support of the warrior band and the bond between its members becomes a matter of survival. This can be as true of modern military units as it was of warrior bands in ancient Ireland or Gaul or Greece. Warrior skills are not trained in solitude, either; martial skills are built through practice combat, tactical scenarios, tests and ordeals. Warriors rely on the warrior band to be the whetstone to their blade. The shared experience of combat both as adversaries in practice and side-by-side in the theater of war creates an incredibly powerful bond between warriors, one that only those who have seen life and death combat will truly understand. The violence, adversity, and intimacy with death that characterize the lives of warriors often isolate them from their more civilian family and community, so that the company of warriors can sometimes be the only place they do not feel alone (though, of course, this experience is highly individual).

In its ideal manifestation, a warrior society also fosters a culture within which its members hold each other accountable, keeping the values of the culture, its codes of honor and conduct intact. Warriors sometimes need to remind each other of what it is they fight for. We need warrior culture for this, but also warrior culture needs to maintain points of contact with the larger culture within which it is embedded. Warriors need rest and time away from the horrors and brutality of the experience. They need opportunities to reconnect to gentler values, to experience compassion, healing, gentility of spirit; to reconnect with the experiences of those who aren't in the fight; and to remember the experiences of the vulnerable, those who can't protect themselves. The warrior band needs to regularly re-experience its embeddedness within a larger social whole to regain a sense of perspective on what combat and warriorship are meant to protect. Civilian society also needs reminding of what it is asking its warriors to undergo, so we can keep an awareness of what is and is not worth sending them to fight for.

These are in part the functions of the periodic rites of re-entry we see in ancient warrior band cultures. This is a responsibility that the larger society has to its warriors, to help maintain these connections, to not just send them out, but to also give them care and support when they are returning, and to help them make that transition. Absent this support and absent the vibrant connection with what the warrior serves to protect, warrior societies can turn inward, hardening into a defensive stance toward the outside world. The effect of life in combat is to begin to see enemies everywhere. We see this in military forces that turn on their own people or reject civilian leadership; we also see it in police forces that become like military occupiers, treating the very communities they serve as if they are the enemy. In part, these situations can be seen as warrior societies who have lost their way, due to modern civilization's fragmented relationship with warriorship. We have often failed our warriors. We need warrior rituals.

Warrior Rituals

Ritual service to warriors is a natural role for priests of the war Goddess. To be of service in this respect, we need to be actively working in community with our warriors. We need not just our priestly training and ritual skills, but more importantly we need to seek to understand the experiences and the needs of warriors. We need to be developing these rituals in collaboration with warriors, not just for them. Rituals of support for warriors are needed for several functions: initiatory rites for people entering warrior service; rites of preparation and blessing for undertaking combat, such as military deployment, and rites of re-entry and reintegration on returning from combat. There is also a need for pastoral support in the care of veterans with trauma after combat service.

Modern polytheist groups have begun to provide for this need. Several leaders in the Celtic Reconstruction religious community developed a model for a Warrior Consecration Ritual, created for a military service member preparing for active deployment.[78] It contains all the important features of such a warrior ritual. The ritual includes a vigil with focused contemplation of a series of concepts central to the warrior ethos; devotional offerings and a baptismal cauldron rebirth rite; spiritual instruction in honor through the modes of sovereignty, warriorship, and poetry; the imparting of a warrior's mark; gifts of talismans and protective charms with a blessing from Brighid; and a warning and blessing from the Morrígan.

The accompanying Warrior Return Ritual created by the group mirrors this rite but focuses on the need to re-integrate warriors with settled society, and de-escalate them from the effects of war and the haunting of battle spirits, following the model of the early Irish warrior re-integration rituals we have examined.[79] A vigil for contemplation of warrior values with visitations from battle spirits; an encounter between the conflict-ridden warrior and representatives of their society, in which the warrior is confronted by naked women, just as in the tales, and asked to recognize how their violence can threaten what is most in need of protection; they are disarmed, bathed three times to "cool" the war-fury; and a purification is performed, with the removal of the warrior's mark, a blessing from the three Brígs (three forms of Brigid), and the use of milk to heal and purify the effects of the battle spirits.

For priestly folk who wish to be of service to warriors and veterans through transition rituals, I encourage reading these rituals in full at the websites of their authors. These represent among the best examples I have seen of modern warrior rituals for practitioners of Celtic traditions. A great many variations can be developed around these core themes, to suit the needs of individual warriors and their communities. It is time that more of us stepped up to support our society's warriors in this way.

---

78 Bernhardt-House, Vermeers, Zelnio et al 2010

79 Bernhardt-House, Vermeers, Zelnio et al 2009

18

Funerary and Ancestral Rites

We have seen how the Morrígna, as divinities concerned with war and warriorship, come into relationship with death and carnage and take a hand in the fates of warriors on the battlefield. We have also seen how, as divinities concerned with sovereignty and the rites of kingship, they become intimately involved in the sacrificial deaths of kings. As tutelary tribal Goddesses, associated with ancestral territorial identity and foundational mythology, they also embody the primal identity of land and people as one, expressed in death and burial customs. In this chapter, we explore funerary customs and mythologies, ancestral elevation and veneration, the cult of the oracular head, and other practices relating to the Morrígna and the dead.

First Death in the Land

Students of the Irish mythological literature often note how the tales dwell on the deaths of the Gods. Most of the Gods, including many of the Túatha Dé, are said to have died and been buried in the land. Some mythological texts contain long passages consisting of little more than lists of the time, place, and manner of death of the mythic characters involved in a great battle, as in parts of the *Lebor Gabála Érenn*. Readers often wonder at this, sometimes questioning whether the Irish Gods are Gods at all, or simply "ancestral figures", since many are accustomed to thinking of mortality as a marker of humanity rather than divinity. In part, this pattern of attributing mortality to the Gods may be an artifact of history; for the medieval Christian authors who compiled the Irish literature, making the characters mortal may have helped to distance them from the pagan nature of the material. By re-framing the Gods as ancestral people, and re-framing their stories as histories rather than pagan myths, it became politically and theologically safer to record them, while bolstering lineage claims for royal patrons.

I believe there is more to these divine deaths than Christian aversion to paganism, however. The way the deaths are told, their lingering over funerary customs and the relationship between death and landscape, suggest to me that something much deeper is at work. A key principle expressed in many of these tales is that in death, the deity establishes a sacred landscape feature or realm, many of which are ancestral in nature. Donn, the Irish God most closely associated with death and whose name means "dark", illustrates this clearly. One of the first kings of the Sons of Míl, as told in the *Lebor Gabála Érenn*, Donn is killed during their arrival in Ireland.[1] His burial mound is raised, and the place is called Tech Duinn, the "House of Donn". Folklore attaches the name Tech Duinn to an island along the coast which by tradition is the place to which souls travel upon death. Through his death, as the first of his people to die in the land, Donn creates the realm of the dead and simultaneously connects the immigrant Milesian people to Ireland by establishing the earthly locus of their ancestral cult.[2] This pattern of divinities being the first of their tribe to die in a land, and thereby establishing ancestral links with the land, is repeated within other groups

1 Macalister 1956 39
2 Lincoln 1991 34

in the Irish invasion cycle.

Among the Morrígna, Macha best exemplifies this relationship to ancestral cultus. In the *Lebor Gabála Érenn*, she is the wife of Nemed, the ancestor of the third wave of the invasion cycle. In the twelfth day after the Nemedians arrived in Ireland, this Macha died, "and hers is the first death of the people of Nemed. And from her is Ard Macha named."[3] Many elements of this account parallel Donn's story: this Macha is the first of her tribe to die in the land; she is buried, and the place of her burial takes her name and becomes a sacred, ancestral cult site. Macalister notes that the mention of Macha's death is an addition to earlier material in the text[4]—an attempt to create continuity of territorial identity by attributing the creation of a sacred ancestral site to the Nemedians, as the earliest mythic founders of the lineage of the Túatha Dé.

But this Macha is not the first to appear in Ireland, and she is not the last. A similar pattern is repeated with a Macha who arrives with the people of Partholon, as one of his ten daughters in the first mythic invasion after the flood.[5] She dies along with the rest of the tribe of Partholon. Later, Macha appears again among the Túatha Dé, as a member of the Morrígna triad in the *First Battle of Mag Tuired*, and as the wife of king Nuada, both of whom are slain in the *Second Battle of Mag Tuired*.[6] Still another Macha appears again among the Ulster tales, as the Otherworldly woman who races the king's horses and curses the Ulstermen with her death in childbirth. The compilers of the later versions of the *Lebor Gabála Érenn* texts identified this Macha with the earlier one.[7] Finally, Macha Mongruad appears in the annals of kings, and though some consider her a distinct persona, it is clear that the authors of several texts sought to identify her with ancestral sites at Ard Macha and Emain Macha through a similar funerary linkage to earlier theophanies.[8]

In each of these many stories Macha engages with the establishment of land, lineage or sovereignty; and in each of them she dies and is identified with the land. We find traces of this with the other Morrígna, too. Badb and Némain, as wives of the war God Néit, are said to have

3 Macalister 1940 131
4 Macalister 1940 194n
5 Macalister 1940 27
6 Macalister 1941 119, 229
7 Macalister 1940 189
8 Gwynn 1924 124, Dobbs 1930 320

been killed in Ailech Néit, the stronghold identified with them.[9] Even the Morrígan has a death-place suggested for her, a mound among the holy places at Brúg na Bóinne, Newgrange, a landscape whose shapes are identified with her body, and the home of her husband the Dagda.[10]

What emerges from all these lives and deaths is a distinctly Celtic mythic pattern: the Gods live and die cyclically; they create the sacred landscape with their mighty deeds, and when they enter into that landscape in death, they also create the place for the human dead to dwell. This indwelling of ancestors in the land, sited at specific consecrated places in the known landscape, manifests the tribal affiliation and claim to the land itself. Human ancestral lineage is traced to these primordial Gods through this funerary relationship to the land. It was not only the medieval Irish who sought to identify the Gods as their remote ancestors—Caesar and other Classical writers noted as a consistent feature of Celtic culture that they identified themselves as familial descendants of a God who was identified with the dead, called by the Romans "Dis Pater", to refer to his Underworld nature.[11] This specifically funerary, ancestral relationship between people, land, and Gods appears to be deeply embedded in Celtic identity.

Beyond this ancestral role held by many of the Gods of the Celts, the Morrígna show a close relationship to death and funerary processes. This is as we might expect for a group of war divinities, and the relationships of the Morrígna to death do appear to center on violent death and the funerary status of the warrior dead.

Guarding Your Death

Just as the warrior's intimacy with violence and battle spirits required ritual containment and protection in life, the death of a warrior is attended by specific ritual patterns. Violent death was, as in many cultures, seen to place the spirit at risk of degradation into one of the battle horrors with which warriors had to contend in life, and mythologies and rituals surrounding the deaths of warriors seem to have been geared toward guarding the spirit from going down this path. The rituals surrounding warriors' deaths are characterized by the presence of

9 Macalister 1941 237

10 Gwynn 2008 19

11 Koch & Carey 2003 23, Lincoln 1991 34

the war Goddess, special funerary treatment, and elevation to the status of heroic ancestor.

Before Cú Chulainn's combat ordeals with the Morrígan, she tells him, "it is at the guarding of thy death that I am; and I shall be."[12] As we have discussed, this amounts to a statement of claim upon him; as a hero seeking to achieve martial glory, he expects to die a hero's death in battle, not a quiet death in bed, and it is this that the war Goddess promises him as part of their pact. This statement can be read both as protective, in the sense that she will ensure he is guarded against an ignominious or dishonorable death, by inciting and guiding him toward a heroic destiny; and as threatening, in the sense that she may be saying she herself will be the agent of his death.

When the time comes, she makes good on the claim. In Cú Chulainn's death-tale, the *Death of Cú Chulainn,* his death is facilitated by the agency of a trio of malevolent crones who in every respect match guises in which the Morrígna are known to appear;[13] and in the later *Brislech Mór* version, one of the trio is named Badb.[14] To make him vulnerable enough for his enemies to kill him, this hag weakens him by means of the *geis*-curse—inducing him to break his *geis* by partaking of the cursed meat of a dog, his totemic animal. His enemies, descendants of men he has slain, then converge on him and finally kill him in battle. If this Badb is read as an appearance of the war Goddess Badb (an identity some scholars reject), we might wonder why she would choose to bring about the undoing of her favored hero. I think that, viewed in the broader context of the warrior's vocation and the chosen path of the hero, we can see that a violent death such as Cú Chulainn's is inevitable, and was always his chosen fate. That she must curse him before this can happen may simply attest to his mighty heroic status.

It also attests to the paradoxical and fatal nature of the warrior's way of life: with every great victory he has created more enemies who must seek his death to fulfill their own obligations to kinship and honor. Further, Cú Chulainn has, in his dedication to the warrior code, committed the atrocity of kin-slaughter when he kills his own son in single combat. Though the extant texts do not explicitly say so, I have wondered if this

---

12 Leahy 1906 136

13 Tymoczko 1981 49

14 O'Grady 1898 243. Note however that whether this is the Badb or another character sharing the same name is a matter of scholarly debate.

crime may be tied to the reason the cursing crones mark Cú Chulainn out for death, just as Conaire becomes marked for his doom when he violates the social code in his acts of kingship, and Badb comes as Cailb the cursing crone to claim him. At the same time, the kin-slaughter of Cu Chulainn fulfills a classic Indo-European motif that may simply serve to demonstrate the costs of too strict an adherence to the warrior code.[15]

In the moment of Cú Chulainn's death at the hands of his enemies, the narrative suggests that his tutelary Goddess guards his death in bird form. Mortally wounded, he has tied himself to a pillar stone using his belt so as to die standing up. He is protected by the Liath Macha, his semi-divine horse (whom we have seen is mythologically linked to the war Goddess Macha) so long as "his soul was in him and his warrior's light remained shining from his brow."[16] When death comes, according to the earliest version of the text, it is signaled by the descent of a bird lighting on the pillar-stone. Tymoczko translates this as "a raven", but the source text simply says *ennach*, "birds".[17] However, a few things suggest that this is not simply any ordinary bird. First, a bird that would be drawn toward battle, and would descend upon a dying man, clearly suggests a carrion bird. Second, the habit of the Morrígna of alighting on pillar-stones in corvid form is a recurrent image in the literature, and the parallel is likely not incidental here. Third, it is significant that both of the signs which mark his status as alive or dead are the visible presence of a bird. He is said to be alive as long as the hero's light continued to emanate from his brow—an emanation that within the same scene is described as a "glossy bird" rising over him,[18] and which we have also seen to be a manifestation of Badb as tutelary war Goddess. That the moment of his death is immediately signaled by the descent of a bird indicates, to my mind, that this is the same bird.[19] The bird of war-fury, his indwelling avatar of Badb, who hovered over him in his heroic ardor, now alights on the pillar as his warrior's light fades in death.

---

15 Thanks to P. Sufenas Virius Lupus for pointing out this theme to me.

16 Tymoczko 1981 61

17 Epstein points out that *ennach* is glossed as "scald-crow" in *O'Clery's Glossary* (Epstein 1998 125).

18 Tymoczko 1981 52, 98n. *Én blaith*, "glossy bird", glossed as "black bird of battle"

19 This interpretation is also favored by Epstein (Epstein 1998 227).

Crying Among the Corpses

The death of a warrior, particularly a great hero or king, is often attended by omens and particularly appearances of the Morrígna with corpses or gory spoils (i.e. valuable armor and war-gear). This is seen in the later *Brislech Mór* version of Cú Chulainn's death tale, in which an Otherworldly woman identified as Badb (or Badb's daughter, depending how the text is read) appears washing his bloody armor in the ford on the eve of his death battle.[20] Related apparitions appear in *Dá Choca's Hostel,* where a red woman washes the gory chariot of Cormac in omen of his death,[21] and the *Dirge of Fothaid Canainne* poem in which the Morrígan washes battle-spoils and entrails.[22] In a related act, the Morrígan shatters Cú Chulainn's chariot on the eve of his death as well, as an omen to warn him of his coming death.[23] These occurrences signal the overshadowing presence of the Morrígna, as active participants in and witnesses to the fates of warriors under their protection.

When we meet the Morrígna in the Irish tales, we are often in the presence of corpses. This is especially true of Badb. In corvid form she is often said to be rejoicing over corpses on the battlefield as a banquet of carrion, as in the *Battle of Magh Leana,* where "blue-mouthed, loud-croaking Badbhs rejoiced; and they were all merry and vociferous at the extent of the tables and the abundance of flesh-spoils which they found upon those cold-prostrate men."[24] An evocative instance of Badb's association with corpses is Cú Chulainn's boyhood encounter where he finds her "crying from among the corpses" on the battlefield, during the night following a battle in which many of his kinsmen have been wounded or killed.[25] In this tale, the corpses do not lie quietly—it is the restless dead in particular who haunt that battlefield, and Cú Chulainn has to wrestle with mutilated, revenant dead men.

The Morrígan, too, haunts battlefields among the corpses after war. The *Fothaid Canainne* poem calls her "the terror of the night", who will come among the dead men on the battlefield—and the dead warrior speaking the poem urges his bereaved woman not to stay, but to take

20 O'Grady 1898 247
21 Stokes 1900a 157
22 Meyer 1910 16
23 Tymoczko 1981 42
24 O'Curry 1855 131
25 O'Rahilly 2011 138

his spoils (that is, his gear) away safely to her house.[26] For, he tells, the Morrígan is already among the corpses, washing their entrails and their spoils, drawing nearer to him. This poem is intriguing for its implication that leaving the body and war-gear of dead warriors on the field might mean in some way placing them in her hands. We have seen this image of the Morrígan or Badb washing corpses or war-gear many times, but it is usually framed as a premonitory vision or warning visitation *before* the battle, as in the instances mentioned above.[27]

The *Fothaid Canainne* poem differs in alluding to the Morrígan's presence washing bloody armor and bodies both before and after the battle. Its language suggests that the pre-battle visitations can be understood as visions of what was to come after the battle, for the dead whose bodies and gear were left upon the field into the night when that field becomes the haunt of the "terror of the night", the war Goddess and the unquiet dead. This framing suggests a role for the Morrígna, especially Badb and the Morrígan, in beliefs about warrior death and their funerary treatment. In a sense, the texts speak to what would be any warrior's hope for his death—that his people would gather his body and war-gear and give him an honorable funeral, which we can expect would involve first cleaning the gore from the gear and washing the body for its funerary rites. The implication I read here is that for those dead warriors whom no one came to claim, it may have been thought that the Morrígan herself would be gathering them in the post-battle gloom, washing their corpses and their spoils in the cold streams.

Funerary Rites

For the Celtic warrior who died on the battlefield, what might that honorable funeral have looked like? Archaeological finds illuminate how the remains of warriors were physically disposed, to a certain extent. As to ritual, the literature may help shed some light on what funerary rites may have looked like. Celtic funerary treatment of warriors appears to have been regionally distinct, with each culture area showing features specific to warrior status.

In Ireland, the rite seems to have usually been burial with a memorial pillar-stone and/or in a chambered tomb, along with head-collection

26 Meyer 1910 16, Borsje 2007 74
27 Stokes 1900a 157, O'Grady 1898 247

and veneration practices. The medieval Irish *Destruction of Dind Rig* tale describes funerary rites in which a warrior or king was placed in his chariot with his weapons, an assembly of mourning was called, burial songs were chanted over him, and members of his family came forward to wail over him. A tomb was then raised over the dead (i.e. a chambered mound) and a memorial pillar-stone was planted.[28] A nearly identical burial practice, including ritual lamentation, a raised mound tomb, and a pillar-stone is described for Macha Mongruad, the mythic warrior-queen.[29] Warrior bands are said to have practiced a more collective form of commemoration with memorial stones: before a raid, each warrior would carry a large stone and together these would be piled into a cairn. At the end of the raid, all the survivors would retrieve their stone; each stone left would then represent a warrior who had been killed on the field, and the cairn would be left as a memorial.[30]

These are, of course, literary accounts, but to some extent they do reflect practices seen in the archaeological record: ground burials and mounds have been found with the entombed bodies of warriors, often buried with their war gear, and in some cases evidence of the separate, special treatment of heads. Cremation and burial or entombment of cremated remains was also often in use in the Irish Iron Age, especially in the earlier period, giving way more strongly to body burial in the later Iron Age.[31]

Ritual lamentation performances have long been important in Celtic funerals, particularly in Ireland. Keening and bewailing the dead are mentioned in the early texts, such as the one above, and their practice continued right into historic times. Vocal lamentation is often described as the role of family members in the funerary process, and this element was important enough that it remains part of the description of funerary ritual even in the most stripped-down versions.[32] Spiritual entities closely connected to the Morrígna were also believed to participate in this keening and wailing; from the folklore of the war Goddesses, in the medieval and later periods the folklore of the "banshee" developed. This term "banshee" is an Anglicization of Old Irish *ban síd*, "woman of the fairy mound". It appears in an early gloss among the epithets for

28 Stokes 1901a 9
29 Stokes 1893 481
30 O'Connor 2013 98
31 Raftery 1994 80, 195
32 Carey 1991 155n

the Morrígna, originally simply denoting her status as an Otherworldly being.[33] Later folklore in the late medieval and early modern periods developed around the belief in Otherworldly female spirits who would appear wailing or keening to warn a family of an impending death, especially a violent one.[34] Often appearing as long-haired women dressed in white, these spirits were seen as the Otherworldly counterpart to the human funerary keeners. Believed to attach to family lineages, they were sometimes even spoken of as ancestors themselves. They were called *beansidhe* or "banshee", or sometimes *bodhbh*, "crow" or *bodhbh chaointe*, "keening crow", especially in the southeast of the country.[35] The continuity of the name Badb clearly attests to the connection between these keening spirits and the Morrígna, but a difference in function is also clear; the banshee's role is limited to, and seems to have grown out of, the funerary function of ritual lamentation, whereas the Morrígna Goddesses embody a broader range of functions and powers.

Excarnation seems to have been a frequent feature of warrior funerary treatment in parts of the Celtic world, especially in Britain and the Continent. Excarnation is funeral by exposure of the body to scavengers, typically carrion birds, to strip the flesh from the bones; in modern language this has also been called "sky burial", as the body is being given to birds. In Celtic contexts it is typically followed by curation of the bones and especially the head. Artwork from Celtic Iberia (modern Spain) depicts excarnation, showing the bodies of fallen warriors being consumed by carrion birds.[36] We also find funerary artwork showing carrion birds in association with warriors at the shrine of Roquepertuse,[37] and skeletal evidence of funerary excarnation at Ribemont, both in Gaul.[38] Contemporary Classical authors, notably the Greeks Pausanias and Aelian, and the Roman Silius Italicus relate that Gauls intentionally left the bodies of slain warriors on battlefields for the carrion birds, which were regarded as sacred, and who were thought to carry the souls of the warriors to the Otherworld.[39] Lucan describes the belief on the part of these Gauls that "those whose flesh

33 Borsje 2007 88
34 Henry 1959 408
35 Lysaght 1996 154, Wood-Martin 1902a 364, 367
36 Aldhouse-Green 2010 240
37 Armit 2012 143
38 Brunaux 1988 17, Beck 2009 261
39 Beck 2009 255-256

the vultures have stripped go up into the sky to join the gods."[40] This practice is described as distinctly reserved for warriors who died in battle, whereas a different funerary rite was given to those who died of illness or natural causes. These carrion birds were, of course, also identified with the war Goddess in bird form—thus, as shocking as the practice was to the Greeks who observed it, for the Gauls, leaving the slain warriors to the crows, ravens, and vultures was a devotional act which honored their relationship with their war Goddess, giving her her due, and ensuring that she might guard their souls on their journey in the Otherworld.

Evidence of excarnation is rare in Ireland, but there are remains of a mortuary enclosure which may have served for exposure of bodies to birds near the "Giant's Ring" in County Down.[41]

The Oracular Head and Heroic Elevation

Ongoing religious veneration of the warrior dead is indicated throughout the sources, including Irish, British and Continental traditions. This is manifest most vividly and consistently in the practice of collection, curation, and devotional treatment of severed heads. Head-collecting was a practice in warfare, which often included taking the heads of slain adversaries as part of the trophies of battle, a practice discussed in Chapter 16 on battle cultus. In a related practice, the severed heads of honored warriors were given ritual treatment oriented toward their elevation as heroic ancestors, who would continue to interact with the warrior community in death. The ubiquitous Celtic motif of the oracular, speaking severed head attests to the importance of this practice. Our most famous example may be the Welsh Brân, but we find the pattern throughout many Irish stories, such as Cú Chulainn's father Súaltaim mac Roích, whose severed head shouted warnings to rouse the Ulstermen from the curse of Macha in the *Táin*.[42]

The *Battle of Allen* yields an intriguing description of a ritual wherein a warrior's head might be venerated: the head of the slain hero Fergal (who, it is worth noting, has been favored by the presence of the Badb

40 Quoted in Brunaux 1988 87.
41 Ó hÓgáin 1999 27
42 O'Rahilly 2011 217, Ó hÓgáin 1999 53

during the battle)[43] is carried in from the battlefield by a contingent of warriors. The head is washed, its hair combed and plaited. It is then wrapped in fine cloth and set in the feast hall, where a huge feast is laid before the head in offering. The head then speaks, giving thanks for these honors; the food is distributed to the people, and the head is taken to its burial place.[44] In a related ritual, the head of Fergal's poet, also killed at the battle, instructs the warriors that he must also be brought into the hall to sing Fergal's funerary song, a *dord fiansa* "warrior's chant", highlighting that chanting would have been important in warriors' last rites.[45]

This careful ritual of gathering in the warrior dead accomplishes a number of things: it separates them from the battlefield, it involves cleansing and beautification, it includes the feeding and honoring of the spirit, and it establishes the ongoing communication between the living and the dead. Speculatively, we might contrast it to the fate of warrior dead whose rites are, for whatever reason, not completed—the head not brought in from the battlefield, the funeral songs not sung, the spirit given no cleansing, feeding, or communion with the living. As mentioned above, the *Fothaid Canainne* poem seems to imply that for the Irish at least, this left the dead to be claimed by the Morrígna, and is treated with some horror. The lore seems to indicate that this treatment might leave the dead as wandering spirits, like the revenant *airdrech*, its head half-missing, with whom Cú Chulainn has to contend in the *Boyhood Deeds* episode,[46] or that they might join the host of *úatha*, horrors and battle spirits, which accompany the Morrígna in their battle functions.

The role of the Morrígna in the fate of dead warriors thus appears to be a complex one. On the one hand, we see the legends suggesting a kind of caretaking of warriors by the war Goddesses, as in Cú Chulainn's "guarded" heroic death. We also see the elevated, heroic dead associated with the Morrígna in the initiatory warrior cult practices. On the other hand, the authors of these tales and poems convey a dread of the dead being claimed by such beings, the "terror of the night", associating this fate with unquiet, revenant dead. These images may reflect regional and tribal differences in beliefs about the dead. I propose that they might also

43 Stokes 1903 55
44 Stokes 1903 65
45 Stokes 1903 63
46 O'Rahilly 2011 138

point to distinct pathways for the warrior dead—to become an unquiet battle spirit or to become an honored heroic ancestor. Both pathways occur within the spheres of power of the Morrígna, but it is up to the human community to ensure that the proper funerary rites are given so as to direct the dead toward ancestral elevation. What is at stake in the funerary rites of warriors is, to some extent, the same as what is needed in any funeral process—the safeguarding of the dead from the vulnerable state of a recently disembodied spirit, to the stable, sacred and empowered status of a revered ancestor. In the case of warrior dead, the risks are specific and more dire in consequence of the violent nature of their deaths and the environment of the battlefield, and so the rites surrounding the guardianship of their deaths are accordingly constructed to carefully facilitate their elevation to heroic ancestors.

The Celtic veneration of heroic ancestors through the preservation and curation of heads is reflected in the archaeological record as well as in literature, and is clearly seen throughout the different Celtic culture hearths. Several of the Gaulish sanctuaries included structures with niches where heads were preserved and displayed in positions of honor, often for long periods of time. At Entremont, stones carved with niches for heads accompany statuary of heroic warriors.[47] Roquepertuse sanctuary, with its great stone portico, held niches for severed heads, including some skulls found intact by the excavators, and showing evidence of violent injury; that is, dead warriors. Here, the heads were incorporated into the fabric of the temple itself, embedded into the masonry and painted over in a continuous fashion with the surrounding stonework—evocatively demonstrating that the warrior dead here were elevated to honored status and made part of the very temple itself, within which the community might continue to venerate and communicate with their spirits as valued heroic ancestors.[48] Skulls have been found preserved beneath houses, in ritual pits, and in burial sites of the Iron Age in Britain and Ireland too.[49]

It is these heroic ancestors who seem to have played such an important role in the instruction and initiation of young warriors, bringing us back again to the warrior initiatory cycle we explored in the previous chapter. As John Waddell observes in his analysis of Irish ritual prac-

47 Aldhouse-Green 2010 133
48 Aldhouse-Green 2010 133-134, Armit 2012 149
49 Ó hÓgáin 1999 28, 50

tice at the Cave of Cruachan, a significant number of heroic warriors have legends linking them specifically to the site (heroes such as Cú Chulainn, Nera, Fráech, Loegaire, Amairgene, and Conall), along with the physical evidence of the memorial pillar-stone of Vraicci (Fráech) being incorporated into the structure. He suggests that warrior initiatory rites were likely conducted here, and included introducing the young initiates to the spirits of their heroic warrior ancestors.[50]

Such rites may have involved the presence of preserved heads or skulls of dead warriors, employed as oracular channels for the spirits of these heroic ancestors to speak with the initiates. A rite such as this may be what is indicated by the poetic practices of *díchetal do chennaibh*, "incantation from heads" and *tenm laida, "illumination of song"* mentioned in medieval texts.[51] Carey points to an intriguing verse in the Bretha Nemed which appears to place these practices in a necromantic context, referring to "a chant which is recited from heads of bodies" (corpses): "It may be that the phrase carried *both* senses: that *díchetal di chennaib* was a type or technique of spontaneous composition which came to be associated with the supernatural properties attributed to severed heads in Celtic tradition."[52] Nora Chadwick notes a frequent association between *tenm laida* and the veneration of severed heads of poets or heroes, typically including chanting to them, offering food, and a placement of honor in a hall. The phrase *tenm laida* can refer either to songs chanted *to* these heads to venerate them, as well as to recitations given *by* the heads after they are awakened and begin speaking.[53]

By such practices, or similar rites of communion between the living and the dead, the wisdom and power of the heroic ancestors could be handed on and embodied in the lives of each new generation of warriors.

For the Souls of the Dead

Care of the dead does not end with funerary rites and ancestral elevation. Devotional rites for the continuing care of the ancestral dead are indicated in the archaeology and literature of Ireland.

50 Waddell 2014 63-66

51 Chadwick 1935, Ó hÓgáin 1999 79. Accounts are garbled and some translations give "revelation from the ends of bones" for *díchetal do chennaibh*. Chadwick gives "extempore incantation" based on Meyer.

52 Carey 1997 45-46

53 Chadwick 1935

We have seen how some of the large burial mounds may not have been closed permanently, but were designed to facilitate continuing ritual engagement. This appears to have been the case at Newgrange, as well as many other burial mounds; it might be more accurate to call sites such as this funerary temples rather than simply tombs. Though most of these funerary mound temples were built in the pre-Celtic Neolithic to Bronze Age periods, evidence shows later ritual deposition of the remains of the newly dead as well as votive offerings such as food, coins, and other valuables. In some places, these ritual deposits continued well into the Iron Age and to the early centuries CE.[54] It is not hard to imagine the value and importance such a ritual would hold for ancient Celtic peoples. Though it is not clear to what extent the dead originally buried in these temples were direct ancestors of the Celtic Irish, we know that Celtic deities and ancestors had been absorbed into the mythologies of these places, and the continued reverencing of ancestral connections was clearly important and had substantial continuity.

Elements of continued ancestral devotion practices survive in the literature and historical record. The important royal fair, the *óenach*, was in many respects a rite of ancestor veneration—one of the meanings of the word is "funerary games". *Óenaige* (plural of *óenach*) were held within each of the historic kingdoms at various intervals, many of them annual. Each major *óenach* was held in a sacred ritual center containing ancestral graves, and with an important funerary legend associated with it; for example, the Óenach Macha, held at Emain Macha, is said to have been established to honor and to "bewail" the legendary Macha, the wife of Cruinn who died racing the king's horses.[55] Some of the other major *óenaige* in Ireland included the Óenach Tailteann, honoring the death of Taílltiu, a Fir Bolg divinity and the foster-mother of Lugh; Óenach Carmán, honoring the death of Carmán, a primordial warrioress slain by the Túatha Dé; and Óenach Tlachtga, honoring the death of Tlachtga, the daughter of Mog Ruith who may have been a solar and storm Goddess. Óenach na Cruachna took place at Cruachan, named for Crochen, an ancestral woman said to be the handmaid of the sovereignty Goddess Étaín.[56] Each *óenach* seems to have celebrated the funerary legacy of a female ancestor or Goddess and took place at a sacred site with funerary features.[57]

54 Waddell 2014 31
55 Gwynn 1924 124
56 Waddell 1983 22
57 Lennon 1988 56, Waddell 1983 21

The feasting, games, and ritual performances were believed to benefit the souls of the ancestral dead to whom the *óenaige* were dedicated, as well as the living. According to one Irish historian, a typical *óenach* began with the burial of the newly dead, raising their burial mounds with the usual ritual lamentation and song. After this followed a fire-lighting with chants and poetic performances praising the dead, reciting ancestral lineage and heroic tales about the honored dead, and offerings honoring the Gods. On the days following, poets and druids would make legal pronouncements and enactments of law. The final days of the *óenach* would be dedicated to honorary games and performances, usually including horse-racing, martial contests, other contests of skill, and poetic and musical performances.[58]

The connections between funerary ritual, female ancestral power, and horse-racing in particular seem to run deep. At the *óenach* of Emain Macha, with its traditions of horse ritual and sacral kingship, horse-racing was a central activity believed to honor the ancestors attached to the place as well as Macha herself.[59] The remnants of an ancestral ritual containing these same elements are described in a later medieval historiographic work. Here, funerary games are held on the hills at Saingel, including a ritual performed by a long line of women, positioned into a circle and leaning with their hands on the ground, with the warriors' charioteers standing behind inciting them. This curious ritual appears to involve women taking the role of horses, just as Macha does in her myth. It may be that the women undertook the role of a female horse divinity acting as psychopomp to aid in the journey of the dead, for the ritual was said to be "for the good of the souls" of warriors slain in battle.[60] We should note that the text attributes this ritual to "the foreigners", i.e. Viking forces, and may not represent any form of Celtic ritual. However, the two cultures shared much in common, and since the ritual takes place at Saingel, the location where another of Cú Chulainn's special horses, the Dubh Sainglenn was said to hail from, we may be looking at a remnant or adaptation of a local tradition regarding the role of women and horse racing in spiritual journeying and ancestral veneration.[61]

58 Lennon 1988 56
59 Waddell 2014 92
60 Todd 1867 83
61 Henderson 1899 39

The Testimony of the Dead

Communication with the dead continues, and can manifest in less direct means than the talking oracular head. We have noted in Chapter 14 above how many divination practices were used to communicate with the dead as much as for prophetic knowledge. For example, the practice of sleeping at tombs of ancestors to seek oracular dreams was documented among the Continental Celts by Nicander of Colophon.[62] This account is supported in the Irish context by the tale of the poet Muirgein, who slept at the tomb of Fergus to seek visions and so recover the story of the *Táin* for the Irish people.[63] Prophetic dreaming at tombs reinforces the notions, found throughout Celtic cultures, that the ancestors remain within the land, that they are accessible through sacred funerary sites in the landscape, and that they have valuable knowledge to impart to the living.

We also read of communications flowing the other direction, from the living to the dead: letters to dead relatives would be placed with the body in the funeral pyre among some Continental Celts who practiced cremation, and the burning of the letter was felt not to destroy it, but to carry it to the Otherworld where the dead would be able to read it.[64] Prayer texts and spell tablets were sometimes addressed to the dead for aid in accomplishing their aims, and deposited in subterranean sites where they would enter into the world of the dead, though this practice may owe something to the influence of Mediterranean cursing traditions.[65]

Divination is consistently a tool for communication with the dead as much as with the Gods and other spirits, and this seems to hold true within Celtic practice as well. In Chapter 14 above we looked at the discovery of what appear to be divinatory lots in the form of polished slips of cattle bone containing inscribed patterns, thousands of which were found together in the megalithic tomb at Loughcrew.[66] Their function has not been identified with certainty and may never be; but Waddell suggests they likely had a cultic purpose, and may have been used in divination or communicating messages to the dead.

There are some intriguing associations between the dead and *ogam* writing and divination. This is explored by Carey, based on a Middle

62 Koch & Carey 2003 10
63 Stohellou 2011
64 Koch & Carey 2003 10
65 Mees 2009
66 Waddell 2014 27

Irish text in which the truth of a person's claim to inheritance of a sacred sword is being tested. In this text, *ogam* writing together with an oath incantation is used to substantiate a claim, and this use of *ogam* is called "the testimony of the dead."[67] An earlier poem also references *ogam* divination, by "the bond of lot-casting", as a method for divining the truth, where it is again linked with the dead: "It is then that the dead corrected the living, in the pure testimony of *ogam*."[68] An early Irish legal text classifies different types of evidence, including a group naming "poem or letter, or boundary or pillar" as "the dead which overswear the living."[69] This refers to written evidence as a whole; but the writings on boundaries and pillar stones are *ogam* inscriptions, and here the connection between *ogam* and the dead becomes manifest. The oldest *ogam* writing is found on pillar stones, most of which are funerary markers.[70] Because of this, *ogam* writing hearkens back to a deep association with the dead, with funerary places, and with Otherworldly knowledge obtained through the agency of the dead. Thus both as written inscription and in its divinatory form, the *ogam* seem to have been used for communication with the dead, particularly as regards the recording and truth-testing of lineal and hereditary claims.

Living Practice: Walking with the Dead

Turning from our exploration of ancient funerary and ancestral rites, we come at last to consider our own deaths, our own rites and practices for honoring the dead. The ritual life of death is among the most profound and important aspects of human religion. Every tradition, to be relevant and of service to human communities, must find its way to engaging with death. People die, and their deaths must be dignified with sacred grace. The living need tools and practices for making the transition to relationship with their dead as ancestors instead of living kin. The dead require spiritual techniques to safeguard their transition to stable ancestral status. Many Pagan and polytheist communities are

67 Carey 1992 2
68 Carey 1992 9
69 Carey 1992 6
70 Ó hÓgáin 1999 114

still in the embryonic stages of developing a culture and practice for death work. It has been my hope to encourage more of our folk to step into building these traditions in ways that serve our communities. In this final section, I offer my observations on integrating death priesting, funerary work, and service to the dead into our living practices.

Death Priesting

Serving as a funerary priest is, I think, the most consequential and weighty of any priestly work I've been called upon to do. The work of a funerary priest concerns both the living and the dead. We have responsibility for offering death rites that present the living community an opportunity for grief and remembrance, for sanctification of the death and placing it in a context of meaning that will allow them to make the emotional and spiritual transition to release the dead to their journey. Equally, we have responsibility to the dead: funerals must also function to sanctify the body, prepare the spirit of the dead for their transition, open the way for them into the Otherworld, safeguard their journey, and facilitate their relationship to other spirits and divinities that oversee their fates in death. Funeral service is equal parts public religious ritual, grief and community counseling, and necromantic spirit work. It requires the utmost grace, poise, focus, and authenticity from us as priests. The consequences of errors in religious practice or social judgment in the context of death priesting can have enormous impacts on the ability of families to process through grief and for the dead to accomplish their journeys.

What I want to share here about funerary priesting is not to give any ritual scripts. Death is too personal and too intimate for that to be of help. It sometimes seems to me that the manner of our dying, and the rituals we create for it, may be the ultimate creative act – the final work of art that places the seal on the great work that our life has been. We cannot, of course, complete the work of art alone, and this is where death moves from the personal to the collective. We rely on the living to bring that final work of art, the funerary rite, to fruition. It becomes a collaboration between the living and the dead. A continued subtle intimacy across the boundary between worlds. Rites of death operate on the same principles as all devotional ritual: a flow of power and life force shared between the physical world and the Otherworld. In the funeral, we create a ritual container and we fill it with power and emotion: love, grief, joy, remembrance, honor, blessing. We raise it up to the dead loved one and to the Gods, and we pour it out as an offering. This outpouring is important, not just for the living, but for the dead. It is why keening and wailing are so ever-present in ancient funerary rites. The living need to give voice to grief, to fully experience it before it can be released. The dead need to know they have been grieved and will be remembered; this is crucial for their ability to move onward. Good funerary ritual reminds us, the living, that we do not need to fear death. It restores an intimacy between us and the ancestral realm. We stand at the moment of transition when the doors between this world and the Otherworld open, and one of our own is entering their ranks. At this moment, the continuity between the living, the land, and the ancestors is as clear as we will ever know it. In funerary ritual, we can glimpse the shining path the dead walk and the realm they enter. We can find trust in the ancestors, we can know that we need not fear that place. Funerary rites can liberate us: we can live without fear, knowing what stands before us at the end of the road.

Reclaiming Death

One of the greatest services we can provide for the dead is the funerary rites that are right and personal for them. The importance of this can hardly be overemphasized. Religious freedom in death, to be given the funeral rites that are sacred to us and that sanctify our deaths, is in a sense the final sovereignty. Denial of agency over our own deaths diminishes and indignifies us. But this is terribly common, because funerary rites do not just consist of the mourning rituals and memorials, but the rites of the body itself, over which we have far less control. I've known a few who have died who were able to be given the funeral customs that were right for them. But I've known many more whose families had to make painful compromises, because the funeral customs that would have been true to their being and needful in their traditions were not allowed or not available. This is a tragedy.

Many of the funerary rites and traditions associated with the cults of the Morrígna are nearly lost to us. Excarnation, collection of the bones, and skull veneration are out of reach to most people due to legal restrictions and the control of the funeral industry. Few people in the Western world still wash and prepare their own dead. It is now common for people in our cultures to go through their lives without ever having contact with a dead person. Instead of the intimate caring for the body by kin, sanctified by the presence of the Washer, the dead are now usually whisked away immediately so we never become comfortable in the presence of death. They are taken to funeral homes run as a commercial industry, to be handled by strangers in cold, ugly rooms and filled with chemicals before being placed in overwhelmingly Christian cemeteries. For many, cremation is the only option available that preserves any resemblance to a funerary rite with the dignity and sacredness of the ancestral. These cultural and legal restrictions stem from a fear and revulsion towards death and decay that we have inherited from Christian culture.

I feel we must reclaim death. We must not fear intimacy with death. We can reclaim death as part of our religious life. We can seek opportunities to sit with its presence, instead of avoiding it. In truth, a great deal of the control exerted by the funeral industry is not strictly legal, but a matter of custom. We can opt out of embalming if we don't want it, and choose natural burial. We can opt to prepare our dead at home—in most places, this is a legal option. Home funerals and even home burial are still our right in many places. There are even a few institutions practicing excarnation in the context of forensic study, where we can have our bodies donated.

We can step into intimacy with death by planning ahead for ourselves, by entering into conversations with our kin and communities. We can also step forward to aid the dying, in the practices of hospice care and death midwifery. As priests and friends of a Goddess embodying death, we can help to open these doors to a fuller and more intimate relationship with death. We have something to offer our communities in the willingness to take action toward reclaiming death as a sacred part of the life of the community.

Ancestor Veneration

We have seen how central ancestral relationships are in Celtic traditions, and in the cults of the Morrígna. Ancestor veneration is a practice that anyone can enter into. We are not limited to our own blood ancestors. We have ancestors in our family lines, but we also have ancestors of place—all those who came before us in our landscapes and established the human relationship to the land. And we have ancestors of spirit—those who preceded us in our spiritual traditions and lineages, ancestors who were pioneers in our vocations, ancestors who fought battles for rights and liberties we need and value, and so many more forms of spiritual ancestry. Hero-cultus is, in a way, its own kind of ancestor veneration; heroes are ancestors who are part divine, or partly deified—they hold a special liminal position of being both human and divine, and by this they invite us to walk a heroic path, bringing us closer to divine status ourselves.

Here I share some practices I have found helpful in developing an ancestor veneration practice.

Devotions

Practices for ancestor veneration closely parallel devotional practices for the Gods. In their essence, the fundamental model is the same: Prayer and invocation, offerings, listening and communication, service. Our offerings may be distinct in ancestor practice, tailored toward the specific nature of our relationship with the ancestor or lineage. We might offer traditional foods from our family's culture, or a favorite treat that a certain person loved. We might offer things that honor the particular sacrifices or gifts of an ancestor. We might offer whatever is best from our own efforts and resources. In the absence of other specifics, classic and simple ancestor veneration can begin with a prayer, a candle lit in their honor, and a cup of clean water, for anyone who has once been human has needed water to drink.

Ancestor Prayer

A prayer inspired by the continuity between the living and the dead, and the courage that it brings.

Ancestors of mine, I bring you life.
I offer you the gift of the living.
For you, for those who will come after us, I will live.
I will live without fear, giving myself fully to life and to love of living.
I will pour out my love as an offering to all you whose being forms the very earth from which I live.
I will live. And when the living is done, I will be dead. I will let go of my body and go into death.
I will join with you and receive the offerings of the living. I will be an Ancestor and love will still move through me.
O ancestors, I share life with you. Grant me long life and I will live.

O ancestors, I guard your memory. Grant me knowledge and I will seek learning.

O ancestors, I stand with you. Grant me courage and I will make you proud.

In your name, ancestors!

Houses of the Dead

Many of us lack the context people had in ancient times of being able to visit the houses of the dead for worship. If our ancestors do have graves or tombs near us, they are often embedded in a distinctly Judeo-Christian context that makes devotional work challenging. As a private analog to the anchoring of ancestral spirits in funerary temples in the landscape, I have developed a practice of building spirit shrines for honored ancestors. Spirit shrines are also employed traditionally in a variety of other cultures, notably many Asian cultures, as well as some African Traditional and Diaspora religions. In my own practice, I use small "house"-like structures such as boxes or lanterns that can be opened or closed. Other traditions sometimes make use of jars or other containers. Spirit shrines as I build them will usually contain some anchor material, such as earth (from a graveyard or relevant sacred place), stones, or when it can be had, relics of the dead, such as ashes, bone, or objects they owned. I include a picture of the ancestral person and any other related things that connect me to them. The spirit house can be consecrated with purification rites, blessings, and an invocation to invite the ancestor to enter into and make a home within the shrine. Whenever it is time honor that ancestor, I open their spirit shrine, set a light in it, make offerings in front of it, and give prayers.

Necromancy

Necromancy is a trigger-word, but it simply means divination through contact with the dead. This is, in fact, just another way of speaking of what the Irish have called the "testimony of the dead". We have seen how the *ogam* script has a special connection with the dead due to its ancient associations with memorial pillar-stones and funerary writing. In truth, any form of divination can be used for communicating with the dead—and it may matter more what kind of oracle the particular ancestor we are contacting finds easiest to communicate through, rather than how well our divination method fits into a particular cultural paradigm. Your grandmother was in the habit of reading tea leaves or playing cards? That will probably be the easiest way for her to speak to you. Want to talk to Cúl Chulainn? Well, *ogam* divination it is, then. Ancestors will often communicate with us through dreams. This, of course, is the practice indicated by the ancient Celts sleeping at tombs. If we cannot go to the tombs of our own ancestors, we can still cultivate necromantic dreams by doing ancestor veneration practices before sleep, and by placing their spirit shrines, icons, pictures or other talismans keyed to their veneration near where we sleep.

The Oracular Skull

The oracular head is, of course, a deeply traditional way of engaging with ancestors in Celtic religion, and very appropriate within a practice connected to the Morrígna. For many of us, a genuine human skull may be difficult to obtain. While they are legal to possess in most places, there are some restrictions on trading them, and ethically sourced skulls are generally quite expensive.[71] If a human skull is not available, we can work with a ceramic, carved, or other crafted replica skull (though I do not recommend resin plastic). Depending on the spirits involved, an animal skull may serve in some instances.

To establish communication and "open the mouth" of an oracular skull, ritual preparation is needed. We can draw on the Irish funerary tales for these rites: our central elements as shown in the lore are cleansing and purification of the skull; anointing, dressing and beautifying it and positioning it in an elevated place of honor; offering it food and drink; and asking it to speak to us. Important for this work is to recognize that any actual skull (whether human or animal) may still have a spirit indwelling in it. This spirit needs to be acknowledged and honored. If we hope to gain oracular communication with any other spirits through the skull, we need to ask the indwelling spirit native to the skull for its cooperation in inviting another spirit through to speak. If we deal honorably with it, it may be willing to assist in this work. We need to be prepared for a "no" answer, or for there to be conditions or reciprocal requests that must be met. As with all spirit work, if we hope

71 Honorable people will want to avoid buying human skulls from any but the most carefully vetted sources. Internet trade in human remains is often supplied by grave desecration and other unspeakable practices in poorer countries, and any materials sourced this way would be an egregious affront to the spirits.

to make an ally of a spirit, we need to treat it as a being with agency and respect its needs and wishes.

To the rites drawn from the funerary tales above, I can add a few more elements which have been shown to me in necromantic dreams. For the opening of the mouth, we can make this ritual more effective by inscribing sigils and incantations for oracular power onto the surface the skull sits on, or onto materials placed beneath it. *Ogam*, as a traditional medium for the voices of the dead, is perfect for such inscriptions, though other scripts such as runic can work also. Depending on the relationship with the skull's indwelling spirit and any specific needs or prohibitions it may have, these inscriptions may be appropriate to apply directly onto the skull. I would also add that protective wards need to be established around the place where the skull is positioned, to keep unfriendly and baneful spirits out, so that when the mouth of the skull is ritually opened they are not invited in. A closable container such as a small cabinet may be needed for the oracular skull, unless it is housed inside a fully protected and sanctified space such as a temple, in order to protect the skull's sanctity at times when it is not actively being venerated.

The War Dead

As the dead who die in war and violent conflict were seen by the ancients to enter into the sphere of the Morrígan, in lived practice as her priests and devotees we often find that we are asked to undertake spirit work to assist them. We should speak here about what to expect in this realm and some of the tools and practices we will need to call upon.

Not all the dead who die in war rest easily. The writers of the ancient tales knew this, and it remains true now. Like the revenant corpse who rises to wrestle Cú Chulainn; like the severed heads that haunt the madman Suibhne Geilt; the nature of war does not lend itself to clean, well-guarded funeral transitions for all the dead. Some move on to take their path through the Otherworld peacefully. Many do not. Some are never found, their fates not known to their warrior companies and their families waiting at home, and so cannot be properly safeguarded through death. Some die in such horror that their souls, wrenched from violated bodies, become lost, confused or enraged. Some cannot let go of the missions they died trying to fulfill, the companions they died trying to save, the loved ones they need to see again. Our ancestors in the warrior cultures of the ancient Celts knew of the risks to the spirits of those who die in war. Priests active in spirit work also know, for when we open the doors to the realms of the Morrígna, we often find that the angry, lost and damaged war dead come flooding through. These spirits make up part of the host of the battle spirits that haunt battlefields in the aftermath.

Not all these war dead are lost. We can offer help to them, and I believe we should, if we can. Here, I share a few lessons and tools gleaned from the experiences of myself and other allied priests of war deities, including collaborative work within the Coru Cathubodua Priesthood as well as friends and colleagues.

Run Deep: Bring backup. Do not attempt working with the war dead without strong spiritual alliances, both Otherworld allies and reliable fellow priests, to work with you. Working with the war dead is spiritually dangerous. We can easily be overwhelmed. The fact is, so many terrible millions of human beings have been fed to the bottomless war machine since the dawn of mechanized warfare, and so few people engage in active spirit work to aid these spirits, that no one person can help them all. Adding to the risk is that there are many unquiet, suffering spirits among them (or they wouldn't need our help). This can make them unpredictable; they can lash out when we contact them, not recognizing that we are here to help. They can attach themselves to us in their urgency to escape an experience where they have been trapped. A great many spiritual harms can befall us when we approach the war dead. It takes a warband to enter their realm. Do this work with allies. Don't go it alone.

Triage: Experience has shown that there are many different kinds of spirits among the war dead. They vary in how pained, confused or enraged they are; how able they are to recognize and receive help; how long they have been dead and suffering. Some are aware of their condition, but some do not even know they are dead. We have encountered some who have been dead and tormented so long that their awareness has degraded to an animalistic state of hungry rage; these are generally not safe to approach directly. Some are more lucid, retaining more awareness of their story and identity; these spirits should be helped first, because they can often be asked to collaborate and help the more dangerous spirits whom we cannot safely approach ourselves. We also meet spirits who are not warriors and who died as civilians caught in the conflict; what they need is often quite different from the needs of warrior dead.

Asking: As with all spirit work, we need to begin by asking what they need. Exercise discretion about this; as I mentioned, some of these spirits will not know they are dead, and we need to tread very carefully about how we introduce that knowledge. The less aware, more degraded souls may not be able to tell you what they need, but the more lucid ones often can, and sometimes they can also tell you what other souls need. We will not always be able to help them with everything they ask for. Sometimes what they need is not our place to provide. For example, it might not be realistic or advisable for us to find their bones and put them to rest somewhere, or track down their granddaughter and tell her their story. Or, what they need may require rituals of a tradition that is not ours to practice. Ask what you can do for them in the moment to help them. In the absence of other specifics, as always with ancestor work, offer water. Milk can be helpful for healing as well. The rites of ancestral elevation can be helpful here: purification, feeding, elevating, and giving honor.

Psychopomp Work: For some spirits, we may be able to actually help them move onward. This is the work of the psychopomp—aiding spirits in crossing over. For this we need to be working in collaboration with Gods or heroic or ancestral spirits who can support such a function. The Morrígna can aid in this. Other Gods we work with can be asked to aid also. Some of the war dead may naturally go to the Morrígna; it has been my experience in this work that she takes many of them into herself, and from there if they are willing they will sometimes join her retinue, working to aid others. It is important, however, to recognize that each of these dead souls may have their own Gods that they need to go to, and our role is to call on whatever resources we have to help them to transition out of their liminal state and find the ancestral realm that is proper to them. We need to tread carefully here around making any culturally inappropriate assumptions. Wars gather in people from many different cultural backgrounds, and each of them has a spiritual destiny. As spirit workers attempting to help them, we need to look for what that is and seek to support it, rather than project our own ideas onto them.

Self-care: We need to place limits on the amount of time, energy and spiritual resources we are giving to this work. As I've said, working with the war dead is overwhelming, as there are far more millions of them than we can ever hope to aid. We do not help them by burning ourselves out. We can set a limit on when and for how long we will be doing this work. Make a guarded container for the tools you use to contact them, so that you can close the connection, protect yourself, and take rest time. Your rites of personal purification and protection will be crucially important here as well.

Trauma Sites: Places in the landscape where battles have occurred often retain an imprint or scar. Sometimes these sites need spiritual work to heal them, and to help release some of the war dead who may be trapped or lost there. We can begin to help these sites, if the same forces that brought conflict to the site are not still in play and it is not still a war zone. We can do cleanup work. We can contact the land spirits and ask what will bring healing. We can make offerings. Again, for healing and restoration, offerings of milk and butter are traditional in our traditions. Depending on the place and the nature of its history, you may be asked to offer something else. As in so many other situations, it is important for us to practice sensitivity and awareness around issues of cultural appropriation. It may not be our place to offer healing at all sites of this nature.

Ancestors and Descendants

The Morrígan speaks of descendants in her Peace Prophecy: rights of descendants, wealth for children, land held secure in longevity and peace... In the work of ancestor veneration, the descendants also arise as worthy of our attention and honoring. In a sense, the descendants, those who come after, are a primary reason for the ancestors' interest in engaging with us. It is for the descendants that they care to see traditions handed on and legacies honored and preserved. It is the descendants who inherit their world and everything they leave behind in their entry into death. For the heroic ethos, the descendants matter too: if the heroic ethos values poetic immortality and the memory of great deeds being preserved, this is only possible as long as there are descendants to remember your deeds and tell your tales.

For all these reasons, in my own practice and within the Coru Cathubodua Priesthood, whenever we invoke and honor the ancestors, we also honor the descendants. We address them together, ancestors and descendants, and make offerings to both together.

Who are the descendants? They represent as a collective all those who will come after us in future generations, and individually those who are to come downline from us within any given lineage, whether familial or spiritual. In another sense, however, we ourselves are the descendants. Each of us is descended from ancestors in a family line, and each of us receives connection from those who came before us in our spiritual traditions. We the living inherit our world from the generations before, and so in the collective sense we are the descendants of all those who lived before us, the collective of ancestors. And just as they did, we will pass on our world, legacies and lineages to those who come after us; so we too are ancestors.

As the living, we stand as the bridge in time between the ancestors and the descendants. We ourselves are both ancestor and descendant. Our work in this position as bridge is to embody and vivify the streams of wisdom and tradition we receive as descendants, to honor them by continuing to build stronger traditions and a better world, and to pass those streams of wisdom and tradition on as ancestors.

Dúnad: Closing

We have undertaken a journey together, seeking the trace of the Great Queen through the time-worn, cryptic layers of story and landscape. I have sought in this book to bring together the threads of both scholarship and inspiration, historical lore and devotional experience. My hope has been to provide as complete a resource of knowledge, study and practice as I could, toward the goal of helping others like myself to increase the depth of their understanding, practice, and connection with the Morrígan. The researching and writing of this book has been my offering both to Herself, and to you, my readers and fellow devotees. But it is also a gift to me; for in fulfilling my commitment to this book, my own understanding and practice have deepened greatly as well. I thank you for supporting this gift by reading my work.

The reading and study of lore can only take you so far, and no further. It is up to you now to take what you may have found of value in this book and bring it to life in your own practice. For though her image and her words fill the pages of literature, the Great Queen does not live in the pages of books. She lives in the world, ours and the Otherworld. In stones and fields that hold the blood of memory, in tongues that speak poetry, in fierce hearts that will not lie still but seek justice, in the lives and struggles and devotions of every one who seeks her. Each of us must encounter the Great Queen on our own terms. Each of us must find our own way into the lore, our own way of embodying its spirit, our own way of giving her a home in our hearts and lives.

Her last message to me to share with you in the completion of this book was this: Listen for my voice. I have heard her voice, as many others also have, becoming more and more insistent in recent years. At the time I am writing this closing, a great many people have observed that the Morrígan has been exceptionally active—calling upon people, gathering her devotees, stirring a sense of purpose in them. She is not the only one; many Gods are being felt more strongly in recent years than perhaps they have been in millennia as the grip of monotheism loosens and the cults of the old Gods are built new. In this rising tide, her voice rings out especially clearly for some of us. She asks us to listen.

We live in changing times. In the time since I began writing this book, several waves of protest and revolution have swept the globe. Fundamental conflicts are being fought over liberty, civil rights, justice, and sovereignty. Institutions long assumed to be fixed are eroding and new forms are arising. The land itself is changing as climate shifts globally. None of us yet knows what world we face tomorrow. Perhaps she knows: perhaps in her prophetic vision she sees the world to come—or the worlds, worlds that stand before us ready to be born and which we stand poised to choose between in our actions now at this cusp of change. Like the worlds of her twin prophecies, the bright world born of justice and the hollow world absent of it. We hold these prophecies in our hands now.

I have often felt, and have heard others say too, that the Morrígan is a fitting Goddess for our times. She holds and teaches the powers and wisdoms we need to be able to face these choices. She sees those who are born on this battlefield. She sees what can rise in us to meet the battle, and calls that forth from within us. We need strengths like these. We need the heroic ethos. We need whatever it is that can grant us the courage to be a force for justice and right action.

We need each other, too. In our myriad individual ways of encountering her, understanding her, and serving her, as communities of devotion we contain a well of diversity and resiliency. Each of us has a part to play in how we contribute to the making of the world. As friends of the war Goddess, there is a kinship in devotion that we can share with one another. It is kinship that gives us the strength and courage to act with grace in the face of adversity and change, and to be a source of spiritual support for our communities.

I hope, then, to inspire readers to seek out kinship and connection with others who have also experienced her call or who are seeking her strength. I hope to connect with many of you myself along the way, and I honor you and thank you for taking this journey with me.

Bennaigid don
Morrígan
Mórda
Sith co nemh
Bidsirnae sith

Pronunciation Guide

This pronunciation guide is not exhaustive, since hundreds of terms in Irish (not to mention other Celtic languages) have been used in the text. Here, we attempt to provide pronunciation and basic definitions for only terms used frequently or which are of significance to the central focus of this book.

The Irish language has evolved in its pronunciation, so that Old Irish pronunciation is different from Modern Irish. This evolution also includes marked variations in regional dialects, so that within Modern Irish, pronunciation varies from district to district. As this is not a linguistics text, we are not attempting to account for all this variation, but simply aiming to provide some basic guidance as to how these words should sound. Since most of the terms here are taken from early texts, in most cases we default to Old Irish pronunciation.

Notation used for pronunciation here is aimed at English speakers, using the following conventions:

ai: as in 'why'
ey: as in 'way'
kh: as in 'loch'
gh: soft g as in 'afghan'
dh: as in 'the'
th: as in 'thin'

áed: aidh
Áed Rúad: aidh ROO-adh
Ailech Néit: AL-ekh neyd
Ailill: AL-ill
airdrech: ARD-rekh
ammait: AM-at
Anu: AN-oo | Variations **Anann**, **Anand**: AN-an

Aoife: EE-fuh
Ard Macha: ardh MAH-kha
armgrith: ARV-gridh
arracht: AR-akht
Badb: BADH-uv | Modern: baiv
badba belderga: BADH-va bel-DER-gha
bánánaig: BAHN-ahn-ig
bancháinti: BAHN-khain-chuh
bandraí: BAHN-dhrai
banfaíth: BAHN-aidh
banfeis: BAHN-eysh
banfili: BAHN-ih-lih
Banshenchas: BAHN-hen-uh-khas
bansíd: BAHN-heedh | Modern variant ***beansidhe***: BAN-shee
bantúaithech: BAHN-DHOO-ah-thekh
Bé Néit: bey NEYD
Beltaine: BEL-chin-uh
Berba: BER-vuh
Bóann: BO-an
bóaire: BO-ar-uh
boccánaig: BOC-an-agh
Bodbmall: BODH-vahl
bodhbh chaointe: BODH-uv KHAIN-chuh
Boudicca: BOO-dih-ka
Brega: BREH-gah
Bres: BRES
brichtu ban: BRIKH-too BAHN
Brigid: BRIGH-id
Brúg Na Bóinne: BROOGH na BOY-nyeh
búadris: BOO-ad-rish
búaida: BOO-ah-dah
Cailb: KAIL-uv
Cailleach: KAIL-yekh
cáintecht: KAIN-chekhd
Calatín: kal-ah-TEEN
cath: KATH
Cath Maige Tuired: KATH MAIG-uh CHYU-ridh
Cathbad: KATH-vadh
Cathubodua: (reconstructed) KATH-oo-BOD-wah or KATH-oo-BODH-vah

cles: KLES
coinnle Bodba: KOYN-luh BODH-vah
conachlonn: KON-akh-lon
Conaire: KON-ar-uh
Conchobor: KON-khuh-var
congain comail: KON-gan KOV-all
Connacht: KON-akht
Cormac: KOR-mak
corrguinecht: KORR-gwin-ekht
crandchur: KRANN-khoor
Crobh Dearg: KROV JER-ugh
Cruachan: KROO-ah-khan
crufechta: KROO-fekh-da
Cruinn: KROO-en | Variant **Crunniuc**: KROON-yukh
Cú Chulainn: KOO KHULL-in
Cú Roí: KOO REE
cúailli Badbhba: KOO-ah-lee BADH-vah
Cúailnge: KOO-lan-yuh
Dá Chích Anann: DAH KHEEKH AN-ann
Dá Chích na Morrígna: DAH KHEEKH nah MOR-reeg-nah
Dá Choca: DAH KHO-ka
Dá Derga: DAH JER-ghuh
Dagda: DAGH-dha
Dáire Donn: DOY-ruh don
***Danu**: DAH-noo | Variant **Danann**: DAN-an
Delbáeth: DELL-vaidh
derg: JER-ugh
día sóach: DEE-ah SO-akh
díchetal do chennaibh: DEE-khed-al do KHEN-av
Dindshenchas: DINN-hen-uh-khas
Dithorba: DIH-thor-vah
Donn Cúailnge: DON KOO-lan-yuh
dord fiannsa: DORDH FEE-an-sah
druí: DROO-ee
dub: doov
Dubh Sainglenn: DOOV SANG-len
Dubthach: DOOV-thakh
Dún Sobairche: DOON SOV-erkh-uh
Emain Macha: EV-ahn MAKH-uh

Emer: EH-ver
én gaile: eyn GAL-yeh
Eochaid: YAH-khidh
Eochu Ollathair: YAH-khoo OLL-ath-ir
Epona: ey-PO-nah
Ernmas: EHR-n-vas
Ériu: EYR-yoo
Étaín: EY-deen
fáilte: FAIL-cheh
fáith: FAI-ith
fé: fey
Féa: FEY-uh
Fedelm: FEHDH-el-iv | Modern: FEY-lim
féle: FEY-luh
Fergus: FER-ghus
fíach: FEE-akh
fíachairecht: FEE-akh-ar-ekht
Fianna: FEE-an-nah
fili: FIH-lih
Findbennach: FINN-ven-akh
Finn: FINN
Fir Bolg: FEER BOLL-ug
fír flathemon: FEER FLATH-ev-on
Fomoire: FO-vor-uh
Fraoch: FRAY-ukh
fulacht fiadh: FUH-lakht FEE-udh
fulacht na Morrígna: FUH-lakht nah MOR-reeg-nah
gaí bulga: gai BUL-gah
geis: GESH | Plural **gessi:** GESH-ee
glám dícenn: GLAV DEE-khen
Gort na Morrígna: GORD na MOR-reeg-nah
Grian: GREE-an
gúdemain: GOO-deh-van
imbas forosnai: IM-bas FOR-os-na
Indech: IN-dekh
Inis Badhbha: IN-ish BADH-va
Lebor Gabála Érenn: LEH-vor ga-VAH-lah EY-renn
Líath Luachra: LEE-ath LOOKH-rah
Líath Macha: LEE-ath MAKH-ah

Lóch: LOWKH
lúan láith: LOO-un LAIDH
Lugh: loogh
Macha: MAKH-ah
Macha Mongruad: MAKH-ah mong-ROO-adh
mag: magh
Mag Féa: MAGH FEY-uh
Mag Macha: MAGH MAKH-ah
Mag mBreg: MAGH MREGH
Mag Tuired: MAGH TYOO-redh
Magh Rath: MAGH RATH
Matha: MATH-ah
Méche: MEY-khuh
Medb: MEDH-uv
mesrad Machae: MESS-radh MAKH-eh
Míl: meel
Morrígan: MOR-reeg-an | Variant **Morrígu**: MOR-reeg-oo | Plural **Morrígna**: MOR-reeg-nah
Mogh Ruith: MUGH ROODH
Muirthemne: MOOR-hev-neh
Nantosuelta: NAN-to-SWEL-tah
Néit: neyd
ném: neyv
Némain: NEY-van
Nemed: NEVH-edh
Nemeton: NEM-et-own
Nemetona: nem-et-OWN-ah
Nemnach: NEVH-nakh
Nera: NEH-rah
Neto: NEY-to
Nia Segamain: NEE-ah SEGH-ah-van
Níth: NEEDH
níthcharpat: NEEDH-khar-bad
nóinden: NOYN-dhen
Nuada: NOO-ah-dhah
Odras: OD-ras
óenach: EE-nakh Plural **óenaige**: EE-nagh-eh
ogam: OGH-am | Modern: OH-am
Rathcroghan: rath-CROW-han

ríastrad: REE-as-tradh
Ró-fessa: ROH-ess-uh
rosc: RUSK Plural *roscada*: RUSK-a-dha
Ross: ross
rúad: ROO-adh
Samhain: SOV-win | Modern: SOW-in
Scáthach: SKAH-thakh
sciath: SHKEE-uth
scoith nía: skoth NEE-ah
síabra: SHEE-av-rah
síd (síth): sheedh | Modern *sidhe*: shee
Síd Cruachan: sheedh KROO-akh-an
Sídaib Féa: SHEE-dav FEY-uh
Sín: sheen | Alternate **Sinand**: SHIN-ann
síthcura: SHEEDH-koo-rah
slán: slawn
Slíab Bodbgna: sleev BODH-v-nyah
Srúb Brain: SROOV bran
Táin Bó Cúalnge: TOYN bo KOO-lan-yuh
Táin Bó Regamna: TOYN bo REH-gav-nah
tarb feis: TARV FEYSH
Tech Duinn: tekh DOO-in
Temhair: TEH-vir
tenm laida: TAY-nyuv LAI-dhuh
Tethra: TETH-rah
tongu a toingend: TONG-oo ah TONG-enn
túath: TOO-ath
Túatha Dé Danann: TOO-ath-ah DEY DAN-an
Tulchine: TULL-khin-eh
Úaim na gCat (Oweynagat): OO-avh na GAT
úatha: OO-ath-ah
Úathach: OO-uth-akh
Ulaid : ULL-idh
Unshin: UN-hin

Readings & Resources

This section aims to provide direction for further reading, research and exploration into the many subject areas we touch on in this book. Many of the recommended sources have already been cited throughout the text of this book. For convenience, I have gathered a few of the most useful sources for each topic here. Authors, titles, and where appropriate, web addresses are included here; full publication information can be found in the Works Cited section.

Part 1: Herself

Chapter 1. The Irish Lore

A large body of Irish source texts were published in English translations in the 19th and early 20th centuries, so many of these are now in the public domain and available to read free of charge. Several online collections provide access to Irish text translations:

CELT: Corpus of Electronic Texts | http://www.ucc.ie/celt/
Mary Jones Celtic Literature Collective | http://www.maryjones.us/
Tech Screpta | http://sejh.pagesperso-orange.fr/celtlink.html

For readers interested in accessing the original journals and collections within which the translations were published, many are also available online (such as *Ériu, Revue Celtique, Irish Texts Society* editions, etc.) For thorough study, this is worthwhile, since the online collections above tend to reproduce only the text and translation, whereas the original publications often included additional notes for context and background to the texts. Many volumes of these journals and collections, especially the earlier ones, can be found and downloaded via

non-profit library sites:
Internet Archive | https://archive.org/
Project Gutenberg | http://www.gutenberg.org/

An excellent ongoing exploration of a wide range of Irish myths, including an in-depth series on the *Second Battle of Mag Tuired* and a great many more, is offered by the following podcast:
Story Archaeology Podcast | http://storyarchaeology.com/

Chapter 2. One, Three and Many

Sources giving perspective on the relationship between the Morrígna:

Carey, John. "Notes on the Irish War-Goddess."

Epstein, Angelique Gulermovich. *War Goddess: The Morrígan and Her Germano-Celtic Counterparts*.

Herbert, Maire. "Transmutations of an Irish Goddess."

Chapter 3. The Morrígan

Sources providing scholarship and discussion related to the Morrígan in particular:

Borsje, Jacqueline. "The 'terror of the Night' and the Morrígain: Shifting Faces of the Supernatural."

Clark, Rosalind. *The Great Queens: Irish Goddesses from the Morrígan to Cathleen Ní Houlihan*.

Epstein, Angelique Gulermovich. "Woman's Word: Threats and Prophecies, Lies and Revelations in Arthurian Romance and Medieval Irish Literature."

Chapter 4. Badb

Sources providing scholarship and discussion related to the Badb in particular:

Bhreathnach, M. "The Sovereignty Goddess as Goddess of Death?"

Borsje, Jacqueline. "Omens, Ordeals and Oracles: On Demons and Weapons in Early Irish Texts."

Donahue, Charles. "The Valkyries and the Irish War-Goddesses."

O'Connor, Ralph. *The Destruction of Da Derga's Hostel: Kingship and Narrative Artistry in a Mediaeval Irish Saga*.

Chapter 5. Macha

Sources providing scholarship and discussion related to Macha in particular:

Carey, John. "Notes on the Irish War-Goddess."

Toner, Gregory. "Macha and the Invention of Myth."

Waddell, John. *Archaeology and Celtic Myth*.

Chapter 6. Anu

Sources discussing Anu often assume identity with Danu and/or the Morrígan, and sometimes may add to confusion instead of being of help. The following are works I found to provide helpful clarity:

Carey, John. "Notes on the Irish War-Goddess."

Kondratiev, Alexei. "Danu and Bile: The Primordial Parents?"

MacLeod, Sharon Paice. "Mater Deorum Hibernensium: Identity and Cross-Correlation in Early Irish Mythology."

7. Némain, Féa and Bé Néit

Very few scholarly works focus any attention on Némain or Féa as distinct from other Morrígna figures. The following works touch on Némain and provide some context:

Carey, John. "Notes on the Irish War-Goddess."

Olmsted, Garrett. *The Gods of the Celts and the Indo-Europeans*. [Note: This work must be read with extreme caution and critical scholarship. Olmsted provides valuable details about inscriptions and some linguistics, but often leaps to conclusions identifying different deities with one another.]

Sjoestedt, Marie-Louise. *Gods and Heroes of the Celts*.

Waddell, John. *Archaeology and Celtic Myth*.

8. Deep Roots: British and Continental Sisters

Several valuable scholarly works explore the relationships between the Morrígna and cognate divinities in Britain and the Continent:

Beck, Noémie. *Goddesses in Celtic Religion - Cult and Mythology: A Comparative Study of Ancient Ireland, Britain and Gaul*.

Bernhardt-House, Phillip A. "Interpretatio Hibernica."

Donahue, Charles. "The Valkyries and the Irish War-Goddesses."

Olmsted, Garrett. *The Gods of the Celts and the Indo-Europeans*. [Note: As above, the same caution applies about reading Olmsted's work critically.]

Waddell, John. *Archaeology and Celtic Myth*.

9. In Her Words: The Poems

In addition to the poems themselves as presented in the medieval Irish tales, a few helpful scholarly papers analyze some of them in more detail:

Carmody, Isolde. *Thesis, Antithesis, Synthesis: An Examination of Three Rosc Passages from Cath Maige Tuired.*

Henry, P. L. "Táin Roscada: Discussion and Edition."

Mees, Bernard. *Celtic Curses.*

Olmsted, Garrett. "Morrigan's Warning to Donn Cuailnge."

Part II: Cult

Chapter 10. Land, Sanctuary, Tomb, and Temple

Many print resources exist focusing on sacred sites within Ireland and elsewhere, and their histories within Celtic religious practice. Here are a few sources referenced from our text:

Brunaux, Jean-Louis. *The Celtic Gauls: Gods, Rites and Sanctuaries.*

Ó hÓgáin, Dáithí. *The Sacred Isle.*

Waddell, John. *Archaeology and Celtic Myth.*

Heritage Guides publish excellent information on important sacred sites within Ireland, which can be ordered here:

Wordwell Books: Heritage Guides | http://www.wordwellbooks.com/

Folkloric and experiential lore about many of Ireland's sacred sites, with photographs and many more links, can be found here:

Voices from the Dawn: The Folklore of Ireland's Ancient Monuments | http://www.voicesfromthedawn.com/

Chapter 11. Iconography and Devotion

Highlighted sources referenced within the text, providing helpful studies on ancient devotional practice and iconography:

Beck, Noémie. *Goddesses in Celtic Religion - Cult and Mythology: A Comparative Study of Ancient Ireland, Britain and Gaul.*

Ó hÓgáin, Dáithí. *The Sacred Isle.*

Green, Miranda. *The Gods of the Celts.*

Additional sources on living devotional and spiritual practice:

Coyle, T. Thorn. *Crafting A Daily Practice: A Simple Course on Self-Commitment.*

Krasskova, Galina. *Devotional Polytheism: An Introduction.*

Laurie, Erynn Rowan. "The Cauldron of Poesy."
O'Grady, Judith. *Pagan Portals - God-Speaking*.

Recordings of the poems of the Morrígan and some of the chants from this chapter:
Poems of the Morrígan | http://bookofthegreatqueen.com/

Chapter 12. Sacrifice

Further reading on sacrifice in the ancient world and among the Celts:
Aldhouse-Green, Miranda. *Caesar's Druids: Story of an Ancient Priesthood*.
Borsje, Jacqueline. "Human Sacrifice in Medieval Irish Literature."
Iping-Petterson, M. *Human Sacrifice in Iron Age Northern Europe: The Culture of the Bog People*.
Lincoln, Bruce. *Death, War, and Sacrifice: Studies in Ideology and Practice*.
van der Sanden, Wijnand A. B. "Bog Bodies: Underwater Burials, Sacrifices, and Executions."

Chapter 14. Priesthood and Sovereignty

Further reading on priesthood, druidic and poetic functions, sovereignty and sacral kingship among the ancient Celts:
Bhreathnach, M. "The Sovereignty Goddess as Goddess of Death?"
Borsje, Jacqueline. "Supernatural Threats to Kings: Exploration of a Motif in the Ulster Cycle and in Other Medieval Irish Tales."
Bray, Daniel. "Sacral Elements of Irish Kingship."
O'Connor, Ralph. *The Destruction of Da Derga's Hostel: Kingship and Narrative Artistry in a Mediaeval Irish Saga*.
Waddell, John. *Archaeology and Celtic Myth*.

For resources on developing meditative trance journeying skills (referenced in this chapter as a prerequisite to the Rite of Sovereignty) see list for the next chapter.

Chapter 14. Oracles and Divinations

Sources on historical oracular and divinatory practice and the Morrígna:
Aldhouse-Green, Miranda. *Caesar's Druids: Story of an Ancient Priesthood*.
Beck, Noémie. *Goddesses in Celtic Religion - Cult and Mythology: A Comparative Study of Ancient Ireland, Britain and Gaul*.
Borsje, Jacqueline. "Omens, Ordeals and Oracles: On Demons and Weapons in Early Irish Texts."

Epstein, Angelique Gulermovich. "Woman's Word: Threats and Prophecies, Lies and Revelations in Arthurian Romance and Medieval Irish Literature."

Additional resources for trance, journeying, oracular possession and preparation, and divinatory practices:

Filan, Kenaz, and Raven Kaldera. *Drawing Down the Spirits: The Traditions and Techniques of Spirit Possession*.

Laurie, Erynn Rowan. *Ogam: Weaving Word Wisdom*.

Paxson, Diana L. *Trance-Portation*.

Paxson, Diana L. *The Essential Guide to Possession, Depossession, and Divine Relationships*.

Simmer-Brown, Judith. "Inviting the Demon."

Zweig, Connie, and Jeremiah Abrams. *Meeting the Shadow: The Hidden Power of the Dark Side of Human Nature*.

Chapter 15. Sorcery

Selected sources from our text on cursing, binding, and oath-swearing:

Borsje, Jacqueline. "'The Evil Eye' in Early Irish Literature and Law."

Carey, John. "The Encounter at the Ford: Warriors, Water and Women."

Koch, John T. "Further to Tongu Do Dia Toinges Mo Thuath, &c."

Mees, Bernard. *Celtic Curses*.

Additional sources on spirit work, magical and cursing practices:

Mickaharic, Draja. *Spiritual Cleansing: A Handbook of Psychic Protection*.

Skallagrimsson, Wayland. *Putting on the Wolf Skin*.

Wilby, Emma. *Cunning-Folk and Familiar Spirits: Shamanistic Visionary Traditions in Early Modern British Witchcraft and Magic*.

Chapter 16. Battle Cultus

A selection of sources referenced in the text with material on Celtic societies in relation to warfare:

Aldhouse-Green, Miranda. *Caesar's Druids: Story of an Ancient Priesthood*.

Brunaux, Jean-Louis. "Gallic Blood Rites."

Irby-Massie, Georgia L. *Military Religion in Roman Britain*.

Koch, John T., and John Carey. *The Celtic Heroic Age: Literary Sources for Ancient Celtic Europe and Early Ireland & Wales*.

Lincoln, Bruce. *Death, War, and Sacrifice: Studies in Ideology and Practice*.

Additional modern sources on war and the warrior ethos:
Greitens, Eric. *The Heart and the Fist.*
Pressfield, Steven. *The Warrior Ethos.*

Chapter 17. The Warrior's Initiation

Selected sources from our text referencing warriorship, warrior rites, and the relationships of warriors and the Morrígna:

Bernhardt-House, Phillip A. "Imbolc: A New Interpretation."
Bernhardt-House, Phillip, C. L. Vermeers, Erin Zelnio, and Erynn Rowan Laurie. "Warrior Consecration Ritual."
Bernhardt-House, Phillip, C. L. Vermeers, Erin Zelnio, and Erynn Rowan Laurie. "Warrior Return Ritual."
Borsje, Jacqueline. "Omens, Ordeals and Oracles: On Demons and Weapons in Early Irish Texts."
Brown, Dorcas R, and David W Anthony. "Midwinter Dog Sacrifices and Warrior Initiations in the Late Bronze Age at the Site of Krasnosamarskoe , Russia."
Henry, P. L. "Furor Heroicus."
Sayers, William. "Martial Feats in the Old Irish Ulster Cycle."
Sayers, William. "Airdrech, Sirite and Other Early Irish Battlefield Spirits."

Additional works on warriorship and warrior practices:

Musashi, Miyamoto. *The Book of Five Rings.*
Thompson, Christopher Scott. *Highland Martial Culture: The Fighting Heritage of Scotland.*
Thompson, Christopher Scott. *The Music of His Sword: Martial Arts of the Pagan Celts.*

Chapter 18. Funerary and Ancestral Rites

A selection of sources referenced in our text relating to funerary and ancestral traditions:

Armit, Ian. *Headhunting and the Body in Iron Age Europe.*
Carey, John. "The Testimony of the Dead."
Chadwick, Nora K. "Imbas Forosnai."
Lysaght, Patricia. "Aspects of the Earth-Goddess in the Traditions of the Banshee in Ireland."
Raftery, Barry. *Pagan Celtic Ireland: The Enigma of the Irish Iron Age.*

Additional resources on death and funerary rites, ancestor work,

and the dead:
Compassion & Choices: End-of-Life Resource Center | https://www.compassionandchoices.org/.
Funeral Consumers Alliance: Your Legal Rights | http://www.funerals.org/forconsumersmenu/your-legal-rights.
Krasskova, Galina. Honoring the Ancestors: *A Basic Guide*.
Lecouteux, Claude. *The Return of the Dead: Ghosts, Ancestors, and the Transparent Veil of the Pagan Mind*.
Slocum, Joshua, and Lisa Carlson. *Final Rights: Reclaiming the American Way of Death*.

Works Cited

Aldhouse-Green, Miranda. 2010. Caesar's Druids: *Story of an Ancient Priesthood*. New Haven: Yale University Press.

Alfoldi, Andrew. 1960. "Diana Nemorensis." *American Journal of Archaeology* 64 (2): 137–44.

Arbuthnot, Sharon. 2010. "Further to the Drink of Death." *Eigse: A Journal of Irish Studies* 37: 134–41.

Armit, Ian. 2012. *Headhunting and the Body in Iron Age Europe*. Cambridge: Cambridge University Press.

Atsma, Aaron J. 2011. "Keres: Goddesses or Spirits of Violent Death." *Theoi Project*. http://www.theoi.com/Daimon/Keres.html.

Beck, Noémie. 2009. *Goddesses in Celtic Religion - Cult and Mythology: A Comparative Study of Ancient Ireland, Britain and Gaul*. Université Lumière Lyon.

Bergin, Osborn, and R. I. Best. 2011. "The Wooing of Étaín." *CELT: Corpus of Electronic Texts*. http://www.ucc.ie/celt/published/T300012/

Bernhardt-House, Phillip A. 2002. "Imbolc: A New Interpretation." *Cosmos* 18: 57–76.

———. 2007a. "Interpretatio Hibernica." *Eolas: The Journal of the American Society of Irish Medieval Studies* 2: 45–61.

———. 2007b. "The Old Irish Impotence Spell: The Dam Díli, Fergus, Fertility, and the Mythic Background of an Irish Incantation." *Journal for the Academic Study of Magic* 4: 304–24.

Bernhardt-House, Phillip, C. L. Vermeers, Erin Zelnio, and Erynn Rowan Laurie. 2009. "Warrior Return Ritual." *Erynn's Journal*. http://erynn.dreamwidth.org/427219.html

———. 2010. "Warrior Consecration Ritual." *The Preserving Shrine*. http://www.seanet.com/~inisglas/warriorrite.html

Best, R. I. 1916. "Prognostications from the Raven and the Wren." *Ériu* 8: 120–26.

Bhreathnach, M. 1982. "The Sovereignty Goddess as Goddess of Death?" *Zeitschrift Für Celtische Philologie* 39: 243–60.

Borsje, Jacqueline. 1999. "Omens, Ordeals and Oracles: On Demons and Weapons in Early Irish Texts." *Peritia: Journal of the Medieval Academy of Ireland* 13: 224–48.
———. 2003. "'The Evil Eye' in Early Irish Literature and Law." *Celtica* 24: 1–39.
———. 2007a. "The 'Terror of the Night' and the Morrígain: Shifting Faces of the Supernatural." In *Proceedings of the Seventh Symposium of Societas Celtologica Nordica*, edited by Mícheál Ó Flaithearta, 71–98. Uppsala: Acta Universitatis Upsaliensis.
———. 2007b. "Human Sacrifice in Medieval Irish Literature." In *The Strange World of Human Sacrifice*, edited by J.N. Bremmer, 31–54. Leuven: Peeters.
———. 2009. "Supernatural Threats to Kings: Exploration of a Motif in the Ulster Cycle and in Other Medieval Irish Tales." *Ulidia* 2: 173–94.
Bray, Daniel. 1999. "Sacral Elements of Irish Kingship." In *This Immense Panorama: Studies in Honour of Eric J. Sharpe*, edited by Carole M. Cusack and Peter Oldmeadow. Sydney: School of Studies in Religion, University of Sydney.
Brown, Dorcas R, and David W Anthony. 2012. "Midwinter Dog Sacrifices and Warrior Initiations in the Late Bronze Age at the Site of Krasnosamarskoe , Russia." In *Roots of Europe - Language, Culture, and Migrations Conference*. Copenhagen: University of Copenhagen.
Brunaux, Jean-Louis. 1988. *The Celtic Gauls: Gods, Rites and Sanctuaries*. Translated by Daphne Nash. London: Seaby.
———. 2001. "Gallic Blood Rites." *Archaeology* 54 (2): 54.
Calder, George. 1922. *Togail Na Tebe: The Thebaid of Statius*. Cambridge: The University Press.
Campanile, Enrico. 1988. "Meaning and Pre-History of OIr. Luan Laith." In *Languages and Cultures: Studies in Honor of Edgar C. Polome*, edited by Mohammad Ali Jazayery and Werner Winter, 89–96. Berlin: Mouton de Gruyter.
Carey, John. 1982. "Notes on the Irish War-Goddess." *Eigse: A Journal of Irish Studies* 19: 263–75.
———. 1991. "The Irish 'Otherworld': Hiberno-Latin Perspectives." *Eigse: A Journal of Irish Studies* 25: 154–59.
———. 1992. "The Testimony of the Dead." *Eigse: A Journal of Irish Studies* 26: 1–12.

———. 1994. "The Irish National Origin-Legend: Synthetic Pseudohistory." *Quiggin Pamphlets on the Sources of Mediaeval Gaelic History* 1: 27.

———. 1997. "The Three Things Required of a Poet." *Ériu* 48: 41–58.

———. 2004. "The Encounter at the Ford: Warriors, Water and Women." *Eigse: A Journal of Irish Studies* 34: 10–24.

Carmody, Isolde. 2004. *Thesis, Antithesis, Synthesis: An Examination of Three Rosc Passages from Cath Maige Tuired*. Trinity College Dublin.

———. 2013. "Poems of the Morrigan." *Story Archaeology Podcast*. http://storyarchaeology.com/poems-of-the-morrigan/

———. 2014. "Rosc from Táin Bó Regamna." Unpublished translation.

Carmody, Isolde, and Chris Thompson. 2012. "The Battle of Moytura 04: Ar Shlicht in Dagdae – On the Track of the Dagda." *Story Archaeology Podcast*. http://storyarchaeology.com/the-battle-of-moytura-04-ar-shlicht-in-dagdae-on-the-track-of-the-dagda/

———. 2015. *Story Archaeology Podcast*. http://storyarchaeology.com/

Carson, Ciaran. 2007. *The Táin: A New Translation of the Táin Bó Cúailnge*. London: Penguin Classics.

Chadwick, Nora K. 1935. "Imbas Forosnai." *Scottish Gaelic Studies* 4 (2): 97–135.

Clark, Rosalind. 1990. *The Great Queens: Irish Goddesses from the Morrígan to Cathleen Ní Houlihan*. Dublin: Colin Smythe Ltd.

Compassion & Choices. 2015. *Compassion & Choices: End-of-Life Resource Center*. https://www.compassionandchoices.org/

Condit, Tom. 2006. "Ireland's Uplands - Archaeological Scenery." In *Islands in the Clouds: An Upland Archaeological Study on Mount Brandon and the Paps, County Kerry*, edited by Frank Coyne, 61–73. Kerry County Council.

Connolly, Michael. 2006. "Fields of View: The Archaeological Landscapes of Mount Brandon and The Paps." In *Islands in the Clouds: An Upland Archaeological Study on Mount Brandon and the Paps, County Kerry*, edited by Frank Coyne, 51–60. Kerry County Council.

Corpus of Electronic Texts (UCC). 2015. *CELT: Corpus of Electronic Texts*. http://www.ucc.ie/celt/.

Corthals, Johan. 1996. "Early Irish Retoirics and Their Late Antique Background." *Cambrian Medieval Celtic Studies* 31: 17–36.

Coyle, T. Thorn. 2012. *Crafting A Daily Practice: A Simple Course on Self-Commitment*. Sunna Press. http://www.solarcrosstemple.org/publishing/sunna-press/

Coyne, Frank. 2006. *Islands in the Clouds: An Upland Archaeological Study on Mount Brandon and the Paps, County Kerry*. Kerry County Council.

Cross, Tom Peete, and Clark Harris Slover. 1936. "The Boyhood Deeds of Finn." In *Ancient Irish Tales*, 360–69. New York: Henry Holt & Company.

Dasent, George W. trans. 1861. "The Story of Burnt Njal." *Icelandic Saga Database*. http://www.sagadb.org/brennu-njals_saga.en

Delamarre, Xavier. 2003. *Dictionnaire de La Langue Gauloise*. Paris: Éditions Errance.

Dobbs, M E. 1923. "The Battle of Findchorad." *Zeitschrift Für Celtische Philologie* 14: 395–420.

Dobbs, Maighréad ni C. 1930. "The Ban-Shenchus." *Revue Celtique* 47.

———. 1931. "The Ban-Shenchus." *Revue Celtique* 48: 163–234.

Donahue, Charles. 1941. "The Valkyries and the Irish War-Goddesses." *PMLA* 56 (1): 12.

Duff, J.D. 1928. *Lucan: The Civil War, Books I-X (Pharsalia)*. London: William Heinemann Ltd.

Duncan, Lilian. 1932. "Altram Tige Dá Medar." *Ériu* 11: 184–225.

Epstein, Angelique Gulermovich. 1992. "Woman's Word: Threats and Prophecies, Lies and Revelations in Arthurian Romance and Medieval Irish Literature." *Proceedings of the Harvard Celtic Colloquium* 12: 184–95.

———. 1998. *War Goddess: The Morrígan and Her Germano-Celtic Counterparts*. Los Angeles: University of California.

Fickett-Wilbar, David. 2012. "Ritual Details of the Irish Horse Sacrifice in Betha Mholaise Daiminse." *The Journal of Indo-European Studies* 40 (3-4): 315–43.

Filan, Kenaz, and Raven Kaldera. 2009. *Drawing Down the Spirits: The Traditions and Techniques of Spirit Possession*. Rochester: Destiny Books. http://www.northernshamanism.org/shamanic-techniques/spirit-possession.html

Flynn, Peter. 2010. "Táin Bó Regamna." *CELT: Corpus of Electronic Texts*. http://www.ucc.ie/celt/online/G301005/

Fraser, J. 1916. "The First Battle of Moytura." *Ériu* 8: 1–63.

Funeral Consumers Alliance. 2010. *Your Legal Rights*. http://www.funerals.org/forconsumersmenu/your-legal-rights

Goldbaum, Howard. 2015. *Voices from the Dawn: The Folklore of Ireland's Ancient Monuments*. http://www.voicesfromthedawn.com/

Gray, Elizabeth A., ed. 1982. *Cath Maige Tuired : The Second Battle of Mag Tuired. Irish Texts Society*. Vol. 2. Kildare: Irish Texts Society.

Green, Miranda. 2011. *The Gods of the Celts*. Stroud: The History Press.

Greitens, Eric. 2011. *The Heart and the Fist*. New York: Houghton Mifflin Harcourt. http://www.ericgreitens.com/books/the-heart-and-the-fist/

Guest, Lady Charlotte. 2014. "Peredur the Son of Evrawc." In *The Mabinogion*, Web edition. Adelaide: University of Adelaide.

Gwynn, Edward. 1924. *The Metrical Dindshenchas Part IV*. Dublin: Hodges, Figgis & Co., Ltd.

———. 2008a. "The Metrical Dindshenchas Volume 2." *CELT: Corpus of Electronic Texts*. http://www.ucc.ie/celt/published/T106500B/index.html

———. 2008b. "The Metrical Dindshenchas Volume 3." *CELT: Corpus of Electronic Texts*. http://www.ucc.ie/celt/published/T106500C/index.html

Henderson, George. 1898. *Leabhar Nan Gleann: The Book of the Glens*. Inverness: The Highland News Printing Works.

———. 1899. *Fled Bricrend: The Feast of Bricriu*. London: Irish Texts Society.

Hennessy, William M. 1872. "The Ancient Irish Goddess of War." *Revue Celtique* I: 32–55.

———. 1889. *Mesca Ulad or The Intoxication of the Ultonians*. Dublin: Royal Irish Academy.

Henry, P. L. 1959. "The Goblin Group." *Études Celtiques* 8: 404–16.

———. 1982. "Furor Heroicus." *Zeitschrift Für Celtische Philologie* 39: 235–42.

———. 1990. "Verba Scathaige." *Celtica* 21: 191–207.

———. 1995. "Táin Roscada: Discussion and Edition." *Zeitschrift Für Celtische Philologie* 47 (1).

Herbert, Maire. 1996. "Transmutations of an Irish Goddess." In *The Concept of the Goddess*, edited by Sandra Billington and Miranda Green, 141–51. London: Routledge.

Homer. 1924. "The Iliad with an English Translation by A.T. Murray, Ph.D. in Two Volumes." *Perseus Digital Library*. http://www.perseus.tufts.edu/hopper/text?doc=urn:cts:greekLit:tlg0012.tlg001.perseus-eng1:18

Hughes, Marilynn. 2005. *The Voice of the Prophets: Abridged Lesser Known Texts*. Lulu.com.

Internet Archive. 2014. *Internet Archive*. https://archive.org

Iping-Petterson, M. 2012. *Human Sacrifice in Iron Age Northern Europe: The Culture of the Bog People*. University of Leiden.

Irby-Massie, Georgia L. 1999. *Military Religion in Roman Britain*. Leiden: Brill.

Jones, Mary. 2014. *Celtic Literature Collective & Jones's Celtic Encyclopedia*. http://www.maryjones.us/

Keating, Geoffrey. 2010. "The History of Ireland." *CELT: Corpus of Electronic Texts*. http://www.ucc.ie/celt/published/T100054/

Kelly, Eamonn P. 2012. "An Archaeological Interpretation of Irish Iron Age Bog Bodies." In *The Archaeology of Violence: Interdisciplinary Approaches*, edited by Sarah Ralph, 232–40. Albany: State University of New York.

Kelly, Fergus. 2003. *A Guide to Early Irish Law*. Dublin: Dublin Institute for Advanced Studies.

Kinsella, Thomas. 1969. *The Táin: Translated from the Irish Epic Táin Bó Cúailnge*. Oxford: Oxford University Press.

Kirk, Robert. 1893. *The Secret Commonwealth of Elves Fauns & Fairies*. Oxford: David Nutt.

Koch, John T. 1992. "Further to Tongu Do Dia Toinges Mo Thuath, &c." *Études Celtiques* 29: 249–61.

———. 2005. *Celtic Culture: A Historical Encyclopedia, Vol. 2*. Santa Barbara: ABC-CLIO.

Koch, John T., and John Carey. 2003. *The Celtic Heroic Age: Literary Sources for Ancient Celtic Europe and Early Ireland & Wales*. Aberystwyth: Celtic Studies Publications.

Kondratiev, Alexei. 1998. "Danu and Bile: The Primordial Parents?" *An Tríbhís Mhór: The IMBAS Journal of Celtic Reconstructionism* 1 (4).

Krasskova, Galina. 2014. *Devotional Polytheism: An Introduction*. Sanngetall Press. http://sanngetallpress.com/

———. 2014a. *Honoring the Ancestors: A Basic Guide*. Sanngetall Press. http://sanngetallpress.com/

Laertius, Diogenes. 1972. "Prologue." In *Lives of Eminent Philosophers*, edited by R.D. Hicks. Cambridge: Harvard University Press.
Laurie, Erynn Rowan. 2007. *Ogam: Weaving Word Wisdom*. Megalithica. http://www.seanet.com/~inisglas/publications.html.
———. 2010. "The Cauldron of Poesy." *The Preserving Shrine*. http://www.seanet.com/~inisglas/cauldronpoesy.html
Leahy, A H. 1902. *The Irish Saga Library, Vol. 1: The Courtship of Ferb*. London: David Nutt.
———. 1905. *Heroic Romances of Ireland, Vol I*. Edited by David Nutt. Vol. I. Edinburgh & London: Ballantyne, Hanson & Co.
———. 1906. *Heroic Romances of Ireland, Vol II*. Edited by David Nutt. Vol. II. Edinburgh & London: Ballantyne, Hanson & Co.
Lecouteux, Claude. 1996. *The Return of the Dead: Ghosts, Ancestors, and the Transparent Veil of the Pagan Mind*. Rochester: Inner Traditions.
Lennon, John. 1988. "Fairs and Assemblies in Ireland." *Before I Forget: Poyntzpass and District Local History Society* 2: 55–62.
Lincoln, Bruce. 1988. "The Druids and Human Sacrifice." In *Languages and Cultures: Studies in Honor of Edgar C. Polome*, edited by Mohammad Ali Jazayery and Werner Winter, 381–96. Berlin: Mouton de Gruyter.
———. 1991. *Death, War, and Sacrifice: Studies in Ideology and Practice*. Chicago & London: The University of Chicago Press.
Lowry-Corry, Dorothy. 1932. "The Stones Carved with Human Effigies on Boa Island and on Lustymore Island, in Lower Lough Erne." *Proceedings of the Royal Irish Academy* 41: 200–204.
Lynn, Chris, Cormac Mcsparron, and Peter Moore. 2002. *Data Structure Report: Navan Fort, Co. Armagh*. Belfast.
Lysaght, Patricia. 1996. "Aspects of the Earth-Goddess in the Traditions of the Banshee in Ireland." In *The Concept of the Goddess*, edited by Sandra Billington and Miranda Green, 152–65. London: Routledge.
Mac Cana, Proinsias. 1970. *Celtic Mythology*. London: Hamlyn.
Mac Firbisigh, Dubhaltach. 1860. *Annals of Ireland: Three Fragments*. Dublin: Irish Archaeological and Celtic Society.
Macalister, R. A. S. 1919. "Temair Breg: A Study of the Remains and Traditions of Tara." *Proceedings of the Royal Irish Academy* 34: 231–404.
———. 1938. *Lebor Gabála Érenn: The Book of the Taking of Ireland, Part I*. Dublin: Irish Texts Society.

———. 1939. *Lebor Gabála Érenn: The Book of the Taking of Ireland, Part II*. Dublin: Irish Texts Society.
———. 1940. *Lebor Gabála Érenn: The Book of the Taking of Ireland, Part III*. Dublin: Irish Texts Society.
———. 1941. *Lebor Gabála Érenn: The Book of the Taking of Ireland, Part IV*. Dublin: Irish Texts Society.
———. 1956. *Lebor Gabála Érenn: The Book of the Taking of Ireland, Part V*. Dublin: Irish Texts Society.
MacLeod, Sharon Paice. 1998. "Mater Deorum Hibernensium: Identity and Cross-Correlation in Early Irish Mythology." *Proceedings of the Harvard Celtic Colloquium* 18/19: 340–84.
McCormick, Finbar. 2007. "The Horse in Early Ireland." *Anthropozoologica* 42 (1): 85–104.
Mees, Bernard. 2008. "The Women of Larzac." *Keltische Forschungen* 3: 169–88.
———. 2009. *Celtic Curses*. Woodbridge: The Boydell Press.
Meyer, Kuno. 1881. "Macgnimartha Find." *Revue Celtique* 5: 195–204, 508.
———. 1885. *Cath Finntraga*. Oxford: Clarendon Press.
———. 1888. "The Wooing of Emer." *Archaeological Review* 1: 68–75; 150–55; 231–35; 298–307.
———. 1889. "The Adventures of Nera." *Revue Celtique* 10: 212–28.
———. 1901. "Brinna Ferchertne." *Zeitschrift Für Celtische Philologie* 3: 40–46.
———. 1906. *The Triads of Ireland*. Dublin: Hodges, Figgis, & Co., Ltd.
———. 1909. *A Primer of Irish Metrics*. Dublin: Hodges, Figgis, & Co., Ltd.
———. 1910. *Fianaigecht*. Dublin: Hogdes, Figgis & Co. Ltd.
Mickaharic, Draja. 2012. *Spiritual Cleansing: A Handbook of Psychic Protection*. San Francisco: Red Wheel/Weiser.
Moriarty, Colm. 2014. "Five Ancient Musical Instruments from Ireland." *Irish Archaeology*. http://irisharchaeology.ie/2014/03/five-ancient-musical-instruments-from-ireland/
Morris, James. 2011. "Animal 'Ritual' Killing: From Remains to Meanings." In *The Ritual Killing and Burial of Animals: European Perspectives*, edited by Aleksander Pluskowski, 8–21. Oxford: Oxbow Books.

Mozley, J.H. 1928a. "Thebaid IV." In *Statius: Volume I*. London: William Heinemann Ltd.

———. 1928b. "Thebaid VIII." In *Statius: Volume II*. London: William Heinemann Ltd.

Mullally, Evelyn. 1999. "The Phantom Army of 1169: An Anglo-Norman View." *Eigse: A Journal of Irish Studies* 31: 89–101.

Musashi, Miyamoto. 1993. *The Book of Five Rings*. Translated by Thomas Cleary. Boston: Shambhala Publications.

Nelson, Max. 2005. *The Barbarian's Beverage: A History of Beer in Ancient Europe*. London: Routledge.

Ó Duinn, Sean. 2014. "The Siege of Knocklong." *CELT: Corpus of Electronic Texts*. http://www.ucc.ie/celt/published/T301044/

Ó hÓgáin, Dáithí. 1999. *The Sacred Isle*. Woodbridge: The Boydell Press.

Ó Tuathail, Seán. 1993. "Excellence of Ancient Word: Druid Rhetorics from Ancient Irish Tales." *Imbas*. http://www.imbas.org/articles/excellence_of_the_ancient_word.html

O'Connor, Ralph. 2013. *The Destruction of Dá Derga's Hostel: Kingship and Narrative Artistry in a Mediaeval Irish Saga*. Oxford: Oxford University Press.

O'Curry, Eugene. 1855. *Cath Mhuighe Leana, or The Battle of Magh Leana; Together with Tocmarc Momera, or The Courtship of Momera*. Dublin: Goodwin, Son, and Nethercott.

———. 1858. "The Sick-Bed of Cuchulainn and the Only Jealousy of Eimer." *Atlantis* 1-2: 362–69, 98–124.

———. 1861. "The Foundation of the Palace of Emain Macha." In *Lectures on the Manuscript Materials of Ancient Irish History*, 527–28. Dublin.

———. 1873a. *On the Manners and Customs of the Ancient Irish, Vol. II*. Dublin: Williams and Norgate.

———. 1873b. *On the Manners and Customs of the Ancient Irish, Vol. III*. Dublin: Williams and Norgate.

O'Donovan, John. 1842. "The Banquet of Dun Na N-Gedh and the Battle of Magh Rath." *Irish Archaeological Society* 6. Dublin: Irish Archaeological Society.

———. 1868. *Sanas Chormaic: Cormac's Glossary*. Edited by John O'Donovan. Calcutta: O. T. Cutter.

———. 2002. "Annals of the Four Masters." Edited by Emma Ryan. *CELT: Corpus of Electronic Texts*. http://www.ucc.ie/celt/published/T100005A/index.html

O'Grady, Judith. 2013. *Pagan Portals - God-Speaking*. Hants: Moon Books. http://www.moon-books.net/books/pagan-portals-god-speaking

O'Grady, Standish Hayes. 1898. "The Great Defeat on the Plain of Muirthemne Before Cuchullin's Death." In *The Cuchullin Saga in Irish Literature*, edited by Eleanor Hull, 237–49. London: David Nutt.

O'Hagan, Terry. 2013. "No Horses for Courses: Christian Horror of Horseflesh in Early Medieval Ireland." *Vox Hiberionacum*. https://voxhiberionacum.wordpress.com/2013/01/17/christian-horseflesh-medieval-ireland1/

O'Keeffe, J. G. 1913. *Buile Suibhne: The Frenzy of Suibhne*. London: Irish Texts Society.

O'Rahilly, Cecile. 1924. *Tóruigheacht Gruaidhe Griansholus: The Pursuit of Gruaidh Ghriansholus*. London: Irish Texts Society.

———. 2010. "Táin Bó Cúalnge from the Book of Leinster." *CELT: Corpus of Electronic Texts*. http://www.ucc.ie/celt/online/T301035.html

———. 2011. "Táin Bó Cúalnge Recension 1." *CELT: Corpus of Electronic Texts*. http://www.ucc.ie/celt/published/T301012/index.html

Olmsted, Garrett. 1982. "Morrigan's Warning to Donn Cuailnge." *Études Celtiques* 19: 165–71.

———. 1994. *The Gods of the Celts and the Indo-Europeans*. Budapest: Innsbruck.

Paxson, Diana L. 2008. *Trance-Portation*. San Francisco: Red Wheel/Weiser. http://www.seidh.org/books/trance-portation/

———. 2015. The Essential Guide to Possession, Depossession, and Divine Relationships. San Francisco: Red Wheel/Weiser.

Pennington, Walter. 1930. "The Little Colloquy." *Philological Quarterly* IX (2): 97–110.

Petrie, George. 1839. "On the History and Antiquities of Tara Hill." *The Transactions of the Royal Irish Academy* 18: 25–232.

Powell, Eric A. 2013. "Wolf Rites of Winter." *Archaeology*, September. http://www.archaeology.org/issues/102-1309/features/1205-timber-grave-culture-krasnosamarskoe-bronze-age

Pressfield, Steven. 2011. *The Warrior Ethos*. New York: Black Irish. http://www.stevenpressfield.com/the-warrior-ethos/
Project Gutenberg Literary Archive Foundation. 2014. *Project Gutenberg*. http://www.gutenberg.org/
Raftery, Barry. 1994. *Pagan Celtic Ireland: The Enigma of the Irish Iron Age*. London: Thames & Hudson.
Ravenna, Morpheus. 2015. *Poems of the Morrígan*. Banshee Arts. http://bookofthegreatqueen.com/
Reinach, Salomon. 1906. "Pourquoi Vercingétorix a Renvoyé Sa Cavalerie d'Alésia." *Revue Celtique* 27: 1–15.
Rhŷs, Sir John. 1906. *The Celtic Inscriptions of France and Italy*. London: Oxford University Press.
Ross, Anne. 1996. *Pagan Celtic Britain: Studies in Iconography and Tradition*. Chicago: Academy Chicago Publishers.
Royal Irish Academy. 2013. *Electronic Dictionary of the Irish Language (eDIL): Revised Electronic Edition*. http://edil.qub.ac.uk/dictionary/search.php
Sayers, William. 1983. "Martial Feats in the Old Irish Ulster Cycle." *Canadian Journal of Irish Studies* 9 (1): 45–80.
———. 1985. "Fergus and the Cosmogonic Sword." *History of Religions* 25 (1): 30–56.
———. 1991. "Airdrech, Sirite and Other Early Irish Battlefield Spirits." *Eigse: A Journal of Irish Studies* 25: 45–55.
Schumacher, Stefan. 1995. "Old Irish *Tucaid, Tocad and Middle Welsh Tynghaf Tynghet Re-Examined." *Ériu* 46: 49–57.
Serjeantson, D., and J. Morris. 2011. "Ravens and Crows in Iron Age and Roman Britain." *Oxford Journal of Archaeology* 30 (1): 85–107.
Simmer-Brown, Judith. 1997. "Inviting the Demon." *Parabola* 22 (2): 12–18. http://buddhism.lib.ntu.edu.tw/FULLTEXT/JR-EPT/simm.htm
Sjoestedt, Marie-Louise. 1994. *Gods and Heroes of the Celts*. Translated by Myles Dillon. New York: Turtle Island Foundation.
Skallagrimsson, Wayland. 2014. *Putting on the Wolf Skin*. CreateSpace. https://somafera.wordpress.com/2014/12/10/putting-on-the-wolf-skin/
Skene, William F. 1868. *The Four Ancient Books of Wales*. Edinburgh: Edmonston and Douglas.
Slocum, Joshua, and Lisa Carlson. 2011. *Final Rights: Reclaiming the American Way of Death*. Hinesberg: Upper Access. http://finalrights.org/

Stacey, Robin Chapman. 2007. *Dark Speech: The Performance of Law in Early Ireland*. Philadelphia: University of Pennsylvania Press.

Stohellou, Erik. 2011. "The Recovery of the Tain: Do Fallsigud Tána Bó Cualnge." *Tech Screpta*. http://sejh.pagesperso-orange.fr/keltia/version-en/fallsigud-en.html

———. 2011. *Tech Screpta*. http://sejh.pagesperso-orange.fr/celtlink.html

Stokes, Whitley. 1862. *Three Irish Glossaries*. London: Williams and Norgate.

———. 1875. "The Ancient Irish Goddess of War, Corrections and Additions." *Revue Celtique* 2: 489–92.

———. 1876. "Cuchulainn's Death, Abridged from the Book of Leinster." *Revue Celtique* 3: 175–85.

———. 1887. "The Siege of Howth." *Revue Celtique* 8: 47–64.

———. 1891. "The Second Battle of Moytura." *Revue Celtique* 12: 52–130, 306–8.

———. 1892. "The Bodleian Dinnshenchas." *Folklore* 3: 467–516.

———. 1893. "The Edinburgh Dinnshenchas." *Folklore* 4: 473–97.

———. 1894. "The Prose Tales in the Rennes Dindshenchas." *Revue Celtique* 15: 277–336.

———. 1897. "Cóir Anmann (Fitness of Names)." In *Irische Text Mit Wörterbuch*, 288–411. Leipzig: Verlag Von S. Hirzel.

———. 1900a. "Da Choca's Hostel." *Revue Celtique* 21: 149–75, 312–28, 388–404.

———. 1900b. "O'Mulconry's Glossary." *Archiv Fur Celtische Lexikographie* 1: 232–324.

———. 1901a. "O'Davoren's Glossary." *Archiv Fur Celtische Lexikographie* II: 197–504.

———. 1901b. "The Destruction of Dind Rig." *Zeitschrift Für Celtische Philologie* 3: 1–14.

———. 1902. "The Death of Murchertach Mac Erca." *Revue Celtique* 23: 395–437.

———. 1903. "The Battle of Allen." *Revue Celtique* 24: 41–67.

———. 1905. "The Colloquy of the Two Sages." *Revue Celtique* 26: 4–64.

———. 1908. "The Training of Cuchulainn." *Revue Celtique* 29: 109–52.

———. 1910a. "The Destruction of Da Derga's Hostel." In *Epic and Saga*. New York: P. F. Collier & Son.

———. 1910b. "Tidings of Conchobar Son of Ness." *Ériu* 4: 18–38.
———. 2009. "The Destruction of Da Derga's Hostel." *CELT: Corpus of Electronic Texts*. http://www.ucc.ie/celt/published/T301017A/index.html.
———. 2010. "In Cath Catharda : The Civil War of the Romans." *CELT: Corpus of Electronic Texts*. http://www.ucc.ie/celt/published/T305001/index.html.
Strachan, John. 1900. "The Notes and Glosses in the Lebor Na hUidre." *Archiv Fur Celtische Lexikographie* I: 1–36.
Suetonius (C. Suetonius Tranquillus). 2006. *The Lives Of The Twelve Caesars, Complete: To Which Are Added, His Lives Of The Grammarians, Rhetoricians, And Poets*. Edited by Alexander Thomson and T. Forester. Project Gutenberg. http://www.gutenberg.org/files/6400/6400-h/6400-h.htm.
Thompson, Chris, and Isolde Carmody. 2014. "Dindshenchas 12: A Magical Mystery Tour." *Story Archaeology Podcast*. http://storyarchaeology.com/dindshenchas-12-a-magical-mystery-tour/.
Thompson, Christopher Scott. 2009. *Highland Martial Culture: The Fighting Heritage of Scotland*. Boulder: Paladin Press. http://www.paladin-press.com/product/Highland_Martial_Culture.
Thompson, Christopher Scott. 2013. *The Music of His Sword: Martial Arts of the Pagan Celts*. Lulu.com.
Todd, James Henthorn. 1867. *The War of the Gaedhil with the Gaill, or The Invasions of Ireland by the Danes and Other Norsemen*. London: Longmans, Green, Reader, and Dyer.
Toner, Gregory. 2010. "Macha and the Invention of Myth." *Ériu* 60: 81–110.
Tonsing, Ernst F. 2014. "A Celtic Invocation: Cétnad nAíse." *E-Keltoi: Journal of Interdisciplinary Celtic Studies* 8: 1–35.
Tymoczko, Maria. 1981. *Two Death Tales from the Ulster Cycle: The Death of Cú Roí & The Death of Cú Chulainn*. Dublin: The Dolmen Press.
Van der Sanden, Wijnand A. B. 2013. "Bog Bodies: Underwater Burials, Sacrifices, and Executions." In *The Oxford Handbook of Wetland Archaeology*, edited by Francesco Menotti and Aidan O'Sullivan, 401–16. Oxford: Oxford University Press.
Volmering, Nicole. 2014. "The Second Vision of Adomnán." In *The End and Beyond: Medieval Irish Eschatology*, edited by John Carey, Emma Nic Cárthaigh, and Caitríona Ó Dochartaigh, II:647–81. Aberystwyth: Celtic Studies Publications.

Waddell, John. 1983. "Rathcroghan - A Royal Site in Connacht." *Journal of Irish Archaeology* 1: 21–46.

———. 2014. *Archaeology and Celtic Myth*. Dublin: Four Courts Press.

Warner, Richard. 2003. "Two Pagan Idols: Remarkable New Discoveries." *Archaeology Ireland* 17 (1): 24–27.

Wilby, Emma. 2006. *Cunning-Folk and Familiar Spirits: Shamanistic Visionary Traditions in Early Modern British Witchcraft and Magic*. East Sussex: Sussex Academic Press. http://www.sussex-academic.com/sa/titles/history/Wilby.htm

Windisch, Ernst. 1905. *Die Altirische Heldensage Táin Bó Cúalnge Nach Dem Buch von Leinster*. Leipzig: S. Hirzel.

Wood-Martin, W.G. 1902a. *Traces of the Elder Faiths of Ireland, Vol. I*. London: Longmans, Green, and Co.

———. 1902b. *Traces of the Elder Faiths of Ireland, Vol. II*. London: Longmans, Green, and Co.

Wright, Thomas, Richard Colt Hoare, and Thomas Forester. 1863. *The Historical Works of Giraldus Cambrensis*. London: George Bell & Sons.

Young, Tomas. 2013. "The Last Letter: A Message to George W. Bush and Dick Cheney From a Dying Veteran." *Truthdig*. http://www.truthdig.com/dig/item/the_last_letter_20130318.

Zweig, Connie, and Jeremiah Abrams. 1991. *Meeting the Shadow: The Hidden Power of the Dark Side of Human Nature*. New York: Tarcher/Putnam.

INDEX

D

G

N

O

P

T

U

V

W

Y

About the Author

Morpheus Ravenna is a spiritual worker, artist, and writer, residing in the San Francisco Bay area. An initiate of the Anderson Feri tradition of witchcraft, she has studied and practiced devotional polytheism and the magical arts for about twenty years. Her primary spiritual practice is her devotion and dedication to the Morrigan, within the framework of Celtic heroic spirituality. She co-founded the Coru Cathubodua Priesthood, a Pagan devotional priesthood dedicated to the Morrígan, and she authors the Shieldmaiden Blog. Her earlier work at Stone City Pagan Sanctuary helped provide a space for land-based Pagan community in northern California, shown in the 2010 documentary "American Mystic."

Morpheus makes her living as a tattoo artist, with a passion for ritual tattoos, folk magic, and tattoo design inspired by historical art and ancient civilizations. She recognizes tattooing as an initiatory art. An accomplished artist, she continues to create devotional artworks in a variety of media including oil and watercolor, ink, metalwork, and more. She also practices medieval armored combat in the Society for Creative Anachronism.

Morpheus can be reached through her website at:
BansheeArts.com

The Coru Cathubodua Priesthood can be reached at:
CoruPriesthood.com

About Concrescent Press

Concrescent Press is dedicated to publishing advanced magickal practice and Pagan scholarship. It takes advantage of the recent revolution in publishing technology and economics to bring forth works that, previously, might only have been circulated privately. We are especially interested in publishing works like this one, focusing on the way and practice of invoking a Deity or set thereof. It is time to rebuild the temples, altars, and rites of the Gods, to bring back our communion with Them and Their many benefits into our world and lives.

Now, we are growing the future together.

Colophon

This book is made of Cochin, and UnZialish using Adobe InDesign. The titling font PF Uncial is by Peter Rempel (http://www.prfonts.com/). The body was set by Sam Webster. The calligraphy facing Chapter 9 is by the author. The cover design and all paintings were created by Valerie Herron. Her website is: ValerieHerron.com

Visit our website at
Concrescent.net

Lightning Source UK Ltd.
Milton Keynes UK
UKHW030409100620
364731UK00009B/1950

9 780990 392712